W9-CCD-409

LINDBERGH
A BIOGRAPHY

LINDBERGH
A BIOGRAPHY
LEONARD MOSLEY

DOVER PUBLICATIONS, INC.
MINEOLA, NEW YORK

Excerpts and selections from works by the following authors and publications were made possible by the kind permission of their respective publishers and representatives:

Excerpts from *Harold Nicolson: Diaries and Letters, 1930–1939*, edited by Nigel Nicolson. Harold Nicolson's Diaries and Letters copyright © 1966 by William Collins Sons & Co., Ltd. V. Sackville-West's Letters copyright © 1966 by Sir Harold Nicolson. Introduction and Notes to this volume copyright © 1966 by Nigel Nicolson. Reprinted by permission of Atheneum Publishers, New York, and William Collins, London.

Excerpts from the article by Charles A. Lindbergh, Christmas, 1967, issue of *Life* magazine. Reprinted by permission of Harcourt Brace Jovanovich, Inc.

Excerpts from September 13, 1941, and October 7, 1941, issues of the *Herald Tribune*. Reprinted by permission of I. H. T. Corporation.

Excerpt from *The Late John Marquand*, by Stephen Birmingham. Copyright © 1972 by Stephen Birmingham. Reprinted by permission of J. B. Lippincott Company.

Excerpt from *The Winds of War*, copyright © 1971 by Herman Wouk. Published by Little, Brown & Company. Reprinted by permission of Harold Matson Company, Inc.

Letters and editorials from April 29, 1941, October 5, 1941, June 6, 1941, and September 6, 1970, issues of the New York *Times*. Copyright © 1941, 1970 by the New York Times Company. Reprinted by permission of the New York *Times*.

Quotations from unpublished diaries and letters of Harold Nicolson. Reprinted by permission of Nigel Nicolson.

Excerpts adapted from Fitzhugh Green's section of *We: His Own Story*, by Charles A. Lindbergh. Copyright 1927, 1955 by Charles A. Lindbergh. Reprinted by permission of G. P. Putnam's Sons.

Excerpts from *The Spirit of St. Louis*, by Charles Lindbergh. Copyright 1953 by Charles Scribner's Sons. Excerpt from *Of Flight and Life*, by Charles A. Lindbergh. Copyright 1948 by Charles A. Lindbergh. Reprinted by permission of Charles Scribner's Sons.

Photo Credits

Minnesota Historical Society, St. Paul, Minnesota: Photographs 1–7; Popperfoto, London, England: Photographs 8, 10, 11, 13, 16, 18, 20–22, 24, 25, 29–32; Mansell Collection, London, England: Photographs 9, 12, 26, 27; Fox Photos Ltd., London, England: Photograph 14; The St. Louis *Globe-Democrat*, St. Louis, Missouri: Photograph 15; Collections of Greenfield Village and the Henry Ford Museum, Dearborn, Michigan: Photograph 17; *Radio Times*, Hulton Picture Library, British Broadcasting Corporation, London, England: Photograph 19; United Press International, New York, New York: Photograph 23; The Associated Press Ltd., London, England: Photographs 28, 37; The New York *Times*, New York, New York: Photographs 33, 34, 36 by Alden Whitman; photograph 39 by Edgar Needham; photograph 40 by Michael Evans; Wide World Photos, New York, New York: Photographs 35, 38.

Copyright

Published in Canada by General Publishing Company, Ltd., 30 Lesmill Road, Don Mills, Toronto, Ontario.

Bibliographical Note

This Dover edition of *Lindbergh: A Biography*, first published in 2000, is an unabridged republication of the book originally published under the same title in 1976 by Doubleday & Company, Inc., Garden City, New York.

Library of Congress Cataloging-in-Publication Data

Mosley, Leonard, 1913–
   Lindbergh : a biography / Leonard Mosley.
     p. cm.
   Originally published: Garden City, N.Y. : Doubleday, 1976.
   Includes bibliographical references and index.
   ISBN 0-486-40964-3 (pbk.)
   1. Lindbergh, Charles A. (Charles Augustus), 1902–1974. 2. Air pilots—United States—Biography. I. Title.

TL540.L5 M63 2000
629.13'092—dc21
[B]

                                           00-022414

Manufactured in the United States of America
Dover Publications, Inc., 31 East 2nd Street, Mineola, N.Y. 11501

CONTENTS

Part Four / Innocents Abroad

Part Five / Peacenik

Part Six / The Mote and the Beam

Part Seven / Out of the Ashes

FOREWORD

In the winter of 1934–35 I was broadening a youthful mind, if hardly elevating it, by working as a replacement reporter and editorial handyman for the New York *Daily Mirror*. It is too long a story to explain how an eighteen-year-old Briton from the English provinces had got himself associated with this raucous American tabloid at one of the shrillest moments of its career, except to mention that it involved a cattle-boat trip from Manchester to Canada, jobs on the Montreal *Star* and backstage at Minsky's Forty-second Street burlesque theater, and an introduction to the *Mirror's* editor by an amiable Irish aristocrat named Viscount (Valentine) Castlerosse. I bring it up here simply to show why, when the *Daily Mirror* moved a considerable portion of its staff to Flemington, New Jersey, at the beginning of January 1935, to cover the trial of Bruno Richard Hauptmann for the murder of the Lindbergh baby, I was a member of the team, and thus saw Charles Augustus Lindbergh in the flesh for the first time. Thereafter, it always seemed as if I were running into him or following in his footsteps.

Not only to young Americans was Charles Lindbergh the greatest hero of the nineteen twenties and thirties. In Britain, too, we pinned his picture over our beds and made fretwork models of the *Spirit of St. Louis*. I remember that in 1927, the year of the famous nonstop flight from New York to Paris, we were living in a Manchester suburb not far away from a great newspaperman of the day, C. P. Scott, owner-editor of the *Manchester Guardian*. I often used to see him cycling to his office in Cross Street, a tweedy, gray-bearded, patriarchal figure, and never failed to tip my school cap to him and say, "Hello, Mr. Scott." One day he hopped off his bike and asked me who I was and what I planned to do when I grew up.

"I'd like to be a great journalist like you, sir," I said.

He then asked me whether I had ever been in a newspaper office, and when I said no, he told me to report to the *Guardian* offices a couple of days hence, and he would arrange to have me shown over. The date fixed was May 22, 1927, which, as it turned out, was the day after Lindbergh's arrival in Paris. Even the staid editorial offices of the *Guardian* were in a tizzy over the reports flowing in from Paris—his hysterical reception by the crowd, detailed accounts of his flight, his first press conferences.

I came away clutching an early edition of the *Guardian* on which Scott had written: "For Leonard Mosley. Perhaps you too will have an article in the *Manchester Guardian* one day." When I got home I wrote in my journal: "Lindbergh has flown the Atlantic. I have been to the *Manchester Guardian*. An auspicious event for both of us."

After that, I always felt I had a sort of family interest in him, and I started a clippings book about his travels and activities, as if I were charting the progress of a hero who was also a favorite brother. I vicariously shared his triumphs and suffered with him over his experiences with public and the press. Among the thousands of letters which were written to him after the kidnaping of his child was one from me and twenty-five of my schoolmates.

To see him in person in court at Flemington, New Jersey, was an emotional experience for me, and what I saw raised him even higher in my estimation. It was part of my job to slip into the courthouse several times during the day to pick up copy from my seniors reporting the trial. He was always there, towering physically and symbolically over all the other performers and spectators at this execrable circus, a rock of rectitude and solidity in a seething, bubbling sea of hysteria and cheap sensation.

I had thought that when I first saw him there, it would be pity that I felt for him in his sorrow. I found myself admiring him, instead. To pity him would have been to insult him. Here was a man to be saluted for his courage, for he was manifestly a man who would always bear what came to him with greater dignity and fortitude than most other men.

Shortly after the end of the trial, I sailed back to England aboard the liner *Berengaria* and discovered that, quite by accident, I was a fellow passenger with Betty Gow, the young Scots girl who had been the Lindbergh baby's nurse. She had been bullied and browbeaten during the trial by the ineffable Edward J. Reilly, chief attorney for the defense, and was in a condition of considerable distress as a result of her ordeal. There followed one of those short, shipboard friendships which was rewarding for both of us, I think (I had my own problems). She knew I had been at the trial and was probably the only person aboard who knew what it had been like, and we talked as two people who have shared a harrowing experience (because I, too, had been profoundly shocked at what I had seen going on in a supposed tribunal of law and justice).

She talked to me about her life with the Lindberghs, and I remember something she said, in her quiet, soft, melodious Scottish voice.

"Colonel Lindbergh is the most honest man I have ever met," she said. "Do you know, he cannot tell a lie, even if he knows the truth is going to hurt—and even if the person he hurts is very close to him? He just has to tell the truth, and he expects other people to tell the truth to him. It would never occur to him that anyone would ever lie to him. He once caught one of Mrs. Lindbergh's aunts telling a tall story, and when he taxed her with it, she said, 'But I was just fibbing, Colonel.' 'Aunt Agnes,' he said, 'there are no such things as fibs, only lies.' She looked quite crushed, poor lady."

I thought of those words in 1938 and 1939. By that time, I was in Germany as a correspondent and was following with some apprehension Charles Lindbergh's visits there. We heard in various roundabout ways what the Nazis were telling the famous flier. Did he realize that they were lying to him? When my friend, Paul Stehlin, who was then an air intelligence officer at the French embassy in Berlin, told me that Lindbergh was happy about the Anglo-French capitulation at Munich and that, later, with war only weeks away, he was trying to promote a Franco-German aircraft deal, I said that what he was probably doing was double-bluffing the Nazis. Stehlin shook his head, but I stayed optimistic.

I flew into Paris from Germany in 1945 just about the time when Charles Lindbergh arrived there with the U. S. Naval Technical Mission, and my office asked me to check the rumors that he was in the city. If so, would I contact him and ask him how Paris in the aftermath of World War II compared with the capital which he had known in 1927. I eventually heard from General Mark Clark (I had been a correspondent with the U. S. Fifth Army, which Clark commanded, in Italy) that he and Lindbergh were lunching that day with Ambassador Jefferson Caffery at the American embassy, and I was there when Lindbergh came in. War correspondents still wore uniforms in Germany in those days, and I had brought no change of clothing with me to France, and I guess it was because he thought I belonged to the military that he stopped and listened to me when I went up and spoke to him. But when he realized I was a newspaperman, the smile disappeared from his face, and he said brusquely, "I have absolutely nothing constructive I could say."

He was about to pass on when his glance caught the paratrooper's wings I was wearing, and in a slightly more amiable tone he asked where I had dropped. I said I had gone in with British 6th Airborne parachutists into Normandy on D day, June 6, 1944. He asked what height we had dropped at, and I said 250 feet. He grinned then, and said that was a sight too low for his liking. He preferred to have height to float around in.

"Not if the air's full of bullets and flak," I said.

He laughed. "I guess not," he said. He reached out his hand, and I shook it. "Glad to have met you. Sorry I can't help you." He passed on. He hadn't asked my name.

I didn't see him during his tour of Germany, but when I went to see Willy Messerschmitt, who built the Me109s, 110s, and 262s for the Nazi Luftwaffe, he said that Lindbergh had been to see him a couple of days before and had given him chocolate, coffee, and cigarettes.

"He is a great gentleman," he said. "He made me feel like a human being again." He paused, and then added: "Do you know, I think he hates the Russians more than we do."

In the postwar years, I still kept tag on Charles Lindbergh's progress. I suppose I had always known in my bones that I would one day write his life story, and what had begun as a youthful fan's souvenir book was now building up into a kind of dossier. Items of this kind found their way into it:

> Cannes, August —, 1973. Had dinner last night at Dolly's villa. Sitting across from me was Sir Charles Wheeler, who sees a lot of the Aubrey Morgans (she's Anne Morrow Lindbergh's sister) in Wales. He said last time he dined there Lindbergh was visiting. Seemed very morose and worried about something. Sir Charles asked him about Nixon, and practically had his head snapped off. Lindbergh said he never talked American politics with Englishmen. He was later told that Lindbergh still feels very constrained when he comes to Britain. Even after all these years, he fears someone will attack him (verbally or physically?) over his behavior toward England in WW2.

Or:

> New York, Feb. 1970. Curious experience today. I came

into Grand Central Station and suddenly had a feeling that there was someone near me that I knew. When I looked around, I saw Charles Lindbergh staring into a bookshop window, but when I came closer to him I realized that he was not looking at the books, but was using the reflection of the light on the window to watch the people behind him hurrying by. He looks a lot older than when I saw him a couple of years ago. He looked slightly annoyed by something, which, I'm told, he does a lot these days, but God, he's still handsome and you can still see the shape of that tall, vital kid we once knew underneath the aging. While I was covertly watching him, with the sort of rueful, mixed emotions I have for him nowadays, I felt the wind of Anne Morrow L.'s passing as she rushed up to him. "Oh, my!" I heard her say. "I know someone who's going to be good and mad. I'm sorry I'm late, Charles." She was wearing a purple suit, a deeper purple sort of jersey, red shoes, and handbag. She nearly always wears purple. Come to think of it, whenever I've seen her, she never wears anything else! He looked down at her, and then the irritated expression cleared and he smiled at her. The smile hasn't changed! They went off—toward the New Haven R.R., I expect.

I practically decided then and there that it was about time I got down to writing about Charles Lindbergh. If he was getting into my bones to the extent that I sensed when he was around, the moment had arrived. But since there were other projects in hand, it was not until 1973 that the dossier on Charles Lindbergh moved to the front of my files. He and it have been with me ever since. On August 26, 1974, the day he died, I was in a small plane flying toward the Eiffel Tower and then turning toward Le Bourget airfield, in imitation of his 1927 flight. News was just coming in from Hawaii as we drove back into Paris in the summer twilight.

"The French people will be very sad," said my companion, a young French pilot. "He was a great hero to them. That flight was a sort of link between us and America, you know, and despite everything, I don't think it has been broken." We drove on in silence, and then he said, "Something went wrong with him later, didn't it? Not just that terrible kidnaping, I mean. Other things. What happened?"

I told him he would have to wait for this book to find out.

At the end of this book, the reader will find a bibliographical essay giving in detail the sources consulted for this biography, the journeys made, the friends and associates to whom I have talked. Here I would like to say how grateful I am to the editors of the New York *Times,* and in particular to my old friend and colleague, James L. Greenfield, for allowing me the facilities of their splendid organization during the researches into Charles Lindbergh's background. I would also like to single out for special thanks Mr. Nigel Nicolson for giving me free access to his father's unpublished diaries and letters and for interrupting his many pursuits to entertain me on two occasions at Sissinghurst Castle; Mr. Tom Harrisson, of the World Wild Life Fund, for his help and hospitality in England, Brussels, and the South of France; and finally, my editor, John Ware, for proving such an amiable godfather to this creation.

Prologue:
The Wound Reopened

On the afternoon of November 4, 1966, Charles Augustus Lindbergh left his office in the Pan American Building in New York City and took the elevator down to Grand Central Station. He had decided to catch an early train home to Darien, Connecticut, not simply to avoid the Friday afternoon rush to the suburbs, but because he wished this to be as long a weekend break as he could possibly make it. It would be his first at home for several months and he knew that his wife, Anne, was growing rueful about his increasing absences. Once upon a time they had flown the world together; now he flew alone. "Charles only touches base now and then," she wrote to a friend. "He is, I think, on his fourth or fifth trip around the world this year. (Someone suggested I should keep in touch with him by satellite.)"

It was true that not even professional air pilots covered much more mileage in the course of an average year than Charles A. Lindbergh. As director and technical consultant of Pan American World Airways he rode with the company's crews on continuing trips to Europe, Asia, and South America. He sat in conference with airways experts and government officials in Washington, London, Paris, and Tokyo. This was only a portion of his manifold activities, which included ecology, wildlife, and conservation, as well as aeronautics, and took him on a variety of missions to every part of the globe.

Once recently he had told his wife that he was "needed" in the Pacific but that it would only be a short trip.

"A month?" she asked tentatively.

"Oh no," he had answered cheerfully. "Just Hawaii and the Philippines—and then back round the world the other way."

In a letter to a friend recounting the conversation, Anne Morrow Lindbergh added "!!?!" by way of personal comment.

Now he was back in the United States for at least five days, and resolved to spend as many of them as possible with his wife in the house on the Tokeneke Trail, near Darien, where the Lindberghs had established themselves in the months following the end of World War II. The house was on Scott's Cove, looking out toward Long Island Sound, and they had come to it in search of the seclusion they had been seeking for most of their life together, and for a refuge in which to recover from the wounds (admittedly some of them self-inflicted) which they had suffered in the years preceding and the months immediately following the outbreak of World War II. It had proved to be a home and an environment which had brought them peace after an era of shared fear, tragedy, misery, resentment, hostility, rancor, hate, and pain. The scars from their wounds were still there, but the ache seemed to have gone, and they were savoring the sweetness of it.

That afternoon of November 4, 1966, an observer watching Charles Lindbergh march across the Grand Central concourse toward the gates of the New Haven Railroad might have had trouble guessing his age. He was, in fact, sixty-four. The lean body and the brisk, long stride were those of someone very much younger, but the used, lined face and the off-white cropped hair, peeping below a trilby hat, seemed to belong to a man at least in his upper sixties. On the other hand, when he paused to allow a luggage-laden old black woman to go past him, and smiled at her as she thanked him, he suddenly looked positively boyish.

In times gone by the loping stride and the transforming smile would have betrayed his identity to the crowd at once, and brought them surging around him, to slap him on the back, to demand his autograph, to shout at him: "Hiya, Lindy!" At that time he was the greatest hero America and the rest of the civilized world had ever known, and he was a fugitive from the perfervid adulation that came with his status. By his solo flight across the Atlantic in 1927 he had not simply been the first man to link New York with Paris in a nonstop flight; he had singlehandedly christened and launched the air age. And the people of the world, instinctively sensing that in a decade of stunts and innovations this was something of immeasurably wider significance, had heaped upon him adulation and honors that a prophet had never before received in his lifetime.

But from that moment on, it went badly wrong. The hero worship turned sour. The hero became disenchanted. Intrusions upon the private life of himself and his wife culminated in the kidnaping and murder of their baby, and in his heart he blamed the excesses of the

American press and the hysteria of the American people for it. Finally, when the war in Europe between the democracies and the Nazis threatened to involve the United States, he emerged from his unhappy seclusion to preach a strident isolationism, a policy of coldhearted expediency, which seemed to many of his fellow countrymen to play into the hands of the dictators. He was charged with dangerous defeatism by his President, accused of racialism by his former admirers, and, when war finally came to the United States in 1941, arbitrarily prevented by the Administration from flying and fighting for his country.

For the once-shining hero, it was a sort of squalid demise. He was consigned to obscurity, and not the kind for which he had been searching. America can be rough with a loser, and Lindbergh had chosen the wrong side and lost. But it was really worse than that, because there were insults and humiliations associated with his disappearance from the public scene that this proud and stubborn man must have found hard to bear. At a moment when he wanted nothing better than to fight, and, if necessary, die for his country, he was kept hanging around the corridors of government in Washington while the Administration took its time in deciding whether he could be accorded the privilege of donning a United States uniform. If he had publicly begged for a military job, no doubt one would have been accorded him—but beg he would not. So the most experienced flier in the nation was banned from the Armed Forces. There were the pinpricks, too. His name was removed from the mountains, the streets, and the airlines which had once been named after him. It could hardly be expunged from the hall of fame, because the feat which had won him a place there was an irremovable bench mark on the history of flight. But otherwise, for much of the civilized world, Charles Augustus Lindbergh was banished and in disgrace.

There were many decent people who, while recognizing his unique qualities as an airman, hoped that they would never have to hear or read about him again, and swore they would never forgive or forget.

But this was 1966, and a quarter of a century had gone by. If you had told the group of Yale students jostling up the aisle that the long lean man on the commuter's train to New Haven had once been called everything from "Copperhead" to "Nazi," it is doubtful if they would have believed you. If they knew Lindbergh at all, they knew him as a friend of the earth, a passionate devotee of conservation, a crusader against ecological barbarism—and how could those activities be reconciled with the appeasement of history's most barbaric tyrant?

As for official Washington, it had long since completed the process of rehabilitation. As far back as 1954, President Eisenhower had given him back his uniform and promoted him in the U. S. Air Force to the rank of brigadier general. The Kennedys and the Johnsons invited him to White House dinners. His autobiography had won the Pulitzer Prize and earned him more than a million dollars. And if he was no longer mobbed by adulating crowds, as he had been in the twenties and thirties, he was now regarded with admiration and respect.

It was all behind him, the black period of his fall from grace, either forgiven or forgotten. And if Charles Augustus Lindbergh still resented what had been done to him and still believed that history would one day vindicate the stand he had taken in 1941 (for, as will be seen, he hadn't changed a single one of his tenaciously held opinions), that could wait until after he was dead. In the meantime, he was content that it was all in the past and, as far as he knew, forgotten. No one thought any more about that wounding period of his life except his wife and himself, and then only when something rubbed against their scars. The idea that someone was about to rip the wounds open again—someone whom his wife admired and he respected—was a possibility that did not occur to him.

He got off the train at Darien, picked up his Volkswagen in the parking lot, and drove through the anonymous entrance of 21 Tokeneke Trail around five in the evening. There was a book pouch among his pile of mail, and when he opened it he saw that the volume inside had been sent to him by the publishers at the request of its author and editor. It was the Atheneum edition of *Diaries and Letters, 1930–39*, by Harold Nicolson, edited by his son, Nigel Nicolson. It had recently been published and he had heard about it. He took it with him to his study and looked forward to going through it that evening. He did not know it then, but he might just as well have been holding a hand grenade, for it was a book that was going to shatter both his weekend and his complacency.

Sir Harold Nicolson was an old friend of Anne Lindbergh's family, the Morrows. In 1966 he was in his eightieth year and his dotage, but in early times he had been famous both in his native England and in the United States as a biographer, essayist, diplomat, and raconteur. His biography of his father, Lord Carnock, an urbane Victorian diplomat, and his study of Lord Curzon, a famous turn-of-the-century foreign secretary, were expertly observed and richly anecdotal accounts of two very different members of Britain's political aristocracy. His wit, his easy flow of conversation, his social, diplomatic, political, and literary con-

nections made him much in demand at all the best London dinner
tables and Bloomsbury *soirées*. In many ways, he was the worst kind of
snob, with a barely concealed contempt for those unfortunate people
who were, in his son's phrase, "outside the elite": "Businessmen, for example, the humbler type of schoolmaster or clergyman, most women,
actors, most Americans, Jews, all coloured or Levantine peoples, and
the great mass of the middle and working classes."

But otherwise, in the society column sense of the term, he knew "ev-
erybody." A glance through the letter C in the index of his diaries re-
veals the names of King Carol of Romania, Lord Castlerosse, Lord
Cecil, Austen and Neville Chamberlain, "Chips" Channon, G. K.
Chesterton, Winston Churchill, Count Ciano, René Clair, Sir Kenneth
Clark, Lady Diana Cooper, Lord Cranborne, and Lady Emerald
Cunard, all celebrities of the day, some of them famous hosts and
hostesses eager for him to adorn their tables, others his fellow guests.

The twenties and the thirties were the years when the doings of British society received a surprising amount of attention in the American
press, and Nicolson was a favored speaker on the American lecture cir-
cuit, where the ladies liked to gather to hear him talk about royalty, the
aristocracy, and literary celebrities. It did not seem to matter—it even
seemed to add a certain zest to the occasion—that his manner was dis-
tinctly patronizing; and of course they could not know that he wrote
disparaging things about them in his diaries and in his letters home.

One of the matrons who attended and enjoyed Harold Nicolson's lectures was Mrs. Elizabeth Dwight Morrow, widow of the late Dwight
Morrow, a well-known American diplomat and statesman. Morrow had
died suddenly in 1931 at the apogee of his career, just at the moment
when a move was gaining strength to have him nominated as Republican candidate for President against Franklin D. Roosevelt in the elections of 1932. Elizabeth Dwight Morrow was not the sort of woman to
indulge in sterile mourning, and she was already busily engaged in social welfare and cultural activities by the time she listened to Nicolson's
lectures in 1933. But she did feel that her husband deserved to have his
diplomatic achievements recognized and that the American public
should know what sort of a man they had lost. She had therefore begun
looking around for a worthy writer to do Dwight Morrow's biography,
and after reading Harold Nicolson's books she decided that she had
found him.

Through an emissary of the international bankers J. P. Morgan and
Company, among whose partners Dwight Morrow had been numbered,
Nicolson was contacted and a proposition was made, and, after an ini-
tial show of diffidence, accepted. In truth, the English writer, despite

his nationality, was a wise choice to write Morrow's life. Nicolson had moved in the same diplomatic circles in which Morrow had secured some of his most notable triumphs and had even, during the London Naval Conference of 1930, sat with him at the same negotiating table. The book he subsequently wrote turned out to be a good one and was well received in the United States.

To research it, Nicolson was invited to be the guest of the Morrow family at their homes at Englewood, New Jersey; North Haven, Maine; and Cuernavaca, Mexico; and he visited all three in 1934 and 1935. Since Charles and Anne Lindbergh were living with Elizabeth Dwight Morrow at the time, he saw a good deal of them, and the period when they were in each other's company happened to be one of the most traumatic in the lives of the young couple. During part of the time a man named Bruno Richard Hauptmann was on trial for the kidnaping and murder of their first child, and Lindbergh was in the courtroom day after day. Nicolson was with them both at the moment when Hauptmann was found guilty and sentenced to die in the electric chair.

Later, when the Lindberghs decided to leave the United States (at the end of 1935), it was Harold Nicolson who found them a refuge in the Weald of Kent, in England, where they could live their lives unmolested; and it was from this base that they began to visit Nazi Germany on the fact-finding trips that were to have such a profound effect upon their political outlook.

Charles Lindbergh was well aware that Harold Nicolson was both a diarist and a copious letter writer. Now that his journals had been published, he would hardly have been human if he had not been curious to discover what the English writer had said about himself, his wife, his family, and his in-laws. After supper that evening, with Anne Morrow Lindbergh waiting with some anxiety on his comments, he settled down to read. For more than one reason, she was extremely nervous about the nature of her husband's reaction. For one thing, she knew that he was a passionately meticulous reader, a believer in literal accuracy, unforgiving of the most trivial mistake or exaggeration.

> On one occasion I urged General Lindbergh to read one of the more than twenty books that had been written about him [wrote William Jovanovich, his publisher]. It was a sympathetic biography that I thought to be unusually free of melodramatic revelations and conclusions. Soon afterwards I received from him a document of seventy-six typewritten pages in which he listed inaccuracies of the book. . . .

How would her father's biographer measure up to her husband's stringent standards?

Almost at once, he pounced upon an exaggeration and denounced it. A few pages further on, and he announced first one error and then, reading rapidly on, another. It was now plain from his exclamations and the expression on his face that Nicolson's journals were, for him, full of irritating and annoying mistakes.

That, at least, was his reaction until he reached page 343 of the book, and then his face went stony. He passed the volume across to his wife, gestured for her to read, and then walked out of the room. He did not come back for a long time, and then only to announce, in a tone of voice she knew only too well, that he was writing at once to Harold Nicolson.

There are two entries on page 343 of the Nicolson *Diaries and Letters*. It was the second and longer of the two which had caught Lindbergh's attention and profoundly disturbed him. It was dated May 22, 1938. This was the time when most people in Europe were beginning to believe that a war between the democracies and Nazi Germany was inevitable, and that Britain and France would soon be fighting. Hitler's armies had occupied Austria, and the Nazi dictator was now threatening the small democratic republic of Czechoslovakia, to whose aid France was pledged to come in the event of an attack. France in turn was Britain's ally and her wars were bound to be Britain's.

It was also the period when Charles and Anne Lindbergh were tenants of the Nicolsons at Long Barn, the farmhouse in the Weald of Kent, not far from Sissinghurst Castle, where Harold Nicolson lived with his wife, Vita Sackville-West, the novelist, and their two sons, Ben and Nigel. The Lindberghs had recently returned from Germany, where they had been warmly welcomed by the Nazis, honored by Adolf Hitler, backslapped by Hermann Göring, and taken on a grand tour of the German Air Force and the factories constructing the planes to reinforce its power. They had been much impressed, both by the planes and by the people. When they returned to England, they hastened to give voice to their impressions, and to their fears for England should a war with Germany come. Since Harold Nicolson was at this time a Member of Parliament and had good connections at Westminster, it seemed to the Lindberghs important that they let him know how they felt. They went to see him, and he recorded the visit this way:

DIARY.   22nd May, 1938

Charles and Anne Lindbergh and Mrs. Morrow [she was on a visit to Britain with her youngest daughter, Constance] come over from Long Barn. Lindbergh is most pessimistic. He says we cannot possibly fight since we should certainly be beaten. The German Air Force is ten times superior to that of Russia, France and Great Britain put together. Our defences are simply futile and the barrage-balloons a mere waste of money. He thinks we should just give way and then make an alliance with Germany. To a certain extent his views can be discounted, (a) because he naturally believes that aeroplanes will be the determinant factor in war; and (b) because he believes in the Nazi theology, all tied up with his hatred of degeneracy and his hatred of democracy as represented by the free Press and the American public. But even when one makes these discounts, the fact remains that he is probably right in saying that we are outmastered in the air.

Victor Cazalet (a fellow M.P. and near neighbor) comes over and we sit on Sissinghurst Crescent in utter gloom. The Germans may force Henlein (leader of the pro-Nazis in Czechoslovakia) to increase his terms to the point where the Czechs cannot possibly accept, and will then intervene. That brings in France, and we shall be faced with the alternative of abandoning France or having a disastrous war.

The news bulletin in the evening is slightly more reassuring. "We have had," the announcer said, "a perfect summer day." True, it is that it has been cloudless and that the sun has poured itself upon the azaleas and the irises. But on the whole it has been the most anxious and unhappy day that I can remember.

On the morning of Saturday, November 5, 1966, Charles Lindbergh drove into Darien and posted a registered letter to Mr. Harold Nicolson at Sissinghurst Castle. (He did not appear to know that he was now Sir Harold Nicolson, nor did he realize that he was old and enfeebled.) The exact contents of this and subsequent letters will not be quoted here because, although Mr. Nigel Nicolson has given consent for his side of the correspondence to be used, Mrs. Anne Morrow Lindbergh has put an embargo on her husband's letters. Suffice to say that the letter was short, sharp, and threatening, and ended by saying that the writer was taking advice and would communicate further.

On November 7, 1966, Lindbergh wrote again, once more to "Mr." Harold Nicolson, complaining bitterly about the "errors" which he felt had been made in *Diaries and Letters*. For instance, why had Nicolson quoted him as saying that German air power was ten times greater than any European power could put against it, when he had simply stated that the German Air Force was stronger than that of all the other countries combined?

But his letter soon made clear that the statement which was troubling him most was the one in which Nicolson had said that he believed in the Nazi theology and hated democracy as represented by the American public. He insisted that the charge was libelous and untrue, and he demanded a public retraction and apology.

Sir Harold Nicolson was fit neither mentally nor physically to deal with all but the simplest correspondence, so after reading Lindbergh's letter to him (he forgot about it almost immediately) his son and editor, Nigel Nicolson, undertook to reply. He addressed his letter to Colonel Charles Lindbergh. (He did not appear to realize that his rank was now that of general.) His attitude was not at all conciliatory.

> Dear Colonel Lindbergh,—Thank you for your letter of November 7th addressed to my father, Sir Harold Nicolson. Although I have shown him your letter and a draft of this reply, he is not really well enough to handle this matter and has asked me to reply for both of us. . . .
>
> You take particular exception to the passage on Page 343 where you are described as believing in "the Nazi Theology" and as hating "democracy" as represented by "the free Press and the American public."
>
> In the first sentence, the word "theology" is loosely synonymous with "ideology." I am quite certain that you never sympathized with the domestic excesses of the Nazi regime, but as your speeches and articles (particularly your article in the *Atlantic Monthly* of March 1940) made clear, you admired their vigour and achievement and saw some historical justification for "the right of an able and virile nation to expand—to conquer territory and influence by force of arms as other nations have done at one time or another throughout history." Later you said that individual liberty is a luxury which can be enjoyed only in stable times. These views, I think, justify the comment that you saw no evil in Germany's methods of recuperation. You did not expect Germany to be beaten in the war and you did not want them to be beaten (see your evidence before the House Foreign Affairs Committee of February, 1941). You saw the Nazi movement as "the wave of the future."

As for my father's remark about your "hatred of democracy . . ." there is no dispute, I think, that you were disgusted by the American press's handling of your private affairs and you were much upset by the cheapness of public reaction to them. Otherwise you would scarcely have left the United States to live temporarily in Europe. To translate your attitude into "hatred of democracy" is no doubt an exaggeration, although I notice that Dorothy Thompson in *Look* magazine of November, 1941, said the same thing more strongly: "I am absolutely certain that Lindbergh hates the present democratic system."

Quotations could be multiplied endlessly, for you spoke and wrote a great deal at that time. But I doubt whether it was your intention when you wrote your letter to revive these old controversies. My father and I would hate to do so since he held and holds your whole family in great respect and affection. Although what you said to him at Sissinghurst on 8th September 1936* and 22nd May 1938 ran contrary to his whole political outlook, he recorded your views without rancour and even with some measure of agreement. Do you really wish to press an old friend to apologise publicly for statements that vary only marginally from the truth? . . . Yours sincerely, Nigel Nicolson.

It seemed that Charles Lindbergh did indeed wish to make Sir Harold Nicolson grovel. Some three or four weeks went by without another word from him, for he was off on another of his jaunts around the globe. But while he was traveling, the newspapers and magazine reviews of *Diaries and Letters* began to appear in the United States, and a great many of them were none too complimentary about the flier's behavior and attitude in the months running up to World War II.

The New York *Herald Tribune* reminded readers that "Nicolson also saw a good deal of Lindbergh during the crisis of 1938–9, when Lindbergh was singing the praises of the German Air Force and finding no fault with the Nazis." The *Saturday Review* mentioned that the *Diaries* offered "some significant glimpses of Charles Lindbergh, not only of his famous tragedy but of his too ardent attachment to the Nazis." And the *New Republic* found that "Sir Harold's record of him as a Nazi sympathizer is no surprise."

---

* Lindbergh had maintained on this occasion that there was no hope for Britain unless she supported the "virile" Germans and abandoned the "decadent" French and the "Red" Russians.

All the bygone controversies, the heated and injurious charges and countercharges, which Lindbergh had hoped had long since gone cold, were now being warmed up again. The image of himself and his wife which he had carefully rebuilt in the postwar years was threatened with being tarnished once more by his calumniators.

He arrived back from his world travels and wrote again, to Nigel Nicolson this time, on December 10, 1966. It was evident that he had been particularly angered by a phrase which Nicolson had used in his letter, the one in which he had charged Lindbergh as seeing the Nazi movement as "the wave of the future." *The Wave of the Future* was the title of a book Anne Lindbergh had written in 1940, at a moment when Britain's fortunes were at a particularly low ebb, in which she seemed to suggest that people must learn to accept nazism, fascism, and communism, because there was no stopping them. The book had caused a great deal of comment, most of it adverse, and one suspects that neither Lindbergh nor his wife now wished to be reminded of its existence.

Once more he insisted that he preferred democracy to any other political system, despite its faults, and it was untruthful and damaging to suggest otherwise. If Sir Harold Nicolson really considered himself a friend of the family, he should withdraw all statements and apologize forthwith, and if he was not well enough to do so, his publishers should do it for him.

In neither the Lindbergh nor the Nicolson household can Christmas 1966 have been a particularly happy one. Anne Lindbergh was tired of this old controversy and must have wondered why her husband insisted on continuing his crusade. At Sissinghurst Castle, whenever he came out of his daydreams, Sir Harold Nicolson would murmur to his son:

"I appear to be in disgrace with Lindbergh about something, but I can't think what."

Finally, on January 17, 1967, after much lonely walking in the woods around Darien and along the shore of Scott's Cove, Charles Lindbergh wrote again. It was a letter composed after what must have been much painful cogitation, and for one as proud and unbending as Charles Lindbergh it undoubtedly cost him more in hurt pride than any other missive he had ever written.

From this letter the peremptory note had completely disappeared, and a man-to-man tone had been substituted for the impression in earlier ones that a lawyer was leaning over his shoulder. He was still irritated by the errors and exaggerations which he claimed to have found in Sir Harold Nicolson's references to him, and cited an incident in the *Diaries* during which he had been described as "vaulting" through a window at the Morrow home, whereas, in fact, he had simply walked through the door. And he harked back repeatedly to Nicolson's charge that he hated democracy and believed in the Nazis. It was not true. Yes, he hated the press. But who could possibly believe that the press represented either democracy *or* the American people? He had always believed in the democratic system, even when it was deteriorating, and he preferred it to any other ideology and would always do so. He had never believed in nazism.

But it was as a friend of Sir Harold's that he was now asking him to do something—something that would repair the damage which the statements in the *Diaries* had done to his reputation. It was not his intention to try to humiliate Sir Harold, but when a man of his reputation had made statements which (Lindbergh insisted) were not true, surely he should be willing to rectify the damage he had done.

It was Nigel Nicolson's turn to write a difficult letter. He was not unaware of the pleading note in Lindbergh's letter. On the other hand, he was convinced that he would be doing his father a disservice if he retracted or apologized for statements which he believed, despite Lindbergh's insistence to the contrary, gave a true picture of his attitude in the vital months before the United States came into the war. Therefore, though well aware of Lindbergh's distress, and anxious not to exacerbate it, he found it impossible to back down. All he could do was try to make his determination to stand by his father as palatable as possible to the man who wanted him to give way.

In the event, the letter which he wrote to Charles Lindbergh on January 31, 1967, was one of which his father would have been proud, had he been able to take it in.

> Dear Colonel Lindbergh [he wrote],—Thank you for your letter of 21st of January. I appreciate its friendly tone, but I still do not feel able to issue in my father's name an apology on the terms which you request. Such an apology would call in question his reliability as a diarist and my responsibility as an editor. Let me deal with these two elements separately.
>
> A diarist is not an historian. Still less is a letter writer. The first writes with extreme rapidity, and with no other reader in mind. The second writes intimately and with the intention to interest and amuse the one person to whom the letter is addressed.† The diary, however, has one great advantage over history, as it is written daily and the mood of conver-

† See page 380.

sations is recorded very soon after they have taken place. It is not direct reporting but it does convey the gist of what the person said, and the effect which his words made upon the diarist. Thus, although my father was not purporting to quote your words directly or exactly, he did commit to paper on that very same day his impression of the way your mind was moving on your return from Germany. He was also trying to work out why your feelings about Germany were so strong, and he attributed that partly to your reaction against the distressing events in which you and your family had been involved in the United States.

It is clear from the passage on page 343 that he was expressing his own opinions ("to a certain extent his views can be discounted . . ."), not quoting what you said to him, so that the most you can charge him with is that he misunderstood your views; one cannot charge him with distorting your words. You also complain that he exaggerated your assessment of the strength of the German Air Force. The expression "ten times superior" is obviously not intended as a mathematical statement. He was not making a technical report. He was conveying by hyperbole, natural to a writer, your impression that the Luftwaffe was a most formidable force.

It was difficult to explain to one as literal-minded and didactic as Lindbergh that writers, particularly diarists, were not always as meticulously accurate as they no doubt should be. As it was, he could only point out about his father's "exaggeration and innocent distortion" that

If he writes "Lindbergh vaulted through the window" when in fact he simply walked through it, he was not intending to falsify a record. He is conveying an impression of your youthful energy, and (in this instance) your dislike of social occasions. Similarly with the telegram passage; in writing to my mother‡ he was indicating the overwhelming pressure to which you were subject. As one might say "Thousands of people swarmed into Trafalgar Square" when, in fact, there were only hundreds. It is in this light that all diaries and letters must be subsequently read. . . .

‡ In a letter to Vita Sackville-West published in the *Diaries*, Nicolson had described "thousands of telegrams" being sent to Lindbergh when there were only hundreds.

It was for Charles Lindbergh alone to decide what action he should take, Nicolson went on.

> You ask me have I any suggestions? Yes, I have one. I suggest you should write to some suitable newspaper in the United States a letter in which you call attention to the passages in the diaries and disclaim the opinions there attributed to you. But, depending on the form of your letter, I reserve the right to reply to it in the same newspaper or elsewhere. If you wish, we might agree beforehand upon the terms of your letter. You might care to send me a draft. . . . Yours sincerely, Nigel Nicolson.

There was no reply to this letter, and from that moment the correspondence ceased. In 1968 this writer asked permission to quote the passage about Lindbergh's political activities and pronouncements as Sir Harold Nicolson had recorded them in his *Diaries*, but this was refused by his publishers "because of Mr. Lindbergh's objections."*

It was rumored that he was preparing a massive refutation of all the accusations against him. It was also said that Anne Morrow Lindbergh and his family were urging him to learn to live with other people's judgments of his prewar activities, no matter how unjust, inaccurate, or hostile they might seem to him to be.

What did it matter, when there were so many other periods of his life that were worth remembering? . . .

* See the author's book, *On Borrowed Time: How World War Two Began* (New York: Random House; London: Weidenfeld and Nicolson, 1969), p. 27.

Part
One
The Makings

CHAPTER

ONE

HUCKLEBERRY SWEDE

One afternoon in the spring of 1971, John T. Rivard, district manager of the Historic Sites Division of the Minnesota Historical Society, looked out of his window and saw that a car had pulled up to the gate of the old Lindbergh house. The house lies on the banks of the Mississippi just outside the small town of Little Falls, Minnesota, and, together with 110 acres of fields and forests surrounding it, was presented as a gift to the state by the Lindbergh family. The gift was made in memory of Charles A. Lindbergh, Sr., father of the flier, former congressman from Minnesota and a considerable character in his own right. It is now a place of pilgrimage for followers of the Lindbergh legend, and its bosky groves and green riverbanks have been turned into a vast picnic and camping area.

Since this was rather too early in the tourist season, and the entrance gate was barred to traffic, anyway, Rivard guessed who the visitor might be even before he recognized the tall gray-haired man climbing out of the car. He walked across the parking lot to open the gate and shook hands with Charles Lindbergh. He was introduced to the man who was with him, Alden Whitman, but was not told that he was a reporter from the New York *Times*.

In the last years of his life, Lindbergh had by no means made his peace with the American press and still viewed most reporters and photographers with intense suspicion and resentment. He still insisted that they twisted his words or quoted them out of context, they took pictures of him and his family from unflattering angles, and their jostling and intrusive flashlights upset him. But Whitman, a veteran reporter of the New York *Times*, he admired as a conscientious newspaperman whose judgment and skill were to be trusted; and he shared, moreover, Lindbergh's love of nature and passionate devotion to ecological causes.

In the spring of 1971 Lindbergh had contacted Whitman and suggested that he accompany him on a transcontinental and trans-oceanic tour of American territories designed to point out to the re-porter, and, through him, to the public "some of the environmental breakdowns" he had witnessed in his lifetime, between the Atlantic coast and Hawaii. They had ranged over Connecticut and New Jersey in Lindbergh's plane, and were now en route to Alaska, Washington, and California, with calls in Minnesota and Montana on the way.

It may well have been simply to indicate to Whitman how times and territory in Minnesota had changed that Lindbergh took him to Little Falls, but one senses that there was a significance behind the visit which had more to do with a feeling in his bones than a desire to make ecological propaganda. When he was alone with John Rivard, he said:

"I had to have a last look at the old house."

It was a curious remark to make, in the circumstances. There was no need for Lindbergh to believe that this need be his last visit. He was sixty-nine in 1971 and made it manifest to everyone that he felt twenty years younger. On this same trip, a few days after leaving Little Falls, he met up with his two eldest sons and challenged them to a race across a Montana cow pasture to prove he was still their physical master, and either he was indeed or they let him think so, for he beat them blind. Throughout the trip he would march briskly for miles through woods and over mountains to demonstrate to the reporter puffing faith-fully behind him, burdened down by his notebook, that he was tireless and on top of his form.

Rivard remembers that a curious remoteness from the rest of them—as if he were distancing himself not only from his companions but from the present time—seemed to settle over Lindbergh the mo-ment he climbed the front steps and re-entered his childhood home. The house has been refurnished with family artifacts in a rough approxi-mation of what it must have looked like from 1906 to 1920, when Charles Lindbergh lived there with his mother, Evangeline Land Lodge Lindbergh, and, more infrequently, with his father, Charles Angustus Lindbergh, Sr. The dining room table is set for a meal, with the Chi-nese dishes his parents bought during their honeymoon in San Francisco. The cookstove still works from the wood in the box beside it, though the stove in the basement that young Lindbergh installed to heat the house is now fed by oil; it is the same stove, though. In the liv-ing room is the swivel chair that his father brought down from his con-gressional office in Washington, and draped over it is a bead shawl embroidered by the local Indians, the Chippewas, who lived in the neighboring woods. Evangeline Lindbergh's room upstairs still has its comfortable bed and family portraits. Across the landing is Lindbergh's room, stuffed with the memorabilia of his boyhood: a box of toy soldiers and armed Indians; his first pair of snowshoes and the license plates of his first motorbikes hung on the wall beside a broken prop from one of his early planes; and pictures of family cars, an ice yacht he built powered by a small engine, an early outboard motorboat with which he explored the Mississippi, and the pump he fixed when he was sixteen years old to bring water to the house and save himself or the hired hand from to-and-froing to the well.

He wandered through the rooms in a sort of moony distraction, down to the old boiler room, and then into the garage where two cars are parked. One is a Saxon Six, which was the Lindbergh family car in 1916, cannibalized by souvenir hunters after Lindbergh's famous transatlantic flight, and later reconstructed with loving care by engineers from the Minnesota National Guard. The other is a 1959 Volkswagen in which he once drove out from Connecticut, sleeping in it (a feat of contortion for a six foot four man) and eating in it en route. He left it behind when he was abruptly summoned back to New York and later presented it to the exhibit, and there it stands beside the old Saxon, sleeping bag still spread across the collapsed spare seat, bully-beef tins littering the floor boards. The curator and the reporter watched him as he came back to the living room level and went to the large screened porch which looks out to a magnificent sweep of the Mississippi as it flows south from its source on Lake Itasca toward Minneapolis, St. Louis, Memphis, New Orleans, and the Gulf. It was here that Lindbergh as a boy did most of his sleeping, hidden under a mountain of blankets against the winter cold and rain, wakened in summer by the fire-and-brimstone flashes of summer storms, the angry red glow of distant brush fires, or the pyrotechnics of the fireflies doing their display of *feux d'artifices* outside the mosquito screens.

He stood there for a time, deep in thought. Then he said abruptly: "No need to go to a motel. We'll stay the night here."

Rivard said, "I'll have your mother's old room made up for you."

He shook his head. "Not necessary. I've got my sleeping bag with me. If you can get me a blanket, I'll bed down in the kitchen."

He walked past them, back into the house, out through the door, and down the steps to the riverbank.

Charles Lindbergh's first conscious memory of the Mississippi was of its black waters turning red in the reflection of a huge fire blazing and crackling on its banks. He was three years old at the time, and the fire was the one that burned his first home to the ground. That was in 1905 and Lindbergh remembered how he began to blubber with fright at the smell of smoke and the sight of the flames, at the desperate shouts of the fire fighters as they sloshed water at the fire and vainly tried to get enough pressure through the hoses to reach the third floor, where the blaze had started. He was snatched up by a maid-cum-nurse and taken to the shelter of the barn, a couple of hundred yards away, where he was kept until nightfall; after which, when it was obvious that there was no hope for the house, he was taken by cart into Little Falls to stay with friends for the night. He sometimes said he could still "see" the flames in his mind as they flickered in the darkness while he was being driven away.

In a way, Lindbergh's vivid memory of the conflagration is significant, for the fire not only burned up the family home but brought to a head the growing estrangement between his parents which was to have a profound effect upon him during the most formative years of his life. His father, Charles Augustus Lindbergh, Sr., was the son of Swedish immigrants to the wooded lakelands of Minnesota which reminded them so much of their homeland. As a child he had been brought up to endure the rigors of early frontier days, and though by the turn of the century he was a well-established lawyer and realtor in Little Falls, it was not too many years earlier that he had had to live with a gun in his hand. With it he supplied the family with meat from the game forests and intimidated the marauding bands of Sioux Indians who divided their time between raiding the friendly indigenous Chippewas and looting or sacking local farms.

Lindbergh, Sr., had been married once before, to May la Fond, daughter of a French Canadian father and an Irish mother, and since she was an admixture of the best qualities of both her parents—proud, passionate, brave, and yet extremely gentle and tenderhearted—she had made her husband supremely happy, as well as having borne him three daughters. But in 1898 May died of an abdominal tumor, just a few days short of her thirty-first birthday, and for a time her husband was inconsolable. As the shock of his beloved wife's death began to fade, he showed an increasing interest in a local kindergarten teacher, Helen Gilbert, whom he had brought into his house to look after his two surviving children (his second daughter had died at the age of ten months). When this caused a certain measure of local scandal, his mother, a stern and God-fearing Swede of the old school, moved into the house with him; and shortly afterward Lindbergh, Sr., departed to downtown Little Falls and took rooms in the Antlers Hotel. There, looking pensively out of his window one day, he saw a young woman gazing at him from an opposite window, and she seemed like the answer to a widower's prayer.

Evangeline Land was in some ways a real-life version of that heroine of Western films, the young, beautiful, cultivated schoolteacher from the East who has come West to bring refinement and enlightenment to the sons and daughters of the rough pioneers along America's frontier. Unlike her Hollywood stereotype, however, Evangeline Land was finding the experience dull rather than exciting, and uncomfortable rather than challengingly rough. It seems more than likely that by the time she saw Charles Augustus Lindbergh, Sr., for the first time, she was just about ready to wash her hands of Little Falls as unworthy of her social and professorial efforts. She had dreamed of teaching social graces to the offspring of two-fisted and trigger-happy miners in some rip-roaring gold or silver town, and Little Falls, an important lumber, fur-trapping, and farming area, had been growing increasingly respectable, and the air was filled with the smell of Swedish home cooking rather than the whiff of gunsmoke. The only drama she had experienced so far was a clash of temperament with her school superintendent, who made it plain that he did not appreciate her highhanded eastern ways.

Matters reached a climax during the winter of 1901. By that time, Eva and Charlie, as they had begun to call each other, were meeting regularly. Since they both lived in the same hotel, she was able to signal from her window when she was leaving her room, and Charlie would walk her to school before going on to his office. They were unofficially engaged by the time she tangled for the last time with the school superintendent. The temperature of the top-floor laboratory, where she was giving a chemistry lesson, was too cold to be borne, she decided, and she picked up the apparatus with which she was working and told her class to follow her downstairs to a lower (and warmer) floor. The superintendent met her on the stairs and ordered her back. She promptly dumped the apparatus at his feet and walked out. Charlie advised her not to go back.

They were married on March 27, 1901. The ceremony took place at the Detroit, Michigan, home of her parents, Dr. and Mrs. Charles Henry Land, and it was Charlie's first meeting with his in-laws. Dr. Land was a dentist whose skills went beyond the mere extraction of aching molars. He had invented the porcelain cap and other orthodontological aids, and had built up a considerable reputation among his peers. It was a big wedding, and among the guests were most of Eva's old classmates from Ann Arbor, where she had majored in chemistry. The couple then left for a honeymoon in San Francisco,

Yosemite Park, and the Garden of the Gods in Colorado. Eight weeks after their return, Eva discovered that she was pregnant.

Determined not to trust herself or her child to the rough ministrations of the local Swedish midwives, she returned to Detroit to have her baby, and there, in the Land home, on February 4, 1902, Charles Augustus Lindbergh was born. By the time she and the infant came back to Little Falls, the home which her husband had been building for them was ready for occupation. It was about two miles south of the town, close to where Pike Creek flows into the Mississippi, and it was in this "richly furnished" three-story residence, "planned with taste and care," that the Lindberghs and their son lived until it burned down three years later. The marriage went up in smoke with the house.

In truth, it had never really worked for more than a few months after the wedding ceremony, because Eva and Charlie were temperamentally quite unsuited to each other. May la Fond, Charlie's first wife, possessed a gentle and romantic disposition which did much to soften and humanize the dreamy, poetic disposition that lay behind his stolid Swedish exterior. His second wife was too young, too self-centered, and too impatient to do likewise. There were seventeen years difference in age between them, but it was more a difference in outlook and attitudes that widened the gulf. Eva was full of *amour-propre* and could not bear to be found in the wrong, teased, or ridiculed. She did not easily forgive anyone who laughed at her when she had made a fool of herself, and Charlie, who had a broad sense of humor, made the mistake of doing so when she tumbled off a horse, fell into the river, or, as happened on one occasion, slipped on the ice in the main street of Little Falls and displayed an inordinate amount of her undergarments. She had a sharp temper and several times showed it in public. After the birth of their son, they rapidly drifted apart.

Since Lindbergh, Sr., was at that time beginning a career in politics— he was elected Republican congressman for the Sixth District of Minnesota in 1907—there was no question of divorce, for his constituents, many of them Roman Catholics, would have been profoundly shocked by it. The couple simply decided to live apart, though to keep up appearances and for the sake of their son, Eva continued to spend periods with her husband in Washington and he came to stay with them in Little Falls whenever he was mending his political fences. They lived separate lives or in separate rooms, and it was an arrangement that seems to have proved less painful to them than to their son.

For a time Charles and his mother lived in the Buckman Hotel in Little Falls, while a smaller house was being built with the insurance money on the site of the one which had burned down. Then they moved for one winter to a rooming house in Minneapolis. It was a period when the boy remembers that he spent most of his time "looking out of windows."* He had been told by his stepsisters about the breakdown in his parents' relationship (or, at least, the fact that they slept in separate rooms), and though he did not realize the full significance of it, he sensed enough about the situation to feel miserable about it. The only bright light in a particularly dark period of his childhood was when he was summoned to Washington and taken to the House for the opening session of the 60th Congress. He was immensely proud of being permitted to sit next to his father among the legislators.

From the moment the new house was finished,† Charles and his mother would follow a routine. Each September they would take the train from Little Falls and travel via Chicago to Detroit, where they would stay two weeks with the Land family. Then they would go on to spend the winter "keeping up appearances" with Congressman Lindbergh. Each spring mother and son would return to Little Falls (again stopping off at Detroit en route) and live for the rest of the year in the house on the banks of the Mississippi. Except for the absence of his father, this was the best time for Charles, because each day brought some new excitement, adventure, or discovery. By the age of six he had his own gun (a gift from his grandfather, a Stevens single-shot .22), and it was the first of many. He taught himself the marksmanship that soon made him expert enough to shoot a duck through the head in full flight (and would one day enable him to win a psychological test of one-upmanship by outshooting the crackshot of the German Luftwaffe with a handgun). He wandered the river and forest on his own, shooting partridge and prairie chickens for the pot, studying woodcraft, collecting butterflies and fireflies, taming a chipmunk, swimming in the creek, catching crayfish, building himself a raft with which to pole himself along the reaches of the great river.

In the letters which he later wrote for the Minnesota Historical Society, Lindbergh gives some revealing glimpses of his lonely childhood.

"In the usual good weather of a Minnesota summer, I spent most of my time outdoors," he wrote. He erected a plank seat in a linden tree, ten feet above the earth, so that he could sit there and scan the opposite bank of the Mississippi, or keep his eye upstream for the first sign of the logs floating down from the lumber camps.

---

* And dropping cats out of them, according to one source. He is said to have taken the landlady's pet tabby and dropped it out of a third-story window "to see if it was true that it would land on its feet." He added gravely: "It is true."

† It is the same one which is now the central pilgrimage point of the Charles A. Lindbergh State Park.

"Sometimes we would go down to the river and walk out on log jams. These log jams were often quite big. As I recall, it was twice each summer that the bateaux and wanigans came through to clear them. Then the 'river pigs' would give exhibitions of logrolling and break up the seemingly unbreakable jams."

Log driving meant free food for the children of the farmers along the riverbank, for, to keep in the good graces of the locals, they were invited to join the "river pigs" at their meals.

"The meals were heavy, good, and unlimited in quantity," he recalled. As one who always enjoyed a more than hearty appetite, he remembered with pleasure the nature and quality of them: "big chunks of meat, potatoes, and carrots, dippered out onto tin plates, if my memory is correct. You could go back for more as often as you wished. And after lunch, you had the privilege of watching as long as you wished the expert plying of peavey and pike pole."‡

When the weather was bad, he would spend most of his time in the house. "For a number of years after the house was built the upstairs rooms were left unfinished with no doors and rough pine floors. I had the entire floor practically to myself. As a result my toys, stone collection, and other articles of interest were well scattered about. I recall two items of particular interest: the rusted barrel of my father's rifle which had been retrieved from the ashes of the first-house fire, and the shell of a snapping turtle on which my father had carved his name. My father told me that after he had carved his name on the turtle he had let it go and that it was found again years later."*

He was a self-absorbed and self-sufficient boy, and so long as he was at Little Falls he always found plenty to do. He was good with his hands from the start, and he built himself stilts, the raft, and a garden hut while he was still only nine years old. He also had charge of a number of regular household chores.

"With week-apart food deliveries from town, an icebox was quite important to us," he wrote. "In addition to meat and vegetables, the icebox let us keep fresh milk which we got from the tenant who ran our farm. It was my job to fill the box with ice, and in the early years this was a formidable task because of the weight of the ice. (I felt it beneath my dignity to split the cakes in half.)"

The icehouse was just a way along from the house, and was filled with big cakes cut from the Mississippi in winter from just above the Little Falls dam.

‡ Charles A. Lindbergh, *Boyhood on the Upper Mississippi: A Reminiscent Letter.* Copyright © 1972 by the Minnesota Historical Society.
* Ibid.

"Of course these cakes were always surrounded by sawdust to keep them from melting during the hot summer months. I would shovel the sawdust off a cake, split it carefully into smaller chunks of a size that would just fit into our icebox, and then with a pair of tongs drag one of the chunks up on top of the sawdust. Since it was too heavy for me to lift up out of the icehouse onto the ground, I had constructed a slide from 2-by-6-inch planks. With a rope attached to the tongs, it was not difficult for me to pull the ice chunks up the slide. Then I would tip my express cart over on its side, push the ice chunk up against it, and tip the cart upright again. I would pull the cart to a stake in the ground well in front of the kitchen steps, to which I had fastened one end of a heavy wire. The other end of the wire I had attached to a ring screw embedded in the house well above the kitchen porch. I would hook the ice tongs to a pulley that ran over this wire and then haul the pulley, with tongs and ice, up on top of the porch. From here it was easy to slide the ice chunk over the floors and into the pantry where we kept the icebox against the north wall. There I had another slide, also made of planks, to get the ice into its compartment."†

It was a contraption and a system worthy of a handy grownup, and Charles Lindbergh was only nine when he thought it out and made it work.

His year was made, of course, when he heard the whistle of the whippoorwill in daytime (the whippoorwill is a nocturnal bird), and he would call to his dog Wahgoosh and race up the road to meet his father, whose call it was. In between his political meetings or sessions at his realtor's office, Lindbergh, Sr., would devote every moment he could spare during his visits to giving his son his whole attention, and a glorious time was had by both of them. They would go off hunting together, or swimming in the creek. It was for his father, in order to have him all to himself, that the boy had built the garden hut down by the river, and his chagrin was great when he discovered that it was too short for his long-legged father to lie down in. When his father had gone back to the house, the boy sawed a hole in the end of the hut, so that if Lindbergh, Sr., stuck his feet through it he could lie down flat. But he never did persuade his father to spend a night there with him.

And then, when he was ten, the internal-combustion engine came into his life, and transformed it.

One day, instead of the sound of the whippoorwill's call, Charles Lindbergh heard the rattle of one of the new automobiles which had

† Ibid.

just begun to be seen around these parts. His father arrived at the house in the passenger seat of a Model T Ford, with a relative at the wheel. He announced that he was leaving it behind at the farm for the use of his wife, and that during his visit he proposed that both he and Evangeline should learn to drive it. Charles, of course, was considered too young to be able to, since his legs were too short to reach the pedals.

Nobody quite knows why, but the Model T was promptly christened Maria (to rhyme with "let's try her"), and for the next three weeks Charles Lindbergh had to go through the mortifying experience of watching his father and mother make a mess of her. Lindbergh, Sr., had no mechanical sense at all, and his estranged wife had not yet caught up with the automobile age. He mistook top gear for reverse and drove Maria into fences or backed her into ditches; his wife was afraid of taking the car out of bottom gear and drove into town with the radiator boiling. Only Charles learned the knack of cranking up the engine when she was cold and avoiding a broken thumb from the kickback.

Cars in those days were still warm-weather vehicles. "One winter driving problem lay in the fact," Lindbergh recalled, "that the spread of sled runners was considerably less than that of automobile wheels, so that even when sleds had packed down the snow, autos couldn't follow in their tracks. It was several years later that state laws required wide-bunk sleds—against considerable opposition from farmers."‡

But in summer, despite the ruts and the absence of routes, riding in the car was a joy for Charles Lindbergh. When his father was at the wheel he did not himself get into the car but stood on the broad running board, hanging on to the struts that supported the removable top.

"I could pick leaves off branches as we passed, and sometimes when the going was slow, scoop up a stone from the road. I liked the wind on my face and through my hair. It was much more fun than riding inside."*

After his father had gone back to Washington, Charles began seriously learning to drive Maria himself. He had fitted out a complicated system of fixed planks in a sort of frame by the barn, on which he would lie down, tuck his feet under the end ones, and start a series of strenuous exercises calculated to stretch his legs and make them long enough to reach the pedals. Whether it was this or just normal growth, but by the time he was eleven years old he found he could push his feet

‡ Ibid. The law requiring sled runners to be at least four feet six inches from center to center was passed by the Minnesota legislature on April 5, 1919, and became law in 1921.
* Ibid.

down to the floor board and still see the road through the driving wheel.

"In the summer of 1913 after I learned to drive, my mother and I often made daylong trips with Maria to Brainerd, St. Cloud, Swanville, Royalton, Pierz, Fort Ripley—to all the nearby towns and villages," he wrote later. "Maria gave us a freedom of travel we had never dreamed of before. Almost always we carried a picnic lunch, and when possible we found a lake shore on which to eat it. Then we would hunt for carnelians on the beach. Several times we found a carnelian arrowhead. . . . None of the country roads were paved, and only a few of the more important highways had even a macadam surface. It was easy to get stuck in sand or ruts with an automobile, especially on the farm and woods roads leading to a lake shore. We often got stuck with Maria, although I soon became expert at judging when we could get through and when we couldn't."†

When Lindbergh, Sr., arrived in Little Falls in the summer of 1913, his son was waiting at the wheel of the Model T as he came out of the depot. The congressman was there to make a tour of the Sixth District as a warm-up for the election of 1914, and after a few experiences of his twelve-year-old son's driving prowess, he agreed to let him act as chauffeur during his speech-making program.

"Most of our driving was done by day, but there were also night drives over country roads. The headlights of the 1912 Ford cars ran on calcium carbide. We carried with us a can of carbide lumps in order to replenish a used charge. The gas generator was on the running board, a polished brass affair, cylindrical and standing upright. The lower portion of the cyclinder contained the carbide calcium lumps. The upper portion contained water. When you needed headlights you turned on a valve that allowed water to drip on the carbide. This generated gas. When the gas reached the headlights, you hinged open their brass-rimmed glass doors and lit the burners. It was hard to get just the right adjustment on the water valve."‡

They got lost frequently in the Minnesotan backwoods, for the roads were not too clearly blazed, and it was easy to miss them in the darkness, or mistake their color. There were blue trails, red trails, yellow trails, and blue and yellow trails marked in paint on trees, and if you missed one you could end up in the wilderness.

"One rainy evening in the country [father], two other men and I got on a road that was so bad, and we got stuck so often, that we gave up trying to reach the town for which we were headed and spent the

† Ibid.
‡ Ibid.

night on the parlor floor of a roadside farm house. The farmer could give us only two blankets, but we kept the stove burning enough to stay warm in spite of our half-soaked clothes."*

They were physically exhausting times for a twelve-year-old boy, but Charles Lindbergh had never been happier. He was spending days and nights at his father's side, and he could not think of anything more rewarding.

Charles Lindbergh took practically no interest at all in the political issues which his father was raising during his campaign tour.

"While I wanted very much to have my father win, my primary interest in his campaign trips lay in the opportunity to be with him and to drive Maria," he wrote later.

In fact, his father was waging the most strenuous campaign so far of his political career in his fight for a fifth term as congressman for the Sixth District. Charlie Lindbergh was an official Republican, but like many another congressman from the western farming states his outlook was strongly tinged with Progressist ideas. It was also true that where his farming constituents were concerned, he was in favor of tariff walls and other methods of market protection. He had strongly opposed President Taft's plan for a Reciprocal Trade Treaty with Canada, on the grounds that though it might open new markets to American manufacturers and give newspaper interests cheaper Canadian newsprint, it would also flood the country with cheap Canadian food, to the detriment of American farmers.

His opposition to this measure, in fact, was so strident that he allowed himself to salt his attack on one occasion with an anecdote which was (for one usually so reticent and respectable in words and behavior) surprisingly rough.

"What is this 'reciprocity' they are asking us to accept?" he demanded. "Let me give you an illustration of what it can mean."

He then proceeded to tell the story of a traveler who, finding himself stranded, asked a farmer for shelter for the night and was told he would have to share a room with the youngest child, since that was the one with the extra bed. The weary traveler settled in for the night and all went well until the early hours, when he felt an urgent need to relieve himself. The lavatory was an outhouse in the garden, the night was bitterly cold, and he would have to pass through the bedroom of the farmer and his wife to get there. So, after much painful cogitating, he went across to the other bed, removed the sleeping child and put it in

* Ibid.

his own, and then urinated in the child's bed. But when he went to move the child back, the cunning traveler discovered that the child had used the occasion to defecate in his bed.

"That's reciprocity!" declared Congressman Lindbergh.

But on most other subjects he was liberal, and sometimes even socialist, in his ideas. He was a fervent opponent of the big money trusts, and in 1913 he published a book, *Banking and Currency and the Money Trust*, in which he attacked the "unfair practices" of such private banking organizations as the Rockefellers and J. P. Morgan, and campaigned strongly to prevent the passage of the so-called Aldrich Plan to create a National Reserve Association.

"Wall Street, backed by Morgan, Rockefeller, and others, would control the Reserve Association," he declared, "and those again, backed by all the deposits and disbursements of the United States, and also backed by the deposits of the national banks holding the private funds of the people, which is provided in the Aldrich Plan, would be the most wonderful machinery that finite beings could invent to take control of the world."†

He was a great defender of American independence but he had a lively suspicion that the big banking trusts and other business interests whom he so much hated and mistrusted were scheming to involve the United States in war, not to preserve the nation's integrity but to protect their financial interests overseas. It so happened that in 1913 the Díaz Government in Mexico had been overthrown by the revolutionary forces of General Victoriano Huerta, who was anti-American and anti-big business, especially foreign big business. Under the Wilson Administration there was a strong movement afoot for armed intervention by U.S. forces, and this, Congressman Lindbergh maintained, would mean war, the enemy of the people's progress.

In a passionate plea against war that would find echo in his son's voice a quarter of a century later (though he might not be listening now) Lindbergh, Sr., cried out:

"War is paid for by the people. It is the slavery and drudgery that follows war that is more damaging than war itself. We glorify the soldier. We appeal to his pride and to his patriotism. The country treats him as a hero, and he is a hero. But what of those who drudge year after year all through life to make up for the destruction of war? . . . I would rather die in action amid the thunder of cannon than by the drudgery that war brings to those who pay the cost. We are safe here in this

† U. S. Congress House Committee on Banking and Currency, *Changes in the Banking and Currency System of the United States*, 63rd Cong., 1st ses., H. Rept. 69, p. 135.

House. The most of us are safe from the burden that war would bring. Are we therefore to be indifferent to the men and women who would really pay the toll? It would be taken out of their daily earnings for the rest of their lives and out of their children's earnings. And what are we to gain? An enormous debt and the loss of valuable lives."‡

These were sentiments that sounded almost socialist to many a stanch Republican, and some of them found themselves more in sympathy with the belligerent line taken by Congressman Lindbergh's Democrat opponent, Dr. J. A. Du Bois, who, though anxious to proclaim his "progressive" ideas, still loyally followed the Wilson line over Mexico. Nor were pro-Allied sentiments pleased when the 1914–18 war broke out in Europe at the height of the campaign, and Congressman Lindbergh at once made his position clear.

"It is true that Europe is ablaze and the destruction of life and property is tremendous," he declared, "but nothing should be destroyed here as a result of the war, so why should we allow the European war to destroy our reason?"

For the moment prointerventionist sentiments were not strong enough to put his seat in danger, but when the results were announced in November 1914, he retained his seat but failed to win by an over-all majority for the first time since he had fought in the Sixth District. He had 47.5 per cent of the vote. Du Bois received 35.2 per cent.

Pro-Allied feelings were growing, and one day soon they would engulf him—with a little help from the congressman himself.

Charles Lindbergh seemed unaware that his father was fighting for his political life. While speeches and arguments were going on, he was too busy tinkering with the internal mechanism of Maria. On several occasions he passed out his father's campaign tracts at meetings, but later confessed that he never did get around to reading them.

‡ In a speech in Congress, *Congressional Record*, 63rd Cong., 2nd sess., p. 6952.

CHAPTER

TWO

DOWN ON THE FARM

In later years, the older citizens of Little Falls recalled Evangeline Land Lindbergh as "a gracious and neighborly lady." But that was after her son became famous, and, in fact, two more inappropriate words could hardly have been used to describe her. Gracious she seldom was with the locals. Neighborly she definitely was not. During the early years of her marriage to Charlie Lindbergh, when they lived in the house that burned down, she often entertained and held card parties. But it can only have been to further her husband's business interests, because after the separation she eschewed town gatherings, invited no one to the house, and saved her social life until she got to Washington and Detroit. Furthermore, she discouraged her son Charles from becoming "too friendly" with the neighbors' boys, and pursed her lips in a silent disapproval which made Charles feel guilty whenever he came back from swimming, boating, or other adventures with the Armstrong boys from the farm down the road.

Evangeline Lindbergh was a physically attractive woman, and she got lots of smiles and salutations when she came into Little Falls with her son in Maria on their weekly shopping expeditions. But she sharply rebuffed any attempts to get to know her better, and adopted a lofty tone of *de haut en bas* whenever she was speaking to someone in the town whom she considered her social inferior, and that was practically everyone.

As a result, a certain element of resentment built up against her, and this may well have been the explanation for the mysterious "shootings" which troubled mother and son's stay at the farm during at least two summers.

It usually seemed to happen after Evangeline Lindbergh had been into town, or ridden across the countryside on one of her regular outings on her horse. She was a good rider, and insisted on using an English saddle rather than the pommeled western version, and since it was rough country, on at least two occasions she came back, once on foot, with torn clothes and a scratched face, having taken a tumble while galloping through the scrub. The shots usually came on the days following these outings.

"My father never happened to be on the farm when one of these incidents took place," Charles Lindbergh recalled later. "The first shooting incident I recall was a bullet whining past our heads as my mother and I were standing on the north side of our house. We immediately went inside. The shooting was obviously to scare and not to kill— almost certainly done for amusement—although a man walking along the road to the north of our farm was hit in the leg by a bullet."*

For most of his life until he met Anne Morrow, his mother was the only female to whom he felt close. He was always extremely protective toward her and, except when his father was there, considered himself the master of the house and responsible for her comfort, companionship, and general welfare. As a result, the mysterious shootings alarmed and angered him, and both at school and during his expeditions to Martin Engstrom's emporium in Little Falls, where he bought gas and spare parts for the car, and drank lemonade in the drugstore parlor next door, he let it be known that anyone who continued to frighten his mother in this fashion would have to reckon with him.

Shortly afterward there occurred what he recalled as "the most serious of the shooting incidents."

"I was poling a raft off the riverbank," he wrote. "Bullets began splashing within five or six feet of the raft, and I heard cracks from a rifle across the river. I poled the raft to shore as quickly as I could, beached it, and climbed up over the bank and out of sight. As I recall, Bill Thompson was with me at the time, though I don't think he was on the raft. [Bill Thompson was a farmer's son from the next homestead.] After the shots from the east riverbank, Bill and I raced across the valley and up the hill to our house. I grabbed my 22-caliber rifle and gave him the 10-gauge cannon. We returned to the valley and crawled (out of sight of the east bank) to [an] earthworks. Pushing through the grass, we saw several men and boys in a clearing across the river from us. As I now recall there were one man—probably a young

* Charles A. Lindbergh, *Boyhood on the Upper Mississippi: A Reminiscent Letter.* Copyright © 1972 by the Minnesota Historical Society.

man—and four or five not fully grown boys. The man was carrying a rifle and all were singing 'Shoot the Old Nigger up in the Tree.' "†

Charles and his companion lay flat on the grass and aimed their guns. They were to aim just wide of the group, he ordered, but close enough "so they would hear the bullet sing."

"I counted to three and on 'three' we both fired. Of course the cannon made a tremendous noise and the zing of the bullet was effective. The group scattered into bushes and trees, and there was no more firing that year."‡

Charles was able to inform his mother confidently that henceforward she would no longer be troubled by "snipers." As if by tacit agreement, neither of them seems to have informed Lindbergh, Sr., of the incidents.

In the summer of 1915 Congressman Lindbergh arrived from Washington with the news that he had been given six weeks' leave of absence from the House in order to lead a two-man expedition to the sources of the Mississippi. He was to write a report on the flooding of the headwaters owing to the malfunction of the system of dams, which was reported to be seriously dissipating the resources of the mighty river. When his thirteen-year-old son asked him who would be the second member of the expedition, his father replied, "You."

The voyage was a landmark in the boy's life, and one of his most grueling experiences. They took a clinker-built boat with them, and rowed or drove it—it had an outboard motor—from the vast network of waterways leading out of Lake Itasca, from whose womb the Mississippi sprang, down to the rapids above Little Falls. They stayed with the Chippewas and Charles was made a member of the tribe. They spent nights with the jacks in the lumber camps, and Charles learned for the first time that his father liked to sing (in a tuneless tenor) and that he had a considerable repertoire of locker-room stories which sometimes made him blush. They pitted their skill as marksmen against each other when they went hunting, and the boy discovered that he could now outshoot his father. They were burned black by the sun and bitten by midges, pestered by flies, and sometimes driven mad by mosquitoes. And by the campfire at night, his father talked, of his childhood in the wilderness, of his pioneer father, and of his political ambitions and motivations.

Those ambitions were about to come up against their sternest tests, and his career in politics would soon be at stake.

† Ibid.
‡ Ibid.

Charles Lindbergh was later to describe his father as "deep, subtle, straight-faced," and his in-laws, the Lands of Detroit, thought him "a rather severe individual, hard to approach and eccentric." He seems, though, to have been much more of a dreamer than any of them ever guessed, and, in politics, a kind of Don Quixote who rarely attacked individuals but was always tilting against the windmills of state and institutional privilege.

In 1916 he announced he was abandoning his seat in Congress at the end of the session and would be fighting in the Minnesota primaries for the Republican nomination for senator. He was beaten and the legend seems to have been cultivated that he was knocked out solely because of his doughty stand against American intervention in World War I. It is true that Lindbergh, Sr., was against American participation, and campaigned strenuously to keep the United States out. But the other three candidates were running similar programs of nonintervention, and even the Democrats were campaigning on the slogan that President Wilson "kept us out of war." Had it been simply a question of Lindbergh, Sr., attacking the "warmongers," it is extremely probable that he would have gotten the Republican nomination from his three less able rivals, Kellogg, Eberhart, and Clapp.

But he insisted on finding an extra institutional windmill against which to tilt during the primaries, and this one was not only impregnable but had powers of reprisal that were to prove fatal to his chances.

He chose to introduce the question of the Roman Catholic Church into the campaign.

An antipapist movement calling itself the Free Press Defense League (about which little information exists today) had been issuing pamphlets in the Middle West charging that the Roman Church in America was subverting freedom of the press, speech, assembly, thought, and conscience. For reasons which even his closest friends and admirers failed to understand, Lindbergh, Sr., decided that he must introduce these matters first into the campaign and then into Congress. He stated that he did not necessarily believe the charges but that he felt they deserved the closest investigation, and introduced a measure into the House to that end. Since he himself did not appear to be convinced of the veracity of the accusations against the church, it seemed to be an incredibly clumsy move to have made during a campaign, especially in a state with a large Catholic vote. He was soundly whipped in the primaries and came in at the bottom of the list.

But more important than that, the Catholic authorities and laity resented his apparent readiness to accept libels against them, and did not forget his stance. In the two years after his defeat in the senatorial race, he increased his opposition to the war, and wrote and financed the publication of a book called *Why Is Your Country at War?* It described the conflict in which the United States was engaged as "senseless" and accused "speculative interests" of tricking the nation into hostilities, and he maintained that idealistic legislation and socialistic ideas would settle quarrels between nations in a manner that could never be achieved by force of arms.

It was a much less expedient stance than his son was to take in the period leading up to World War II, and there was considerable support for it among thoughtful people in places far beyond the isolationist states of the Middle West. In 1918 he decided to carry his campaign to the people by putting himself forward as the Nonpartisan League candidate in the Minnesota Republican primaries for governor of the state, and it was one of the roughest campaigns in Minnesotan history. Not only did all the prowar elements gang up against him—and, of course, these were powerful, since America was now in the war—but his "smears" (or what the church and many people thought were smears) against Roman Catholics came back to haunt him.

His refusal to take an anti-German stance, his attacks on the press and on supporters of the Red Cross all combined to rouse antagonism. He was pelted with rotten eggs at meetings, he was accused of disloyalty to his country, his book was confiscated, and at one time he was arrested apparently on the grounds of "sedition," though the actual charge was never made. More important, prayers that "Lindbergh shall not be governor" were said in Catholic churches all over the state.

On June 17, 1918, a record number of voters turned out and voted for Lindbergh's rival, J. A. A. Burnquist, by 199,325 votes to 150,626, and to all intents and purposes (though he did try to make a comeback later) it was the end of Charlie Lindbergh's political career on a national scale. He himself later came to admit that his ham-handed introduction of the Roman Catholic Church into his campaign arguments and his congressional speeches had been a blunder far more damaging to his chances than his outright opposition to the war.

Evangeline Lindbergh was willing to be with her erstwhile husband and act as his hostess in Washington so long as he was an up-and-coming member of the House, but when his defeat in the senatorial primaries of 1916 washed up his career and he went back to the capital as a kind of lameduck congressman, there only until the following March, and then only to clean up his office, she saw no reason to go along and help him to pick up the pieces.

Instead, she proposed to her son that they embark on an adventure that would give them both "a change of air." The shooting incidents earlier in the year appear to have worried her and left her restless. She summoned her brother, Charles, from Detroit—after her son, Charles Land was always the man to whom she was closest—and announced that they would go to California together for the winter. Moreover, they would go by automobile.

To help him get around in his Senate campaign, Charlie Lindbergh had sent his wife the money to buy a new car to replace Maria, now showing signs of mechanical palpitation and what their son called "infernal combustion." She bought a Saxon Six from Farrow's Garage in Little Falls in the spring of 1916, and it was just about as up-to-date as you could get. It had an electric starter, for one thing, a six-cylinder engine, and was much better sprung. A handyman was called in to build a garage to house it in, and when the primaries were over and his father had gone back to Washington, Charles got down to the serious business of grinding the valves, replacing the piston rings, and generally overhauling it for the momentous journey. It would be the first time he had ever been west of Minnesota.

They started out in August 1916, and the weather couldn't have been worse. In 1934, at the age of seventeen, the author drove across the American continent for the first time, and even then there were large stretches of the route along Highway 66, which the Lindberghs seem to have followed, where the banked-up roads became pure sludge after a heavy rainstorm, and on the stretches of macadamed highway it was disaster if an approaching truck forced your nearside wheels onto the verge, which only too often was as treacherous as quicksand. It was certainly much worse in 1916, and since Charles Lindbergh drove the whole way ("neither my mother nor uncle had learned to drive the Saxon"), it must have been a test of his nerve, skill, and endurance. According to their plans, they hoped to make the Pacific Coast in ten days to two weeks. It took them four times as long. But all Charles Lindbergh says about it is:

"We encountered a great deal of bad weather and many miles of poor roads—sometimes literally impassable, as in Missouri where we had to stay at a small-town hotel until the clay road dried up. Our trip to the coast took forty days."*

Uncle Charles returned to Detroit after a short stay in California. Mother and son took a cottage at Redondo Beach and Charles was enrolled in the high school there. School records reveal that he was not

* *Boyhood on the Upper Mississippi.*

a particularly keen or outstanding pupil. In any case, he had never favored school lessons. Like George Bernard Shaw, who once said that his
education was interrupted from the ages of six to seventeen while he
went to school, Charles Lindbergh preferred to teach himself and
resented being taught by others. He was self-conscious in front of other
students and showed himself openly bored when they failed to understand or got wrong something he had already boned up at home and
knew thoroughly.

So he played hooky on several occasions and wandered along the
beach, looking for shells, or dug into the sage-covered bluffs overlooking
the sea for stones which he and his mother collected called serpentines,
green in color, which, the boy decided, "looked like the waves of the
sea when polished." He recalled later that the serpentines were responsible for the one and only time in his life when he was arrested. He had
spent the afternoon with his mother on the bluffs digging among the
salvias for the stones they both prized so much. Why they collected so
many—unless his mother was selling them—is hard to understand, but
after several strenuous hours they had filled a large bag with them, and
they were both extremely tired. The bag was too large for them to carry
home, so Charles announced that he would go back to the cottage for
the car while his mother stood guard over the serpentines.

They kept their Saxon Six in a local garage, and by the time the boy
and his dog Wahgoosh reached it, darkness had fallen. When he tried
the lights of the car, he discovered they would not work, and he was
obliged to drive back to the beach with only a spotlight on the wind-
shield lighting his way. As luck would have it, a policeman patrolling
the sidewalk on the outskirts of Redondo saw him, flagged him down,
and told him he was arresting him for driving on one light. He was persuaded to allow the boy to go on and pick up his mother, but was
handed a ticket to appear in court next day.

There it was discovered that not only was he playing hooky from
school but was underage (he was fourteen) and not allowed to drive in
California. He was let off with a caution when his mother put in a plea
for him, during which she did not fail to invoke the name of Congressman Lindbergh as her husband and the boy's father. But thereafter,
whenever they were within city limits, Evangeline drove (badly) until
they were out of sight of the law and the boy could take over again.

They liked California and they would probably have stayed on there
had not a telegram arrived from Detroit in the late spring of 1917 to
say that Evangeline's mother had cancer and could not be expected to

live long. They hurried to Detroit to see her, and later she was brought to the farm at Little Falls, where her daughter could look after her.†

They had decided to spend the winter on the farm, and it would be the first time they had done so. The United States was now involved in World War I, and ex-Congressman Lindbergh forecast a dire period for the nation and general food shortages. He told his son that he thought the farm should be stocked with sheep and cattle the following spring, and that he and his mother should prepare to make themselves self-sufficient.

It was a prospect that filled Charles Lindbergh with a grave sort of pleasure. At fifteen, going on sixteen, he considered himself quite grown-up and well able to look after his mother and himself. He had by this time taken over all the duties except the sexual ones that would have been performed by her husband, and save for the periods, increasingly rare, when his father was in residence, he took all major decisions about the house and the farm.

The only thing which interfered with his status as master of the house was the fact that he was still going to school, and that first winter of 1917–18 it riled him to have to set off every morning by bike or, if the snow was too thick, on foot to Little Falls High School. The other students were the same age as he was, but they seemed such kids, only interested in japing or flirting with the girls in the class, whereas he had *serious* things to do.

"That was the first winter anyone had lived in our house, and considerable preparation was required," he wrote later. "We had storm windows put on and the upstairs rooms further finished. . . . With the help of neighbor boys, paid by the hour, I had dug an open well in the basement's northwest corner. It seems to me we went down about twenty-five feet. . . . I installed a small gasoline engine and pump in the basement and a pressure tank—doing all the plumbing myself."‡

Martin Engstrom came out from Little Falls to put in a hot-air furnace, but it burned up so much wood that they rationed their supplies to keep only a modicum of heat in the basement and the bedrooms, and lived and kept warm through the winter in the kitchen and the sewing room, both of which had wood stoves. Evangeline and her mother shared a bedroom. Charles slept on the screened porch, no matter how cold it was (and it reached forty degrees below on the farm at one period).

"I would undress in the warm sewing room," he recalled, "put on an

† She lasted another eighteen months and, still in her daughter's care at Little Falls, did not die until January 6, 1919.

‡ *Boyhood on the Upper Mississippi.*

old fur-lined coat of my father's, open the window and climb through it
onto the bed. The bed was piled high with blankets and quilts. Often
Wahgoosh would sleep with me. On some very cold nights the stars
were extraordinarily bright. I would look out at the constellations before falling asleep. At intervals a tree, stressed too much by the cold,
would crack through the still night like a rifle shot."*

Evangeline Lindbergh disagreed with her husband's attitude toward
World War I and was intensely patriotic, like her family in Detroit. If
Charles had any feelings at all, he shared those of his mother. Certainly
the war sounded exciting to him. He was reading a serial in *Everybody's
Magazine* called "Tam o' the Scoots" by the British writer Edgar
Wallace, and it was all about a young Scotsman with the Royal Flying
Corps on the western front who becomes an ace pilot.

"I think this story had considerable effect on my decision to enlist in
the army when I was old enough and so become a fighter pilot myself,"
he wrote later.

In the meantime, he sat up nights under the kerosene lamps working
out plans for the future of the farm. He had decided that the farm
should be mechanized, and he had already—without consulting his father until it was done—ordered a La Crosse three-wheeled tractor with
a two-gang plow. He had traveled around the district talking to neighboring farmers, and once they realized that this grave-faced boy was serious when he talked about "stock for my farm," they had advised him
what to buy and where to go for it. He had determined on a herd of
Red Polled cattle, Duroc-Jersey hogs, Shropshire sheep—and Leghorn
chickens and Toulouse geese for his mother to look after.

But how could he take on the chores that would be involved so long
as he was still going to school, trying desperately to keep up? Except for
physics and mechanical drawing, he was doing badly, and there just
wasn't time to work around the farm and also do his homework. He
hated the humiliation of the classroom each morning when he had to
display an empty notebook or present his hastily scribbled, and too
often erroneous, homework to the teacher. He was never able to bear
the sneers of his contemporaries, and he several times did battle with
boys who dared to mock him for his setbacks, though there was nothing
he could do except burn with slow anger over the sniggers of the girls.

By the beginning of 1918 his marks were so low that he became convinced that he would never pass his final exams and graduate, and that
would be a humiliation almost too much to bear. And then luckily, the
war let him off the hook. A nationwide propaganda campaign had

* Ibid.

begun to increase food production, but farm labor was being drafted into the Army for service in France, and workers were scarce. It was announced one day by the high school principal that any boy wishing to leave school and volunteer for farm work would be given full academic credit for the period while he was away and would not have to submit to examinations.

Charles Lindbergh left high school at once, and never went back again except at the end of the school year in 1918, to collect his diploma. By that time he was a full-fledged farmer in his own right. He cherished the memory of the days when the herd of heifers and the flock of sheep his father had ordered for him arrived at the depot in Little Falls, and practically half the town turned out to watch how he handled each of them in turn as he drove them back to the farm on the riverbank. "Didn't let a single stray get away," he said later.

He had bought himself a couple of ponies from a neighboring farm to help him to get around in winter, and one of them, Queen, had never been broken to a saddle. He managed to get his father's old western saddle on her and, after a couple of spills, got her sufficiently tamed to bear him on her back—"though she never could resist suddenly bucking now and then." The other, Prince, he rode about the countryside until they were caught in a blizzard riding back from Pierz one night, and the pony collapsed and died of exhaustion as the boy was leading him by the reins through the driving snow.

The farm became his life, and it seemed as if his life would become the farm. Though he was still only sixteen years old, the pattern of his future looked as if it had already been shaped and this is how he would live and work until he died: a farmer, on bigger and better farms, maybe, with a wife and children as well as his mother to help him, but nothing more nor less than a Minnesotan farmer. He was up before dawn to operate the brand-new milking machine in which he had invested. He was always building something: styes for the hogs, a small suspension footbridge across Pike Creek, a duckpond for the Toulouse geese. By this time, his mother was too busy watching life ebb out of old Mrs. Land, now in the painful terminal stages of her illness, to feed the geese and chickens, so he took over that chore, too, prepared swill for the hogs, helped the cows to calve, collected stray lambs, mucked out the stable, stopped the hogs from bashing their young against the walls of the styes, ploughed, planted, and reaped, tinkered with the machines, and laid out a work program for the hired man.† His only out-

---

† By agreement with his father, he had put a seventy-year-old retired lumberjack named Daniel Thompson in the tenant's house in return for odd help around the farm. "Thompson was, of course, an expert axman," Lindbergh wrote later. "He could fell

ings were to market or to neighboring farms to buy and sell animals, pick up supplies. He was working at all hours in subzero temperature, he slept in subzero surroundings, but, except when he had to swim the swollen creek to rescue a sheep or cow, he was never cold and always fighting fit.

At night he lay in his cot on the porch, studying the constellations in the night sky, listening to the wind or the snapping twigs or the Mississippi flowing by, and he dreamed that he was Tam o' the Scoots doing battle with the Hun above the western front in France. But at 5 A.M. his alarm bell rang, and he was off through the snow in his gum boots, black serge britches, leather coat, and fur cap pulled down low over his ears, ready for another day of wrestling with the crude practicalities of life on a small Minnesota farm.

And then, on November 11, 1918, while he was bidding for cattle at a farm auction in Morrison County, someone handed the auctioneer a note and he shouted to the small crowd of bidders around him:

"Gentlemen, I have good news. The war is over!"

And though he did not realize it at the time, so was Charles Lindbergh's career as a farmer.

---

a tree with amazing speed, considering his age. I had to restrict his activities in this respect, because he tended to look on trees as overgrown weeds."

CHAPTER

THREE

BARNSTORMING

Evangeline Lindbergh had no doubts about what she wanted her son to do now that the war was over. She was a great believer in academic qualifications and took a poor view of the way Charles had used prevailing conditions to get his high school diploma without working or sitting for it. Now he must remedy the situation by getting himself a college education, after which he could come back to Little Falls and set up as an engineer or become a bigger and better farmer (with herself to look after him, of course). His father seems to have misread his character completely, for though he agreed about the college education, he thought that afterward Charles should go to work in an office.

All Charles Lindbergh knew was that he was restless and that somehow the end of the war was forcing decisions on him. Until the armistice, he had quietly planned (he did not tell his mother about it until years later) to go off and enlist in the Army Air Corps the moment he was old enough, and his ambition was to end up as a fighter ace in France. When that hope was frustrated, he did the next best thing by buying himself a twin-cylindered Excelsior motorbike from Martin Engstrom, and gunned it around Little Falls with a daredeviltry that scared the wits out of everyone but himself. It was as near to flying as he could get at the moment.

He had rarely failed to take his mother's advice, and he knew it would please her if he agreed to go to college. So during the spring of 1919 they spent their nights together studying college prospectuses. Charles Lindbergh later said he finally chose the University of Wisconsin "probably more because of its lakes than because of its high engineering standards. Then, as now, I could not be happy long away from water." But in fact his mother's own plans had probably just as much to do with it. She was determined not to cut the umbilical cord yet, and that meant that when Charles left Little Falls she must move with him. It could only be done if she found a job, because her erstwhile husband was now no longer in a position to give his wife and son an allowance. His affairs were going badly. A magazine he had started, *Lindbergh's National Farmer*, was losing money rapidly, and what remained of his resources was being spent in a vain attempt to resuscitate his political career.

So when Charles Lindbergh enrolled at Wisconsin U, it was not only because of the proximity of the lakes but also because his mother had found a post as a science teacher at Emerson Junior High, in Madison. Once the decision was made, he turned the farm over to tenants (making it a condition that Dan Thompson be kept on as handy man) and filled in the time until he was old enough to go to college by taking on the local agency for the milking machine he had used on the farm.

"It was a difficult and rather heartbreaking procedure, giving up the stock and machinery and seeing my methods and hopes give way to the methods and hopes of others," he recalled later. "But it gave me more time to spend on the milking-machine agency. This agency was disappointing in the end. There wasn't enough demand for milking machines to make them attractive from a business standpoint. Farmers were interested, but the cost of a milking machine was high in relation to their income. Some were afraid it would reduce their yields of milk and eventually damage the cows."*

In the summer of 1920 Evangeline went ahead to Madison and found a shabby but cheap apartment on the top floor of a brownstone house on North Mills, three blocks away from Wisconsin U. Charles stayed on alone at Little Falls to see in the new farm tenants and do some last-minute clearing up. Then kick-starting his Excelsior, he zoomed round the house and along the river's edge just once, and sped off down the lane for Minneapolis and Wisconsin. It was not the last time he would see the house which had wombed him for fifteen of his eighteen years, but he would never live there again for more than a day or two.

He came back by himself one day in 1921, when he was trying to work out in his mind how to break some bad news to his mother, and he wandered around the house, a Colt .45 in a holster strapped around his waist. He was going through a phase when he liked to imagine himself the fastest gun in the West (he was already the champion marks-

---

* Charles A. Lindbergh, *Boyhood on the Upper Mississippi: A Reminiscent Letter.* Copyright © 1972 by the Minnesota Historical Society.

man at Wisconsin), and he spent hours practicing quick draws. Searching through the empty rooms for imaginary enemies, he accidentally pulled the trigger after one draw, and put a bullet through the door between hallway and kitchen—where the hole can still be seen today. He was irritated to discover, when he examined it, that it was too high to have killed an adversary had one really been there.

A couple of years later, in 1923, when his way of life had changed radically, he dropped into Little Falls from the sky and landed in a meadow west of the farm.

"Daniel Thompson was there to meet me, ax slung over his shoulder in the manner so familiar to me in the past, tremendously impressed by my airplane, and impressed still more by the fact that I was flying it," he wrote later. "I felt nostalgia then if ever I felt it in my life, for I knew the farming days I loved so much were over. I had made my choice. I loved still more to fly."†

The bad news he brooded about in the house during his 1921 visit was how to tell his mother that he was dropping out of college after just over a year. It was to please his mother that he had consented to go, and he had sensed that he wasn't going to like it, but he hadn't realized just how frustrating and time-wasting he would find it. For one thing, he hadn't realized how *frivolous* his fellow-students would prove to be, only interested in drinking, smoking, dancing, girls, and having fun. It was the beginning of the jazz age, and Charles Lindbergh was the odd man out—a strict abstainer from both alcohol and tobacco,‡ with a tin ear, no sense of rhythm, and two left feet, a feeling toward girls that varied between awe and contempt, and, just to be contradictory, a fierce antagonism toward the college rules and regulations by which the authorities tried (and failed) to control the activities of the students.

"They treat you here as though you were a baby," he complained. "Presumably a man comes to college because he wants an education. Why, then, all this taking of rolls, daily assignments, checks on your personal life, and so on?"*

It was difficult to know why he was complaining, because in his opinion most of the students were a bunch of grown-up babies, anyway. It was true that, given his antipathy to being taught and supervised, Charles himself would probably have benefited by a more relaxed,

---

† Ibid.
‡ He also never drank coffee or colas.
* A remark recalled by one of his classmates and reproduced in *The Hero*, by Kenneth S. Davis (Garden City: Doubleday, 1959).

English-style of undisciplined curriculum, but he could hardly have expected Wisconsin to change its methods just to suit his temperament. As it was, he often refused to turn in his papers even after he had written them, on the premise that his professors ought to be able to divine that he had understood and absorbed their lectures. When he comtemplated the three years that lay ahead of him, he found the prospect hard to bear. He became increasingly divorced from the life of the campus. Whether it was because he lived with his mother and went home to her each night, he was one of the few students at Wisconsin who never had a girl friend, and went through three semesters without a date with a member of the opposite sex.

Years later, when he sat with her on the committee trying to keep America out of World War II, Charles Lindbergh had to confess to Lillian Gish that he had never seen one of her films, though while he was at college she was one of the great stars of the day. He thought stars like Theda Bara and Gloria Swanson were "shameless" and would certainly have never gone openly to one of their films, and he was disgusted when he saw that some of his female classmates were practicing Bara's famous "shimmy" and doing their hair in cowlicks down the cheek like Swanson.

He made two friends at college, Richard Plummer and Delos Dudley, and what attracted him to them was the fact that they were the only other students on the campus who rode motorbikes. Riding with them through the woods beyond Lake Mendota gave him the only happy moments of his college career. He had become a superb and nerveless rider and led his companions on cross-country runs through scrub that scratched their faces and tore their clothes, over bluffs and along river beds, and often over obstacles so formidable that they got off and pushed while he skidded round and mocked them for their lack of pluck.

Dudley later gave an example of Charles Lindbergh's inability to resist a challenge or back out once his skill and courage were at stake. The three students were walking on one occasion down a street lined with houses, one of which was the home of the president of the university. The street plunged steeply down to a cross street along which ran a tall fence, and Plummer remarked that a motorcyclist would be in trouble if his brakes failed on the hill, because he would crash directly into the fence. Charles Lindbergh was silent for a moment, and then he declared that he was convinced he could ride his motorbike down the hill without brakes and still make the sharp turn at the bottom. They scoffed at him and declared that it was impossible.

That settled it. "The only way to prove that it can be done is to do it," he said.

"It's a damn fool thing to do," said Plummer. "You'll end up in the hospital, or dead."

But when Lindbergh insisted, they went down to the bottom of the hill and posted themselves there "to pick up the pieces." As Dudley later recounted it to Kenneth Davis:

"They watched apprehensively as he started his motor and pointed the cycle downhill. Apprehension mounted into actual terror as the cycle plunged downward, faster and faster, with Lindbergh stubbornly refusing to touch the brakes. By the time he reached the bottom, his speed was so tremendous that, for all his skill, he couldn't quite complete the turn. The machine plunged into a gutter, its rider was thrown violently against the fence. Plummer and Dudley ran toward him, sure that he was seriously injured, but before they could reach him he had got to his feet. Bruised and bleeding, but with no bones broken, he stood calmly looking up the hill.

"'You know,' he said in an interested tone, 'that wouldn't have happened if I'd gunned the motor just as I made my turn.'

"Then, to the almost speechless amazement of his friends, he walked over to his undamaged machine, picked it up, and rode it to the top of the hill. Again Plummer and Dudley watched in helpless anxiety as he made his downward run. Again his speed at the run's end was terrific. But this time, as he reached the cross street, he did 'gun the motor,' and this time, though barely, he completed his turn. . . ."†

His success with this challenge encouraged him to think of even more daredevil feats with his beloved motorbike. As Evel Knievel was to do fifty years later, he dreamed of flying with his machine through space. He confided in 1922 to his two friends that he was thinking of taking his bike up to the top of the college ski jump, ride down it, and fly through the air until he landed (upright, he hoped) on the frozen surface of Lake Mendota.

Fortunately, before he could work out the details, a letter arrived at the North Mills apartment that radically changed all his plans. He had already told his mother that he was thinking of becoming an airplane pilot, and she had immediately written to his father and pleaded with him to dissuade Charles from such a dangerous and unproductive project. At no time did she raise any objections herself with her son, but Lindbergh, Sr., did write at once to point out to Charles that even in

† Ibid.

peacetime insurance companies refused to insure pilots, that in more ways than one it was a dead-end profession.

But Charles had already written to the Nebraska Aircraft Company, which made Lincoln Standard planes in Lincoln, Nebraska, and advertised that it would give flying instruction to all potential buyers. He had pointed out that he was not in the market for a plane (not yet, anyway), but that he would be prepared to pay for instruction. Now here was a letter telling him that he would be accepted as a pupil in return for a fee of five hundred dollars. He wired back his acceptance and followed it with a letter and a money order deposit; and only then did he tell his mother that it was all fixed, that he was leaving college, and that he had made up his mind to fly.

In later years, pupils at the high school in Detroit where Evangeline Land Lindbergh taught were to nickname her "Stone Face" and this was one of the occasions that demonstrated the accuracy of the sobriquet. She was afterward to confess that "it all but broke my heart" that Charles was dropping out of college; and, even worse, he was to a great extent dropping out of her life. She had followed him to Madison but she knew without asking that this time he was going on alone, and she was not the sort of woman to ask anyone—not even her son—to take her where she suspected she would not be wanted. After twenty years, he was cutting the umbilical cord at last, and things would never be quite the same between them again.

"All right," she had said when he had first broached the subject of becoming a pilot. "If you really want to fly, that's what you should do."

Now she looked at her son and said, without expression in her face or voice:

"You must go. You must lead your own life. I mustn't hold you back. Only I can't see the time when we'll be together much again."

On March 22, 1922, he said good-by without regret to Madison and Wisconsin U, climbed aboard his Excelsior and rode off to start a new career. He arrived, after several mishaps en route, at the gates of the Nebraska Aircraft Company in Lincoln on April 1. By that time his mother had packed up and returned to Detroit, where she would make her home for the rest of her life.

Charles Lindbergh was twenty years old, but it would be a long time before any other female would come into his life.

"The novice has a poet's eye," Charles Lindbergh once wrote. "He sees and feels where the expert's senses have been calloused by experience."

Within a year of that spring of 1922, he would be able to read the landscape of the Middle West plains and hills from the air as surely as if he were walking them on foot, and all the objects on the ground, every shading of the fields, the bend of trees in the wind or the angle on the line of a farmer's wife's Monday morning washing, the height, the shape, and the color of the clouds would be mere facts filtering through his eyes to the computer in his mind. But on his first few flights‡ it was all new and exciting, and more fascinating than any other experience in his life so far, a voyage, as he was later to say, to an unmortal space crowded with beauty and pierced with danger.

He did not lose his sense of ecstasy and fulfillment for several weeks after his instruction as a pilot began; but he came down to earth with a bump when he realized that his tutors were going to fail in their obligations toward him. When he arrived at the Nebraska Aircraft Company's hangars on April 1, 1922, the president of the company, a brisk, cheerful, unreliable character named Ray Page, at once asked Lindbergh to hand over the balance of the five hundred dollars he had agreed to pay for his tuition. He didn't know it then, but Page needed the money to help pay the week's wages and was already in the process of selling off his training planes.

The pilot assigned to teach him was a morose character with a shock of black hair and a face lined and stained dark brown by the elements. His name was Ira Biffle and he had once been an instructor for the U. S. Army Air Corps with a reputation for expertise in handling planes under any conditions. But his closest friend, a fellow pilot, had spun in and died in a crash, and Biffle had thereafter lost his nerve. He hated flying from then on, and left the ground with the utmost reluctance.

Charles Lindbergh's first glorious flights were done in the company of another of Page's pilots, just to give him the feel of flying, but when Biffle took over, the pleasure began to fade. The instructor was a hard taskmaster, impatient with mistakes, apt to call his pupil down and curse him even before he started to carry out the orders he had been given. This, however, he didn't mind. So long as he was learning, so long as he was being allowed the privilege of handling a plane, he didn't care how roughly anyone dressed him down.

But soon Biffle began to skip lessons. His pupil accepted his absence when it was blowing too hard or raining, and he would spend his time around the workshops watching the mechanics at work, learning how to mend tail skids, wing struts, shock absorbers, how to lap a propeller shaft to its hub, how to warp valves and clean spark plugs. On good days, however, he was impatient and resented not getting the teaching

‡ For the record, Charles Lindbergh took his first airplane flight on April 9, 1922.

he had paid for with his savings. When Biffle finally turned up, he would explain that the air had been too turbulent at midday and make a rendezvous for later in the afternoon. Lindbergh would park his motorbike and lie down under a wing, watching the sky, not daring to leave the field in case Biffle turned up—which sometimes he did, when they practiced landing and take-offs. But only too often he wouldn't appear at all and explain next morning:

"It was just too rough, Slim." It hadn't been. "Let's try at sunrise tomorrow—that's the smoothest time of day."

At which, when Lindbergh mentioned his date to the workmen, they would roar with laughter. "*Sunrise?* Biff *never* starts work before eleven."

But his pupil would get there at sunrise, just in case.

There was a sixteen-year-old kid named Bud Gurney working around the Nebraska Aircraft Company plant, doing odd jobs in return for enough for his keep. He was mad about planes* and spent all his waking hours around the hangars, picking up tips about planes, snatching rides whenever they were going, and listening to the gossip in the workshops. He had a gregariousness that was completely lacking in Lindbergh, and though he was four years younger, he took it upon himself to be responsible for the welfare of this thin, shy, plane-struck youth. He was also one of the first to give him the nickname of "Slim" that was to stay with him in the years to come.

It was Bud Gurney who warned Slim that Ray Page was doing a deal to sell the company's training plane to a barnstorming pilot named Erold Bahl, and that if he didn't get his lessons finished and take his solo soon, there wouldn't be a plane for him to fly in.

Up to this point Charles Lindbergh had done about eight hours in the air and was showing great aptitude, but had not yet been allowed to go solo. When he approached Ira Biffle for a further round of lessons, plus a chance to take up the plane alone, the instructor informed him that so far as he was concerned, his pupil had had his money's worth.

"I'm taking off for a new job tomorrow," he said. "Got business interests to attend to."

Nothing that Lindbergh said would move him. He refused to go up with him again. As for going solo:

"You'll have to get Page to okay it," he said, "before I can turn you loose."†

---

* Gurney later became a senior pilot for United Air Lines.

† Despite his anger toward Biffle at the way he treated him, Lindbergh bore him no resentment. When Biffle was ill and dying in poverty in 1934 in Chicago, a newspaper mentioned that a fund was being raised on his behalf. Lindbergh sent a check for fifty dollars and a get-well note.

But Page was unwilling to allow a student, no matter how promising, to take up and possibly damage a plane which he had already sold. Not unless Lindbergh was prepared to put up a five-hundred-dollar bond to cover him in the event of a crack-up. That, however, was the kind of money he no longer had. There was still a cache of two or three hundred dollars left in his bank account in Little Falls, but he was holding on to that in readiness for the day when he would be able to buy and fly his own plane. In the meantime, he pleaded and argued with Page, pointing out with some justice that he was still owed some hours of lessons from his original five-hundred-dollar tuition fee. Page shrugged his shoulders in a manner which asked the young man what he was going to do about it. Lindbergh knew only too well that there was little he could do.

That was mid-May 1922, and it was a black period. He had spent nearly all of the money he had brought with him to cover his food and lodgings. It looked as if his ambition to be a pilot was going to whimper away to nothing. Would he have to go back to his mother and admit that he had failed? If the thought occurred to him, he put it rapidly out of his mind. Going back on a decision was something he would never do.

Then one morning a small man in a business suit, a white celluloid collar, and a peaked cap drove onto the field and parked his roadster by the hangar. He demanded to see "my plane" and was taken to the Fokker biplane in which Charles Lindbergh had learned to fly but failed to solo. He had it wheeled out onto the grass, signaled Bud Gurney to give the props a turnover, and climbed into the cockpit. Spurning the helmet that all the other pilots wore, he simply turned his cap back to front and headed the plane down the field and up into the blue. For the next thirty minutes he had even the old hands among the mechanics out of the hangar to watch him demonstrate what the plane could do when a self-confident pilot was aboard. Charles Lindbergh watched him in a kind of ecstasy, because this was the kind of flier he dreamed of emulating, whose skill could turn a machine into a bird.

His name was Erold Bahl and he was a member of a growing breed of pilots called barnstormers. When he landed and had seen his plane safely back into the hangar, Lindbergh approached him and hesitantly asked him whether he could tag along as a helper during Bahl's forthcoming tour.

The older man shook his head. "I don't need any help where I'm going—county fairs, town fetes, that sort of thing," he said. "There's always someone around to help you push the plane."

Lindbergh took a deep breath. "It won't cost you anything. I'll pay my own expenses."

Again Bahl shook his head. And then something about the look of this callow youth, the air of quiet desperation that seemed to hang around him, touched his sensibilities.

"What's your name, son?"

"I'm Slim Lindbergh. I've been learning to fly here, but now it looks as if they've run out of training planes. And trainers," he added bitterly.

Bahl said, "I guess it'll be all right for you to tag along. If you can look after yourself, that is."

A smile that would one day be famous broke across the young man's face.

"When do we leave!" he cried.

All over the Western world in those days, barnstorming pilots were bringing the thrills of flying to the people. In Scandinavia a German air ace named Hermann Göring, who would one day hang a medal round Lindbergh's neck like an albatross, was stunting a Fokker monoplane over the heads of cheering crowds. In England in summer every beach or field near a holiday resort had its visiting pilot offering five-minute flights at five shillings a time. In the United States no town or county fair was complete unless the day was rounded off by a display from a visiting flier, plus the hawking of rides at five dollars a flight.

Erold Bahl was a good and prudent pilot whose stunts, no matter how spectacular they might look from the ground, never went beyond the capabilities of the plane or his skill as a flier. For four weeks in May and June 1922, they toured the farm lands of Nebraska, Kansas, and Colorado, alighting on a farmer's meadow near a small town, drumming up trade by an exhibition of low flying over streets and houses, and then hawking tickets for rides. Lindbergh proved himself so useful as a mechanic, handy man, and ticket-tout that Bahl soon decided to pay his expenses, and in gratitude his young helpmate thought long and hard how to give even more spice to his pilot's show. Finally, when he was sitting in the front cockpit one day, he made up his mind, and when they landed he proposed to Bahl that next time they flew low over towns or villages, working up trade, he should climb out onto the wing and wave to the crowds down below.

In a way, it was a challenge to himself as well as a gesture to Bahl, because he had a complex at that time about exposing himself on isolated heights. He had a recurring dream in which he was falling, falling, falling from a tall building or peak, and the terror and sickness he felt was such that it woke him up, trembling and in a cold sweat. All Bahl said to him was:

"You can climb out of the cockpit if you want to, but watch your step on the spars, and don't go farther than the inner-bay strut the first time."

It was a nerve-racking experience, and he never really learned to like wing-walking. For a time the ordeal even seemed to increase the fear he felt in his nightmares, and he would need an even greater challenge to exorcise his terrors. But thereafter during the tour he regularly climbed out and waved to the crowds from the wing. By the time they got back to Lincoln, Nebraska, he had more than earned his keep, but all Erold Bahl was able, or willing, to pay him was what he had cost in food and bed. With the tour over, he faced the problem of his future again, particularly where the money was coming from to pay for his next meal. He moved from his five-dollar-a-week to a two-and-a-quarter-a-week room in the town and got himself a job helping the mechanics at the factory for a wage of fifteen dollars a week. He was at a dead end again, or so it seemed.

But then a contraption came into his life that cured his nightmares, gave him a thrill even more intense though not as permanently satisfying as flying, and revived his flagging spirits. It was a parachute.

CHAPTER

FOUR

CATHARSIS BY
RIP CORD

Anyone who has made (or been obliged to make) a descent by parachute will probably come to the conclusion that Charles Lindbergh, in
his subsequent writings, was guilty of overdramatizing the first occasion
he ever jumped out of an airplane. He considered the experience "beyond the descriptive words of men—where immortality is touched
through danger, where life meets death on equal plane; where man is
more than man, and existence both supreme and valueless at the same
instant."

It is true that a first parachute jump is an occasion to be savored and
remembered, and some have been known to compare it to the joys of
sexual intercourse. But Lindbergh went on recalling and writing about
the experience so often in later years that it quite obviously represented
a much greater challenge than it does to most men. Even in 1922
baling out of a plane by parachute was not particularly dangerous. One
surmises that what transformed Lindbergh's first jump into a psychological landmark in his life was the terrible fear the contemplation of
doing it aroused—and the ecstatic relief that he achieved by overcoming
his fear, and jumping.

It was in June 1922 that Charlie Hardin and his young wife, Kathryn,
arrived in Lincoln, Nebraska, and announced that they were going to
give an exhibition of wing-walking and parachuting. They came at the
invitation of Ray Page, who was drumming up publicity for his aircraft
factory, and they gave value for money to the throng gathered below to
watch them. Kathryn, a former circus aerialist, didn't just walk the
wings of a plane but also stood on her head or swung in space beneath
the wheels by her teeth. But Slim Lindbergh was neither attracted by

her charms (and she was quite pretty) nor impressed by her gravity-defying acrobatics. What touched his imagination was the spectacle when Charlie Hardin climbed out onto the wing and flung himself from the plane while it cruised two thousand feet above the field, and he saw the parachute burst into flower above the tiny figure of the man twisting in space.

He never referred to Kathryn in any of his writings except as an adjunct of her husband on the ground. But Charlie Hardin flying through the sky! It was a never-to-be-forgotten sight: "A few gossamer yards grasping onto air and suspending below them, with invisible threads, a human life, a man who by stitches, cloth and cord, had made himself a god of the sky for those immortal moments."*

He went back from the field and shut himself in his room and thought about what he had seen and of the determination growing in his mind. He knew he would have to make a parachute jump himself, and the realization filled him with "anticipation mixed with dread, of confidence restrained by caution, of courage salted through with fear."

Next day, when the workers at the factory broke off for lunch, he went into the hangar and found Hardin and his wife busily working away with sewing machine and shears, making new parachutes from yards of muslin. The Hardins made their living not just by parachute jumping but by selling them to pilots, and to a certain extent their exhibitions were a sales talk for the safety of their product. Charlie Hardin boasted in his publicity that he sometimes dropped with five, even ten, different parachutes strapped to him, and he allowed these to open one by one, with a free-fall between each, before he finally floated to the ground. All to demonstrate that for a resolute man there was nothing to it.

"I want to jump—and I'd like to make it a double jump," Lindbergh blurted out.

Kathyrn Hardin halted her machine. Charlie Hardin looked hard at the young man and fingered his long, curly black mustache.

"A double jump! You want to do a double jump the *first* time?" he asked, with such astonished skepticism that Lindbergh blushed and quickly said:

"I've read about the multiple jumps you make. It isn't more dangerous with two chutes than with one, is it?"

Hardin swiftly shook his head. He was in business to prove that any kind of parachuting was safe. He hastened to say that it wasn't the danger, it was just that Lindbergh was a beginner, and he had never heard

* Charles A. Lindbergh, *The Spirit of St. Louis* (New York: Scribner's, 1953).

1. Charles Lindbergh was born in Detroit but spent his boyhood at a farm in Little Falls, Minnesota, on the banks of the Mississippi. The house and 110 acres of farm land and forest surrounding it were presented by the Lindbergh family to the state of Minnesota and in 1931 named the Charles A. Lindbergh State Park, in memory of Charles Lindbergh's father.

2. Charles Lindbergh had a deep affection for his boyhood home at Little Falls, Minnesota, and took a close interest in its restoration. He is here seen checking on the arrangement of furniture and bibelots in the family dining room during a visit in 1971.

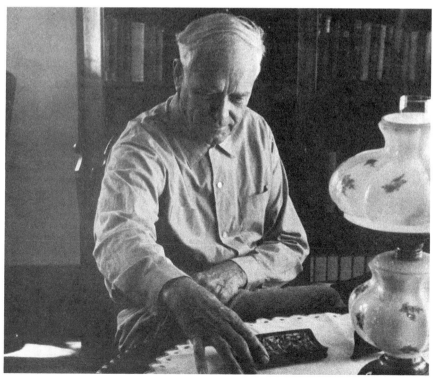

3. Charles Augustus Lindbergh, Sr., was Republican congressman for the Sixth District of Minnesota, to which he was first elected in 1907. Here he is seen with his son in a photograph believed to have been taken about 1910.

4. Evangeline Land Lodge Lindbergh, Charles Lindbergh's mother, was a schoolteacher newly arrived in Little Falls, Minnesota, from the East when she first met Charles Augustus Lindbergh, Sr., then a local up-and-coming lawyer. They were married in March 1901, and their son, Charles, was born the following year, when this photograph was taken.

5. Always fond of dogs, Charles Lindbergh had several of varying breeds during his boyhood in Little Falls, Minnesota. This one was called Dingo.

6. It was Charles Lindbergh's father who taught him hunting, shooting, and forest lore on expeditions which they took together along the Mississippi River lands of Minnesota, whenever Congressman Lindbergh could get away from Washington. This picture of father and son on a hunting trip together was taken in 1911, when Charles Lindbergh was nine years old.

7. Charles Lindbergh fell in love early with the internal-combustion engine and could drive a car at eleven. He bought his first motorcycle at sixteen and soon became a daredevil rider. This photograph of him on his twin-cylindered Excelsior was taken while he was at the University of Wisconsin in 1921.

8. Charles Lindbergh's mother loved flying with her son and once went with him on a barnstorming tour through the Middle West in the early 1920s. This picture of mother and son about to make a flight together was taken later.

of a beginner making his first jump with two parachutes. But if the young man was a possible buyer of a parachute—and Lindbergh quickly said that he might well be *afterward*—then okay, he could make his double jump, first time or not.

Next day Lindbergh arrived in the Hardins' work corner in the hangar with the news that he had arranged for a plane and a pilot—that afternoon. Would they get his double parachute ready? He was ready to jump.

It was late in the afternoon when Charlie Hardin finished fixing the chute bag to the right wing of the plane. He and his wife had had to hurry to get the great lengths of muslin and shrouds packed and ready, and, at the last moment, Charlie had found himself out of the twine with which he usually fastened one chute to the other when a double jump was being made. He rummaged around until he found some package string, and made do with that, wrapping it round three times to give it strength.

Lindbergh climbed into the front cockpit in his parachute harness, gave the sign to his pilot, and they were off.

To make a parachute jump in those days (a voluntary jump, that is), you had to climb out on the wing, fix your harness to the chute bag, and then wait until the pilot gave the signal. Until that moment you hung in space held up only by a wire, your parachute shrouds leading up into the chute bag, and a bowknotted lace tying together the lips of the bag and preventing the chute from emerging.

At two thousand feet, the pilot signaled Lindbergh that his time had come. Gingerly, he crawled from the cockpit and edged along the right wing and, fighting the wind, managed to hook up his harness to the shrouds. Then, with the aid of a wire, he lowered himself over the side, hung there for what were seconds but seemed hours long, until the pilot throttled back and put up his thumb. He pulled the bowknot loose and he was going down, the muslin flapping out above him and suddenly and magically blossoming into a great white canopy that swung him peacefully in the sky.

This is the moment when all parachutists know the feeling of relief that is almost too sweet to bear, and all you want to do is dangle forever in space. But if you savor the experience too long, you can hit the earth with a terrible thud. In Lindbergh's case, his peace was so great and his fears so dissipated that he almost forgot that he had arranged to make a double jump. He must cut away the canopy that was hammocking him so deliciously in the sky, fall free once more, until the second chute caught him up and cushioned him once more.

He reached up, cut the first parachute away with his bowie knife, and began to fall. The earth was rushing up toward him rapidly now, and his body was twisting, so that the setting sun on the far horizon seemed to be a circle of red. And still the second parachute did not open. He waited for the harness to tighten against the straining chute.

"But why *doesn't* it tighten?" he began asking himself. "It didn't take so long before—Air rushes past—my body tenses—turns—falls—good God—"†

In that moment of returning panic, the chute opened at last and he was floating down to earth and suddenly rolling in the grass, safe back on the ground.

Hardin, Bud Gurney, and Ray Page hurried across and helped him to his feet. Hardin's face was gray.

"I sure didn't like the way that second chute came out," he said. "I was afraid the break cord was too light—but it's all we had." He breathed a long sigh of relief. "That's the longest fall I've ever seen one of my chutes take."

On the way back into town that night, Bud Gurney told Lindbergh that the second chute should have been tied to the first by twine, so that the second chute would be pulled clear before the twine snapped. But the grocery string which Hardin had used instead had broken even before it came out of the bag, and the second chute stayed in a wad of muslin and needed hundreds of feet of air before it opened out. Hence the long and alarming delayed drop.

"How do you feel?" Bud asked anxiously.

"I've never felt better," said Lindbergh.

It was true. He already, as always, had an appetite like a horse and that night he had six eggs instead of his usual four, ate a whole T-bone steak, and followed it with a great hunk of apple pie and ice cream. He went to sleep the moment his head touched the pillow.

"There wasn't a dream in memory," he said later.

The parachute jump had purged him of his nightmares. Not that night nor any night thereafter did he ever dream again that he was falling through space, and sick with terror. Actual experience had cured his subconscious dread.

Perhaps he can be forgiven for making so much of the experience in the years to come.

In many ways, practical as well as psychological, the successful triumph over ordeal by parachute changed things for Charles Lindbergh. He acted (and the men around him reacted) rather like a teen-age boy

† Ibid.

preening himself after his first sexual experience. He felt and was treated as if he had lost his virginity and become a man at last: "I'd stepped to the highest level of daring—a level above even that which airline pilots could attain," he wrote later. "I'd left my role of apprentice far behind."

As always, his aim was to possess and fly a plane of his own, and for that he needed more experience in the air and the opportunity to solo; and the fact that he was now a parachute jumper was a considerable aid in getting him air time. He had by now picked up enough mechanical knowledge in the Lincoln factory to be able to take care of the average aircraft engine of the time, and the fact that he could also wing-walk and parajump made him attractive to barnstorming pilots touring the state and county fairs.

He had parlayed the flying lessons he was owed, plus a week's wages and twenty-five dollars in cash for one of Hardin's parachutes. In mid-July 1922 he teamed up with a pilot named H. J. Lynch, known to his fellow-fliers as Cupid, a rancher named Banty Rogers (who owned the plane Lynch flew), a dog named Booster, which was mad on flying, and a Lincoln-Standard biplane. Except for occasional visits, Rogers stayed on the ranch, but Lynch and Lindbergh—and Booster on Slim's lap in the front cockpit—trekked from Kansas, the Nebraska Badlands, and the Big Horns of Wyoming to Montana, with Lindbergh doing a triple job as mechanic, wing-walker, and parachutist.

He had picked up the tricks of his new profession as a stuntsman with great speed, thanks to a crash course from Charlie Hardin. He learned how to hang below a wing by his teeth (thanks to a thin wire hooked from the plane to a harness concealed beneath his flying jacket). He practiced spilling air from his chute to avoid trees and how to land on marked-out targets. He became adept at stand-up landings from two thousand feet. And as he and Lynch flew from fair to fair, he refined his technique, so that, by the time they reached Wyoming, he walked out onto the wing and stood there for the first time while Cupid Lynch put the plane into a loop. He was standing on the top wing, and the crowd below gasped when, at one point, he stumbled to his knees. But he did not fall.

Thereafter he got top billing on the posters they scattered from the air upon the towns and villages they were about to visit. "Daredevil Lindbergh" was what they called him, and the stunts he was now performing needed a nerve far stronger than the one which had dared the first parachute jump. But from now on, he seemed to have no fears. He insisted that the wing-walk during a loop was as safe as if he were still strapped into the cockpit, because he had taken all precautions—metal heel caps, like those on roller skates, with straps to hold his feet in place, and a heavy leather belt around the waist attached to cables on the wing pins.

"There was really little danger involved," he wrote later. "I might fall down (I did as we came out of the loop) but I would never fall off."

When the weather closed in and the barnstorming season came to an end, Slim Lindbergh said good-by to Lynch and Rogers and went back to stay the winter with his father in Minneapolis. He paid a couple of visits to Little Falls, but it was the wrong season of the year to stay in an empty house, and, except for Martin Engstrom, he had no one he particularly wished to see. He mooned away the winter, talking plans with Lindbergh, Sr., and convincing his father that he had now found his métier, that henceforward flying would be his life. He must have been convincing, because when spring came in 1923 Lindbergh borrowed nine hundred dollars from his Little Falls bank, and his father signed the guarantee of the loan. The money would be used, he explained, to buy himself a plane and keep him while he was getting established as a barnstormer. He left Minneapolis at the end of March and went first to spend three weeks with his mother in Detroit; and from there he went south to the auctions at Souther Field, Georgia, where the U. S. Army was selling off surplus equipment, including World War I planes.

He bought himself a Curtiss "Jenny" with a 90-horsepower engine, a top speed of seventy miles an hour (provided there was no headwind), and a ceiling of seventeen hundred feet. It cost him five hundred dollars, twice as much as he expected to pay, and it was a broken-down-looking old thing. But Charles Lindbergh was no fool and he knew what he was buying. He had checked it carefully, put his head into the engine cowling, and was satisfied. Later that year, a man named Fred Fair saw Lindbergh's Jenny in a field near Boulder, Colorado, and described it as "a wreck if ever I saw one. It creaked. The canvas was tattered and frayed edges fluttered in the breeze, but the engine purred smoothly and it circled gracefully in flight."

Since no license was needed in those days for an airplane pilot, Lindbergh had only needed to assure the auctioneer that he could fly for the Jenny to be handed over to him, with a full tank of gas, his very own airplane. He climbed aboard and began to realize that he was soloing in a strange plane whose controls were new and characteristics completely unknown. He almost crashed it at once by taking it off the ground too soon, and he came down with a bounce that almost wrecked the landing gear. But Lindbergh was one of those men who rarely make the same mistake twice, and by the end of the day he had mastered the tricks of his plane, and was tasting at last the delights of flying as he wished, with no one looking over his shoulder, and doing it in a plane of his own. He could henceforward go where he liked, and the great expanses of the United States were open to him.

That spring and summer he lived the happy-go-lucky life of a gypsy flier all over the small-town regions of the middle of America. He flew through Minnesota, Kansas, Wyoming, Missouri, and as far west as Colorado and as far south as Texas. It was a rough life and he found that you didn't get rich on it at five dollars per passenger a ride. There was no room in the Jenny for a suitcase so he had no change of clothes, and made do with a toothbrush and a razor and a cake of soap. His nails were always broken and his hands pitted with black oil from tinkering inside the engine. But he looked back later on that summer as the fulfillment of a dream.

In Boulder, Colorado, he heard one day that the Denver Interurban Railway was offering a thousand dollars to the first flier who would land a plane on the St. Vrain Glacier, in the Rockies northwest of Boulder. It was all part of a publicity campaign thought up by a Boulder engineer to draw attention to the scenic beauties of the region. When he heard that there was a pilot down on the cow pasture outside the town willing to accept the challenge, the engineer, Fred A. Fair, went down to see him, and so met Charles Lindbergh. He later described him as "a hungry-looking youngster with a bashful grin. He looked me in the eye and said: 'Sure, I'll land on the glacier. I'll guarantee it. I know I can do it. I certainly could use that thousand dollars."

He saw Fair looking at his plane, which was rather decrepit by this time, and added:

"I don't care if I never get her off there. You can see for yourself it wouldn't be much loss."

Fair was attracted to the young man and would have liked to see him do the job, but was suddenly stricken by a sense of responsibility. Despite Lindbergh's self-confidence, what if something went wrong and the kid was killed? Was the publicity worth the risk?

"I didn't want to hurt his feelings," he said afterward, "but that ship looked like a suicide ship to me."

So he turned him down. But Lindbergh's evident disappointment stayed in his mind like grit, and worried him over the years. After Lindbergh became famous later, and there was a move to name a Colorado peak after him, Fred Fair came up with the suggestion that a mountain tip twelve thousand feet high, looking down on the glacier where he once was ready to land, should be named after him, and Mount Lindbergh it became.

There were triumphs as well as disappointments. In Brainerd, Minnesota, he fixed a flag to the top of a pine tree and neatly snatched it off with a hook between his undercarriage, an operation, had he been a foot too low, which would have ripped his wheels off and probably crashed him into the forest. He tried a similar feat of ultra-precision flying afterward in Uvalde, Texas, hometown of John Nance Garner, sometime Vice-president of the United States, and wasn't quite so lucky. He was flying west and lost his way. He was practically out of gas by the time he came over Uvalde, and he decided to put his machine down in the center square of the town. That was all right. He landed safely and went off with cans to the local garage to refuel. But could he take off again? The square was not big enough, but there was a street leading off it long enough to give him taxiing length. The only trouble was that halfway down were two telegraph poles, and they were just wide enough apart to leave a three-foot margin between the wing tips of Lindbergh's plane.

He decided to try it, anyway. He was heartened and encouraged by the crowd of Texans who had gathered to watch him, and assured him that they would help him out if things went wrong. He had willing help in backing the plane down the street to a point where he was convinced it was safe to start his run. He revved the engine, signaled the chocks to be pulled, and raced down Uvalde's main street, his eyes glued to the telegraph poles and the mid-point between them.

What he hadn't reckoned with was the poor surface of the street. There was no macadam in those days, or pavement. At a crucial point his wheels went into a rut, and the wings lurched. The plane hit one of the poles, whipped around, and hurled the nose into a hardware store on the sidewalk, coming to a horrid halt amid a crescendo of crashing plates, glass, and cutlery. He had been six inches on the wrong side of the pole, and when he crawled out of the cockpit he found that the Texans were good sportsmen and appreciated the narrowness of his luck.

"A great moment, a great moment!" the hardware storesman said, and waved Lindbergh away when he offered to pay for the damage. "It was worth every broken plate in the store."

But there was one bad moment. In the summer of 1923 he landed the Jenny in the western meadow at the farm at Little Falls and went into town to tell his father and his father's political campaign manager that he had arrived to help in the election. Lindbergh, Sr., had decided to make a last attempt to get back into national politics, and planned to secure nomination in the primaries coming up for Minnesota's seat in the Senate. He had hoped, as he had done in the past, to get the backing of the Nonpartisan League and go forward in the elections as Farmer-Labor candidate, but there was a revulsion of feeling among politicians in the state against the ex-congressman, whom they had begun to consider too doctrinaire, too intellectual, too "literary." (The fact that he had written books was actually held against him.) As a result, he was being forced to fight the primaries on his own, with no official backing, and no financial support. All posters, campaign letters, and other election expenses had to come out of his own pocket.

Charles flew in from Little Falls to join his father's campaign at Marshall, Minnesota, enabling Lindbergh, Sr., to speak about the force of the future and point dramatically into the sky, as the Jenny hove into view, and say:

"There is my son!"

Shortly thereafter the would-be senator experienced his first ride in a plane. "Armed with a bundle of hundreds of sheets of campaign literature, Lindbergh [Sr.] climbed into the open-front cockpit of the 'Jenny.' As was customary in the early biplanes, Charles, Jr., the pilot, took his place at the controls in the cockpit behind his father. By prearrangement, Lindbergh was to throw out the bills when his son rocked the plane and nodded. He did so when the signal was given, but instead of throwing the leaflets a few at a time, Lindbergh threw out the whole stack of literature at once and the bundle sharply hit the plane stabilizer. Fortunately, no damage was done, but as Charles Jr. observed many years later, 'the distribution of the literature in the town wasn't very broad.' He recalled that 'my father's face was quite serious when he looked back at me after the thud.' "‡

If Charles's arrival was intended to give a boost to his father's campaign, it was not to last long. On June 8, 1923, he revved up ready to take off from a field on the Miley farm, west of Glencoe, Minnesota, but halfway down the meadow the Jenny suddenly swerved into a ditch and broke up both the landing gear and the prop. Lindbergh, Sr.'s, biographer writes that conflicting accounts of the accident appeared in the local papers.

"The Litchfield *Saturday Review* stated that the mishap occurred during takeoff, but the McLeod County *Republic* at Glencoe reported that it took place during an attempted landing."*

‡ Bruce L. Larson, *Lindbergh of Minnesota: A Political Biography* (New York: Harcourt Brace Jovanovich, 1971).
* Ibid.

There were strong rumors, which Charles Lindbergh seems to have believed, that sabotage was involved, and that someone had tampered with the rudder of the Jenny. Why anyone should have bothered to damage Lindbergh, Sr.'s, chances is a mystery, because he was a loser from the start. There was still a backwash of disapproval in Minnesota for his anti-Catholic, antiwar stand. He campaigned for nationalization of public services and other socialistic and welfare measures that were ahead of their time, and was therefore smeared with the brush of being communistic. There was no likelihood that he could ever be adopted as senatorial candidate over his chief (and well-endorsed) rival, Magnus Johnson.†

Lindbergh, Sr.'s, head hit the control board during the crash and smashed his glasses, and he staggered from the wreckage with his face covered in blood. He wiped his face clean and went on to a meeting at Litchfield by automobile, while his son stayed with his plane until a new prop and wheel struts could come from Minneapolis. It was the end of his attempt to help his father get elected. When the returns came in, Johnson was at the top, with Lindbergh once more at the bottom.

But if the old man was down, he was not yet out. The following year, he decided that he must try one more time to get back into political office. He put himself forward as the Farmer-Labor candidate for governor of Minnesota, and this time did not solicit his son's help in the campaign.

He was not needed, in any case. The campaign had hardly begun when Lindbergh, Sr., was taken seriously ill and rushed to the Mayo Clinic, in Rochester, Minnesota, where he was found to have a deep-seated brain tumor, an inoperable one. He died in St. Vincent's Hospital, Crookston, Minnesota, on May 24, 1924.

By that time his son was a flying cadet in the U. S. Army at Brooks Field, San Antonio, Texas. He got compassionate leave to come up to Rochester to see his father before he died, and again for the funeral at the First Unitarian Church in Minneapolis. Lindbergh, Sr., had asked in a letter to his daughter, Eva, that he be cremated after his death ("Don't give me any of those marble monuments"), and some years later Charles Lindbergh took the ashes with him in his plane and scattered them over Melrose, Minnesota, where his father had spent his childhood. It was a thoughtful filial gesture, but, in truth, one that

† But it is true that his son did annoy Johnson supporters during the campaign by hawking for customers at places near their meetings, and, on one occasion, during a big rally at Glencoe, refusing to stop flying passengers noisily around the park during the speeches.

Lindbergh, Sr., would hardly have appreciated. The Melrose he had known was surrounded by virgin forest, thick with wildlife, its skies black with duck at dawn. His incinerated remains fell on urban farm lands—and were not exactly welcome, either, among certain stanch Republican farmers who considered him a revolutionary and a Red.

CHAPTER

FIVE

FIREWORKS

For most of the gypsy pilots barnstorming across the United States in those days there were plenty of distractions to be found in the small towns where they set down their flying crates for the night. In some ways, they were the pop stars of the time. Most of them were young, fit, and filled with a devil-may-care *joie de vivre,* and to the populace whom they distracted with their stunts their profession was still novel enough to be considered romantic and death-defying. Among the spectators there was always one town belle eager for a free ride and an experience of aerobatics—and suitably grateful later. Barnstormers seldom got together because there was rarely enough trade for two planes at the town and county fairs where they made their living; but when they did meet up—on an open day at the National Air Show, or at the air factories where they flew in for spares and repairs—their conversation was mostly a mixture of narrow escapes in the air and close encounters on the ground, of the day the engine conked out at a thousand feet and the night they had the farmer's daughter in the hayloft. To hear them talk, they were flying Lotharios with a female conquest in every small town in the Middle West.

It is doubtful if Charles Lindbergh envied them their boastful victories over the opposite sex, real or fanciful. By the very nature of his upbringing, he had developed into something of a prude. It was not simply that he was an abstainer from alcohol, tobacco, and other "stimulants." He had solemnly tried whiskey, beer, cigarettes, cigars, and coffee, and had subsequently eschewed them because he considered they were physically weakening and would affect his nervous system, to the detriment of his instinctive reactions to danger. He had drawn up a list of rules by which he felt he should live, and resolved to keep a close watch for any weaknesses in his character by examining himself each day.

"I came to the conclusion that if I knew the difference between the right way to do something and the wrong way to do it, it was up to me to train myself to do the right thing at all times. So I drew up a list of character factors."

He made a list of sixty-five, including such qualities as Alertness, Altruism, Ambition, Aptitude, Balance, Brevity, Concentration, Diligence, Enterprise, Foresight, Honesty, Intuition, Judiciousness, Manliness, Orderliness, Precision, Quiet-temperedness, Reserve, Solicitude, Tact, Unselfishness, Vigor, Watchfulness, and Zeal.

"At night I would read off my list of character factors, and those which I had fulfilled satisfactorily during the day I would mark with a red cross; those I had not been called upon to demonstrate that day would get no mark. But those character factors which I had actually violated each day I would mark with a black cross. I began to check myself from day to day and compare my 'blacks and whites' from month to month and year to year. I was glad to notice that there was an improvement as I grew older."*

He had no objections to the girls who swirled around his plane and giggled at him as they clamored for his autograph, only that none of them managed to measure up to his standards. If he had accepted the overt invitations of one or other of them, what would he have talked to them about, anyway, except airplanes? He knew nothing about jazz, his favorite song was still "Home on the Range," he could neither dance nor play a ukulele, and he hadn't the time or money to go to the movies. He was now twenty-two years old, tall, thin as a lath, dashingly handsome. Most women must have found him attractive, especially when he flashed his smile. But whether by shyness or indifference, or because he shared his mother's contempt for "flappers and that type of girl," he never allowed any of them to come near him. Perhaps it was because none of them measured up to his mother.

It must, therefore, have got awfully boring sometimes for him to spend his nights alone in a boardinghouse room, marking up his merit chart, or sleeping under the wing of his plane, or talking to some farmer about the inevitable subjects of crops and weather. There is evidence to suggest that it was sheer loneliness that drove him, about this time, to make an important decision. But first of all, before he made it, he telegraphed his mother.

* From an interview given in London after his transatlantic flight.

Evangeline Lindbergh was still teaching school in Detroit, and though she kept up a steady correspondence with her son, she must have been missing him dreadfully. At one moment she had written to Little Falls to ask for a job in the high school there, knowing that if she got it she would be closer to Charles, but with no luck. The school superintendent with whom she had once tangled had long since left, but he had managed to leave behind an impression of her (quite unjustly) as a troublemaker, and she was curtly informed by the management that there was no vacancy. Plodding on with her classes in Detroit, she kept up with her son's adventures from his letters. In one of her own to him she reminded him that one day she hoped to be able to make a flight. Ever since Charles had gone off to become a pilot, she had dreamed of the day when the two of them would be able to take to the air together.

Now she was overjoyed to get a telegram telling her to meet him at Janesville, Minnesota. He would be barnstorming in the area. She would just be beginning her school holidays.

She left by train and he met her at the depot and drove her to the pasture where the Jenny was parked, and if she was daunted by its appearance—it was patchworked where part of the fuselage had recently been eaten by cows—she said no word. Her son handed her a flying jacket and a leather helmet and helped her into the front cockpit, and then they were bouncing down the field and off on a tour of the region. It lasted for ten days, and as often as possible, Evangeline Lindbergh was up in the air with her son, stoic at first and then increasingly attracted by the rigors of a barnstormer's life and the hazards and excitements of flight in Charles's decrepit flying machine. She threw leaflets and tear sheets overboard to advertise their coming. She bargained with the farmers for permission to use their fields. She hawked custom in the towns and sold tickets for the flights. But best of all, she flew with her son and learned from him, as he proudly demonstrated them, the crafts of the air pilot, and how to read the clouds, the wind, and the ground for the telltale signs that often meant the difference between a safe landing and a crash.

It was a good period for both of them. After Charles had dropped out of college and gone off on his own, there had been a period of coolness, almost amounting to bitterness. The mother-son relation had always been so tense and possessive that (at least on Evangeline Lindbergh's side) it was not possible to normalize it without an interim period of resentment and regret. Her only great love had walked out of her life, and it was hard to bear.

But ten days and nights of having her son to herself once again (and the crowds and customers didn't matter) was enough for her to sense that, in fact, her son, Charles, had never gone away, and that such was her influence on him that for the rest of his life he would judge, and react, to all other people as if he were seeing them through her eyes.

"Most mothers worry about the mistakes their sons are going to make, the girls who are going to make fools of them," said Eva Lindbergh, eldest daughter of Charlie Lindbergh's first wife. "My stepmother never needed to do that. She knew Charles, and knew that every girl he met, when he wanted to meet one, he would compare with her."

Such was Charles Lindbergh's estimation of his mother that a girl would have to be something of a paragon before he went any further than simply sizing her up.

The only trouble was that when Evangeline Lindbergh had gone back to school in Detroit, she left behind a son who was lonelier than ever. It was a poor time of the year for a gypsy flier. The weather was growing cool and folks no longer wanted to take flights in open cockpits.

Punting along in his Jenny one afternoon and trying to work out where to fly next, he remembered the item he had read in the local paper that morning about the International Air Races, which were just starting at Lambert Field, St. Louis. On an impulse, he decided he would go and see them, and banked his plane south.

It was the first time he had ever seen so many modern planes or mixed with sophisticated fliers, and they made him feel like a hayseed. Right from the start, he goofed. In the wide-open spaces where he was used to flying he almost always had the sky to himself, and he blithely trundled his Jenny toward Lambert Field and started to land. Unfortunately, one of the races was in progress, and startled and angry steward planes zoomed onto him like angry bees and shooed him away, forcing him to put down on a hilly pasture overlooking Lambert.

A couple of days later, having been allowed to land on Lambert at last, he decided to take a spin over the field and started his craft. He revved it up, as usual, forgetting that he was no longer in a grassy cow pasture but on the hot, baked earth surface of a Missouri airfield. The bunch of international fliers and officials behind him got the full burst of dust right in their faces, and they choked and spat with rage.

"God Almighty! Where did you learn to fly?" shouted an irate air race official, hands, face, and clothes yellow with dust. "Get out and lift that tail around. Hold that throttle down while you taxi!"

But there were compensations for the humiliations. There were more types of planes to be examined than he had ever imagined existed, and he walked around them for hours on end, wide-eyed, eager, and curious, and not a strut, tail plane, engine cowling, or wing set missed his keen examination. To add to his pleasure, he ran into the tousle-haired kid, Bud Gurney, who, despite being four years his junior, had fathered him and counseled him during his tuition days at Lincoln, Nebraska. Bud was now an itinerant parachute jumper, working the county fairs as Lindbergh had done in order to make flying time, gain experience, and save up to buy his own plane. He had ridden a freight train into St. Louis and hoped to do a drop at the air show in order to cover his expenses.

"Who's flying you?" Lindbergh asked.

Bud hadn't found a plane yet to take him up. He looked hopefully at his friend.

"Slim, will you take me up? I want to do a double jump."

It was arranged that if Lindbergh could get his Jenny up high enough with a double parachute aboard, he would be carrier for Bud when he did his show on opening day. Meantime, they wandered round Lambert together, and, as always, Bud thought up schemes for his friend and introduced him to pilots he would otherwise have been too shy to meet.

On the second day of the show, Bud came rushing up to his friend.

"I've found a guy who'd like to buy your plane," he said. "All you've got to do is teach him how to fly it."

They had already discussed whether he should sell the Jenny. The novelty was going out of the barnstorming game, and rides were increasingly hard to sell. Some gypsies had put down their price to two and a half dollars a flip, and there was one flier around who had found business so bad he was taking farmers' wives aloft for a crate of eggs. Besides, winter was coming on, and he would need a billet for the cold weather. Several of the pilots around had suggested solutions to his problem, and one was that he should stick around Lambert after the races and start instructing there. The region was full of people who wanted to fly. He had over two hundred flying hours to his credit, and in those days he didn't need a teaching certificate.

Now Bud had come up with a solution to what he could do with the Jenny if he decided to stay on. They went over together to talk to the young Iowan who was interested in the plane. Lindbergh set a price on the Jenny, with a solo flight guaranteed, and the deal was closed. In return for a down payment he agreed to begin instructing as soon as the air meet was over.

They went over to a hot-dog stand to celebrate, and Bud and Slim ate T-bone steaks for supper that evening.

Next day, though, it wasn't so good. The posters had been pasted for

Bud's double jump, and in the afternoon, with his friend aboard, the double-parachute sack tied to the wing, Lindbergh coaxed the Jenny to its maximum height of seventeen hundred feet. But it wasn't really high enough. The second parachute was slow in opening and the free fall before it flowered was so long that when Bud Gurney hit the ground he smashed an arm and a shoulder and had to be rushed to a hospital.

"Slim took it worse than I did," Bud Gurney said later. "It wasn't his fault. It was my carelessness. But he kept blaming himself for my heavy fall—and he insisted on giving me a stake for when I got out of the hospital."

It was while he was wandering forlornly around Lambert after this incident that Lindbergh caught the eye of Marvin Northrop, who at that time had a small aircraft manufacturing firm near St. Louis. Northrop remembered the tall, thin character in a leather flying cap, a rumpled coat, thick stockings, and breeches, all covered with thick Missouri dust.

"He looked not so much forlorn as just plain damn lonely," he said later. "I went over and started talking to him."

Lindbergh seems for once to have been eager to unburden himself, and he told Northrop all about his barnstorming tours, his plans for selling the Jenny and instructing during the winter, his ambition to become an airline pilot. But what should he do next, until commercial flying really got going in the United States and he could find the kind of job he wanted?

"Why don't you sign up with the Army as an air cadet?" said Northrop.

Lindbergh replied that some Missouri National Guard pilots had already given him a sales talk about that—how he would learn more about the technics and mechanics of flying in three months with the Army than a couple of years gypsy flying.

"It's true," said Northrop. "I know it's true, because I was an air cadet myself, and look where it's got me."

He went on to point out that Lindbergh didn't have to make a career of it. The moment he had won his commission, he could decide whether to stay on or go on the reserve.

"You get all the flying you want—and they pay you for it," Northrop said.

He watched the young man's face as he said it, and realized that the U. S. Army had a customer.

"I did it because I knew the kid needed experience, and where better to get it in those days?" he said later. "But I also did it because I

guessed it was about time he came back and lived with people. I figured
him for a loner, but even loners have to come in from the cold sometimes. Another few months of barnstorming in the sticks, and he'd be
talking to himself. The guy needed buddies."

That same night, Charles Lindbergh wrote off to Washington for application papers. On March 15, 1924, he traveled to Brooks Field,
Texas, to sit for examinations as a flying cadet, and four days later he
was in the Army.

He learned a lot in the Army, about planes, about flying technics,
about himself.

There were 104 cadets reporting to Brooks Field for the air course in
March 1924. A year later 18 of them had stayed the course and were
lined up to receive their wings and commissions as second lieutenants
in the U. S. Army. Charles Augustus Lindbergh was top of his class,
and not simply in his skill with planes. There was a great amount of
theoretical work connected with the course, and that meant studying,
listening to lectures, examinations, all of which he still hated. But he
decided that this was one occasion when he was not going to drop out,
and he gritted his teeth and bested all his fellow cadets in oral tests,
written tests, and, of course, actual flying.

The course was a tough one, and included all the kinds of flying that
never came a gypsy pilot's way: formation flying and high altitude maneuvers, strafing, bombing, gunnery, and photography as well as precision landing and take-off. In these last two arts, of course, Lindbergh
didn't have to learn much, because by that time he could get a plane
airborne out of practically anywhere—providing there weren't telegraph
poles in the way, of course.

Halfway through the course, the cadets moved over from Hisso-Jen-
nies to De Havillands, and Lindbergh had his first experience of what it
was like to fly a really powerful machine. You could fly a D.H. to over
twelve thousand feet, and see half across Texas to Mexico and the Gulf.
But the instructor warned that the D.H. was a tricky and choosy craft
which was not up to being thrown around or stunted. Too tight a turn
or too abrupt a dive and you were apt to leave your wings behind. The
warnings didn't prevent most cadets from trying their craft to the
limits, and whenever he was in the sky alone, Lindbergh could never
resist putting on his own private exhibition of aerobatics; and once,
when he glimpsed another D.H. below him, he dove in and practically
scraped the other's tail, and for the next twenty minutes simulated a
dogfight that had the other D.H. yawing all over the sky. It only slowly
dawned on him that there were two men in the other plane, which

meant that one of them must be an instructor, and that if a report went in, he would be fired. None was ever filed. Maybe the other pilot was giving a bootleg flight to his brother.

The nearest he came to being washed out of the course was when an instructor examining his plane found damage to the wheel axle and tell-tale grass and seeds sticking to it. He was accused of taking off from a prohibited field and not reporting a mishap. He knew he was not guilty and that the cadet who had used the plane later in the day was probably the culprit, but under the honor system he could only insist that he hadn't done the damage himself. He was about to be flunked for indiscipline when the other cadet owned up.

It cannot be said that he was a popular cadet, but his comrades came to admire him, and respect him, even if they did not learn to like him. The only attempt to haze him, when he escaped from a group who tried to throw him into a nearby pond, led to drastic reprisals. Four of the hazers found itching powder in their pajamas, and the fifth, the ringleader, discovered himself in bed with a live snake.

"It wasn't venomous, was it?" the cadet cried, after he had flung it through the bunkhouse window.

"Yes, but not fatally," Lindbergh replied.

A sergeant who snored too loudly when he was drunk returned one night to find his bed had been shifted from the bunkhouse to the roof. A skunk was let loose in a classroom. Life in the Army stirred Lindbergh's appetite for practical jokes, and they got rougher as he grew older.

The only time when it looked as if Lindbergh was not going to emerge successfully from the course was on March 6, 1925, just before he was due for passing out. On that day he took off from Kelly Field, Texas, on a nine-ship formation flight of SE-5s. After preliminary training, he had been given the option of choosing bombing, reconnaissance, or pursuit flying as his speciality, and he had chosen pursuit. The SE-5s were the Army's fighter planes at that time.

The squadron under the leadership of an army pilot, Lieutenant Blackburn, had been ordered to intercept and attack a formation of De Havillands cruising at five thousand feet above the clouds, and what happened next is best told in Lindbergh's own words. They were part of an official report which he wrote afterward and one which was picked up and reprinted in the New York *Evening World*.

"I was flying on the left of the top unit, Lieut. McAllister on my right, and Cadet Love leading," he reported. "When we nosed down on the DH, I attacked from the left and Lieut. McAllister from the right. After Cadet Love pulled up, I continued to dive on the DH for a short time before pulling up to the left. I saw no other ship nearby. I passed above the DH and a moment later I felt a slight jolt followed by a crash. My head was thrown forward against the cowling and my plane seemed to turn around and hang nearly motionless for an instant. I closed the throttle and saw an SE-5 with Lieut. McAllister in the cockpit a few feet on my left. He was apparently unhurt and getting ready to jump."

The two planes had locked together, with the wings intermeshed and the fuselages approximately parallel. Lindbergh's right wing had been smashed up and folded back, pressing over the forward right-hand corner of the cockpit.

"Then the wings started to mill around and the wires began whistling," he went on. "The right wing commenced vibrating and striking my head at the bottom of each oscillation. I removed the rubber band safetying the belt, unbuckled it, climbed out past the trailing edge of the damaged wing, and with my feet on the cowling on the right side of the cockpit, which was then in a nearly vertical position, I jumped backwards as far from the ship as possible. I had no difficulty locating the pull ring and experienced no sensation of falling."

The interlocked fighters were by this time tumbling fast down to earth, and for a time Lindbergh was falling beside them, only a few yards to one side of the mass of swirling wings and fuselage.

"Fearing the wreckage might fall on me," he wrote, "I did not pull the rip cord until I dropped several hundred feet and into the clouds. During this time I had turned one-half revolution and was falling flat and face downwards. . . . I saw Lieut. McAllister floating above me and the wrecked ships pass about 100 yards to one side, continuing to spin to the right and leaving a trail of lighter fragments along their path. I watched them until, still locked together, they crashed in the mesquite about 2,000 feet below and burst into flames several seconds after the impact."

Since he was the only one around those parts who was an experienced parachutist, he could not resist a bit of one-upmanship about his landing.

"Next I turned my attention to locating a landing place. I was over mesquite and drifting in the general direction of a plowed field which I reached by slipping my chute. Shortly before striking the ground I was drifting backwards, but was able to swing around in the harness just as I landed on the side of a ditch less than 100 feet from the edge of the mesquite. Although the impact of the landing was too great for me to remain standing, I was not injured in any way. The parachute was still held open by the wind and did not collapse until I pulled in one group of shroud lines."

He added: "During my descent I lost my goggles, a vest pocket camera which fitted tightly into my hip pocket, and the rip cord of the parachute."†

The two pilots were sent up in new planes almost immediately to make sure they hadn't lost their nerve. Ten days later they joined their comrades at the passing-out parade and were gazetted second lieutenants in the U. S. Army. Charles Lindbergh had written to Washington to apply for a permanent commission in the Army,‡ but in the meantime he resigned from active service and automatically became a member of the reserve corps.

On March 25, 1925, with his last army pay in his pocket, he was driven to the depot at San Antonio. Now he had to decide where he was going to go and what he was going to do. His father was dead. He would like to have seen his mother, but saw no prospect of a pilot's job in Detroit, and it was no time for spending unnecessary money on railroad fares.

He marched up to the ticket office and bought a one-way trip to St. Louis, Missouri. There was something about that city—and particularly Lambert Field—that gave him a feeling in his bones that St. Louis held the key to his future.

Aviation in the United States in 1925 had just received a boost from Washington that would soon be turning many a gypsy pilot into a professional flier with a regular job, and Charles Lindbergh was one of them. Until that year, what airmail services existed in America were run by army planes and personnel, and in 1924 the Army had even inaugurated a transcontinental service from San Francisco to Long Island, with branch routes from New York to Washington, St. Louis to Chicago, and Chicago to Minneapolis. But the service ran at a loss, and the railroads were constantly complaining that it was unfair that their own postal services should have to compete with a government-subsidized system. In any case, wasn't this the land of free enterprise? What right had the U. S. Government to be meddling in private business?

A measure was therefore introduced into the House by Congressman

---

† Reprinted in *Swedes in America, 1638–1938* (New Haven: Yale University Press, 1938), chapter entitled "Aviation," by John Goldstrom. It is interesting to note that Lindbergh abandoned this version for a much more dramatized one in *The Spirit of St. Louis.*

‡ There is no record that he got a reply.

Clyde Kelly handing the airmail system back to the private aircraft companies. It was a bill designed to save money for the Treasury and appease the railroad men, and only a few foresighted air pioneers realized that it was going to change everything, so far as commercial flying was concerned.

Charles Lindbergh had decided that he would pick up a few instruction jobs, taxi flights, passenger trips, and the odd barnstorming expedition out of Lambert Field while he looked around and found out what was going. Within a few days of his arrival he was approached by the Robertson Brothers (Bill and Frank), a couple of war veteran fliers who had formed a small aircraft company at Lambert and were shooting for the airmail contracts that were now coming onto the market. Eventually they saw themselves taking over the transcontinental route, but the franchise for it would not be available for a couple of years. In the meantime, they had made a bid for the St. Louis–Chicago route, and though he was still only twenty-three years old, Charles Lindbergh had built up a solid enough reputation for the brothers to offer him the job of chief pilot.

It was an if-and-when offer, since they hadn't yet got the contract and couldn't pay anything until it was theirs, but Lindbergh was sufficiently enthusiastic (he shared their views about the future of commercial aviation) to tell them they could count on him, if and when.

In the meantime, he mulled over a letter he had received from Wray Vaughn, president of an organization calling itself the Mil-Hi Airways and Flying Circus, which operated out of Denver, Colorado. Vaughn offered Lindbergh a job at four hundred dollars a month if he would join the gang. It was quite big money in those days, but Lindbergh was more interested in the location of the company. During his army career, and on his barnstorming visit to Boulder, Colorado, he had become interested in the air currents which are encountered around canyons, over glaciers, and high mountain ridges, and a flying job out of Denver would give him a good opportunity of studying "the effect of turbulence, about which aviators knew so little and speculated so much." It would enable him to attach a serious purpose to what sounded like just another stunting job. He had his eyes on different goals now, and he had reached the stage when it was no longer enough for him to throw a plane around the sky merely for the entertainment of himself and customers on the ground below. He wired acceptance of the offer, and when he reached Humphrey's Field outside Denver and met Wray Vaughn and the Mil-Hi outfit, it was as he suspected. The "circus" consisted of an old Hisso-Standard biplane with a green dragon painted on each side of its fuselage, and underneath its carnival costume it turned out to be a crate in which he had barnstormed three years earlier; even the dents in the cockpit seat still fitted the shape of his rear end.

He soon found out why he was being paid four hundred a month. Not only was he expected to take up passengers on five-dollar flights, but in the evening roman candles and streamers were attached to his wings and he was off into the black sky to give a fireworks display. It was bad enough taking off and landing at airfields by night at that time, and the wise pilot came down to earth with the setting sun. Operating out of farmers' fields was much trickier and more dangerous; you took off in the limited beams from the headlights of a customer's car, and when the time came to land that wasn't much help, because your eyes had been blinded by the glare of the fireworks. You trusted to luck and instinct and the length of the field—if you could find it again.

Wray Vaughn was the sort of man who would take any risk for an extra buck, and on one occasion his appetite for money almost cut short Charles Lindbergh's career at twenty-three. At the time, Wray was accompanying his pilot and it was he who insisted on staying late at one town to accommodate four extra customers who wanted rides, and so earn an extra twenty dollars. It was late in the evening by the time they were ready to leave for the next town, where they had a contract to give a fireworks display.

Lindbergh didn't know the area and the sun was setting, and he suggested that they should scrub the engagement. Since he was being paid two hundred and fifty dollars for the fireworks show, and the contract was good until midnight, canceling out was something Vaughn would not countenance. He swore he knew the area like a book, but it soon developed that it wasn't a book he remembered very well. The landing ground was beside the golf links, he said confidently. Lindbergh, staring down hard at the darkening ground below him, replied:

"Yes, but where is the golf links?"

Finally, he decided to risk a landing in what looked like a stubbled field, and they were in luck. They were down safely. But they were five miles away from the town, and it was dark now. Lindbergh was still for forgetting the whole thing, but not Vaughn. He would not be flying from now on, only collecting the check from the town clerk. He raced over to the road, flagged down an approaching car, and asked for a lift from the driver for himself and his pilot. The two men arrived in town, announced their presence, and busied themselves collecting the fireworks and paraphernalia that were needed for the show.

It was half past nine when they got back to the plane. It was too dark for Lindbergh to study the ground from which he would be taking off. In any case, he was too busy helping Vaughn to get the racks fixed and the roman candles attached to them, and all he had time to do was walk across the stubbled field and test its texture with his feet. It was half past eleven before everything was ready—and by that time, he pointed out to his boss, most folks in country areas had gone to bed. But Vaughn insisted. A contract was a contract. Provided he could get the fireworks blazing in the sky before midnight, they were due two hundred and fifty dollars.

But how to get aloft? A farmer in an old model car promised to turn the beams of his lights down the field to give Lindbergh a flight path, and it looked as if things would be all right as he trundled his ancient crate down the pasture for a run. But by the time he turned, the beams had started shortening—the car's batteries were low and running down rapidly. The flier had to disembark and tell Vaughn to shine his torch on a haystack, to give him a landmark to concentrate on, and it was by that faint light that he finally got his loaded plane into the black sky. He was over the town by eighteen minutes before midnight. For the next quarter of an hour he was busy cruising around the night sky, dipping his hand into a box by his side, pulling the caps off colored bombs and streamers, rubbing the ignition caps and tossing them over the side of the plane. And praying that a sudden gust of wind didn't blow one of the lighted fireworks back against the plane.

At long last, he pulled the switches that lit the roman candles and dove on the town, banked, looped, spun in a trail of red, white, green, and yellow sparks like some drunken comet, and all he was thinking about was how he was going to get down again.

At last the candles burned out and he was flying in darkness again. He lit the dashboard light and looked at his watch. It was 11:57. Vaughn could go and collect the check. He had fulfilled the contract with three minutes to spare. But first he had to find the field from which he had taken off, and then follow signals from Vaughn's torch to guide him in the direction in which he should land. After flying in the gaudy blaze of the fireworks, it was like looking for a needle in a haystack. Could that be it far below—the tiny glow that looked like a cigarette tip on which a smoker is puffing? If it wasn't, then Wray Vaughn would have to get another plane and another pilot, because he had to go down anyway.

He set the old crate's nose down toward the flicker in front of him, eased slowly on the stick, and prayed as he descended into the black pit below him. . . . And all he said afterward was: "Thank God for the length of Colorado fields."

And then there arrived a telegram: COME AT ONCE. It was signed by Frank Lambert. That meant the airmail contract must be coming up. He handed in his notice to Wray Vaughn, and took the train at once for St. Louis and Lambert Field. He would henceforward be delivering the United States mail.

CHAPTER

SIX

MAIL RUN

On the wall of the small office which Charles Lindbergh used at Lambert Field when he started the St. Louis–Chicago mail run in 1926 was a quotation adapted from Herodotus:

"Neither snow, nor rain, nor heat, nor gloom of night stays these couriers from the swift completion of their appointed rounds."

The Robertsons got word from Washington early in the year that they had won the contract, and they promptly called in Lindbergh. He was given full charge of the operation and told to pick two other pilots to serve under and share the run with him. He was also given a plane and told to take off and plot the route between St. Louis and Chicago, picking his own landing fields, ordering the equipment for them, and starting dummy services in readiness for the official opening. He chose two army cadets from his class at San Antonio to fly with him, Philip R. (Red) Love and Thomas P. (Nellie) Nelson, both of whom had often been in the air with him and whose skill and reliability he felt he could trust. Between them, they flew over and picked out nine landing grounds on the route to Chicago, and arranged for gas dumps to be established and a certain amount of night lighting for when it might be necessary. Since the Robertsons had blown almost all their capital on planes (ten De Havillands, four stand-by De Havillands, and two Curtiss Orioles), only minimum amounts could be spent on ground equipment.

The airmail contract stipulated that the company must be in business before the end of April 1926, and on the fifteenth of that month Charles Lindbergh took off just before dawn from Chicago on the inaugural flight. He made it without incident. In the afternoon he loaded mail at St. Louis and began the return journey to Chicago at 4 P.M., landing at Peoria and Springfield, Illinois, en route, to pick up more mail. He wrote several letters to relatives for the inaugural flight north, and undoubtedly one of them went to his mother, but the only one which was ever made public was the one released by his uncle, John C. Lodge, in which he scribbled that he was "very short of time" and that he was expecting to land in Chicago at 7 P.M., which he did, with a full load of mail.

Summer weather was pretty stable that year in the Middle West and the service went through without incidents of any serious character for the next four months. One report indicates that 98 per cent of the flights made the connection with the transcontinental services at Chicago. No one minded the airmail surcharge if this was the efficient and speedy way in which it was going to work.

On September 15, however, Lindbergh got the first indication of what it was going to be like to run a regular airmail service when the winter weather began to close in. On the regular four o'clock run north, he landed at Peoria and took off again at six o'clock with a full load. There was no weather service to warn him that fog was rolling in across the plains toward Chicago, and soon it was so thick that it blanketed Maywood Field, where he was supposed to land, to a height of nearly a thousand feet. It was the first big weather hazard the company had experienced, and to meet it searchlights were turned skyward and great oil fires lighted in the hope that they would pierce the thousand-foot cover and give a signal to the airmail plane circling above them.

Lindbergh saw nothing. He cruised through the darkening mist for half an hour, hoping that he might find a pocket to dive through; but when one did not appear, he turned away and decided to fly back south in search of an area clear of fog. He was not too worried. He figured that he had fuel enough for another hour's flying, not counting his emergency tank. What he did not know was that a mechanic in St. Louis had taken out the usual 110-gallon tank to repair a leak and replaced it with an 85-gallon tank. Suddenly his engine stopped in mid-air. He switched over to his emergency, but that would only give him another twenty minutes of flight—and the way things looked down on the ground, the mist did not seem likely to clear away by then. In his official report, which he wrote later, he went on:

"I decided to leave the ship as soon as the reserve tank was exhausted. I tried to get the mail pit open with the idea of throwing out the mail sacks, and then jumping, but was unable to open the front buckle. I knew that the risk of fire with no gasoline in the tanks was very slight and began to climb for altitude when I saw a light on the ground for several seconds. This was the first light I had seen for nearly two hours, and as almost enough gasoline for fifteen minutes' flying remained in the reserve, I glided down to 1,200 feet and pulled out the flare release . . . the flare functioned but only to illuminate the top of a solid bank of fog, into which it soon disappeared without showing any trace of ground."

He now had seven minutes of gas left in the emergency tank, and becoming conscious of the glow of a town through the fog, he nosed the plane up and made for open country.

"At 5,000 feet the engine sputtered and died," he went on. "I stepped up on the cowling and out over the right side of the cockpit, pulling the rip cord after about a 100-feet fall. The parachute, an Irving seat service type, functioned perfectly; I was falling head downward when the risers jerked me into an upright position and the chute opened. . . . I pulled the flashlight from my belt and was playing it down towards the top of the fog when I heard the plane's engine pick up. When I had jumped it had practically stopped dead and I had neglected to cut the switches. Apparently when the ship nosed down an additional supply of gasoline drained to the carburettor."

He was uncomfortably aware from the noise that the plane was coming toward him, and soon he got the horrid feeling that it was playing hide-and-seek with him.

"Soon [the ship] came into sight, about a quarter of a mile away, and headed in the general direction of my parachute. I put the flashlight in a pocket of my flying suit preparatory to slipping the parachute out of the way if necessary. The plane was making a left spiral of about a mile diameter, and passed approximately 300 yards away from my chute, leaving me on the outside of the circle. I was undecided as to whether the plane or I was descending the more rapidly and glided my chute away from the spiral path of the ship as rapidly as I could. The ship passed completely out of sight, but reappeared in a few seconds, its rate of descent being about the same as that of the parachute. I counted the five spirals, each one a little further away than the last, before reaching the top of the fog bank."

As he drifted through the thick wet bank of fog, he began methodically to make preparations for the moment he hit the ground, which he now calculated to be about a thousand feet down. Since he could see nothing above or below him, he had no idea what kind of terrain it was that was waiting for him, and when he reached for his flashlight, with which he hoped to light the last few yards of his descent, he discovered that it was gone, probably whipped away by the wind.

"I crossed my legs to keep from straddling a branch or wire, guarded my face with my hands, and waited," he wrote later. "Presently I saw the outline of the ground and a moment later was down in a cornfield. The corn was over my head and the chute was lying on top of the corn stalks. I hurriedly packed it and started down a corn row."

The priority was to discover what had happened to the plane—and the mail it contained. The fog was still thick and he had some difficulty finding a farmhouse, and even more difficulty explaining to the farmer —who had heard the crash—that he was the pilot of the plane and was looking for it himself. It was eventually discovered about three miles away, having just missed another farmhouse and skidded for eighty yards on its left wing through a cornfield. The mail pit had broken open, but the mailbags were intact. They were taken to the local post office and put aboard the 3:30 A.M. train for Chicago, and only then did Charles Lindbergh have time to attend to his cuts and bruises.

The crash was an item on the AP wire service out of Chicago, but it made no more than a paragraph or so in the press. It seems curious that no newspaper at this time seems to have considered the establishment of an all-weather airmail service as a good story. No reporter rode along with the mail pilots, and no one, therefore, really realized how rough it could get. It was remarkable how seldom blizzards or tornados forced them to cancel flights, and between them Lindbergh, Love, and Nelson kept up a standard of delivery that was frequently above and beyond the terms of their contract, for they often flew in conditions when all other planes were grounded, and when the transcontinental service with which they were connecting in Chicago failed to come through.

His two fellow mail pilots constantly complained of the cold when they were flying, and piled sourdough underwear and leather coats around them in an effort to make the conditions bearable. But Lindbergh, who didn't even possess an overcoat, seemed impervious to the weather. He once flew his station manager, O. E. Scott, from St. Louis to Chicago on a November ride when the temperature was well below zero up in the air, and Scott was soon so close to collapsing from the cold that he frantically indicated to his pilot that he should land the plane. When they did so, Lindbergh seemed quite surprised that his passenger was cold. He hadn't noticed it himself, he said.

It was in pretty appalling conditions that he took off by night on November 4, 1926, and once more failed to get through. He had landed at Springfield, Illinois, and was in the air again for Peoria when snow began to fall and was soon so thick that he could no longer see lights on the ground, even when he came down to two hundred feet. He had flown in from Chicago early that same afternoon and remembered that conditions had been clear around that area, and he decided to press on, figuring that there would be a better chance of making an emergency landing further north than if he turned and tried to make it back to St. Louis. He had enough gas for an hour and ten minutes flying time plus twenty minutes in the reserve.

"For the next half hour the flight northeast was at about 2,000 feet altitude and then at 600 feet," he wrote in his official report. "After passing over the light of a small town a fairly clear space in the clouds was encountered. I pulled up to about 600 feet, released the parachute flare, whipped the ship around to get into the wind and under the flare, which lit at once. Instead of floating down slowly, however, it dropped like a rock. I could see the ground for only an instant and then there was total darkness."

He flew on until there was about ten minutes of gas in the pressure tank, and made the decision to bale out, once he had taken the ship up to a high enough altitude.

"The main tank went dry at 7:50 P.M. and the reserve twenty minutes later," he wrote. "The altimeter then registered approximately 14,000 feet, yet the top of the clouds was apparently several thousand feet higher. Rolling the stabilizer back, I cut out the switches, pulled the ship up into a stall and was about to go over the right side of the cockpit when the right wing began to drop."

In such a position, it was only too likely that the plane would speed up, start to spin, and strike his parachute. So he climbed back into the cockpit and took the controls again until he had righted the plane. Only then did he dive out of the left side of the plane, into a seventy-mile-an-hour gale at thirteen thousand feet.

The chute opened normally, at first. It was snowing and very cold. For a minute or so the parachute descended smoothly and then, in Lindbergh's words, "commenced an excessive oscillation which continued for about five minutes and could not be checked." It meant that the canopy above him began to shake violently, tossing him wildly about the sky, while he struggled with the shrouds and tried to control it.

"The first indication of the nearness of the chute to the ground," his report went on, "was the gradual darkening of the space below. The snow had turned to rain and, although the chute was thoroughly soaked, its oscillation had decreased. I directed the beam from my five-hundred-feet spotlight downward, but the ground appeared so suddenly that I landed directly on top of a barbed wire fence without seeing it."

The fence helped to cushion his fall and the barbs did not penetrate his flying suit. The chute was blown over the fence and billowed out across a muddy field in the wind, but he edged round with the shrouds until he had collapsed it, after which he carefully folded it up into its pack and, carrying it over his shoulder, tramped off across the fields in the rain and sleet toward the nearest light.

That night the mail was not sent on. The wreckage of the plane was not found until next day, when Lindbergh sighted it from another ship he had picked up in Chicago. The mail was intact, though some of the letters got stained with oil from the leaking engine.

This time even the New York *Times* used the story, though they misspelled the pilot's name "Lindberg." The correct name went into the records, for he was the first pilot in the United States ever to have made four emergency parachute jumps from a plane.

The Robertson airmail contract was paid by the U. S. Post Office according to the number of pounds of mail the company's aircraft carried, and that meant they packed the planes with every letter and package they could cram aboard. It was a pleasant bonus when registered mail was included in the load, because the registered bags were secured with stout locks weighing two pounds apiece, and these added a welcome sum to the monthly dividends. At first, lack of money stopped the Robertson planes from carrying more than one aircraft flare—maybe if he had had two aboard, Lindbergh might have been able to land his second "lost" plane instead of parachuting out of it—or fitting starboard and port navigation lights, but even when they could afford to fit them, these flight aids were discarded if it meant loading an extra mailbag.

The company ran on a shoestring all through 1926. To save electricity, they used short-burning oil flares instead of floodlights for the flight paths on terminal and emergency landing fields, and Lindbergh stressed to his two assistant pilots that there was a penalty to be paid each time the mailbags failed to make the whole journey, so that it had to be a desperate situation and not just a moment of uncertainty before they decided to come down short of their destination.

To outward appearances, Charles Lindbergh did not seem to be affected by what must have been the strains and stresses of the situation. Twenty-four years old, in peak physical condition, he lived, ate, and slept flying and would have scoffed at anyone who suggested that he felt any pressures on his job. On days off, he hired out to fly passengers around the state, and that fall, when a great hurricane hit Florida, flew a reporter from the St. Louis *Post-Dispatch* to Miami by night and through the storm, just to earn a few extra dollars for himself and his bosses. He also stunted for the crowds at the St. Louis motorboat races

on the Mississippi that summer and thrilled them by diving and dipping
his wheels in the water as he skimmed past them.

He had no private life and scoffed at his aides if they developed interests outside their aircraft and their jobs. Phil Love had to sneak away
to talk to his girl friends, because, whenever he telephoned them in
Lindbergh's presence, he would have to do so to the accompaniment of
yells, falsetto shrieks, and clashing pans. Lindbergh's talent for practical
joking, which had first begun to develop in the Army, now took a sadis-
tic turn. Back from a date, Love would crawl into bed to find it filled
with frogs or lizards. When he failed to awake at the sound of the
alarm clock, he would have the bedclothes ripped back and Lindbergh
would be standing over him, pouring on him a bucket of ice-cold water.
His old friend Bud Gurney, back from a night out and thirsty from the
heat and liquor, took up a jug of what looked like iced water and
poured it down his throat. Lindbergh had substituted kerosene and
Gurney was rushed to a hospital with a badly burned stomach and
throat.

Nelson, Love, and Gurney all shared rooms with Lindbergh at one
time or another during this period, but moved out when it became obvious that he was a monomaniac about flying and resented them if they
interested themselves in anything else. On one occasion Love and his
girl friend, aroused at last by Lindbergh's constant harassment of their
association, spread ball bearings over the floor behind the front door
and draped themselves over the sofa in a passionate embrace when they
heard him coming. He opened the door, gazed at them in angry amazement, and then stepped forward and skidded to a spectacular collapse
across the floor. He climbed to his feet and went into his bedroom
without saying a word. They had also arranged a split bed for him, and
it collapsed with a thud as he crawled into it. But when they peeped
through the bedroom door, Lindbergh did not seem to have noticed.
He was fast asleep on the split bed, or appeared to be. Next day, however, he suggested that Love go and bunk elsewhere in future, and
things were never really the same between them again.

In truth, as the letters he wrote to his mother will reveal when they
are released, he was living under a considerable amount of tension at
this time. There is little doubt that the practical jokes were a way of
blowing off excess pressure. He had no other way of relaxing. When
things were going too well in the air, he almost resented it. One day,
flying in perfect weather toward Chicago, he expressed disappointment
that there were no turbulences or emergencies to challenge him. It was
simply a question of holding on to his course and plugging on. "There's
nothing else to do, nothing to match yourself against," he decided.

"There hasn't been even an occasional cloud near enough to burrow through. Skill is no asset. The spirit of conquest is gone from the air."

It was on such occasions that he fretted and became restless, and wondered if he was going to spend the rest of his life flying mail between St. Louis and Chicago. He knew, of course, that nothing was less likely, but he used these hours of eventless boredom to goad himself and dream. Unlike other young Americans of his time, who were dreaming of becoming president of General Motors or even President of the United States, he was dreaming of bigger and better airplanes which he would fly further than any man had done before.

Later on he described those pensive hours in the cockpit as the time when he played a game called Suppose. *Suppose* someone was to refine a new kind of gasoline which didn't weigh down the plane so heavily, and when he filled up on it he could fly his ship not just for hours but for days? *Suppose* they had one of those new-type Wright-Bellanca planes which were just coming into production? Experts said they carried an incredible load. With three Wright-Bellancas they wouldn't need to keep on flying back and forth between St. Louis and Chicago. They could fly direct from St. Louis to New York, and maybe carry three passengers as well as the mail. *Suppose* he had a Bellanca of his own, to do with what he liked, go where he wished? He could show those ignorant, land-locked folks down there that planes were not just for stunting, barnstorming, crashing, expensive toys only good for putting on a show. He could load it with gasoline in special tanks and fly it anywhere, break all the records for altitude, distance, length of flight. *Suppose* it was loaded down with gasoline and nothing else? "I could fly on all night, like the moon," he told himself. He could break records across the country, or span the continents.

He could even fly from New York to Paris.

It was as casually as this, he was later to say, that the notion came into his mind of making a transatlantic flight. But the more closely one studies the man, the more unlikely it seems that Charles Augustus Lindbergh ever did anything casually.

CHAPTER

SEVEN

PROMOTION

On the afternoon of September 16, 1926, Charles Lindbergh left his
room in the Congress Hotel in Chicago and went to a movie house on
the Loop to see a film called *What Price Glory?* starring an ugly but
amiable Irish actor called Victor McLaglen. Even though he could now
afford the price of a ticket, Lindbergh was still not much of a movie-
goer, but he was taking a day off after his crash and parachute jump of
the day before, and the ballyhoo about *What Price Glory?* had been so
great that even he had heard of it. He was interested to see what "revelations" it promised about life among the doughboys along the western
front in World War I.

Film shows in those days were almost always preceded by newsreels,
filling the same function as television news programs do today, and one
of the items in the program on this occasion gripped Lindbergh's attention, because it was about airplanes. Or rather, about one airplane. It
was a huge (for those days) biplane built on Long Island, New York,
by an aviation pioneer named Igor Sikorsky, and when it was wheeled
out of its hangar and into the view of the camera, at least one man in
the audience opened his eyes wide in surprise and admiration. The
Sikorsky plane had three engines and propellers and had been built to
carry a crew of four over the ocean to Europe. When, in a subsequent
shot, Lindbergh saw the beautiful monster taxi down the runway of
Roosevelt Field and take off, he had little doubt that the Sikorsky was
capable of making the journey.

Newsreels had not yet been wired for sound, and all that could be
gathered from the brief captions in between the shots was that the
plane would be competing for the Orteig Prize and that it would be

piloted by an ace French pilot named Capitaine René Fonck. Lindbergh was apt to be patronizing about men who failed to measure up to his own height, and he must have grinned at the shots of Fonck, for he was a tiny neat manikin, not much more than five feet two, who looked like a Gallic stereotype almost to the point of caricature. But there was no doubt about the authority he exuded once he sat at the controls of his magnificent machine.

He grinned and mouthed words at the camera, and the subtitle came on the screen:

"Paris, here I come!"

What Price Glory? faded into triviality compared with the significance of those words, and Lindbergh hurried away after it was over to buy newspapers and magazines and try to find the answers to the questions the newsreel item had raised: What was the Orteig Prize? Who was René Fonck? What chance did he have of making the flight from New York to Paris?

It was not difficult to find the answers, because the newspapers were full of them. It is surprising that Charles Lindbergh had not heard of the Orteig Prize before, because it was not exactly new. It was named after the man who had originally proposed it, Raymond Orteig, a fat and friendly Frenchman who operated the Brevoort and Lafayette hotels in New York City, and it offered $25,000* to any flier or group of fliers "who shall cross the Atlantic in a land or water aircraft (heavier than air) from Paris or the shores of France to New York, or from New York to Paris or the shores of France, without stop."

Orteig had made his offer through the Aero Club of America after he went to a dinner honoring Captain Eddie Rickenbacker, the U.S. ace, when he came back from flying over the French battlefields in World War I. The speeches had contained lots of flowery oratory about Franco-American friendship and the brotherhood of the air which had been established between fliers of the two nations over the western front. Rickenbacker had looked forward to the day when airplanes would link the two peoples not only in battle but also in peace, by flights between their countries. Impressed, Orteig had proposed a prize for the aviator or aviators who pioneered the route.

But that offer had been made in 1919 and stipulated that the flight must be made within five years. There were no takers. A flight of such magnitude was beyond the limits of the planes of the day.† Early in

---

* Worth about five times that amount today.

† It was true that in 1919 two British fliers, John Alcock and Arthur Whitten Brown, had flown from Newfoundland to Ireland, where they crash-landed in a bog. It was a tremendous achievement for its time but the distance was under 2,000 miles, whereas New York to Paris was 3,400.

1926, however, egged on by a French newspaper, Orteig had renewed his offer and almost at once René Fonck had appeared on the scene to announce that Sikorsky was building him a plane especially designed to make the transatlantic flight. He had gathered together considerable financial backing in both France and the United States, and he seemed an eminently suitable pilot to make the journey. He had a considerable reputation in France as one of the great aces of the war, with several members of the Richthofen Squadron among his victims, and he had since made many long-distance flights in Europe.

After testing the Sikorsky all through the summer of 1926 with ever-increasing loads, Fonck was now, in September, ready to start off on the great adventure. All he was waiting for, the newspapers said, was a spell of good weather, and then: *Paris, here I come!*

The more he read about the Fonck project, the more thoughtful and skeptical Lindbergh became about some of the aspects of it. First of all, why were four men being used on the flight? Who needed four men to fly a plane, even a huge plane like the Sikorsky? They could only add to the load. There were other things that were going to add to the load, too, from what he read in the newspapers. Fonck announced that he was taking along two kinds of radio sets, a long-wave and a short-wave apparatus, and at that time they weighed a lot. Why couldn't he manage with one? Then the interior of the plane, apparently, had been decorated in red leather and the cabin even contained a bed. And could it really be true that each member of the crew was taking along presents for friends in Europe, and that they were going to cook themselves a hot dinner—with a real stove?—en route?

No wonder the pay load was now announced at 28,000 pounds. It sounded too much even for a plane with three engines. Lindbergh, who would have ripped out every unnecessary gadget and decorative strip and thrown out at least two members of the crew, grew increasingly doubtful. He had looked so capable in the newsreel, but was Capitaine Fonck really a serious flier?

On September 20 it was announced from New York that weather conditions were favorable over the Atlantic, and at dawn the following day the great Sikorsky was wheeled out of its hangar on Roosevelt Field, Long Island, and pushed to the end of the runway. Right from the start, things went wrong. The tail skid slipped from its dolly as the plane was being taken out, and the rudder was damaged. A few minutes later, the auxiliary landing structure was bent in swinging the plane around and had to be straightened.

Nevertheless, the engines started smoothly, and after taking a last package aboard (it contained, of all things, a dozen American-made croissants), René Fonck waved good-by to Raymond Orteig and his backers and gunned the great ship down the runway. He needed to reach eighty miles an hour for lift-off, and it became obvious to the experts watching him pass the halfway mark along the runway that he was not going to make it. Suddenly things began to happen. Bits of the plane broke away. A wheel from the auxiliary landing gear broke off and began to drag. The tail bounced high into the air and then thudded down onto the grass.

It was the obvious moment to cut the motors and call it a day, but for some reason Fonck carried on. Still well below take-off speed, the monster thundered toward the end of the field and finally plunged through the fencing and crashed twenty feet down to the bottom of a gully, its tail high in the air. A few seconds later, flames shot up to the sky. The Sikorsky was carrying 2,380 gallons of gas, and it had ignited.

Fonck and his American copilot, Lawrence W. Curtin, scrambled clear, but the two other members of the crew were trapped in the cabin and burned to death.

No one read the reports of the disaster more avidly than Charles Lindbergh, and long before all the details were out he had made up his mind. Fonck's misfortune was his opportunity. The Orteig Prize was still there to be won by some enterprising pilot who could learn from the Frenchman's mistakes. Why shouldn't Charles Lindbergh be the first man to fly from New York to Paris—and do it alone?

In the next few months, Charles Lindbergh changed his nature, not for the last time. Normally he was a solitary, taciturn man who rarely sought the company of his fellow human beings, and sometimes positively shunned them. He had no party manners. He was impatient with those who differed from him. He hated making polite conversation. But once he got an idea in his mind or a project that needed selling, he was prepared to meet anyone, slap every back in sight, turn on his smile and his charm, and listen patiently to the emptiest small talk—but only if it brought him nearer to the attainment of his objective.

The more he thought about it, the more convinced he was that he could win the Orteig Prize, provided he had the right sort of plane, providing he flew alone. As he plodded back and forth along the mail route from St. Louis to Chicago, he worked it all out, first of all in his mind and then on paper. But could he convince other people, people with money, that it was feasible and that they should back him?

Somewhat to his own surprise, he discovered talents in himself as a promoter. Among his spare-time activities, he had taken to giving instruction to a number of well-connected businessmen in St. Louis, and the craze for flying was catching on. Nearly all these men were not only rich but city-boosters as well, eager to put the name of St. Louis on the map. So why not convince them that he was worth backing by emphasizing that it would be a St. Louis enterprise and that if he succeeded everybody in the world would be talking about their town? He made an appointment first with Earl Thompson, a local insurance broker, who was skeptical at first. That was natural, Lindbergh told himself; he had to be conservative by reason of his profession. Thompson didn't seem to believe that a transatlantic flight could be made in a single-engined plane, which was the kind Lindbergh wanted to fly. But Lindbergh came away at the end of the evening convinced that Thompson was interested and could be talked around. The insurance broker had not failed to be impressed by the fact that young Lindbergh was willing to put up $2,000 out of his own savings toward the purchase of a plane.

Every spare moment between his airmail duties now was spent in rehearsing his arguments and trying them out on anyone who would listen. The first one to come in definitely with an offer of a check was Major Albert B. Lambert, an aviation pioneer after whom St. Louis's airport is named. Taken by Lindbergh's enthusiasm, he agreed to donate $1,000 to the fund. On hearing this, Frank Robertson, Lindbergh's boss, said he would come in, too, and also introduced his pilot to the editor of the St. Louis *Post-Dispatch*, the city's most influential newspaper, in the hope of persuading him to back the enterprise. But on this occasion Lindbergh's enthusiastic sales talk fell on stony ground. Once the editor heard that his visitor planned to attempt the Atlantic crossing by himself, and in a single-engined plane, his tone became frigid. He had heard about Lindbergh's reputation as a barnstormer, a wingwalker, and a parachutist. This was just another stunt, and a newspaper with the reputation of the *Post-Dispatch*, he pointed out severely, could not possibly associate itself with stunts. Especially stunts that were almost certain to fail.

But others connected with the newspaper world of St. Louis had more faith. Harry F. Knight, who had interests in the *Post-Dispatch's* rival, the *Globe-Democrat*, promised money and the backing of the newspaper.‡ When Harold Bixby, a local bank president, heard about this, he came forward with a check. And, after thinking it over, Earl Thompson decided that there was something about Lindbergh's vigor, enthusiasm, absolute self-confidence, and certainty about his project that deserved backing, and he signed a guarantee as well.

‡ Lansing Ray, owner of the paper, and Harry Knight's father came in later, as did Frank Robertson's brother, Bill, and Lambert's brother, J. D. Wooster Lambert.

He now had $15,000 in checks or firm promises, and that, he calculated, was enough to buy the plane and start the project in motion.

But which plane?

Certainly not a Fokker, which was one of the planes he had been considering. A Fokker salesman happened to visit Lambert Field about this time and Frank Robertson took Lindbergh to meet him. He listened to the plan, looked Lindbergh over, and decided that there was going to be no glory for his company in anything this young man might achieve. He shook his head.

"Mr. Fokker wouldn't consider selling a single-engined plane for a flight over the Atlantic Ocean," he said sharply. And Lindbergh could all but hear him adding under his breath: "Especially to a nondescript like you."

He got even worse treatment when he tried to buy one of the new Wright-Bellanca monoplanes, which he knew would be ideal for making the flight. The only model available had come into the hands of a flashy promoter named Charles Levine, who led Lindbergh to believe that he would sell him the plane for $15,000. But when he got a check for that amount from his backers and rushed with it to New York, he found that there were conditions attached to the sale. Levine reserved the right to choose the crew, and Lindbergh guessed from the attitude of the man on the other side of the desk that when the time came to choose, Levine would not choose him. He walked out of the office, angry at the fruitless, unnecessary journey and the waste of time, because time was now of the essence if he was to win the Orteig Prize.

Other aspirants were beginning to appear, and most of them seemed to have far more resources and be far better known than he was. Capitaine René Fonck, undismayed by his disastrous crash, had bounced back into the competition and had let it be known that Sikorsky was building him a new giant plane. The Army Air Corps announced that they had authorized the Huff-Daland Company to sell a stripped-down bomber to Lieutenant Commander Noel Davis for the flight. There were also rumors that no less an aviation personality than Commander Richard E. Byrd, who had made a reputation by flying over the North Pole the previous year,* was planning to enter the race. Lindbergh began to understand why the Fokker salesman had been so contemptuous of him, for the rumors also added that Byrd would probably use a trimotored Fokker.

And not only in America were the competitors coming on the scene. In Britain, France, and other parts of Europe there were reports of avia-

---

* There are now doubts that he did, in fact, do so.

tors making plans for transatlantic flights. Compared with Lindbergh, they seemed to be in an advanced state of preparation. They had unlimited supplies of money from their backers (Byrd's trimotored Fokker alone would cost $100,000), and their spokesmen all declared that they were all but ready to take off. Whereas, as yet, Lindbergh hadn't even found his plane.

The winter of 1926-27 was a bad one for Charles Lindbergh. One by one, different aircraft companies turned him down. He could not seem to convince them of the feasibility of his plans or of his own standing as a flier. In fact, as it turned out, of all the competitors for the Orteig Prize he was the only one who was concentrating on practical details and confronting all the probable hazards of the enterprise. All the others, despite their heavy, authoritative-sounding pronouncements, were just playing around, as yet. But Lindbergh was not to know that. He took them seriously.

For the moment he could not afford to take too much time off from his mail-flying job, and sometimes it was hard and frustrating. The twice-daily journey through snow and icy conditions was definitely not pleasant in an open-cockpit plane, not even for someone of Lindbergh's imperviousness to the cold. Although he might be able to endure the rigors of the weather, sometimes his plane could not, and he was forced to put down on one of the emergency landing strips, and wait the night out until conditions improved. He dare not cut the engine in case it froze up overnight, so he had to stand by in the bitter darkness and idle the engine, stamping around to keep warm, watching the frozen minutes tick by from seven in the evening until dawn next day, when he could take off again.

One thing which must have helped to keep him warm at this time was the faith of his St. Louis backers. Other people might be skeptical about him, but Bixby, Knight, Thompson, et al., once having given him their pledge and their money, sustained him in other ways. It was in January 1927 that his morale seems to have reached its lowest ebb. It had by then become obvious that if he was to have the right plane, he must arrange to have it built. But who would build it to his specifications and within the budget that his backers had set? He had circulated a large number of aircraft firms with the specifications of the craft he was seeking, and he had only one affirmative reply. The Ryan Aircraft Company, of San Diego, California, maintained that they could build the plane he wanted and do it well within the money in the kitty.

But who had ever heard of Ryan Aircraft? Could they be taken seriously? And even if they could, how long would they take to build the aircraft?

Too long, he decided. He went to see Harry Knight and confessed that he was becoming convinced that it just couldn't be done. The plane would never be ready in time. By the time one was built, the Orteig Prize would have been won by his competitors. He therefore suggested that the syndicate abandon the idea of competing, and that they concentrate their efforts on another project—a transpacific flight, say. Maybe they could persuade someone to put up a prize for that.

Harry Knight looked at the young man and felt sorry for him. "I knew what it had cost him to say what he had," he said later. "He had set his heart on winning the Orteig Prize, and now here he was telling me he was ready to give it up. I wasn't going to let him. I said: 'Let's stick to the Paris flight, Slim. That's the idea we started out with.' I told him to wait in my outer office and I picked up the telephone and called Harold Bixby at the bank, and I said: 'I've got Slim Lindbergh with me, and I think his morale could do with a boost. Why don't you and me take him out to lunch?' We took him off and Bixby talked to him like a father while he ate his meal. I must say the state of his morale didn't seem to have affected his appetite, and by the time he'd finished he was a lot more cheerful. Maybe that's because we had made him a proposition."

The proposition was that he give up his mail-flying job for the time being and get himself out to San Diego and find out whether the Ryan Aircraft Company could really build him a plane to fly the Atlantic.

On February 24, 1927, Harry Knight received the following telegram from San Diego:

BELIEVE RYAN CAPABLE OF BUILDING PLANE WITH SUFFICIENT PERFORMANCE STOP COST COMPLETE WITH WHIRLWIND ENGINE AND STANDARD INSTRUMENTS IS TEN THOUSAND FIVE HUNDRED EIGHTY DOLLARS STOP DELIVERY WITHIN SIXTY DAYS STOP RECOMMEND CLOSING DEAL—LINDBERGH

Knight wired back:

YOUR WIRE STOP SUGGEST YOU CLOSE WITH RYAN FOLLOWING TERMS. . . .

They were in business.

On March 3, taking a break from work in the Ryan plant on Barnett Avenue, San Diego, Charles Lindbergh saw his name mentioned for the first time in the newspapers in connection with the Orteig Prize. But it was well down in the story:

> New York, March 2—Rodman Wanamaker, who once financed a project to fly the Atlantic Ocean which was prevented by the war, will back Commander Byrd's attempt to fly non-stop from New York to Paris next spring. A huge three-engined Fokker monoplane, now under construction, is to be used for the trip. It is expected that the machine will be ready by May, which is the earliest month weather conditions will be suitable for a transatlantic flight.
>
> In carrying out his project, Commander Byrd will make use of the most advanced instruments and navigational devices known to science.
>
> This spring may see a race between American and French pilots for the honor of being first to fly between New York and Paris. The Sikorsky Company announced recently that a big plane was being built for the Atlantic flight. Although the company would not comment, it is reported that the pilot will be Capt. René Fonck, the French ace who crashed on Roosevelt Field on an attempted take-off for Paris last September.
>
> A number of American pilots, including Noel Davis, are known to be planning on competing for the Orteig prize of $25,000 which will be awarded to the first aviator to fly between New York and Paris without stopping. Charles A. Lindbergh, a St. Louis mail pilot, has filed the latest entry, according to the National Aeronautic Association. He will pilot a single-engined Ryan monoplane, and plans to make the flight alone.

It was Harold Bixby who had suggested that the plane be christened *Spirit of St. Louis,* and by mid-April it was almost ready to be wheeled out of the workshop. No one realized more than Charles Lindbergh how lucky he had been in choosing the Ryan Aircraft Company to build his ship. By pure chance, he had stumbled upon a small group of expert and dedicated designers, engineers, and craftsmen. Both Franklin Mahoney, the president, and Donald Hall, chief engineer and designer, had welcomed as a challenge the rough plans Lindbergh brought to them, and the moment the contract was signed they abandoned everything else, including their private lives, to its fulfillment. On one occasion Lindbergh had to send Donald Hall home after he had spent eighteen straight hours at the drawing board without a break, protesting that if Hall kept pushing himself this hard he would have a physical breakdown and ruin the project.

Lindbergh was sharing an office with him and, in fact, was working just as hard not only on the design of the plane but on preparations for his flight, plots of his route, and all the other details and decisions which had to be settled. They were all young men and their exuberant enthusiasm compensated them for lack of sleep, snatched meals, constant physical and mental effort.

For a time they were all dogged by the fear that before they could get the plane into the air there would be an announcement from New York —or maybe from Paris—that one of their rivals had taken off and was on his way across the Atlantic. But at the beginning of April news began to come in that, bad though it was for their competitors, must have encouraged them to believe that they might still be in time to compete.

First came a dispatch from New York that the trimotored Fokker in which Commander Byrd planned to fly had crashed on its test flight, injuring all those aboard, including Byrd himself, except the test pilot, the great Anthony J. Fokker. The plane was not beyond repair and the injuries to its passengers were slight, but it meant that these particular rivals would not be ready to leave just yet. In the Wright-Bellanca which Lindbergh had been so eager to buy from its owner, Charles Levine, two crack pilots, Clarence D. Chamberlin and Bert Acosta, had taken off two days before the Fokker crash and did not land again for 51 hours, 11 minutes, and 25 seconds, beating the world endurance record by nearly six hours. That would be long enough to take them all the way to Paris, and they were obviously the rivals to fear. On April 24 the Wright-Bellanca was officially christened *Columbia* and Clarence Chamberlin climbed aboard for a celebration flight. He lost a wheel on take-off and had to make a crash landing. Once again the damage was reparable, but for Lindbergh it was the gift of time.

Forty-eight hours later another competitor was out of the race, this time permanently and tragically:

Hampton, Va. April 26—Lieut. Commander Noel Davis and Lieut. Stanton H. Wooster lost their lives today in the last of the trial flights of the huge trans-Atlantic plane in which they were to attempt to fly to Paris next week.

The tragedy occurred when the machine was carrying almost the equivalent of its full load for the trans-Atlantic trip. Those on the ground saw a huge splash as the big machine

came down in an area of marsh land, not far from Langley
Field.

Both Commander Davis and Lieutenant Wooster were exceptionally skillful aviators.

On the day that Davis and his comrade died the *Spirit of St. Louis*
was gingerly wheeled out of the Ryan factory, but only by canting it
over on its side. Ten feet had been added to its wingspan after work
had started, and no one had remembered to take the dimensions of the
factory doors. It turned out to be a most complicated maneuver involving derricks, guys, and pulleys and much anxiety. But it was a somewhat different emotion which everyone felt when the plane was finally
lowered onto a waiting truck. The Ryan Aircraft Company was a small
organization, and every employee, from president to latrine-cleaner, had
had a part in building this ship, and, as Lindbergh wrote in his diary
later:

"[It was] as though some child of theirs was going away to war.
Their part was done. For them, the flight had started. For two months
theirs had been the active part, while I stood by watching their crafts-
manship. Now, the roles are reversed, and I'll have the field of action.
Now, the success of their efforts depends upon my skill; and my life
upon their thoroughness."

On April 28, 1927, on Dutch Flats, below San Diego, Charles Lindbergh signaled chocks-away to those on the ground below him. A young
mechanic named Douglas Corrigan† nipped under the wing and
pulled them away. Lindbergh gunned the plane and rolled it over the
baked clay surface of the field, then gave it full throttle.

In seven and a half seconds it was off the ground, and the *Spirit of
St. Louis* was flying for the first time.

In the next two weeks, Charles Lindbergh cherished the *Spirit of St.
Louis* and became convinced that it was going to carry him successfully
across the Atlantic. It was, as those who look at it in the Smithsonian
Institution in Washington will acknowledge, an ugly-looking duckling.
Its wheels hung down below its body as if they had been attached by a
joiner doing a quick carpentry job. Its flat, untapered wings were balanced across the fuselage like a plank on a performing seal's neck, and
behind them the pilot's view ahead was concealed by the big gasoline
tank. For safety's sake, Lindbergh had put it between him and the engine, so that, in the event of a crash, he would not become the meat in

† Who became known, some years later, as Wrong-Way Corrigan after his own
flight across the Atlantic.

a very unpleasant sandwich; but this meant that if he wanted to see what was in front of him, he would have to lean out and look sideways. When he put the plane through its paces, he found that the nose dropped in a stall and showed no tendency to come up again. When he took his feet off the rudder and steered with the stick, the fuselage veered the opposite way to the ailerons. It certainly wasn't a *stable* plane, but then it hadn't been designed for stability, but to get one man 3,500 miles across a very rough ocean.

And certainly, the plane had speed—up to 128 miles an hour, when he took it up to its limit. Maneuverability, too. A navy plane came out from North Island base, and for ten minutes the two planes played fighter-pilots. Lindbergh turned the *Spirit of St. Louis* inside his opponent several times before breaking off, though that, of course, may have been because Lindbergh was an experienced pursuit pilot. Still . . . though the plane would never qualify in appearance or performance as a graceful swan, it would never be an ugly duckling to Charles Augustus Lindbergh.

On May 4, 1927, he took off from San Diego Bay on his final speed and load tests. On a measured course in the mist of a California dawn, he made 130 miles an hour cruising fifty feet above the water. He couldn't have asked for better.

He flew on to Camp Kearney, where Donald Hall, the designer, was waiting for him, and on the way he scribbled details of the performance on the data board. Suddenly a gust of wind snatched it out of his hand and it fluttered earthward and landed in the bushes short of a clearing. It would have to be retrieved. The details were needed for the official report; otherwise he would have to make the tests all over again.

At Camp Kearney their faces fell when he told them of the mishap. But leaving them to prepare the *Spirit* for its load tests, Lindbergh called for another plane, and waving other volunteers aside, hopped into a Hisso-Standard and took off for the spot where the data board had landed. It would be a tricky landing and take-off in the small clearing, and he was not willing for anyone else to risk it. After two attempts, he was back, grinning cheerfully, the data board in his hand.

Time was running short now, and there was a whole roster of tests to be made. On each run they poured an extra 50 gallons into the tank of the *Spirit*, and as the load started to get heavy so did the strain on the ship. The run lengthened and the wheels bounced up and down on the loose stones covering the runway. When they increased the load to 300 gallons, it took Lindbergh twenty seconds to lift the ship off the ground, and he could feel through the fuselage the beating that the tires were taking from the rough stones on which they were rolling. It was even worse when he came down.

He looked at Donald Hall and Hall stared back, and it was obvious that the same thought was in their minds. The intention was to run two more flights, with 350 and 400 gallons (which is what he would be carrying when he made the actual flight). But on a surface like this, was it wise to go on? What if a tire burst now? It would wreck the whole project.

"Charlie,"‡ said Donald Hall hesitantly, "I'd like to get one for three hundred and fifty gallons. But if you think the surface is too rough, we can probably get by with what we've got."

He added that when the last landing was made, the wheels were smoking.

Mahoney, president of Ryan, came over, shaking his head. "It's landing with all that gasoline that worries me," he said. "I'm for calling it enough."

It was a risk to stop there, for one day soon he would have to take off with a very much heavier load. But wasn't it an even greater risk to carry on?

He sighed, then grinned and shrugged his shoulders.

"We'll call it enough," he said.

That night he telegraphed his partners and backers in St. Louis that all tests and checks had been satisfactorily completed, and that he was starting eastward aboard the *Spirit of St. Louis* in forty-eight hours.

Two days later he wrote in his diary:

"The *Spirit of St. Louis* is standing ready in its hangar. My plans are complete. All San Diego details have been attended to: my bills are paid; my bank account is closed. The rubber boat is lashed down tightly in the fuselage. Tires are pumped to just the right pressure. The center wing-tank is full. It's early on the morning of the 8th of May."

All he was waiting for now was for a storm area to clear over the Rocky Mountains, and then he was off. As he waited, he glanced through the morning paper and saw a story on the front page that shattered him.

NUNGESSER OVER THE ATLANTIC, said the headline. DUE IN NEW YORK TOMORROW.

As the sun rose over the horizon this morning, Captains Nungesser and François Coli started their heavily overloaded Levasseur biplane, *L'Oiseau Blanc* (The White Bird), rolling

‡ Nobody at Ryan ever called him Slim.

over the ground at Le Bourget Aerodrome, Paris, for the start of their transatlantic flight westward to New York.

There was a breathtaking moment during the long take-off when Captain Nungesser tried to lift his machine, but failed. He was successful, however, on the next attempt, and the white plane rose slowly, to disappear into the western sky.

If all goes well, Captains Nungesser and Coli are expected to land in New York tomorrow.

So that was that. After all the agony and effort to get the *Spirit of St. Louis* ready in time, they had been beaten in the last hours. Nungesser and Coli were old hands and were unlikely to have picked a dud to fly the Atlantic. By tomorrow it would be all over and the Orteig Prize would be theirs.

As news of the Frenchmen's flight spread around the airfield, other fliers and mechanics came over to commiserate with Charles Lindbergh. He gave no outward sign that he was distressed. But Donald Hall and Mahoney, who had driven out from town, had come to know the young flier pretty well over the past two months, and the very blankness of his face told them how much he must be stricken. Hall said softly:

"I almost hope they don't make it."

"Don't say that!" Lindbergh's face had flushed angrily, and the other two men knew from it and from the sharp tone of his voice that he must have been thinking the same thing, and felt guilty about it.

"Aw, Charlie," Mahoney said, "we know how you feel."

Lindbergh had some maps and a data pad in his hand. When he saw Mahoney looking at them, he said:

"I've been going over the transpacific idea again." He spread a map over the hood of Mahoney's car, and began jabbing with his finger. "It's the route beyond Honolulu I'm worried about. I can arrange for gasoline dumps on the islands, but how am I going to find them? I don't suppose anyone has a radio out there for me to pinpoint on."

"Charlie," said Donald Hall, "let's wait to see whether they make it."

By next day, it seemed as if Nungesser and Coli had indeed made a successful crossing. The San Diego papers reported that *The White Bird* had been sighted off Cape Race and reported by a U.S. destroyer. Throughout the day, radio stations interrupted their programs to announce that the Frenchmen had passed over Portland, Maine, and one breathless report from New York even went so far as to declare that they were over Boston.

Public interest was stirred. There was something about the challenge of the flight that quickened everyone's interest, and in New York excitement started growing. Crowds gathered on the Battery when the rumor spread that Nungesser and Coli would fly over Manhattan and do a victory roll before putting down on Long Island.

But then hours went by and there was no more news of the Frenchmen, no more sightings.* They had vanished, in Lindbergh's words, "like midnight ghosts." When twelve hours had passed beyond the time limit their gasoline supplies would have allowed them and they were still unreported, it became obvious that they had come down somewhere in the Atlantic, and search parties were being organized.

Charles Lindbergh put away his maps of the Pacific and told the mechanics to roll out the *Spirit of St. Louis* for its flight to New York.

Two more competitors were out of the race for the Orteig Prize. But their tragic and unsuccessful challenge, far from daunting them, had galvanized the other competitors. Repairs were being rushed on Commander Byrd's trimotored Fokker. The Wright-Bellanca was already in flying condition again after its mishap with its landing wheel, and there were rumors from Long Island that Clarence Chamberlin was getting ready for an imminent departure for Paris.

Charles Lindbergh was 2,400 miles away on the other side of the American continent. But perhaps if he made a record journey, he could still get the *Spirit of St. Louis* to New York in time.

He took off from San Diego on May 10, 1927, and made a record run to St. Louis, flying by night over the Rockies. On Lambert Field he had another example of the good will and understanding of his backers. Harry Knight and Harold Bixby came out from the city to join him at breakfast and asked him how long he was staying over. Since the flight was in part to boost St. Louis, there had originally been plans for an elaborate christening ceremony for the plane, followed by lunches, dinners, and speeches. But they understood at once when Lindbergh pointed out that time was pressing. He left the same day.

Seven hours after taking off from Lambert Field, he was circling over Mineola, Long Island, and straightening up for the landing approach on Curtiss Field. Practically every photographer and reporter in New York seemed to be waiting for him. It was his first taste of the media in Manhattan, and he didn't like it. The cameramen pushed and shoved each other and shouted instructions at him as he posed, and he was astonished when some of them crouched or kneeled or lay on the ground to get angle pictures. The reporters asked him what he considered were ridiculous questions.

* It later became evident that all the previous sightings had, in fact, been mistaken.

"Do you carry a rabbit's foot?"

"What's your favorite pie?"

"Have you got a sweetheart?"

"How do you feel about girls?"

He wrote later:

"Each moment I feel more uncomfortable. It's not like San Diego or St. Louis."

He didn't realize it then, but from now on things were not going to be like San Diego or St. Louis ever again.

Part
Two
Wings to Lift
a World

CHAPTER

EIGHT

THE FLYING

FOOL

On the morning of May 13, 1927, Dick Blythe came into Charles Lindbergh's room at the Garden City Hotel, Garden City, Long Island, and tossed the day's newspapers on the bed.

Dick Blythe was a public relations man for the Wright Aeronautical Corporation, and he had been assigned to handle Lindbergh's dealings with the press. The Wright Corporation was in a commanding position so far as the Orteig Prize was concerned. Each of the three planes now vying for the prize—Byrd's Fokker, now named the *America*, Chamberlin's *Columbia*, and the *Spirit of St. Louis*—had Wright engines, and if any one of them successfully made the crossing, the company would reap the benefits.

So it was nurturing the press relations of all the contenders, even those of Charles Lindbergh, whose chances until now they had considered remote. But like the newspapers, they had been impressed by the speed and efficiency of his transcontinental flight from San Diego. And, furthermore, the guy seemed to have a strangely attractive and exploitable personality.

"You've stolen the show," Dick Blythe said. "The boys don't know what to make of you."

Lindbergh picked up a copy of the New York *Times* and saw his name in headlines on the front page of that august newspaper.

LINDBERGH HERE, READY FOR SEA HOP, the headline read, and they had spelled his name right this time. Underneath the story began:

What promises to be the most spectacular race ever held—
3,600 miles over the open sea to Paris—may start tomorrow

morning. Three transatlantic planes are on Curtiss and
Roosevelt Fields, within a short distance of each other, ready
to take the air. . . . Observers at the field look to Lindbergh
as a dark horse in the race. He arrived yesterday afternoon,
ahead of schedule, after a fast seven and a quarter hour flight
from St. Louis. The trim, slender lines of his silver-coated
monoplane impressed pilots and mechanics alike. . . .

When he arrived at Curtiss Field after breakfast and went into the
hangar to work on his engine, he quickly discovered what it was like to
be a celebrity in New York. Cameramen and reporters in even greater
numbers than the day before were waiting for him, and he was all for
telling them to get out of his way and his sight. He was dissuaded by
Dick Blythe, and it was just as well, because half an hour later Commander Byrd and Giuseppe Bellanca, the designer of Chamberlin's
plane, arrived to shake the young flier's hand and wish him well. Lindbergh was surprised to discover that they were prepared to do it several
times over for the benefit of the photographers, and lost neither their
patience nor their smiles when they were ordered around and told how
to pose. He was appreciative of the sporting gesture his rivals had made,
and even more so of Byrd's offer to let him use Roosevelt Field for his
take-off. Curtiss Field would be by no means long enough when he was
fully loaded, but Byrd had hired Roosevelt for his exclusive use and had
spent large amounts of money improving and lengthening its runway,
and he was under no obligation to offer it to his competitors.

He thanked Byrd profusely for his generosity and went back to work
in the hangar, only to be interrupted once more by Dick Blythe, this
time holding a copy of the *Daily Mirror* in his hand and a rueful look
on his face.

"You're not going to like this," he said.

There was a picture of Lindbergh occupying most of the front page,
and it was not a particularly flattering one; he had been caught with his
mouth open in what looked like an asinine grin. Evidently the *Mirror*
did not share the idea that he was a "dark horse" or been impressed by
his transcontinental flight. FLYING FOOL HOPS TODAY, the headline over it
read.

Charles Lindbergh took the printed word seriously, and the headline
brought an angry flush to his cheeks. The epithet was insulting and the
statement was untrue, because the weather was bad and he had no intention of "hopping" today. What kind of a place was it where newspapers said such things and took so little care with their facts? When
he started to go over the other stories in the papers, they continually

made mistakes. They got the place of his birth wrong, they said he had learned to fly in about half a dozen different places, they said his friends called him "Lucky," and that he took off and landed his plane with a periscope because he could not see directly ahead.

"I'm disgusted," he told Dick Blythe, and that cynical young man discovered with some surprise that he was not using the word lightly. He *was* disgusted. He was even more so later that evening when a bell-boy delivered a telegram to his room:

ARRIVE NEW YORK TOMORROW MORNING. MOTHER.

Not because she was coming, of course, but the reason behind her journey.

Evangeline Lodge Lindbergh was having her baptism of press publicity, too, and liking it as little as her son. To all questions about her and where she lived, Lindbergh had refused answers, but enterprising reporters had tracked her down to Detroit and were now besieging her in her home. Some of them telephoned to ask her how she felt about her son's suicidal mission, what sort of emotions were aroused in her when she contemplated the fact that her son might die within the next twenty-four hours, whether she was going to see him before he took off and bid him "one last good-by."

Normally a stoically unresponsive type, at least to approaches of this kind, she had at last succumbed to the fears that the questions had raised in her, and she had decided on an impulse to make the journey to New York. By the time the telegram arrived, it was too late for her son to stop her, and amid all his other occupations and anxieties he now had to contemplate a rendezvous with his beloved mother in the full blaze of publicity on Curtiss Field.

He met her at Garden City station, and, chased by reporters, took her back to the field to see the *Spirit of St. Louis.* They stayed in the hangar alone for an hour, and police barred everyone else from entering. Then they came out and posed for photographers but refused to embrace or touch each other while the cameras were clicking.* Then Evangeline said she didn't want to cause her son any more trouble, she knew he had a lot to do, and went quietly back to Detroit.

Shortly afterward, her son took the *Spirit of St. Louis* for a trial flight. When he came in to land, a group of cameramen got in the way of his approach, and he broke the plane's tail skid when he had to slew

* One tabloid newspaper, undeterred, posed two characters kissing each other passionately and then pasted the two Lindberghs' faces over them.

to avoid them. His fury over the incident was exacerbated by the story one of the papers made out of it, inferring that the mishap had been his fault:

> So terrific was his speed that in landing he slightly damaged the machine's tail skid. Undismayed by this accident, which he considered trivial, Lindbergh hopped out wearing a broad smile: "Boys, she's ready and rarin' to go!" he said.

What appalled him was the language they put in his mouth.

"These fellows must think I'm a cowpuncher just transferred to aviation," he complained.

He squirmed with rage when another tabloid called him "a lank demon of the air from the wide-open spaces."

Outside the hangar, it was raining and the weather forecast for the North Atlantic was bleak. The longer the fliers had to wait for it to clear, the more the story built up in the newspapers. It was now becoming a publicity man's dream, and hucksters were running a shuttle service between New York and the Long Island airfields with their clients, hoping to pose them with the protagonists or their planes. Lindbergh heard that one P.R. man was planning to get a picture of his protégée, a dancer and starlet, doing the splits along the propeller of the *Spirit of St. Louis*. Once someone had explained to him what the splits were, he spent a happy half hour speculating on the anatomical consequences of such a feat, but made it clear that she would get near his plane over his dead body.

Not everything about the wait was annoying. Dick Blythe took him to Theodore Roosevelt's estate overlooking Oyster Bay, where the late President's son showed him his father's books and trophies and gave him letters to friends in Europe. Anthony Fokker and Al Williams, two of his great aviation heroes, stopped by to say hello. He was introduced to Harry F. Guggenheim, who ran the Fund for the Promotion of Aeronautics, and they took to each other at once.

"I want to see you when you get back," Guggenheim said, although he confessed later that he thought the young man would never reach France, and he would almost certainly never see him again.

Charles Lindbergh was never one to take snubs or rebuffs lightly, and he had not forgotten how Charles Levine, owner of the Wright-Bellanca plane, *Columbia*, had treated him in the early days of his search for a transatlantic plane. Now he must have been pleased to hear that the egregious Levine was having his own share of setbacks. He had ruffled the feathers of Clarence Chamberlin and his copilot by demanding that if they won the Orteig Prize in *Columbia* they must contract to hand over half the prize money to him. He had also been making several changes in the crew, and had sacked the navigator. The navigator had gone immediately to court, demanded, and been granted, an injunction preventing the *Columbia* from taking off without him. Levine would not rescind the dismissal. The plane could not move until he did so.

It was not exactly unpleasant to know that Byrd, too, was having administrative difficulties. The *America* had now been repaired, the crew had recovered from their injuries, and all was ready except for the insistence of the chief financial backer, Rodman Wanamaker, that the plane undergo meticulous airworthiness tests—and these, unless Byrd succeeded in getting them called off, could take time.

It was a relief to know that so far as the *Spirit of St. Louis* was concerned, he was the only person concerned with the decisions.

"You just leave the finances to us," Harold Bixby had said, "and we'll leave the flight to you."

They had kept their word. He had had yet another touching example of their faith in him within the past few hours. He had telephoned Harry Knight to point out that if he was to steal a march on his rivals, he must be ready to leave at any moment, as soon as there was a break in the clouds over the Atlantic. But one of the rules of the competition for the Orteig Prize was that sixty days must pass between the official entry and the commencement of the flight, and Lindbergh's entry had not been in that long. If he took off now, he could be ineligible, even if successful, for the $25,000 purse.

"To hell with the money," Harry Knight had said. "When you're ready to take off, go ahead."†

Dick Blythe had arranged a typical publicity man's ploy, and on May 19, 1927, he told his client that he was taking him for a night out on Broadway, to see the hit musical of the moment, *Rio Rita*. What was more, he added, they were going to watch it from the wings, backstage. One can imagine the visions which must have been passing through Blythe's mind and those of his theatrical confrere of the photographs in the next day's papers, of this naïve young man draped in the arms, legs, and bosoms of pretty show girls, and maybe the headline over it: FLYING FOOL SAYS HIYA RITA!

---

† Through Lansing Ray, of the *Globe-Democrat*, Lindbergh had signed to write his story of the flight for a syndicate of U.S. newspapers at a sum which would cover his backers' expenses, but, in fact, they never demanded a share in his earnings beyond their initial investment of $13,000, even though they soared way beyond that amount.

Lindbergh, who cannot have guessed what he was in for, agreed to take a night off, since the weather reports were still unpromising, and even thought "it ought to be great fun." They drove into Manhattan from Long Island that evening. It was raining and mist was hanging so heavily over the city that they could not see the tops of the buildings as they drove along Forty-second Street. Nevertheless, Ken Lane, a Wright engineer who was a member of the party, thought it might be a wise idea to phone in to the weather bureau and check how things were developing. Blythe knew a building where he could use the phone and they waited at the curb while he went in to call. When he came back Lindbergh saw from his face that he had news. Doc Kimball of the weather bureau, with whom Lindbergh had established a rapport and come to trust, said that there was a sudden change of front over the Atlantic and the weather was clearing.

Blythe saw a publicity man's dream going down the drain and gestured at the pouring rain in disbelief.

"Of course conditions aren't good all along your route," he said. "They say it may take another day or two for that."

Maybe, he went on, they could all go to the theater and make another call from there. He did not know his man. All thoughts of *Rio Rita* had gone out of Lindbergh's mind, and all he could see through the Manhattan mist and rain was the weatherman's touch of lightening sky along the western horizon. He had already told the driver to turn round and get back lickety-split to Long Island. There was much to do.

For one thing, he had to get the *Spirit of St. Louis* from Curtiss Field to Roosevelt, and it was now too late to do it by air, in this weather. It would have to wait until morning and daylight, and by that time Byrd's *America*, which was already on Roosevelt Field, could have taken off for Europe, providing he had heard the same weather forecast and was acting on it.

While Lindbergh stopped for supper at Queensboro Plaza, Lane went on to Curtiss to round up friends and get the *Spirit of St. Louis* fueled up with a preliminary load, and thoroughly inspected. Mahoney, president of Ryan, had arrived at Curtiss from San Diego and would help to see that the plane he had built was in top shape. By the time Lindbergh reached the hangar, men were busily at work in the glare of floodlights, and he went across to Roosevelt Field—it was separated from Curtiss by only a short route across the fields—to find out how the opposition were getting on.

To his surprise they were not getting on at all. Of course Chamberlin and the *Columbia* crew were still grounded by their sacked navigator's injunction, but surely Byrd and his associates must be aware that the weather was changing out in the Atlantic. What were they waiting for? Sunshine?

It was a moment when his airmail pilot's training was coming to his rescue, and he must have had a feeling in his bones that it would win him the day. He looked up at the sky, what little he could see of it through the driving rain and misty blackness. The prospect looked vile. But how many times last year had he watched the rain driving across Lambert Field or the snow blizzarding over Maywood, heard the radio report that all planes throughout the area were grounded, and decided to take off? He had said to himself: "No flight—no pay," so he had taken a chance. Wasn't this the same situation? If he didn't go now, he would lose the prize. The big boys would beat him if he waited for sunshine. The only advantage he had over them was that he was one man risking no one else's life but his own, whereas they had to think of each other—and had never flown mail through Midwest blizzards, anyway.

Besides, he trusted Doc Kimball, and there was still time until dawn to change his mind.

Meantime, what he needed to do was get some sleep. He had the prospect of a forty-hour flight in front of him during which he would not dare to sleep. He must be up at 2:30 A.M. if he was to take off at dawn. That gave him two and a half hours, because it was just going on midnight now, and it would have to be enough.

He went up to his room and instructed a friend to stand guard in the corridor, so that no one could disturb him. Down below, he could hear the reporters and photographers engaged in a noisy series of poker games. Somehow the news had spread that he was planning a dawn take-off and they had swarmed in to witness it, and since they did not have a transatlantic flight before them they were planning to stay up all night.

At 12:40 A.M., shortly after he had dropped off to sleep, there was a knock on the door and he started up. His friend on guard outside came in, and to Lindbergh's anger, all he said was:

"Slim, what am I going to do when you're gone?"

And then, mumbling apologies, suddenly aware of his stupidity, he had backed out of the room. But by then it was too late and getting back to sleep was impossible. He lay on the bed, trying to relax, until they called him at 2:15 and he started to get dressed.

When he got down to the hangar, at 3 A.M. it was still raining and the glare of the floodlights was thrown back by the mist. Except for the last workers on the plane, everyone stood around, shoulders hunched against the steady downpour. But there was good news. He would not have to wait until dawn to fly the *Spirit of St. Louis* across to Roosevelt

Field. They had found a side road across the fields from Curtiss to Roosevelt, and they could tow the plane across.

The weather forecast hadn't changed much from the night before. But it was clearing along the American coast and over the Atlantic, and there were only local storms in Europe. He looked across the field at the hangars where Byrd's *America* and Chamberlin's *Columbia* were housed. There were lights in the *Columbia* hangar but no sign of any flight preparations. In any case, they were still grounded by the court. *America's* hangar was in total darkness.

Maybe they had more information about the weather than he had. Lane, the Wright engineer, shook his head.

"They don't see how they can take off with this low ceiling over New York," he said.

To Lindbergh it seemed that what mattered was not how low the ceiling was here but how high it was over the Atlantic and Europe. Still, the prospect certainly did look filthy. He watched as they removed the tail skid, attached the *Spirit of St. Louis* to a lorry, and began tugging it through the mud across the fields toward Roosevelt. To the man who was shortly going to fly it, its appearance was awkward and clumsy, incapable of flight—"shrouded, lashed, and dripping."

Led by a couple of motorcycle cops, the procession moved off, reporters, cameramen, a handful of onlookers. To Lindbergh it looked "more like a funeral procession than the beginning of a flight to Paris."

The wind changed direction just after daybreak. The *Spirit of St. Louis*, loaded now and weighing 5,250 pounds—a thousand pounds more than it had ever carried before—had been rolled down to the end of the runway on Roosevelt Field to take advantage of the slight head-on breeze. And now it had swung around the other way. True, it wasn't a stiff wind, but it was blowing at five miles an hour on his tail, and that wouldn't help the take-off at all—not with a load like this.

Should he order the plane towed to the other end of the runway? But the wind might change again. In any case, he would have to be towed by tractor because taxiing would overheat the engine, and the runway was soft already from days of rain; a tractor and the 5,250 pounds worth of plane would cut it into ruts. He couldn't afford to have his speed cut down on the take-off by softening the surface further.

He nodded to the mechanic and they started the engine. Dr. Johnson once said that the knowledge that a man is about to be hanged in a fortnight concentrates his mind wonderfully, and at this moment Charles Lindbergh would have appreciated the appropriateness of the remark. The knowledge that within the next few minutes this engine would decide his fate sharpened every faculty in his body. He stood looking up at the mechanic and listened to the engine's note, and it seemed as if there was a lack of vibrancy, a decibel or so missing from its full-throated roar.

The mechanic climbed down. At full throttle, the engine was thirty revolutions low, and that meant he would not have all the power he expected—and needed.

"It's the weather," the mechanic said. "They never rev up on a day like this."

But Lindbergh was conscious of the worry on his face and in his voice, and he carried it with him as he climbed into the cockpit. This was the mechanic who had been over every inch of the plane to make sure it was in peak condition—and now he looked apprehensive. Because now the moment had come for Lindbergh to make the final decision, to take off or wait for another day. It was still raining. The telephone wires at the end of the runway were only just in view. The ground underneath was soft, cloggy clay. The soaked plane must be that much heavier with moisture. And the engine was running thirty revolutions low.

He was aware of eyes watching him on either side, the eyes of men who have seen pilots take the wrong decision before and crash on takeoff. They would understand if he decided to call it a day. On the other hand, the weather was clearing over the Atlantic, and if he waited until tomorrow, the big boys would be back in the race.

He buckled his seat belt, pulled his goggles over his eyes, and nodded down at the men on the wheel chocks. He saw them yank on the ropes and felt the wheels go free as he revved on the throttle. But underneath was so soggy that he was hardly moving, and helpers had to leap forward and push on the wing struts to get him going. He had a feeling as if he were driving an overloaded truck.

And then gradually the speed increased. At the hundred-yard mark the last man dropped away from the wing struts and he was moving on his own. Ploughing through the mud, concentrating on the runway ahead, holding the wheels down hard until the right moment for takeoff, he suddenly felt lifelike blood gushing and quickening in the stick and he had to push hard on it to keep it forward.

Now he was halfway down the runway at the point of no return. He must decide now whether he was going to make it, or whether he should dethrottle and hope to coast to a stop before he reached the gully at the end where René Fonck had met his Waterloo. But he knew there was no question now of allowing himself to stop, that psychologically the point of no return had been long since passed.

He felt the tail go up and then the wheels leave the ground, but seconds later they were touching again. He splashed through a puddle of water, but skimmed the next one, and suddenly he was airborne. A thousand feet ahead were the telephone wires. He would just clear them, he calculated, and did, by twenty feet. Was he really off at last? Were five thousand pounds of gasoline, silver metal, and man really being carried by those tiny wings?

He looked over the cockpit and saw a golf links and people looking up. He pulled the throttle back, tried the controls, and found that they were taut. He banked cautiously and headed the plane northward toward the Great Circle route he had traced out on his map.

Down below, the watchers saw the silver plane clear the wires and disappear into the mist, and as the throb of his engine came back strongly to their ears, quite a few of them said, with surprise as well as relief:

"By God, he's made it!"

It was 7:54 eastern daylight time. The *Spirit of St. Louis*, pilot Charles Augustus Lindbergh, was en route for Paris. May 20, 1927.

CHAPTER

NINE

THE FLIGHT

When modern fliers think about Charles Lindbergh's flight across the ocean, the picture that probably comes into their minds is of a tiny silver monoplane, a speck in the limitless sky, battling with the turbulent clouds tumbling against each other high above the Atlantic. There were certainly periods in the flight when he had to fight the *Spirit of St. Louis* up to its maximum altitude to pass over the storm and cloud conditions confronting him, but in fact, for much of the way, he hugged so close to the sea that he often had to remind himself of the danger of running into the masts of passing ships. He had scoffed at reports that he used a periscope for taking off and landing his plane, but he had one aboard and used it for looking ahead when he was airborne. It was a simple affair run up for him by one of the workmen at the San Diego factory, two flat mirrors set at the right angle in a tube, which he could lower from the left side of the fuselage.

He pushed it out now as he cleared Rhode Island and approached the Atlantic Ocean. It was just after 9:30 A.M. on a fresh, misty morning. He brought the plane down from 600 feet to 150, took off his goggles, and leaned back in the cockpit to study the chart on his knees. Now that he knew his competitors were still earthbound on Long Island and he would not need to race them to Paris, he throttled the plane down to one hundred miles an hour. The consequent saving in gasoline would give him a fifty-hour range for what should not be much more than a thirty-six-hour flight.

Providing he made the right calculations, that is. The moment had come for him to begin the test that could settle whether he steered the right course for Paris or perished somewhere in the North Atlantic. He had rejected a radio aboard his ship because of his weight problem, and his only instruments for guiding him over the ocean were a compass, a sextant, and the chart on his knees.

He had chosen to follow the Great Circle course to save himself mileage, but that meant meticulous navigation. Until now, Charles Lindbergh had been a land pilot. Whenever he had got lost over the American continent, he had been able to look at the ground below him and pick out landmarks to give him clues to his whereabouts. Now, for the first time, he was flying over a vast stretch of ocean with no railroad lines, no rivers, no mountain peaks, to guide him on his way. All he had was the line on his chart and the marks he had inked in beside it to show him the way.

It said at the first mark that twenty miles after passing the Massachusetts coastline he must change his course to 71° magnetic. That moment was now approaching, and he made the necessary adjustment, but first looked at the direction of the wave caps down below to calculate and allow for the drift of the wind.

If he had calculated right, and if he changed direction again to 74° magnetic after flying one hundred miles, his course in the next two hours would take him across the ocean to the shores of Nova Scotia. One more change of direction and he would sight the mouth of St. Mary Bay below him. It was important that he make his target with reasonable accuracy and calculate exactly any margin of error, so that he could allow for it in his future reckonings. Once he left the American continent, there were thirty-seven more of such adjustments— nearly all of them over water—to be made before he sighted a large tall tower which would, he had been assured, identify Paris for him.

He was later to say that this was the moment when he was struck by his arrogance in attempting a flight of such magnitude over such a lonely ocean. Why should he be so certain that a swinging compass needle would lead him to safety? Why had he dared to stake his life on the belief that by drawing a line on paper and measuring its arc and its length, he could find his way through the shifting air to Europe? Why had he been so sure that he could hold the nose of the *Spirit of St. Louis* on an unmarked point on a uniform horizon and find Nova Scotia, and Newfoundland, and Ireland, and finally an infinitesimal spot on the earth's surface called Le Bourget?

He glanced at the mirrors of his periscope to make sure that there were no ships' masts or smokestacks in the way.

It was an indication of the time he lived in that he needed to ask himself these questions about his flight. In the world of the 1970s, when men and women have rowed, drifted, singlehandedly sailed, and done practically everything else but walk, swim, or waterski across the Atlantic, it is perhaps difficult to appreciate the nature of the challenge Charles Lindbergh was making, and the remarkable response and support it was getting from the public.

It was not simply a question of making the first transatlantic flight. Alcock and Brown had already done that. It was not a question of demonstrating that the air age was reaching its adolescence, and America and Europe were about to be connected by one single giant step. If Lindbergh had failed to take off, Byrd in *America* and Chamberlin in *Columbia* would have shown the feasibility of it. Both of them completed the flight shortly after Lindbergh. But it is doubtful that, even if one or other of them had done it first, the hopes and hearts of humanity would have ridden with them, as they did with Lindbergh. They were so obviously organization men, with rich financiers to pay their large expenses, with crews to give them companionship and aid over the Atlantic, whereas Charles Lindbergh flew alone and there was something almost mystical about his challenge to the elements.

The quality of the challenge was perhaps best summed up in a cartoon which appeared, on the evening of his flight, in the St. Louis *Post-Dispatch*, whose cartoonist most evidently did not share his editor's opinion of Charles Lindbergh as a mere stuntsman. Daniel R. Fitzpatrick's cartoon showed an expanse of heaving, empty sea and above it a baleful sky stretching back to a limitless horizon—and in the middle of that sky, a very tiny plane. It was a cartoon that twanged a chord in people's hearts, and wherever men and women saw it they caught their breath. In the tawdry world of 1927, the bright sparks of the jazz age generation, in between boozing their way through the last months of the boom years, were apt to make overnight heroes of anyone who squatted longer on a pole, swallowed more goldfish, or gorged more frankfurters than anyone else had done before.

And now suddenly they were confronted by the real thing, a genuine hero, who looked, sounded, behaved like one, young, clean, handsome, untainted by the freneticism of the time. He had arrived out of nowhere without fanfare and he had taken off without fuss. He had stayed aloof and been unaffected by the shoddy carnival swirling around him during his stay in New York, and had simply ignored the skeptics and scoffers who called him a Flying Fool and said he would never make it. Maybe he wouldn't. But there was something so confidently godlike in his demeanor that to some religiously minded Americans it was almost as if he were a Messenger for them, carrying the Word. To others he was a rebel against the shabbiness, cynicism, cheapness, and injustice of their flashy world, challenging the system by which they lived. The more the experts swore he would kill himself, the more their dreams rode with him. And from the moment the *Spirit of St. Louis* took off from the mud of a Long Island airfield into the misted sea, he became a symbol of their own hopes and ambitions, a bright light in a murky world.

To millions of simple people, he was no longer flying for himself but for humanity; he was not simply flying to Paris but blazing the trail to a better life.

If he failed, they would sigh sadly and realize that their hopes for him had been too good to be true. But if he made it, a halo would not be too much for him.

On the night of Friday, May 20, 1927, as the *Spirit of St. Louis* headed out to sea from Newfoundland, a crowd of 40,000 people gathered in Yankee Stadium in New York to watch a heavyweight boxing bout between Jack Sharkey and Tom Maloney. When the pugs had climbed into the ring, the referee, Joe Humphreys, stood between them and signaled to the multitude in the arena to give him their attention.

"Ladees and gentlemen," he called out, "before we come to the big bout of the evening, I want you to rise to your feet and think about a boy up there tonight"—he thrust an arm dramatically skyward—"who is carrying the hopes of all true-blooded Americans. Say a little prayer for Charles *Lindbergh!*"

At the mention of the name, a hush fell over the stadium that even overawed and silenced the candy-barkers. Never before or since can 40,000 boxing fans have worn such reverent expressions on their faces. Even the pugs looked soulful.

By that time it was nearing dawn in Europe and the newspaper presses were rolling. The flight was already front-page news, although, as *Paris-Soir* wrote, "it is considered doubtful by the experts that a single flier can stay awake and alert long enough to challenge successfully the dark forces waiting to do battle with him over the Atlantic."

In the United States, radio bulletins were being broadcast every hour whether there was any news or not.

Evangeline Lindbergh was getting the news of her son's progress from telephone reports from the Detroit *Free Press*. She had taken her classes as usual at school, but it must have been a trying day for her. The pupils were excited and failed to pay attention. Outside the windows she could see clusters of reporters. It was in the hope of persuading them to call off their vigil that she consented to allow the *Free Press* on Friday night to put out a statement in her name.

"Tomorrow, Saturday, a holiday for me, will either be the happiest day of my life, or the saddest," the statement read. "Saturday afternoon at three o'clock I shall begin looking for word from Paris—not before that. Perhaps I shall not worry, however, if the hours of Saturday afternoon drag along until evening. But I know I shall receive word that my boy successfully covered the long journey. . . . It will be a happy message."

It seems unlikely that Evangeline Lindbergh ever made such a statement. Even at such an emotional moment, it was quite untypical of her. But no doubt she had a debt to pay to the *Free Press*. After that, however, she was not heard from again. She shut her doors and windows to the reporters, refused to see anyone, and spent the weekend locked inside her house.

No plane had ever flown over Newfoundland before without landing, and though Lindbergh had no fuel to spare to circle over the capital of St. John's, he did dive down to two hundred feet over the ships in the harbor and noticed a rower in a whaleboat break rhythm at the sight of him. Then he was heading away in the thin light of sunset from the last island of the American continent. There were two thousand miles of ocean ahead of him before the next landfall in Ireland.

He made meticulous notes in his log of his speed, altitude, wind velocity and direction, course, drift, visibility, engine revs, oil temperature and pressure, fuel pressure and mixture. He was reasonably satisfied with his progress so far. He had covered eleven hundred miles in eleven hours, and despite having to make two detours over Nova Scotia to avoid storm regions, his navigation had been reasonably accurate. But now that he was over the open water, he would have to steer with greater care than ever before. His dive over St. John's had, in fact, been a touch of vanity, for he should not really have been over the Newfoundland capital at all. It was ninety miles off his Great Circle course and he had made the detour because he could not resist flying over the city and demonstrating to the populace that he was just passing over. His reward had been one oarsman's momentary reaction. Now he must pay for his whim by readjusting hs calculations, compensating not only for magnetic variation and wind drift but for having started from too far south.

Normally, that would not have been much of a chore. But he was beginning to sense that he was tired. He had been flying for eleven hours, but it was nearly thirty-six hours since he had had any real sleep. Now he was riding into night over the Atlantic. There was no room in the cockpit to spread out his chart to make the new calculations, and he must try to estimate wind velocity from the last glimpses of the waves below him, assess the possibilities in his head, and hope to rectify his mistakes in the morning.

Out of the gathering darkness, a pyramid of dazzling whiteness thrust up at him and then he was into a vast field of icebergs. Mist clung to them like skirts, transparent at first, so that he could still see their shapes, and then gradually thickening and rising until only their peaks were visible. Soon the mist had turned to fog and he eased the stick back and began to climb, to make sure that a mountain of ice would not suddenly loom in his flight path. When he looked back now, the last light had disappeared from the western horizon and it was night.

When Charles Lindbergh had flown the *Spirit of St. Louis* across the American continent from San Diego to Long Island, he had deliberately chosen to do the bulk of the journey by night, to measure his own skills as a navigator and test the qualities of his plane. For long periods of the flight, he avoided checking his course by the lights of towns or the occasional beacon below him, and he had discovered things that were now proving invaluable over the Atlantic.

The *Spirit of St. Louis* was a solid, fast, splendid plane which had, so far, done everything that Lindbergh had asked of it. But as has been mentioned earlier, it was not a *stable* plane. When left to itself, it drifted off course. Like a high-strung horse, it demanded every moment of its rider's attention. It was possible to fly it by instruments once darkness had fallen, but only by the most meticulous concentration. A moment of inattention, and it was wandering off on its own.

In the twenty hours or so of flying that lay ahead, could Charles Lindbergh guarantee that he could give his craft every single moment of concentrated guidance? He was tiring. Instrument flying is a wearying business at the best of times, and the freshest mind can drift for moments at a time. How could he possibly manage to remain awake, his eyes glued to the dials for every second? Yet if he slept even for seconds, it could make a difference to his course that could easily prove fatal.

The alternative to instrument flying was steering by the stars, and there were strains and hazards connected with that, too. The higher rolled the banks of fog, the higher he must climb to keep his eyes on the constellations, and that meant he must watch out for icing-up on his wings.

Since it was impossible for him to look directly ahead in the *Spirit of St. Louis*, he must read the stars by tilting his head right back and reading them directly overhead. It made his neck painfully stiff. The continual movement of staring directly upward and then glancing down to check his instruments made him feel as if he were "dangling at the end of a rope," and he could feel the plane turn slightly with each movement.

He could feel the cold creeping in as he climbed higher and higher to keep track of the stars, which kept blinking in and out and seemed to be deliberately trying to get away from him. It was the fourteenth hour of his flight. He leveled off at 10,500 feet and could feel a chill seeping through his flying suit and flesh to his bones, and the misery of it brought him suddenly alive to the danger into which he had put himself. When he took off his gauntlet and thrust a bare hand over the side of his cockpit, he felt the flesh being pelted with sleet. He grabbed for his flashlight and shone it on the wings, and saw the warning patina of shiny ice covering the surface. The sleet sliced thick through the beam of the torch, and at any moment could seize up the breathers of the plane.

Instinct told him to go into a dive and get down to warmer air fast. Wisdom and experience, fighting his panic, persuaded him to move with caution. In the black night of the Atlantic a too abrupt descent out of the cloud bank engulfing him could take him hopelessly off course; he forced himself to bank carefully and feel his way down and around the cloud pillar and the swirling sleet inside it until he reached the clear night sky and could see the stars again. He knew now that there was a storm area in front of him, thunderheads much higher than the 10,000 feet at which he was flying, blocking his path eastward. Should he try to go around them? How could he tell how far south they stretched, how low they came, and how high they reached, when he had no radio connection with the rest of the world and no one to tell him the state of the weather? All he was aware of was that "great cliffs tower over me, ward me off with icy walls." They were an obstacle in his path like mountains, but with forms that changed.

"There'd be no rending crash if my wing struck one of them," he thought. "They carry a subtler death . . . to plunge into these mountains would be like stepping into quicksand. They enmesh intruders. They're barbaric in their methods. They toss you in their inner turbulence, lash you with their hailstones, poison you with freezing mist. It would be a slow death, a death one would have long minutes to struggle against, trying blindly to regain control of an ice-crippled airplane, climbing, stalling, diving, whipping, always downwards towards the sea."

He weaved his plane in and out of the towering clouds, his head thrown back to concentrate on an overhead star, and suddenly felt so tired that he wondered whether he was awake or asleep, alive or dead, a spirit in a spirit world.

Over the left side of his plane, he became aware of a light in the sky. It was the moon, rising where he had least expected it to. Slowly but with growing strength, it threw a glow across the seascape and gave the black clouds ahead of him form, texture, dimension. It was the most moving moment of his flight, a revelation to his spirit as well as to his eyes, and its cool yet benignant light seemed to give a benison to him and the *Spirit of St. Louis.* . . .

It was the eighteenth hour and he had passed the point of no return. From now on, it would be nearer to fly on to Ireland than back to the American continent.

It was the moment he had planned to eat and take a drink from his water bottle, but for once in his life he wasn't hungry. Dick Blythe had ordered him two ham, two beef, and an egg and mayonnaise sandwich and had them wrapped in greaseproof paper for the journey, and normally he would have demolished them in hurried mouthfuls. But the thought of food at this moment left his appetite unstirred, and the thought of a drink made him remember that he hadn't peed since climbing aboard. He had brought along an aluminum container with a large cork in it especially for that purpose, and now he used it. The relief was so great that he relaxed and lost command of his eyelids.

He shook his head violently and prized his lids open with his fingers. He stared at the instrument panel and could make no sense of it. He flexed his muscles, bounced in the cockpit, stamped his feet, leaned out and gulped in cold air. He banished all thought of sleep from his conscious mind and concentrated on the thought that if he did not stay awake, he would die. . . .

When next his eyes opened, or, rather, became capable of seeing, he realized that his compass needle was off ten degrees. It was not the moon which was illuminating the sky now, but a suffusion of light in the east which signified that dawn was coming. In terms of New York time, it was still 1 A.M. But here in the Atlantic, dawn was coming up— and he was off course, suddenly aching in every limb, and desperate for sleep.

But thank God for the fact that the *Spirit of St. Louis* was *not* a stable plane. Each time he dropped off, he could feel it nudging him as it swung off course and he would start up and correct the error on the needle. Then he was back in a dream again, and the *Spirit*, its reins loosened, would gallop off freely across the sky until the capriciousness of its movements nudged him awake again. . . .

With the coming of morning, he brought the *Spirit of St. Louis* down out of the clouds and set it on a course at 1,000 feet at one hundred miles an hour. It was raining and he was just beneath the cloud cover, and able to see the froth flecking the dark green waves beneath him. He had been nearly a whole twenty-four hours in the air now, and aware only of pain in his seat where he had sat too long, pins and needles in his arms and legs, and a sense of vagueness. The steady throb of the *Spirit's* engines had been broken down by blunted senses, so that through the cotton wool in his ears there seemed to be a half dozen voices coming at him from the air, and vaporish forms kept swirling toward him from out of the sky and inviting him to join them. All feelings of apprehension had gone by now, and when he leaned out of the cockpit the rain struck his face like a cooling shower.

In later years they would have said that he was no longer flying an airplane, he was on a "trip."

"I'm on the border line of life and a greater realm beyond," he felt, "as though caught in the field of gravitation between two planets, acted on by forces I can't control, forces too weak to be measured by any means at my command, yet representing powers incomparably stronger than I've ever known."

He was a practical young man of twenty-five, and when he analyzed them later, he was startled by the nature of his visions, and yet comforted by them.

"I'm so far separated from the earthly life I know that I accept whatever circumstance may come. In fact, these emissaries from a spirit world are quite in keeping with the night and day. They're neither intruders nor strangers. It's more like a gathering of family and friends after years of separation, as though I've known all of them before in some past reincarnation."

In the twenty-seventh hour, he came out of his trance and looked down to the sea below him. Was that a piece of driftwood? And that speck on the water two or three miles to the southeast? A boat?

He had been flying blind, half-asleep, half-awake, not quite certain yet whether he had returned from the world of fantasy in which he had been traveling. He had lost his bearings for the moment, physically as well as mentally. But if that was a boat down below him, and if those others were part of the same fleet, in fact fishing trawlers drifting and bobbing up and down on the oily surface of the ocean, then that was a sign as certain as a dove with an olive branch in its beak that he was nearing land. But what land? And in what direction did it lie?

Like he used to do in his barnstorming days, he put the *Spirit of St. Louis* into a dive and brought it to within fifty feet of the water, and at that height he buzzed the nearest trawler, banking over the mast at just the right moment so that he could look over the side of the cockpit down onto the deck. But down below nothing happened. No one appeared on deck. The noise of the engine and the whistle of the wind in his wings and struts must have been enough to raise the dead or the devil, but it stirred no life in the trawler.

He straightened up and zoomed across the water toward the next boat in the fleet, and as he approached he could see that there was no one on the deck of this one either. With the noise he was making, it was hard to understand. Had they never seen a plane before, and was he scaring the wits and the movement out of them? Were they hiding from him?

The thought had barely gone through his head when he noticed that someone aboard the second boat was watching him. A man's head was thrust through one of the portholes and a pale face was turned up toward him. The sight of the face suffused him with joy. It was the first human face—or any living face, for that matter—he had seen since he had left Long Island twenty-seven hours before, and it was like coming back into the world of men after an eon in another universe.

He felt the urgent need to communicate, to re-establish the connection with humankind which had been severed during his long night over the ocean. In his barnstorming period, when he had sometimes lost his way on a cross-country flight, he had often taken his Jenny down below treetop level, throttled back the engine, and asked a worker in the fields for directions. Now he closed the throttle of the *Spirit of St. Louis* and put it into a glide which took him to within fifty feet of the man staring at him from the porthole of the fishing vessel. Above the sough of the wind in the struts, he shouted at the top of his voice:

"Which way is Ireland?"

For a few moments he concentrated his gaze on the face in the porthole and then had to wrench it back to his controls as the plane showed signs of stalling. He opened the throttle, got speed up again, climbed, and banked. Once more he swooped low and approached the fishing vessel. The face in the porthole was still watching him. But there was no change in expression, no sign whatsoever of a response. And neither on this nor any other of the vessels did anyone come on deck. In his mood at this moment, he was hungry for some sign of human comradeship. Nerves frayed by sleeplessness and exhaustion, he wanted, needed, the comfort and encouragement of men on the decks below waving to him, so that he could wave back and thus signal his acknowledgment of their acceptance of him back in the normal world.

But no acceptance came. He might just as well not have been there.

Was he there? Were *they* there? Was the face staring up at him real, or just another phantom from his strange visions of a few hours before? But these were certainly not fantasy vessels, like the shapes in his dreams.

"They're tangible," he told himself firmly, "made of real substance like my plane—sails furled, ropes coiled neatly on the decks, masts swaying back and forth with each new swell. Yet the only sign of crew is that single head, hanging motionless through the cabin porthole."

It reminded him of his childhood, when his mother used to read him "The Rime of the Ancient Mariner." This still, silent vessel was like "a painted ship upon a painted ocean."

He was tempted to keep on flying around and over the boats until he forced some recognition out of them, and then reminded himself of practicalities. He was wasting fuel and time. It was 10:52 A.M. New York time but almost 3 P.M. here. He needed the daylight. Disappointed, dispirited, he banked his plane, and without another glance at the silent fishing fleet he opened up the throttle and pointed the *Spirit of St. Louis* eastward again toward what he hoped was Europe.

An hour later came a sight to lift his heart. First land loomed up like a cloud on the northeastern horizon, then the shape of a coastline that he recognized from his chart as Valencia and Dingle Bay. He had made the southwest coast of Ireland sixteen hours after leaving Newfoundland, two and a half hours ahead of his calculated time. What's more, there were villages down there, and people were coming out into the streets and actually looking up and waving to him.

"Here are human beings," he noted with quickening pleasure. "Here's a human welcome. Not a single detail is wrong. I've never seen such beauty before—fields so green, people so human, a village so attractive, mountains and rocks so mountainous and rocklike."

Now indeed he was back in the world of men, and from now on it was terrain over which he could fly without fear, or phantoms.

The word had already gone out from Ireland that Charles Lindbergh had passed over. In the thirty-first hour of his flight he was signaled over Cornwall. An hour later, just as the sun was disappearing over the horizon, the *Spirit of St. Louis* roared over the French coast and was cheered by a small but enthusiastic crowd as it passed over Cherbourg Harbor at a thousand feet.

Both plane and pilot had already flown their way into the record books of aviation history. For one thing, the Orteig Prize should already be theirs, since the rules simply specified a nonstop flight from New York to the shores of France *or* Paris. For another, in flying 3,400 miles across the Atlantic, they had broken the long-distance record for heavier-than-air machines.* But it was something more than prizes or records that was stirring the imaginations of multitudes as news came through that Lindbergh had spanned the ocean. Every newspaper in the world was replating for a new front-page lead. Every editor was wishing he had bought the Lindbergh story. Every reporter was dreaming of helping him write it. And every Parisian in Paris was determined to be there to welcome him when he landed in France.

At 9:52 P.M. he sighted the Eiffel Tower and circled over it once. The lights of Paris glowed all around him, a patch of starlit earth.

It was quite dark now. Some hours back he had worried about landing in Paris in the dark, but now he was in a state of euphoria. All sleepiness had left him, and excitement had driven the aches out of his body. But where was Le Bourget?

"It's a big airport," they had told him. "You can't miss it. Just fly northeast from the city."

But he did miss it, the first time. He had to fly north of Paris, turn around, and come back before he decided that the black square of earth, one patch of it lit by floodlights, the whole of it marked by what seemed to be moving lights, had to be Le Bourget. But just in case, he decided to do a sideslip landing to cut down the length of his run.

The *Spirit of St. Louis* touched down in the darkness and Charles Lindbergh revved the plane around to taxi it across to the floodlit patch of concrete by a group of hangars. He had to abandon that idea. He was suddenly aware that a great concourse of people was moving toward him, their hands in the air, waving. When he tugged the cotton wool out of his ears, he could hear them shouting. They were calling his name: *Lindbergh! Lindbergh! Lindbergh!*

He had flown from New York to Paris in thirty-three and a half hours. The time was 10:24 P.M. European time, Saturday, May 21, 1927. From now on, Charles Augustus Lindbergh was going to discover what it was like to be the most admired man in the world.

* In November 1917 the German Zeppelin L59 took off from Jamboli, Bulgaria, in an abortive attempt to bring succor to German troops fighting in East Africa. The airship turned back over the Sudan, covering nearly 4,000 miles in all.

9. Charles Lindbergh took off from Roosevelt Airfield, Long Island, at 7:54 A.M. on May 20, 1927, and landed at Le Bourget, Paris, thirty-three and a half hours later, the first man to fly the Atlantic nonstop singlehanded. This picture was taken just before the take-off beside his plane, *Spirit of St. Louis.*

10. *Spirit of St. Louis* was built by the Ryan Aircraft Company at their factory in San Diego, California. It had a top speed of 130 mph, could carry four hundred gallons of gasoline, and had a range of nearly 4,000 miles. New York to Paris is 3,500 miles.

11. The building of *Spirit of St. Louis* was a race against time, and the plane was never fully tested before Lindbergh took off from San Diego, California, to cross the continent and reach New York in time to compete for the Orteig Prize. One gadget he tested en route was a periscope, since his gasoline tank otherwise prevented him from seeing directly ahead.

12. It was dark when Lindbergh and *Spirit of St. Louis* landed at Le Bourget Airfield, in Paris, and no pictures were taken of the arrival of the plane. But a few days later, when he flew into Croydon Airport, London, the photographers were waiting. And so was the crowd.

13. Charles Lindbergh got a hero's welcome wherever he went in Europe after his triumphant flight, but nothing equaled the fervor of New York's acclaim when he rode up Broadway on June 13, 1927. It was estimated that he was greeted by 4.5 million spectators and eighteen hundred tons of ticker tape were showered on his head.

14. Back from his triumphant transatlantic flight, Charles Lindbergh flew to Mexico City in December 1927 and spent Christmas with American Ambassador Dwight Whitney Morrow and his family. Here he is seen with Mr. and Mrs. Morrow and their youngest daughter, Constance. Anne Morrow, the middle daughter, whom he subsequently married, had not yet arrived from college in the United States.

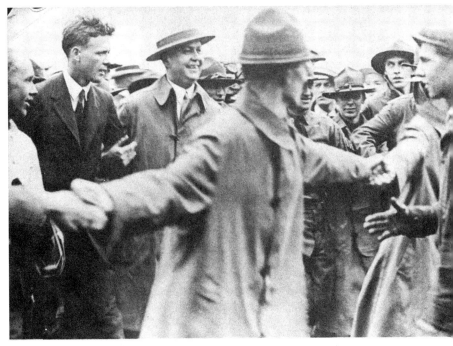

15. Lindbergh was greeted warmly at Lambert Field in St. Louis by Mayor Victor Miller one month after the triumphant New York–Paris flight. It was fitting that he go back to that city to be received by its people because it was a group of St. Louis businessmen who had given him strong financial and moral support for the flight.

16. During his nationwide tour, Lindbergh landed in Detroit and was there received by Henry Ford, the pioneer automobile builder. Ford had never been up in a plane and had always refused to fly, but persuaded by Lindbergh's charm and confident air, he finally agreed to make his first flight with the nation's hero.

CHAPTER

TEN

HERO

It is a measure of how Charles Lindbergh's feat was received in Europe that not only did the masses make their admiration for him plain in a series of hysterical demonstrations, but the kings and presidents who governed them flung open their gilded doors to him. The French have always seemed to regret that Lafayette and De Grasse helped the United States to achieve independence, which, they hint, was both premature and undeserved, and at the time of Lindbergh's arrival they were going through one of their particularly lively phases of anti-Americanism. There were fears both in Washington and in the embassy in Paris that the American flier's arrival would only serve to exacerbate the bitter regret French people felt over the disappearance of their own transatlantic fliers, Nungesser and Coli.

They misread the mood. For once there were no differences between people and rulers over their attitudes, and statesmen shared their enthusiasm with their constituents. A souvenir hunter snatched Lindbergh's helmet from his head as he clambered out of the cockpit of the *Spirit of St. Louis* and waved it to the crowd. He was immediately identified by the frenetically happy mob as the flier and borne away on their shoulders; meanwhile, a trio of French aviators surrounded the real Lindbergh and smuggled him off the field to their car, which they drove by side roads into Paris. U. S. Ambassador Myron T. Herrick and French officials had to make do with the unwilling impostor.

It was a typical French gesture that before taking him to the American embassy his three rescuers drove him up the Champs Élysée and "parked at the curb of a circular area in the center of which was a great stone arch," Lindbergh remembered later. "My friends took me through the arch." He had never heard of the Arc de Triomphe nor did he know that it was the tomb of France's Unknown Warrior, though his companions did try to explain the significance of "the ever-burning flame." But though he spoke no French and his companions very little English, he caught on that this was a place revered by Frenchmen and he stood there for a few moments in silent tribute.

The only food he had eaten since leaving Long Island were the beef, ham, and egg sandwiches Dick Blythe had bought him at Queensboro Plaza two nights before, and these he had consumed while flying down the French coast and inland to Paris. He was now revenously hungry again, and while he waited for Ambassador Herrick to catch up with him he sat down to a steak dinner which the embassy staff prepared for him.

Meanwhile, all hell was breaking loose at Le Bourget. Herrick, realizing that he had been handed an impostor instead of the real Lindbergh, had ordered a search and finally decided to make his way back to Paris. He had to buck mad traffic jams all the way. Meanwhile, a battle was going on among newspapermen at the airport to get hold of telephones.

A veteran correspondent of the old Paris edition of the Chicago *Tribune*, Waverley Root, remembers that United Press had cannily made a deal with someone at Le Bourget for exclusive use of all public telephone lines.

"Every booth was occupied by someone hired by UP to keep the line open and the door shut against the competition," he said. "Taking no time out to admire the foresightedness of this organization, the representatives of rival news-gathering institutions reacted by overturning the booth occupied by the chief UP correspondent, leaving it doorside down, on the floor, within it the imprisoned correspondent in the company of a useless phone whose wires had been ripped away."

Hank Wales, Paris correspondent of the *Tribune*, was meanwhile cabling an exclusive interview with Lindbergh, which made the front page of his paper long before all the others and earned him a bonus of five hundred dollars.

"It is painful to be obliged to record," said Root, "that the interview was a fake. Wales, a wily operator, had decided that it would be a waste of time making the long trip to Le Bourget when he could just as well stay in his office and write a story on what Lindbergh would be likely to say. Being nobody's fool, he made arrangements with the embassy, where he was on the best of terms, to make sure that Lindbergh would neither deny that he had given an interview nor utter anything subsequently which would contradict what Wales, a volunteer speech writer, had decided he ought to say."

It was 3 A.M. when the American ambassador finally made it back to his embassy, and after greeting the hero and congratulating him, he persuaded him to give a press conference to reporters who had been waiting to speak to him. He was bright, alert, answered questions shortly but straightforwardly. He finally went to bed, wearing Herrick's pajamas, at 4:15 A.M. It was sixty-three hours since he had last slept. He did not come conscious again until noon, by which time the whole world was in a fervor about him.

ALL FRANCE IN DEEP JOY AT CHARLES LINDBERGH'S BRAVE FLIGHT, cabled Ambassador Herrick to Washington on the evening of the flier's first day in Paris. IF WE HAD DELIBERATELY SOUGHT A TYPE TO REPRESENT THE YOUTH, THE INTREPID ADVENTURE OF AMERICA . . . WE COULD NOT HAVE FARED AS WELL AS IN THIS BOY OF DIVINE GENIUS AND SIMPLE COURAGE.

He seemed almost too good to be true. Not only had he proved himself an incomparable flier and insuperably brave, but he was young, handsome, polite, and, it seemed, instinctively modest. He grinned charmingly and waved to the crowds waiting to greet him outside the embassy. Herrick had arranged a series of public appearances for him and was delighted to have on his hands not a gauche hick from the Middle West backwoods but a young man who seemed to be "normal and comfortable in every situation."

In some ways he was a diplomat's dream. At a dinner given by the French Aero Club at which Louis Blériot, first man to fly the English Channel, was a guest, he called Blériot one of his "mentors" and went on to say that his flight had been "easy" compared with the dangerous difficulties which the lost French fliers, Nungesser and Coli, had faced in their fated flight from East to West.

He went to the Élysée to receive the Cross of the Légion d'Honneur from the President. He addressed the French Assembly and told a story which Herrick wrote for him about Benjamin Franklin's interest in the first French balloon when he was ambassador to Paris. (The French deputies had been supplied with a translation of his remarks in advance, since he spoke in English.) He visited Napoleon's tomb in the Hotel des Invalides, rode through the streets before a half million people to receive the Gold Medal of the Municipality of Paris, auctioned his autograph for fifteen hundred dollars in aid of French veterans, and was to be everywhere seen waving American and French flags from balconies.

His most perfervid admirer was Ambassador Herrick, for whom

Charles Lindbergh had become almost a winged god brought temporarily to earth.

"I am not a religious man," he said, shortly after Lindbergh's arrival, "but I believe there are certain things that happen in life that can only be described as interpretation of a Divine Act. . . . Lindbergh brought you the spirit of America in a manner in which it could never be brought in a diplomatic sack."

Not quite so extravagant was King George V of England, but he told his courtiers that Lindbergh was "quite a feller." When the flier had been rescued from the hysterical crowds which greeted him at Croydon Airport on his arrival in Britain, he was taken to the American embassy and told that the King wanted to receive him in audience. The American envoy, Ambassador Alanson Houghton, happened to be on vacation and his place was taken by the chargé d'affaires who was, Lindbergh recalled later, "a boiled shirt who was rather in a state because I was in an ordinary business suit and had no frock coat" in which to be received by the King.

In the car on the way to Buckingham Palace, the chargé kept nervously instructing Lindbergh in court protocol, how and when he was to bow, and above all else when he was to walk backward.

"He got me kind o' scared by the time we arrived," Lindbergh said later. "And there at the door was a lord who said that the King wanted to see me alone. So I was taken into his room and I remembered to bow and we sat down."

The young flier and the aging King-Emperor sat facing each other for an awkward moment, and then the monarch leaned forward.

"Now tell me, Captain Lindbergh," he said. "There is one thing I long to know. How did you pee?"

It was a question which, Lindbergh said later, "sort of put me at my ease."

"Well, you see, sir," he said, "I had a sort of aluminum container. I dropped the thing when I was over France. I was not going to be caught with the thing on me at Le Bourget."

Everything now went somewhat overboard. In the United States both people and politicians watched with mingled pride and impatience the hysterically enthusiastic reception Charles Lindbergh was receiving in Paris and London. It was a challenge to their own capacity for hailing a hero, and they could not wait to set him up on a bigger and better bandwagon than anything Europe could provide.

But when was he coming home? The politicians, who have never been loath to share a layman's limelight, wanted him back fast before his novelty wore off. (They did not seem to realize as yet how durable this latest hero would prove to be.) Congressmen and senators beseeched the President to get him back fast, and there was dismay in Washington when Ambassador Herrick informed the White House that Lindbergh was not planning to come home just yet. He was making plans to fly the *Spirit of St. Louis* across Europe and Asia and come home by the back door across the Bering Strait into Alaska.

"But that will take months," groaned the Secretary of War, Dwight F. Davis. He had already arranged to promote Captain Lindbergh to colonel's rank in the Air Corps Reserve, and was determined to milk every last drop of prestige out of the hero's return for the benefit of the Army.

The Navy was not averse, either, to winning public approval by associating itself with the man of the hour, and Secretary of the Navy Curtis D. Wilbur went to President Calvin Coolidge with a suggestion which he immediately, and eagerly, accepted. He sent a cable to Ambassador Herrick to inform him that the U.S. cruiser *Memphis* had been ordered to Cherbourg and instructed to pick up Lindbergh and his plane and transport them back to the United States at once. It was inferred that if Herrick wished to remain in the President's good graces, he must overcome any objections Lindbergh might have to this proposal.

Everybody wanted him back, big business included. The Wright Aeronautical Corporation had by now permanently assigned Dick Blythe to handling Lindbergh's public relations, and given him an assistant, Harry Bruno, to help him deal with the flood of offers which were now coming in for the use of the flier's name. American hoardings and newspaper and magazine pages were already picturing Lindbergh in profile or full face, with such diverse messages underneath as: "I was able to carry very few things in my *Spirit of St. Louis* but I took special care not to forget my faithful Waterman which was most precious to mark the route on my maps."

He had signed contracts before taking off with Mobiloil, Vacuum Oil, AC Sparkplugs, and Wright at an average of $6,000 a recommendation, and the companies were now cashing in. His name was having a magic effect upon their sales and share values, and they were anxious to have him on the spot to help whip up their campaigns. A thousand other hucksters with other propositions were now queuing up for the hero's signature, and they were willing to pay high for his endorsement: up to a half million dollars for a cigarette endorsement, a million dollars for a film, $300,000 for a phonograph record of the flight, and anything from $100,000 upward for a claim that he used a certain shaving cream, hair oil, soap, or hat and gloves. Altogether offers amounting to $5 million had come in. One group of businessmen had even approached Blythe and proclaimed their willingness to deposit $1 million to Lindbergh's account "with no strings attached" in order to "preserve his independence and keep him untainted by commercialism." Like most of the other offers, this one was turned down. But the cry for the hero's return was clamant, and finally even Charles Lindbergh found it impossible to resist it—especially after Ambassador Herrick pointed out to him that President Coolidge was his Commander in Chief and his "request" that the flier come home in the *Memphis* was not one to be lightly ignored.

On the afternoon of June 10, 1927, the cruiser *Memphis* passed through the Virginia Capes into Chesapeake Bay and was greeted by a welcoming committee of four destroyers, two army blimps, and forty aircraft of the Army, Navy, and Air Corps. It was a precursor of things to come.

Dick Blythe came aboard by tender and the two went belowdecks for a conference in which the publicity man gave his client a breakdown of the program that lay before him, a list of the offers which had been coming in, and his recommendations. It was a short but highly practical conversation, which might have surprised some of the more starry-eyed of his admirers.

"Charles Lindbergh was never averse to cashing in on his flight," said Harry Bruno, Blythe's partner, later. "Once he realized how everyone was reacting to it, and to him, he resolved a plan to make it solve his financial problems, and made sure that he was never short of a dollar again. But that doesn't mean to say that he gave us carte blanche to endorse anything in his name. Just the opposite. He kept a tight hold on everything we were doing for him, and made sure that the only recommendations he made were for articles or projects directly associated with his flight or his interests. But for those we were to ask as much as the market would bear."

Blythe had brought with him a new army uniform with colonel's eagles on the tabs, and was amused to notice that his client was not without his touch of vanity. He immediately donned the uniform (it had been run up for him by army tailors from measurements in his record file) and took a look at himself in the mirror.

"Not so bad . . . for a mail pilot," he said.

With a good public relations man's instinct for the right effect, Blythe looked at the slim young colonel and shook his head.

"You can't wear it," he said.

At the expression of angry astonishment on his client's face, he said:

"Look, dumbbell. Up to now you weren't an army man, or a navy man, but a plain civilian with a job, and your way to make in the world. Nobody could claim you and nobody could be against you."

"I was always a captain in the Air Reserve," Lindbergh said.

"But you went to Paris as a civilian," Blythe said. "The public remembers you in that old blue serge suit. You can get a new one, but you don't wear the uniform. Look, you're aboard a navy vessel yet there isn't a man in the crew who isn't on your side. But suppose you put on an army uniform . . . ?"

"Why couldn't I wear a navy overcoat over this?" asked Lindbergh.

Blythe gestured through the porthole. Even in the bay in the late afternoon, it was as hot as an oven.

"People would think you had gone crazy," he said.

A stubborn look came on Lindbergh's face. "I've got to wear the uniform. It was made for me and I've been ordered by my superior officers to have it on when I land. I have no choice."

"It's a lousy fit," said Blythe.

"Where doesn't it fit?" Lindbergh asked. In fact, it fitted perfectly. He had the kind of body that doesn't change much over the years, and his measurements had been followed precisely.

"It's terrible," Blythe insisted. "No superior officer can expect you to wear a uniform that looks so bad."

Lindbergh stared at him in perplexity, looked at himself in the mirror, then swiveled his eyes back to his publicity man. His face broke into a grin.

"I got you," he said.

President Coolidge had summoned Evangeline Lindbergh to come to Washington to partake in the home-coming celebrations for her son, and with typical lack of fuss she had traveled by train without informing the presidential aides of what time she would be arriving. They managed to find her at a hotel in Baltimore and she dined with the President and his wife on the night of June 10.

It is doubtful if she was looking forward to the ceremonials on the following day. The mother of the hero is an indispensable requirement on an occasion of this kind, but Evangeline Lindbergh was not exactly a typical American mother. But since her son was not exactly a typical American hero, either, perhaps that did not matter. She was, in any case, told to hold herself in readiness for the great occasion on the morrow.

For most of his tour of America, Charles Lindbergh not only had publicity men but also a paid Boswell to chronicle the details of his return. A writer named Fitzhugh Green was, with Lindbergh's consent, paid ten thousand dollars to chart his progress from the moment he touched the American shore, and he was guilty of one of those opening remarks, with its dying fall, which will always be cherished by connoisseurs of great occasions.

"Casear was glum when he came back from Gaul," he wrote, "Napoleon grim; Paul Jones defiant; Peary blunt; Roosevelt abrupt; Dewey deferential; Wilson brooding; Pershing imposing. Lindbergh was none of these. He was a plain citizen dressed in the garments of an ordinary man."

It was true to the extent that Lindbergh had taken Dick Blythe's advice and donned a blue serge suit, instead of his colonel's uniform. All around him, otherwise, was extravaganza. The United States Armed Forces had put into the air practically every craft they possessed, and as the *Memphis* wharfed at the Navy Dockyard at Alexandria fifty pursuit planes and a squadron of biplane bombers came over, and the dirigible U.S.S. *Los Angeles* passed over the decks of the cruiser.

"By eleven o'clock the saluting began," reported Fitzhugh Green. "Vice-admiral Burrage, also returning on the *Memphis,* received his customary fifteen guns from the navy yard. The President's salute of 21 guns was exchanged. Firing from the cruisers' battery and from the shore stations lent a fine rhythmic punctuation to the constantly increasing noise from other quarters."

When the gangplank came down, Admiral Burrage went ashore and a few moments later returned with Evangeline Lindbergh on his arm.

"Instantly a new burst of cheering went up," Fitzhugh Green reported. "But many wept—they knew not just why. For a few minutes mother and son disappeared into a cabin aboard the *Memphis.* It was a nice touch; something more than the brass bands and cheering. And it somehow symbolized a great deal of what was being felt and said that morning in our country's great capital."

He went on:

"When the parade reached the natural amphitheater of the Washington Monument the hillsides were jammed with a great gathering of men, women and children. On the high stand that had been erected, the President of the United States and Mrs. Coolidge waited to receive the man who but three weeks and a day before had been a comparatively unknown hopping off for Paris by air. . . . When Lindbergh mounted the stand the President came forward and grasped his hand. Those closest to Mr. Coolidge say that rarely has he shown the unrestrained cordiality he put into that simple greeting."

Then came the speeches.

Calvin Coolidge was not exactly an inspiring President, and there was nothing in his speech to welcome Charles Lindbergh that would move anyone to praise his wisdom, percipience, or oratorical expertise. No one would ever have guessed from its content that it concealed beneath its mundane words a heart genuinely moved by the young flier's feat. It went on for a long time. It ended when Coolidge took a handkerchief from his pocket, mopped his brow, and thus gave a signal to his aides that he was in the midst of his last sentences.

"And now, my fellow citizens," he declaimed, "this young man has returned. He is here. He has brought his unsullied fame home. It is our great privilege to welcome back to his native land, on behalf of his own people, who have a deep affection for him and have been thrilled by his splendid achievement, a Colonel of the United States Officers' Reserve Corps, an illustrious citizen of our Republic, a conqueror of the air and strengthener of the ties which bind us to our sister nations across the sea."

He reached behind him to the tray an aide was holding. "And, as President of the United States, I bestow the Distinguished Flying Cross, as a symbol of appreciation for what he is and what he has done, upon Charles Augustus Lindbergh."

He pinned the decoration on the chest of the young man standing beside him, waved his hand in a call for silence, and then settled back to listen to the hero speak.

Lindbergh rose and said:

"On the evening of May 21, I arrived at Le Bourget, France. I was in Paris for one week, in Belgium for a day and was in London and in England for several days. Everywhere I went, at every meeting I attended, I was requested to bring home a message to you. Always the message was the same.

"'You have seen,' the message was, 'the affection of the people of France for the people of America demonstrated to you. When you return to America take back that message to the people of the United States from the people of France and of Europe.' I thank you."

His audience sat back, stunned at the abrupt end of the speech. It is, in fact, the shortest response to a speech of a President of the United States in the history of the Union. Charles Lindbergh sat down to a heavy silence followed by applause loud enough to crack the skies open.

That night Lindbergh dined with the Cabinet. On June 13 he received a life membership of the Aeronautical Association, and went on to New York for the gaudiest celebration of all.

"It was estimated that 300,000 people were massed in the vicinity of the Battery when the *Macom** hove alongside," Fitzhugh Green reported. "Lining the streets clear to Central Park was a multitude that was variously estimated from 3,000,000 to 4,500,000. Scores of people were in their places before 8 A.M. on Upper Fifth Avenue. Lindbergh did not pass them until 3 P.M. Traffic was disrupted. Police control was strained to the utmost. As evidence of the almost unanimous turnout for the occasion, the Police Department of the City issued special instructions to all citizens about leaving their houses protected against thieves, something that hadn't been been done for a generation."

He added:

"When the cavalcade with Lindbergh leading started up Broadway there came the famous New York 'snow storm' consisting of a myriad of paper bits and confetti streamers floating downwards from the skyscrapers. Photographs do scant justice to the spectacle. At the City Hall Mayor [James J.] Walker expressed the city's sentiments with a felicity that deserves their record here. He spoke more informally than most had spoken in Washington; by the same token he echoed through his easily forgiven eloquence much that the inarticulate thousands waiting without the lines would like to have said."

In fact, the best moment came toward the end of a long speech when Walker, a charming character but a Tammany mayor who was helping to steal the city blind, looked up from his script for the first time and said:

"Colonel Lindbergh, New York City is yours—I give it to you. You won it."

He had also won the Orteig Prize. It is true that he had taken off in the *Spirit of St. Louis* before the end of the sixty days between entry and flight, but Raymond Orteig and his committee decided to bend the rules. He was handed the $25,000 at a small ceremony on June 16, 1927, and a few days later a similar sum was "awarded" him by Vacuum Oil Company. Considering the way their sales were booming as a result of his endorsement, they could have afforded to give him a million.

Next day he flew to St. Louis to celebrate with the backers who had made the enterprise possible, and for the benefit of an ecstatic crowd he took up a plane and gave a superb exhibition of aerobatics. But he was already beginning to show signs of irritation and boredom with the extravagant hero worship he was now encountering everywhere.

"I was so filled up with this hero guff," he told Dick Blythe while they were in St. Louis, "I was ready to shout murder."

---

* Official yacht of the mayor of New York.

By this time gifts were flowing in for him from all parts of the world, from monarchs, presidents, governments, societies, and private individuals. There were tokens of great beauty (such as a pair of lovely silver sixteenth-century globes from William Randolph Hearst, some Orrefors glass from Sweden), some touching curiosa (crocheted egg-warmers, portraits of the hero or his plane carved in ivory, fashioned out of matchsticks, embroidered in silk), and lots of monstrous and expensive junk (gold busts, gold medals, gold Bibles, gold, silver, and platinum scrolls), but not much that a man of taste would wish to cherish.†

There were not only gifts but letters and telegrams, and among the 2 million pieces of fan mail which were now beginning to flow his way, at least 5,000 contained poems celebrating his flight. Throughout the nation, towns, streets, mountains, and, of course, babies were being named after him. And even his father's admirers were hailing his son. From Minnesota came a long poem which ended with the words:

> Lindbergh here and Lindbergh there
> Lindbergh! Lindbergh! everywhere!
> Lindbergh wins our favor
> Lindbergh's brave beyond compare.
> Was his father braver?

† Lindbergh and his mother, who received her share of presents, eventually presented them to the Missouri Historical Society, and they are to be seen today on display in the basement of the Jefferson Memorial in St. Louis.

CHAPTER

ELEVEN

"WHO? LITTLE ME?"

Charles Augustus Lindbergh was now the most famous young man in the world, and nothing was too good for him. Honors, citations, and memberships were piled upon him. Congress voted him the Medal of Honor, the first time it had been awarded for a feat unconnected with war. A hastily written account of his flight (called *We*) quickly became a best seller and earned him $100,000 in royalties. Syndication rights from articles in the New York *Times*, from which the *Times* refused to take any profits, brought him in another $60,000.

If he was still by no means a wealthy hero, he was beginning to realize that he would never be poor again. In the meantime, he was enjoying the privileges that only fame or money can buy. There was no man in the world who would not have considered it an honor to be his friend, and hardly a woman who would not have married him.

In the summer of 1927 he set off on an air tour of the United States in the *Spirit of St. Louis* as part of a campaign to publicize air travel, and by the time he touched down again on Mitchel Field on October 23, he had covered 22,350 miles, led a parade in eighty-two different cities, and stayed at least one night in each of the forty-eight states on the North American continent. He was paid $50,000 for making the tour, but he did it less for the money than because he earnestly believed that showing himself and the *Spirit* to the people, and always arriving on time no matter what the weather,* would prove to them that the air age had arrived and they should become part of it. It was a grueling chore, and though he loved the flying parts of it he came to hate the

---

* He flew through snow, rain, and fog and only missed one date (in Portland, Maine) during the whole tour.

cheering crowds, giggling girls, autograph hunters, reporters, and photographers, and soon began to treat the first three with icy disdain and
the latter two with anger and contempt. Now that he no longer needed
publicity, he was quickly disenchanted with the public side of being a
hero. He got a sort of cynical satisfaction out of openly showing how
little he thought of the whole business, out of demonstrating that no
matter how roughly he treated them they could not help coming back
for more.

He was now becoming the high priest of what Sir Harold Nicolson
would later describe as "the Lindbergh religion." Its devotees came in
all shapes, sizes, and sexes, but a great many of them were women. He
could be pretty rough with women reporters who insisted on asking him
his opinion about love, marriage, or girls ("What's that to do with aviation?" was his stock reply), but particularly with the middle-aged and
the spinsterly he would sometimes make a gesture, smile, offer them a
ride in his plane, which won their hearts and all their sisters who heard
about it. Nicolson recalls meeting one such in St. Louis. She worked for
the Missouri Historical Society and had come in contact with Lindbergh after being given charge of his trophies and souvenirs in the
Jefferson Memorial Museum. She had never forgotten that he had been
particularly nice to her.

"She sort of makes an idol of me," Lindbergh told him. "I dread
going to St. Louis."

Nicolson found out why when he visited the Jefferson Memorial to
see the extraordinary exhibits in the collection, and was shown around
by Lindbergh's adoring acolyte. In a letter to Vita Sackville-West he
wrote:

> [She] did not in any sense approve of levity in the face of
> the exhibits. I did not feel like levity. I never derive amuse-
> ment from the stupidity of other people, only an interested
> sadness. . . . I said to her (not being very agreeable, per-
> haps): "Have you ever met Colonel Lindbergh, Miss ———?"
> She cast her eyes up to where from the gallery of the museum
> depended the Stars and Stripes. In that look was deep love
> and an appeal to God to forgive my ignorance. A momentary
> reflection as to the terms in which that ignorance might most
> effectively be exposed. She found those terms and her eyes re-
> turned to Mother Earth with sweet forgiveness in them. "I
> have," she said, "*flown* with Colonel Lindbergh. Since that
> day I've never quite returned to earth. I remain" (and here

again her eyes sought the roof) "in the air." She did indeed, poor old trout.

It was Nicolson at his most snob, but his paragraph did encapsulate a typical Lindbergh female fan of the time, and their numbers were legion. It did not help to abate their ardor that he was unmarried, and they waited with palpitating anticipation for the day when some girl would get him, and meanwhile dreamed that the lucky girl was themselves.

In fact, it was a period when Charles Lindbergh showed so little interest in the female sex that he was introduced to the girl he eventually married, and only vaguely remembered her afterward. At the dinner with President Coolidge to celebrate his arrival back in the United States he had met, among the other guests, a shrewd, able, and ambitious Republican named Dwight Whitney Morrow. Impressed by the young flier's simplicity, enthusiasm, and lack of guile, Morrow resolved to make his further acquaintance and invited him to visit him at his home at Englewood, New Jersey. Before they retired to the politician's study to talk, he introduced Lindbergh to his wife and his three daughters; he flashed them his famous smile but barely seemed to notice them. One of them was his future wife.

Gossip writers and female matchmakers were baffled. Here was a good-looking young man of twenty-five who seemed healthy, virile, full of spirit, but never went out with a woman. The only close female companion in his life was still his mother, though he nowadays saw very much less of her. When other members of the female sex were around, he seemed tongue-tied and ill at ease, impatient to get away. Among young men of his own age, he was exuberantly at ease, like a cowboy in a bunkhouse, full of tricks and practical jokes, always ready for a jape. As Harry Bruno put it: "You had to be wary and watch him all the time, in case he'd put a fish in your camera, a blunt blade in your razor, or switched the keys in your typewriter. It could get tiring at times." But unlike the boys of the bunkhouse, when he rode into town he never took off with a girl, but stayed resolutely around the men. Was he terribly shy? Or just indifferent? Or was he sickened by the female sex because some of them made spectacles of themselves by stealing his underwear from the laundry, scooping up his leavings as souvenirs after he had eaten in a restaurant, or purloined the pillow slips from the hotels he stayed in and pinned them, unwashed, on their walls?

One thing he was discovering as the pressures of fame crowded in on him was the need for privacy, a place where he could relax without fans or photographers† popping up and annoying him. There were plenty of rich men who were more than willing to provide him with a haven, and one of the most congenial proved to be a millionaire aviation enthusiast, race horse owner, and philanthropist named Captain Harry F. Guggenheim. The Guggenheim family was of Swiss-Jewish origin and had made a vast fortune in mining, thereafter devoting much money and time to the organization of foundations for the propagation of research and knowledge. Harry Guggenheim ran the Foundation for Aeronautical Research and it was this organization which had provided the financial backing for Lindbergh's forty-eight-state tour with the *Spirit of St. Louis*. When he had first met Charles Lindbergh just before he took off for his transatlantic flight, Guggenheim had invited the young flier to contact him "when you get back," but had been convinced at the time that he would never see him again.

Now he set himself up as Lindbergh's mentor in the social arts and in accustoming him to what he termed his "new status as a public figure." Guggenheim would have easily qualified for the list of best-dressed men if the publicity men had thought up the rating at that time; he was a snappy dresser and filled his wardrobes with a large variety of suits and uniforms, shoes, boots, shirts, ties, and cravats. He sent his protégé to his tailor for a new tuxedo, his first suit of tails, and replacements for his blue serge suit, but he never did succeed in convincing Lindbergh that a gentleman should have a different suit for every day of the week, and preferably change them morning, afternoon, and evening.

Captain Harry, as he was generally called, and his then wife, Carol, lived in a baronial Norman-type mansion which sat on the cliffs at Sands Point, on the north shore of Long Island, and it was appropriately called Falaise.‡ Behind it was a 350-acre estate with dower houses, stables, woods, and pastures where he raised pheasants, a small landing field where he kept his private plane, and a twenty-one-mile road system. The atmosphere inside the house was somewhat oppressive, with huge fireplaces, heavy Gothic furniture, and a plethora of Madonnas and artistic curiosa which the Guggenheims had bought in Europe on their honeymoon; but outside was a magnificent terrace overlooking a private beach, and, beyond, a glorious view across the Sound to Connecticut and the Bronx.

† The war with the press which would last for the rest of his life had now begun in earnest. "Smile!" the cameramen would say as he posed beside his plane. "What for?" he would snap back, and glower at them.

‡ *Falaise* is French for cliff. The house and domain were left to the Nassau County authorities by the Guggenheim estate and are now a museum.

Lindbergh was invited to make Falaise his home while he rushed through the writing of his first account of his transatlantic flight, *We*, and the bedroom suite he was given, looking out over the Sound, was henceforth considered his own and never occupied by anyone else. He was delighted by the protection the domain and its servants gave him from the prying eyes of fans and reporters, and in between his writing chores he wandered freely around the estate, punted on the Sound with Captain Harry, fished, or bathed.

When he relaxed at weekends, the Guggenheims assembled for him lunch and dinner parties whose guests were deliberately picked to further Lindbergh's education and advancement. It was a house on this part of the so-called Gold Coast that Scott Fitzgerald set *The Great Gatsby*, but though this was the Prohibition era the parties the Guggenheims gave were vastly different from Jay Gatsby's kind of whoopee. Drinks were available, but no one was likely to be invited who would have offended Lindbergh's teetotal standards by becoming tipsy or inebriated, a state toward which he had the liveliest antipathy. When the male guests trooped down for coffee and cigars to Captain Harry's smoking room and spread themselves in the leather armchairs beneath his racing cups, hunting prints, and photographs of his thoroughbreds, Charles Lindbergh was almost always the youngest of the group but by no means out of place. There would be bankers like Dwight Morrow and Thomas Lamont of J. P. Morgan, airline pioneers like Juan C. Trippe and Orville Wright, millionaires like Clarence Mackay and John D. Rockefeller, Jr., publishers like George Palmer Putnam, politicians like Herbert Hoover, Theodore Roosevelt, Jr., and Frank B. Kellogg.

Most of them were Republicans, and if he did not share all their conservative opinions, Charles Lindbergh found much in their conversation and ideas with which he was in accord. He was as worried as they were about the behavior of the nation's youth, concerned about crime and corruption, and solid for all measures they recommended to preserve the financial and social status quo and halt the decline in American morals and the sanctity of family life. His father would not have been found dead in the company of several of them whom Charles Lindbergh found congenial. He was still only twenty-five years old, but his fellow guests found him "remarkably mature in his judgments," as Rockefeller put it, and they hadn't much doubt that he would vote Republican at the next election.

But first he went to Mexico, at the suggestion of Dwight Morrow.

Dwight Whitney Morrow was a small, untidy man with deep blue eyes, uncombed hair, baggy trousers, and a disarming manner which concealed one of the shrewdest political brains in the United States. The son of a God-fearing Allegheny schoolteacher, he had, with few social or financial advantages, worked his way from a Pittsburgh lawyer's office to a senior partnership in J. P. Morgan and Company, the international bankers. He was rich, happily married, with a son and three daughters, and lived on a large estate at Englewood, New Jersey, where Lindbergh had visited him.

But Morrow was ambitious. In the years before, during, and after America's entry into World War I, he had filled several important positions for the U. S. Government both in Washington and in Europe, and when his old Amherst classmate Calvin Coolidge became President on the death of Warren G. Harding in 1923, Morrow expected and many a Capital tipster forecast that he would soon be a member of the Cabinet. And who knows where that would lead to?

It did not happen. It was not until 1927 that he was rewarded for his loyalty to the administration by being offered the ambassadorship to Mexico, where, as was usual at that time, U.S.-Mexican relationships were badly in need of some repair work. Morrow was aware that Mexico was regarded as the graveyard of the American diplomatic service, but he accepted because he believed he could re-establish a rapport between the two peoples—as indeed he did.

He was prepared to use any ploy to win him the regard of the Mexican people, and when he met Charles Lindbergh at the presidential dinner to welcome him back, he had an inspiration. Why not persuade the popular hero to visit Mexico? He invited Lindbergh to his home and put the proposition to him, and got an immediate yes from the flier. He had finished his book. He had had a splendidly lazy time since with the Guggenheims on Long Island, doing the odd bit of flying in between social engagements with his powerful new friends. Now he felt the need to flex his flying muscles again.

He told Morrow he would fly the *Spirit of St. Louis* nonstop from Washington to Mexico City, the first time it would ever have been done, and when the new ambassador hastily said it sounded too dangerous, Lindbergh replied:

"You get me the invitation, and I'll take care of the flying."

The official invitation from President Plutarco Elías Calles of Mexico came in shortly afterward, and Lindbergh took off from Bolling Field at 12:26 P.M. on December 13, 1927. He arrived the following afternoon to find that a grandstand had been erected on the flying field, and that President Calles had come to welcome him and hand him the keys of

Mexico City. Practically the whole of the population of the capital was there, too, and for the next week he was feted wherever he went, the most popular North American to have visited Mexico for generations.

For the moment, only two of the Morrow children, the youngest ones, Dwight and Constance, were at the embassy with their parents, but on December 21 Anne, the middle daughter, and Elisabeth, the eldest, arrived by train from the North (they were both students at Smith) to spend Christmas in Mexico City. By this time not only was Mexico mad about "Colonel Lindy," as they called him, but the ambassador himself had fallen under the young man's spell, too, and not simply because he was earning him political and diplomatic dividends. "He is a beautiful boy," he kept saying. His wife was more distant toward the hero (she always would be), but she fell in with Dwight Morrow's wishes when he suggested that Lindbergh be asked to stay on over Christmas, and it was Mrs. Morrow who telephoned Detroit and asked Evangeline Lindbergh to come down and join the party.

Constance had been getting on with Lindbergh like a favorite sister. Perhaps because he regarded her as still a schoolgirl, he relaxed with her, and even allowed her to tease him (she continually called him Lindy because she knew it made him wince). But once the two older girls were in the embassy, Constance complained that he had "stiffened" and become self-conscious. Anne Morrow, who was four years younger than Lindbergh, kept calling him a boy, "a shy cool boy," whenever she thought about him or wrote about him in her diary. He became tongue-tied whenever she and Elisabeth were around and sometimes passed them in the embassy grounds and deliberately did not look their way. Constance, who was mildly scornful, said it was because most of the girls he had ever met had fallen all over him and it embarrassed him. Anne agreed that they were stupid and silly.

Actually, she had already fallen for him herself, though for the moment she was refusing to admit it, even to her diary.

Anne Morrow was twenty-one years old in 1927, but looked younger. She was a tiny brunette with an elfin figure and an air of shy fragility which was apt to bring out the protective instincts of everyone who met her, men and women alike. She was a gay, sensitive, intelligent girl and her frailty was more apparent than real. It was a joke in the family that though she presented herself as a timid mouse to the outside world, in fact she had the courage of a tigress, plus a dogged determination that was not prepared to let anything or anyone stand in her way when she wanted something badly enough.

She was, however, the last person to have recognized these characteristics in herself. Each night she confided to her diary or, when she was at college, in her letters to her mother her unworthiness or inferiority when compared with her cheerful, uninhibited younger sister, Constance, or her regal and beautiful elder sister, Elisabeth. So far as Charles Lindbergh was concerned, she told herself she could not possibly build up a rapport with this "boy," because she was "so fuddled, so ignorant" that anything she might say to him would be trivial and superficial, "like pink frosting flowers," whereas Elisabeth was so wonderful and "so natural" with him, and Constance "so keen and intelligent, never loses her head—steady and intelligent—more like him than the rest of us." With a humility that would have made female liberationists squirm, she asked herself dolefully how he could possibly spare a second for her humble, unworthy self when her more beautiful and brilliant sisters were on hand.

Mrs. Elizabeth Dwight Morrow was the only one impervious to the heady perfume of hero worship with which the embassy was now redolent, and she watched with amusement (and, it must be imagined, a certain amount of concern) the catalytic presence of Charles Lindbergh reacting on her three daughters. It would have been an exciting Christmas for them even if he had not been there, because this was their first experience of a winter in the rarefied atmosphere of Mexico City, with so many new sights, sounds, and smells to savor; to have the added effect of the world's most eligible young man on their awakened emotions must have been devastating for them, especially as he was around them during his stay for almost twenty-four hours of the day. He accompanied them on picnics to the floating gardens of Xochimilco. He took them for flights over the city, the mountains, and the lakes in the trimotored Ford plane which had brought his mother from Detroit. He talked to them about his flight, his contempt for his fans and the press, his faith in aviation.

At first they treated him like a child whose confidence they were trying to win, being extra careful not to "frighten" him and say something that would make him stiffen up. But then, as he and they gained confidence, they began to relax and joke and argue with him. By the time he flew off to continue a flying tour of South America, he had won the hearts of all three of them.

Anne was besotted. In her diary at the beginning of January 1928, she was already writing screeds trying to explain his "greatness" both to herself and to those people who knew him only from "the newspaper prejudice." She scribbled down his qualities: his *tremendous power over people, unconscious, untried for;* his *dignity,* his *youth,* his *clean-cut freshness—nothing smeared—keen sharpness;* his *complete absence of falseness, never a tinny sound, as one might expect in a vulgar phrase, or badly kept fingernails;* his *tolerant good humor;* his *smile;* his *small-boy-hands-in-pockets-looking-straight-at-you attitude.*

Yet when she heard that her father had invited him to stay with them that summer at North Haven, Maine, where the Morrows had an island home off the coast, she was cast down. With her sisters there, what chance had she got?

"Oh, I know so well just what it will be like," she wrote in her diary. His attention would, of course, be caught by the cool beauty, charm, and serenity of Elisabeth, who had the knack of making him at ease. "I will back out more and more, feeling in the way, stupid, useless, and (in the bottom of my vain heart) hoping that I will be missed. But I am not missed."

She had been jealous of her sister's easy conquests before, but this one seemed likely to cause her special pain.

"Oh, I don't see how I can face this and fight it all over again," she wrote. "I dread this summer."

But if she had read them, these defeatist-sounding sentiments would probably not have fooled her mother, who must have been aware that her middle daughter had already decided that she wanted Charles Lindbergh, and that against the tactics she was using neither of her other daughters stood a chance. For what real interest could Colonel Lindbergh have except affectionate sympathy for her eldest daughter, Elisabeth, who was the genuinely frail member of the family, prey to every fever that was going, and doomed to die soon?* As for Constance, pretty and charming though she might be, she was the kind of exuberant tomboy, the potential New Woman of the 1920s, whose independent spirit and self-confidence were likely to scare the hero out of his wits.

Whereas Mrs. Morrow had not missed the fact that Anne had paid particular attention to Evangeline Lindbergh during her stay at the embassy in Mexico City. The two had built up a rapport with each other through a shared feeling for the son, and it had become unusually strong by the time the visit was over—so strong that, in an unusual outburst of self-revelation, Evangeline Lindbergh had confessed to Anne the depth and strength of her love for her famous offspring. "I just like to be in the room with him, I just like to be there and see him," she confided to the girl. ("Yes, I know—I feel that way too," Anne wrote in her diary that night.) Anne Morrow and Evangeline Lindbergh were a generation apart, but the younger of the two had firmly established the

---

* She died in 1934.

fact that they shared a common interest, and it was likely to cement more than their own friendship in the future. Especially if Charles Lindbergh, who was not unobservant himself, had noted the fact that this shy, timid girl and his beloved mother got on so well.

As it turned out, Lindbergh never did make North Haven that summer. He was too busy arranging for his future, and most of 1928 was spent either in the air or in conference with aviation officials with whose concerns he now proposed to make his career. The South American good-will tour which he had made after leaving Mexico City was an enormous success so far as it concerned the United States Government's plan to show the flag by having it carried by a popular hero, but for Charles Lindbergh it was to prove both hazardous and exhausting. Several times, since he was a stickler for keeping his dates, he had to fly through dangerous storms in order to be in the right spot at the right time, and on his home leg from Havana to St. Louis he was at one time reported overdue. But the hazards he did not really mind, relished them, in fact, because they were part of the thrills of flying; what exhausted him were the crowds who followed him wherever he went, badgered him for his autograph, jostled him; and what angered him were the reporters, who never left him alone, and to whom he now became increasingly distant, curt, and finally downright rude.

In Washington to see President Coolidge after the South American tour, he came out of the White House with a lesser hero named Lieutenant Lester Maitland, who had recently flown to Hawaii. They began walking across to the War Department, and as the waiting crowd fell in behind them, Maitland said:

"Don't you get fed up with this, Slim?"

"I can stand it," Lindbergh said, smiling tightly, "just so they don't push me."

He said it out loud and the hangers-on just behind him heard him plainly. One young man moved forward, pushed hard on Lindbergh's shoulder, and said to the crowd: "There! I touched him!"

The flier swung around, his face stony and white with anger. His fists were clenched and Maitland thought he was going to hit him. But finally he got control of himself and muttered:

"I'm going to quit! I've got to! I'll go out of my mind if they don't stop pushing me."

In some ways he had become obsessed with the idea that he could simply announce that he had finished with being a public hero, and all attention would immediately cease, the limelight switched off him. He would henceforward become a private citizen who could walk down the street unmolested, who could fly where he liked, visit whom he liked, without being dogged by reporters and cameramen. He would devote the spring of 1928 to a final series of "official" or "semiofficial" activities, and then finish: end of episode—on to next hero.

In the weeks after his arrival back from South America he allowed himself to be involved in a succession of events which attracted much public and press attention, and he put up with the resulting crowds and publicity with a grudging but willing acceptance. In a way, he considered, it was his "farewell tour." He came to Washington to receive from the hands of President Coolidge the Medal of Honor which Congress had voted him, and afterward gave free rides in his plane over a period of a week for most Congress representatives and their families. His mood of cynical acceptance was jolted when, hearing that one of Byrd's crew, Floyd Bennett, was gravely ill with pneumonia in a Quebec hospital, he volunteered to fly serum from the Rockefeller Institute in New York through a blinding snowstorm. He got the serum through at considerable risk to his own neck, only to hear that Bennett had died anyway and that the Quebec authorities were not grateful but offended at his effort, since they had plenty of serum anyway.

He planned as the climax of his "farewell tour" his flight from St. Louis to Washington, where he presented the *Spirit of St. Louis* to the Smithsonian Institution after a nonstop flight. The ceremonies over, he put on his hat and took the train back to New York. Four weeks later it was announced that he had joined Transcontinental Air Transport† as technical director, and he appeared at a press conference to talk about his job.

It was, he decided, the last time he would have any dealings with the press until he had something of value to say about aviation.

He was being naïve. Only three weeks before he had had a salutary example of how he would remain "news" to the press and public, no matter how much he wished it otherwise. He had taken off early in May from Ford Airport in Detroit to fly down to Curtiss Field in New York, and had given strict instructions that no one was to talk about his flight, particularly to the press. But when he landed at Curtiss that evening he forgot to report his safe arrival to Ford; they put out a general alarm, and airmail planes along his route were asked to look out for his wrecked or stranded machine. He had meanwhile forbidden Curtiss to announce his arrival, and though they were being bombarded with inquiries they refused all statements. It was not until late in the evening that they admitted he had landed hours before. He chuckled over

† Later, after the incorporation of Western Air, to be known as Trans World Airlines.

LINDBERGH MISSING as a headline in the morning papers, for it confirmed his opinion of press inaccuracy, but he did not seem to realize that he was primarily responsible, and that, whether he liked it or not, he was still the most famous man in the world over whose fate the public and the newspapers—especially in this case—displayed legitimate anxiety.

He became particularly angry with newspapers which claimed he was getting a swelled head ("My hatter says my size is still the same") and of "backing into the limelight" by deliberately creating secrecy over his flights. He insisted that in future he would see reporters only when he had something to say to them about "the only subject I know, avia-tion." Otherwise, he wished to be left alone by the crowds and unreported in the press.

But on October 3, 1928, he was back in the limelight of his own voli-tion, and the reason had nothing at all to do with flying. He had intro-duced his name for the first time into American politics. As his new and powerful Republican friends had prophesied after those cosy eve-nings in Guggenheim's smoking room on Long Island, he came through with an endorsement for their candidate in the presidential election. He sent a telegram to Herbert C. Hoover, the Republican nominee, saying:

> THE MORE I SEE OF YOUR CAMPAIGN, THE MORE STRONGLY I FEEL THAT YOUR ELECTION IS OF SUPREME IMPORTANCE TO THE COUNTRY. YOUR QUALITIES AS A MAN AND WHAT YOU STAND FOR, REGARDLESS OF PARTY, MAKE ME FEEL THAT THE PROBLEMS WHICH WILL COME BEFORE THE COUNTRY DURING THE NEXT FOUR YEARS WILL BEST BE SOLVED BY YOUR LEADERSHIP.

There were some Minnesotans who remarked that if his father had not been cremated he would be turning in his grave, for Herbert Hoover stood for most of the things Charles Lindbergh, Sr., had fought against all his political life. But one man who was vastly pleased by the endorsement was Dwight Whitney Morrow.

Charles Lindbergh had become *"le seul saint devant qui je brûle ma chandelle"*‡ for Anne Morrow now. She quite often bought *Popular Aviation* at the newsstands, and was boning up on the arts of flying by studying a book called *Airmen and Aircraft*. This last depressed her be-cause it set out the requirements of an aviator and they seemed to be so ridiculously contrary to her own qualities. She went through the list: *in-*

‡ "The only saint before whom I burn a candle."

stantaneous coordination between muscles and thoughts, ability to withstand physical and mental strain, complete lack of fear while flying, readiness to take risks, calm, level-headedness at all times, adaptability. She told herself that the only qualification she possessed was *good eyesight*, and, sighing with despair, concluded that she had more in common with a ditchdigger, a newspaper vendor, a fruit-store man, or her Italian dressmaker than with beloved Colonel L.

Nevertheless, with her usual but unacknowledged tenacity, she continued her pursuit of aeronautical knowledge. After classes she drove out to a local airfield where a man in charge of the planes answered her questions and finally invited her into the cockpit to work the controls. Another day, she persuaded a pilot to take her and a college mate up in the plane, and came down hair tangled, but ecstatic. It was one way of staying close to the absent hero.

In the midst of her dreams, however, she did not lose her solid sense of application, and her work at college showed no sign of neglect whatsoever. Just the opposite, in fact. She won the Elizabeth Montagu prize for a paper on Madame d'Houdetot and later the Mary Augusta Jordan prize for an essay. She read W. B. Yeats, Ezra Pound, A. E. Housman, the *Book of the Duchesse, Canterbury Tales,* Marcel Proust, Alice Meynell, Emily Dickinson, Edna St. Vincent Millay, James Elroy Flecker, John Masefield, Honoré de Balzac, and Charles Baudelaire. She wrote poems, some of them about the joys of flying. She went out with boys from Amherst but found them too young and "platitudinous."

She confided to her diary: "I want to be married, but I never, never will."

And then, on the morning of October 3—the day he had sent his telegram to Herbert Hoover—Charles Lindbergh called the Morrow apartment in New York. Anne answered the telephone.

So began a surreptitious courtship designed to keep secret from the newspapers the palpitating gossip item that he had at last found himself a girl. He was anxious to take her up for a flight over New York, but "we can't go to any of the fields or we'd be engaged the next day." He added, with some embarrassment: "I've been engaged to two girls in one week and I haven't seen either of them." They arranged to meet in the New York apartment of a Morrow family friend and then drove in his Franklin tourer to the Guggenheim estate at Sands Point.

There for the first time Anne Morrow saw the other side of her shy boy hero. She was amazed at how easily he had made himself at home at "the swell Guggenheim place (gatehouses and towers and lawns and peacocks!)" and at the self-confident way he got on with the family. She had expected to stop somewhere for a hamburger or a sandwich, and she was already dressed for the flight in riding trousers, leather coat, street shoes, and gray golf stockings. She found herself being led into the impressive dining hall for a posh luncheon party with the Guggenheims. She daren't take her jacket off because her jersey underneath was shabby, and she "boiled" in it—"oh, it was priceless, I and the Madonnas!" she wrote to Constance.

She waited with the Guggenheims while Lindbergh went off to Roosevelt Field to collect a plane, and the family proceeded to "horrify" her "with tales of 'Slim's' practical jokes. (They all call him 'Slim')." Then he brought a silver biplane Moth down on the Guggenheim landing strip, presented her with goggles and a helmet, and took her off for a breath-taking flight over New York and New Jersey. Soon he was visiting her regularly, teaching her how to fly a plane, and actually coming back to the Morrow's New Jersey home where (with the housekeeper, Mrs. Graeme, as chaperone) they drank ginger ale and "argued about Al Smith.* I told about Dwight voting for Al Smith. He said to me, grinning, 'Your father is voting for Hoover and *he's* pretty right about things' and also—with a delicious laughing grin—'*Terrible!* These sons voting against their fathers!' "

She was giving her sister Constance a blow by blow, or rather flight by flight, account of her meetings with Lindbergh, and she was at first inclined to spatter her letters with such phrases as "it should have been you" (in the plane or at supper) or "he really likes us," emphasizing that she meant not just herself but all three of them. Sometimes she expressed doubt that any of them could actually have anything in common with him, since he was "terribly young and crude in many small ways." She was occasionally appalled by his gaucheness, especially when he agreed with her about liking poetry and proudly told her that his favorite poet was Robert W. Service. ("That just hurt *terribly*.")

She now had code words for him when writing to her sisters, and the favorite one was Boyd:

> I have a great deal to write to you about Boyd, more than you can think possible. . . . I sat next to a Mr. [Cornelius Vanderbilt] Whitney (a friend of Sandy's) who knows Boyd quite well. I had a divine evening pretending I *didn't*, and leading him on, by disparaging remarks, to praise Boyd. . . . Boyd said that you *never get over* that feeling of serenity and sense of proportion that ⤲ gives you.

* Hoover's Democrat opponent in the presidential election.

At the beginning of November 1928, she left to stay with her parents in Mexico City, and on November 8 Charles Lindbergh landed there. He airily told reporters that the only explanation for his presence was the fact that his first visit had so favorably impressed him that he had determined to come back as soon as possible. He spent the next fifteen days with the Morrows and Anne, including a weekend at their new home in Cuernavaca. He even persuaded Mrs. Morrow to go for a ride with him in his plane. Besotted was too weak a word now for Anne Morrow's condition. She was "completely turned upside down, completely overwhelmed, completely upset. . . ." After he left she reported that "I'm in a complete coma now . . . I sleep till twelve every morning and take naps in the afternoon!"

But the embassy went on strenuously denying that there was any romance between "Colonel Charles Lindbergh and a member of the Morrow family." Anne went on ridiculing the idea that it could possibly be her in whom the great hero was interested.

Toward the end of December, however, she wrote to Corliss Lamont, a family friend:

"Apparently I am going to marry Charles Lindbergh. It must seem hysterically funny to you as it did to me. . . . Wish me courage and strength and a sense of humor—I will need them all."

It was not until February 12, 1929, that reporters were summoned to the American Embassy in Mexico City and handed a statement. It said:

"Ambassador and Mrs. Morrow have announced the engagement of their daughter, Anne Spencer Morrow, to Col. Charles A. Lindbergh."

There was no elaboration of the announcement and no date given for the wedding. But on May 27, Evangeline Lindbergh, who had been working for some months as a temporary teacher at the American College in Constantinople, Turkey, returned to the United States, and the Morrows informed a few of their close friends and relatives that they were giving a small reception for her at their home, Next Day Hill, Englewood, New Jersey, to which they had now returned.

The last guest had barely arrived when Mrs. Morrow ushered them into the dining room and told them to gather around Dr. William Adams Brown, pastor of the local church. Charles Lindbergh was already standing near him, and almost immediately Anne Morrow, carrying a bouquet of columbine and larkspur, entered on the arm of her father. By that time even the slowest wits among the guests realized that they were witnesses at a wedding, and one that would make headlines in newspapers around the world on the morrow.

It was a short wedding service with no music, and the bride and groom stayed only long enough to cut the wedding cake, which was trundled in, and join the guests in sipping ginger ale and water. Then they went upstairs, changed clothes, and motored out of the estate gates under the gaze of unsuspecting reporters.

Not until long after they were gone did Arthur Springer, Dwight Morrow's secretary, walk to the gate of Next Day Hill and beckon to the newspapermen to approach him. He had a paper in his hand and he read out:

"Mr. and Mrs. Dwight W. Morrow announce the marriage of their daughter Anne to Charles A. Lindbergh at Englewood, New Jersey, May 27, 1929."

A torrent of questions poured out of the mouths of the astonished reporters, but the secretary shook his head.

"That is all," he said firmly, and turned on his heel and went back past the bodyguards into the estate, ignoring the anguished cries of: "Where are they honeymooning? What did she wear?"

Presently the car containing the Reverend Dr. Brown came out of the gates, and the padre was eventually prevailed upon to stop and answer some questions. But he had to hurry, he said; he had a service that evening, and he hadn't told his wife what he had been doing that morning.

What did the bride wear for the wedding? he was asked.

"Oh, my word," he replied, "I didn't look at her dress. I was looking at her face. But her dress was charming."†

Did the bride cry during the ceremony?

Emphatically, Dr. Brown shook his head. "How silly," he said disdainfully. "Gentlefolk do not behave that way."

He was not very observant. As Anne Morrow Lindbergh confessed afterward, the tears were there. She could still hardly believe it was happening to *her.*

† She wore a white wedding gown with a cap of Brussels lace with a short veil. The bouquet was of spring flowers picked by Elisabeth earlier in the morning.

Part
Three
Into the
Abyss

CHAPTER

TWELVE

A LIFE OF RELENTLESS

ACTION

Like Lucy Snowe in Charlotte Brontë's *Villette*, Anne Morrow knew what she was letting herself in for when she married Charles Lindbergh, and could say along with Lucy: "[Charles] and I intended to be married in this way almost from the first; we never meant to be spliced in the humdrum way of other people." Or, as she put it in her own words:

"And there he is—darn it all—the great Western strong-man-open-spaces type and a life of relentless action! But after all, what am I going to do about it? After all, there he is and I've got to go."

In some ways, the Morrow girls were not unlike the Brontë sisters in their talents, sensitivities, and closely knitted loyalty to each other and mutual pride. Although they had all of them been smitten by Lindbergh's charm and magnetism, and flattered by his pleasure in being with them, they by no means felt that Anne had got the better part of the bargain by marrying Charles. And even Anne herself rather resented the way in which people kept coming to congratulate *her* on the marriage and telling her what a lucky girl she was. They were an unpretentious family, and they laughed along with all the other guests when one of the secretaries, at an embassy party, sang a song which included the lines: "She was only an ambassador's daughter, but he was a Prince of the air." Nevertheless, privately they bridled.

Even Anne considered that she had married her intellectual inferior. He hardly ever seemed to have read a book except ones on aviation. He had no feeling for words and seemed to prefer doggerel to poetry. His knowledge of music was elementary and his liking for it apathetic. He still could not resist playing those stupid schoolboy practical jokes. He seemed altogether lacking in the attributes of an educated young man of the kind she had been brought up to recognize. When she said in one of her letters to him, *"J'ai besoin de vous voir, et de vous voir encore—et de vous voir toujours,"** and added, *"Don't* let anyone translate this," she must have wondered afterward how otherwise he was going to discover what she was telling him, because she was only too well aware that he knew no French and could not learn it. In the same letter she added a phrase in Greek from *Anabasis* which she did not translate, but which meant: "Without you every road lies through the shadows." He did not read Greek either. There was an interesting psychological touch to the fact that she was confiding herself to him in words of love and surrender, but at the same time asserting her cultural superiority by couching them in languages he did not understand.

It says a good deal for Charles Lindbergh's regard and admiration for his new wife that he did not seem to resent these indications that she was something of an intellectual snob. She could be devastatingly patronizing on occasion ("The average noncollege woman can talk for hours without a letup," she wrote after meeting some housewives in Kansas City). She was apt to judge every man she met by how he would fit into the directors' room at J. P. Morgan. (After a transcontinental flight, they stayed with a banker in San Francisco and she wrote: "He is a keen man-of-the-world, discreet, kindly, cultured—the kind we know in the Firm. . . . I recognized [the timbre] immediately. I have not seen anyone like him on this trip, and I felt at home.")

Lindbergh put down her attitude to the sheltered life she had led as a Morrow daughter, her horizons confined to Next Day Hill, Smith College campus, and Wall Street bankers' drawing rooms, and he quietly set out to broaden them, mentally, emotionally, physically. In the months that followed their marriage, he embarked on what could only be considered an intensive course of re-education, and it did not always go smoothly. There were occasions, as she made clear in her letters and diary entries, when she was desperately homesick for the strong matriarchal hand of her mother and the companionship of her two sisters.

Charles Lindbergh made it clear to her from the start that his idea of a wife was in no fashion one who sat at home and waited for him, who had a life apart from his own. Where he went, she must go, too—and it was he who decided where they were going. As time went by, she came somewhat ruefully to regard her relationship to him as roughly equivalent to a faithful page accompanying a knight in shining armor ("What ho, cup-bearer!"—"Yes, sire, here I come!"). There were more spiteful

* "I need to see you, and to see you again—and to see you always."

friends who, when they saw her hauling the baggage from a plane while he stood talking to officials, likened them to an officer and his batman. In fact, what he proceeded to do was treat her exactly as he would have done a close male friend and associate (except when they got to bed, of course), and expected from her all the useful help he would have received from such a working partner.

But that meant learning new skills and facing situations, often really dangerous ones, with which she had not only never been confronted before, but had never even had nightmares about. For instance, he expected her to fly with him not as a passenger, for then she would be taking up weight and space, but as a member of the crew of his plane. So she had to learn to work a radio, become touch-perfect in Morse code, which was the means of communication between air and ground in those days; and she, who was bad at figures and knew nothing about electronics, had to sweat out an intensive course in radiophony. She had to learn to read a chart, so as to be able to tell her pilot-husband where they were when they were flying in darkness or over the sea.

What might have proved to be the hardest task he gave her was that of qualifying as a pilot, so that she could take over from him if need be. But there she was lucky. She was mad about flying. The act of flying was an experience which uplifted her both physically and spiritually. Her instructor was Charles Lindbergh himself, and he was a perfectionist. He told her bluntly that he would rather have her a nonpilot than a poor pilot, and sometimes he had her flying out of Roosevelt Field, six, eight, even ten hours a day, landing and taking off, landing and taking off, till her hands were falling off with exhaustion. Each time she came down with a thud, and breathed a sigh of relief that they were down at all, he would say: "Not good. Take her up again." But when she made a perfect landing, he smiled at her and that made it worthwhile.

By the middle of 1929, she was a qualified navigator and radio operator, and she was charting their progress by map and radio across the American continent, and helping her husband to break the record for a transcontinental flight.

That exciting, exhausting, sometimes terrifying first year of marriage did not just change her life and her point of view. It also revealed to her the qualities in her husband which made her ashamed of ever having thought him her inferior. As their intimacy developed and he began to reveal himself to her, she was filled with admiration for the variety of his knowledge and the wealth of his ideas. He taught her how to read the stars and the contours of the earth over which they were flying. He was interested in subjects she had never given much thought to, like space research and deep-sea diving. He seemed to have inherited his maternal forebears' fascination with science, and was always setting up problems to be solved, gadgets to be invented. He knew about animals, wild and domesticated, and could talk to her for hours about grasses, trees, and flowers.

It was true that he did not yet have the gift of words, but she resolved to teach him that. It was true that he could not master foreign languages. It was true that he was still awkward with strangers and uneasy in company. But so far as she was concerned, he was a poet who wrote his verses in the sky and did it with his own kind of music. He was no longer to her a daredevil flier but a dedicated craftsman, with aeronautics as his art. She knew now that he knew beauty, felt as deeply, and dreamed as hopefully as she did.

By the end of that first year, she was no longer reconciled to having to spend the rest of her life with him but gloriously excited about it, despite the discomforts, inconveniences, and dangers that seemed to accompany this strange husband of hers wherever he went. It was with eager anticipation that she began planning with him projects and adventures which, twelve months earlier, would have seemed to her crazy, suicidal.

And amid all her other activities in that crowded year, she succeeded in becoming pregnant as well.

The first appearance that the Lindberghs made after their honeymoon was at a Long Island airport with their friend Harry Guggenheim. Captain Harry had now appointed Charles as a consultant to the Guggenheim Aeronautical Foundation on a retainer of $25,000 a year, and the occasion was yet another in the foundation's crusades to convince the public of the safety and efficacy of air travel. The appearance of the hero and his new wife was what circus barkers would have described as the "come-on," and their appearance drew not only the crowds but the press as well.

One of the cheekier reporters present at the conference which Lindbergh gave was resolved not to confine the occasion to aviation, and thought he would get a snappy reaction from the flier if he asked him an impudent question:

"Is it true that Mrs. Lindbergh is pregnant?"

A more sophisticated person would have shrugged it off as a cheap but forgettable impertinence. Lindbergh was not sophisticated. He would have resented it as an intrusion into his private life if one of the reporters had asked him what he had eaten for breakfast. To hear a question about something so intimate as his relations with his wife and her condition shocked him profoundly.

His arms went ramrod straight against his sides, his fists clenched, and his face was flushed with anger as he turned away. Once more the American press had confirmed his worst opinions of them.

He was still raw at this time from the way in which their behavior had interfered with his honeymoon. After slipping away from Next Day Hill (with Anne lying on the floor of the car to deceive the reporters at the gate) they had gone to a cabin cruiser anchored for them off the Long Island shore, and they set sail for what they hoped would be a peaceful cruise to Maine. Two days later, when they came into York Harbor, Maine, for fuel, they were spotted by a flying boat with reporters and cameramen aboard, and from that moment the chase was on.

One motorboat with a cameraman aboard cruised around them for seven hours. The reporter had come up to the porthole in the early hours and after shouting, "Is this the Lindbergh boat?" declared that he and his colleagues would leave the honeymooners alone if only they would come out on deck and pose for a session of photographs. Lindbergh stubbornly and furiously refused. For the rest of the morning and afternoon their boat was rocked as the press boat cruised round and round them, until finally they fled out to sea, dragging their anchor behind them, and spent the night on a fishing bank out of sight of land. It was a rough night, crockery was smashed, Anne was sick.

Charles Lindbergh did not forgive American newspapers for their behavior toward him. He was now obsessed by what he called "the evils" of the press. He could not seem to see that where the press was entirely free there were bound to be irresponsibles, and excesses, and he stubbornly refused to accept that, like death and taxes, they were inevitable. He adamantly refused to be more co-operative, even when friends told him that in this way he would cease to be a "forbidden" object and gradually lose his news value. He did not wish to ameliorate the situation, he said, he just wanted to be left alone.

This growing sense of resentment at the way he was being "persecuted" he soon passed on to his wife, and it considerably marred her happiness in being married. One of the first things he did after they became engaged was to warn her to watch her words in future.

"Never say anything you wouldn't want shouted from the housetops," he said, "and never write anything you would mind seeing on the front page of a newspaper."

For someone who liked to share every thought and activity with other people, it was an inhibiting prohibition. If she had been less anxious to please him, less dominated by the magnetic quality of his personality, she might have refused such a restriction on her very nature and personality. Out of love for him and a desire to help him preserve the privacy he so much cherished, she fell in with his wishes. "But what a sacrifice to make never to speak or write deeply or honestly!" she wrote long afterward.

But obsessions are catching, and soon Anne Lindbergh was a victim of the persecution complex herself. So far as the newspapers were concerned, of course, the more they deliberately avoided publicity, the more the news value grew; like orchids or orangutans hiding in the forests, they had rarity value and everyone wanted to know about them. Had they posed for engagement pictures, wedding pictures, and on their boat during their honeymoon, it might not have guaranteed them freedom from all press intrusion, but it would certainly have called off most of the photographers scrambling over each other in search of scoops.

Obsessions feed upon themselves, too, and Anne Lindbergh became frightened of talking to anyone, in case they should sell what she said to the press—as, indeed, they often did. From this developed a loathing for people, especially the crowds who followed them when they appeared in public. When she saw what she called "the *leer* of recognition" on someone's face, she stared at them in as insulting fashion as she could manage and called them "you *brutes*" in her mind. She became afraid of going out on the streets "because of people leering and nudging and craning their necks and following. Oh, it is brutal."

One weekend the two of them went up to visit a friend in Milton, Connecticut, and in the afternoon decided to go shopping in the town with Anne's sister, Constance. The two Lindberghs decided to disguise themselves. Anne pushed her hair under a floppy hat which she wore on the back of her head, smeared herself heavily with lipstick, and wore goggles. Charles put on a shabby cap and also wore goggles. Constance stayed her extremely pretty and natural self. After a time, Anne wailed that people were *still* looking at them.

"Yes, dear," said Constance ironically, "they're wondering why such a nice girl is going around with such awful hicks."

They disguised themselves often after that. Once they went to the theater to see the Spanish dancer La Argentina. Anne had her hair bobbed and wore lipstick and glasses. Charles oiled his hair down, put burned cork on his eyebrows, and proposed to wear a false mustache, but left it off at the last minute.

They were of course recognized and word spread that they were in the theater, and Charles Lindbergh immediately got up and left. Anne stayed and confessed later: "As a matter of fact, people were much nicer than I imagined." But they now found that the glances even of "nice people" made them uneasy and took the pleasure out of things.

The doctors confirmed in November 1929 that Anne Lindbergh was going to have a baby, and they began to plan seriously for a permanent home in the country somewhere within reach of New York and the Long Island flying fields. But first, despite Anne's recurrent bouts of sickness, they flew to California to pick up the plane in which they planned to break the transcontinental flight record to New York.

While there they dined in Hollywood with the biggest movie stars of the day, Mary Pickford and Douglas Fairbanks, at their home "Pickfair".† They also renewed acquaintance with Amelia Earhart, a flier whose fame was growing ever since she had become the first woman to fly the Atlantic in 1928.‡ She was a tall, slim, attractive girl whose short, boyish hair and friendly grin had encouraged some of the newspapers to call her "Lady Lindy" and this embarrassed her. After she had met Anne Lindbergh for the first time the previous spring, she wrote her a letter in which she said:

> I had no chance at the banquet of the Ohio Federation of Women's Clubs to thank you for your graciousness in absolving me from blame in the ridiculous "Lady Lindy" publicity.
> I believe I have never apologized so widely and so consistently for anything in my life, excepting possibly having been born. The title was given me, I believe, probably because one of us wasn't a swarthy runt. You understand my dislike of the title isn't because I don't appreciate being compared to one who has abilities such as Colonel Lindbergh has, but because that comparison is quite unjustified.

In fact Anne Lindbergh, who rightly thought Amelia Earhart was "a most amazing person—just as tremendous as C," was startled at how much alike she was to her husband.

"Oh, I've got the kind of face that looks like everybody," Earhart remarked.

She commiserated with the Lindberghs over the penalties attached to being famous. "It's no fun to have one's clothes torn," she said. "It's simply ghastly to be *pinched*."

† They jokingly decided they would call their own home "Spengustus" after their middle names, Spencer and Augustus.
‡ She disappeared on a flight across the Pacific in 1937.

But she came to the conclusion during the four days she saw the Lindberghs that Charles was certainly an odd character, and gave the man who later became her husband (George Palmer Putnam) a savory account of one of his practical jokes:

> Anne, the Colonel and AE [Amelia Earhart] were fellow guests at the home of Jack Maddux in Hollywood. One night they were sitting about close to the icebox. Anne and AE were drinking buttermilk. Lindbergh, standing behind his wife munching a tomato sandwich, had the sudden impulse to let drops of water fall in a stream on his wife's shoulder from a glass in his hand.
>
> Anne was wearing a sweet dress of pale blue silk. Water spots silk. AE observed a growing unhappiness on Anne's part —but no move toward rebellion, not even any murmur of complaint. AE often said that Anne Lindbergh is the best sport in the world.
>
> Then Anne rose and stood by the door, with her back to the others, and her head resting on her arm. AE thought, with horror, that the impossible had come to pass, and that Anne was crying. But Anne was thinking out a solution to her problem, and the instant she thought it out, she acted upon it. At once—and with surprising thoroughness.
>
> With one comprehensive movement she swung around and —quite simply—threw the contents of her glass of buttermilk straight over the Colonel's blue serge suit. It made a simply marvellous mess! Lindbergh's look of utter amazement changed into a tremendous grin, and he threw his head up and shouted with laughter. The joke, very practical, was on him!
>
> AE always suspected that no more of Anne's wardrobe ever got spotted—at least in that way.*

Even the newspapers by now knew that Anne was expecting a child, and by the time the Lindberghs' plane took off for the transcontinental flight both press and public were watching it with rather more than technical interest. By the time they took off on Easter Sunday 1930, Anne Lindbergh was in her seventh month of pregnancy, and though the newspapers did not know this they did suspect that she was approaching the crucial period. It was a rough journey and probably the

---

* George Palmer Putnam, *Soaring Wings: A Biography of Amelia Earhart* (New York: Harcourt, Brace and Co., 1930).

most difficult and frightening flight she had yet made with her husband. There had been much newspaper discussion over recent air crashes in bad weather, and Lindbergh was out to prove that regular air travel was still possible even in storm conditions so long as the pilot flew over the clouds at high (for the time) altitude.

He made his point and broke the record despite storm conditions for most of the journey. But he had to take his plane to a height which, in her condition, Anne Lindbergh found extremely trying. They had no oxygen. She was painfully sick. She was tempted several times to plead with her husband to land, but restrained herself and moiled in considerable pain for at least four out of the fourteen hours.

As the flight had been well publicized beforehand, by Lindbergh himself among others, reporters were waiting for him to land and expected to get his story. But Anne's condition made him change his mind. While she hid in the plane, he dismissed the whole flight as a routine one and refused to be interviewed about it.

"He wasn't just curt, he was damned rude," said Rena Terrington, one of the reporters.

The reporters suspected that he was trying to conceal something from them. As indeed he was. Anne Lindbergh, obsessed by the notion that her distressful condition would do harm both to her husband and to aviation, had pleaded with him to get rid of the press. Instead of doing it with a smile and a statement, he tried to drive them away. So some of them stayed on long enough to see his wife being carried out of the plane and put into a car, obviously very much the worse for wear.

When stories to this effect appeared in the newspapers, they were vehemently denied by spokesmen for Lindbergh. But in this case they were true—as Anne Lindbergh admitted, forty-three years later.†

All this only served to exacerbate the state of war which now existed between the Lindberghs and the press. In May, Anne moved into her parents' home at Englewood, and as her time grew near, American newspapers began reacting like their British counterparts when the monarch or the heir to the throne is about to father an heir. The parallel is not too inexact, for in public regard Charles Lindbergh was viewed very much with the same loyal affection as Britain's Prince of Wales. The British, however, were apt to handle these things with more efficiency, and a spokesman would have been on hand with regular bulletins if the Prince had found himself in a similar situation.

In the case of the Lindberghs, their antagonism was now so bitter

† See Anne Morrow Lindbergh, *Hour of Gold, Hour of Lead* (New York: Harcourt Brace Jovanovich, 1973), p. 10.

that they tried to deny that anything was happening at all. Anne Lindbergh wrote to her mother-in-law to tell her that "we both feel" that considering the way the newspapers had behaved "they should be given no announcement." They were not sure whether her accouchement and the birth could be kept secret until the baby's official registration, but they were certainly going to try.

She told Evangeline Lindbergh that they would send her a code signal when the baby was born. ADVISE ACCEPTING TERMS OF CONTRACT would tell her that the baby was a girl. ADVISE PURCHASING PROPERTY would tell her that it was a boy. Both messages would be signed REUBEN LLOYD. They had tentatively decided to call the child Anne if it was a girl, and it went without saying that its name would be Charles Augustus if it was a boy.

On June 22, 1930—which happened to be Anne Lindbergh's twenty-fourth birthday—a happy Charles Lindbergh went into Englewood to send a telegram to his mother:

ADVISE PURCHASING PROPERTY. REUBEN LLOYD.

Charles Augustus Lindbergh III had come into the world that day, and despite the buffeting his mother had taken over the past few months, he was a bonny, healthy child.

His joyful parents kept the press waiting for two weeks, and then revealed the Christian names of their son and heir. The reporters were also handed some photographs of the boy which Lindbergh had taken himself.

CHAPTER

THIRTEEN

THE FAT LAMB IS

STOLEN

For the first few months after the birth of her child, Anne Morrow Lindbergh knew what it was like to be married to a comparatively serene and happy man. Once the fuss of the baby's birth was over, both press and public declared a sort of truce with the Lindberghs and there was a surcease from the constant ogling and publicity which grated so much on their nerves.

Charles Lindbergh discovered with some surprise that he could even appear on the streets of New York without starting a riot—providing he didn't hang around in one spot, that is. Anne rediscovered the pleasure of going to concerts and went overboard in a letter to her sister Constance about the delicious joy of listening to César Franck alone among the rest of the *accompanied* audience, like having an exotic fruit to oneself.

The fact that she had suffered some physical discomforts after the birth of Charles hardly seemed to matter,* compared with the bliss, the unbadgered connubial bliss, of a comparatively normal life with husband and son.

Not that Lindbergh stayed at home to cosset her while she was recovering from the accouchement. By this time he had become not simply a flier, or even an expert on aeronautics, but something of an *homme d'affaires*. If he had not yet quite achieved his first million dollars, he was getting pretty close to it. The firm with which he had first become associated after his transatlantic flight, Transcontinental Air Transport, retained him as chief technical director at a salary of

* A breast abscess developed while she was feeding the child, and she had to go into hospital to have it lanced.

$10,000 a year. But much more important, he was given 25,000 shares in TAT at ten dollars a share, which was ten dollars a share below their market value before he joined the firm and twenty dollars below afterward—his name added that much prestige to an organization. He was advised to sell some of these shares and did so.

Juan Trippe, president of Pan American Airways, had also retained his services as a technical adviser at $10,000 a year, and he was given stock options with this company, too. Altogether he made $400,000 out of selling his premium shares in the two companies, and still retained considerable interests in them.

Then, too, there was the money he made through his connection by marriage with the House of Morgan. Those were the cosy days when the big bankers looked after their own with no fear of congressional or senatorial committees coming down on their necks. J. P. Morgan kept its relations sweet with prominent people, or with its protégés, by putting lucrative opportunities in their way. The bank had what it called a "preferred list" to whom it offered blue-chip stocks at discount rates. They were given the opportunity of buying at a quarter to a third below the figure quoted on the New York Stock Exchange, and there was no restriction on their selling at the market price immediately afterward. Charles Lindbergh's name was added to the roster. He joined General John Pershing, John J. Raskob, Thomas Lamont, and Newton D. Baker in buying Allegheny Corporation at fourteen dollars below the quoted share price. He figured in other purchases at bargain prices with Bernard Baruch and Calvin Coolidge. He added a considerable amount to his fortune this way.

He now needed an expert to look after his "interests" and a Morrow family friend, Colonel Henry C. Breckenridge, volunteered to become his legal adviser and general counselor. He worked hard, well, and profitably for him, and became a close friend.

So there were now definitely no financial worries connected to the Lindberghs' future, and he got on with the process of living and flying. He spent a good deal of time in conferences along the transcontinental routes which TWA was now covering. He had met and become absorbed with a French biologist, Dr. Alexis Carrel, who was experimenting with artificial transplants, and he regularly joined him in his work at the Rockefeller Institute in New York. He had flown continually over the wooded hill country of southern New Jersey and finally bought some land near Hopewell, where he planned to build a house for his family. He had picked up another scientific pioneer in the person of Robert H. Goddard, who had the mad idea of making rockets capable of carrying mail (or bombs) over long distances, and he was busily trying to interest Captain Harry and the Guggenheim Foundation in his spectacular but expensive experiments.

In between, he flew off to South America to check a route for Pan American Airways, and began planning with Anne the flight which they were to make as soon as she had recovered, by the Great Circle route over the Arctic Sea to China. It was a well-filled life and all it lacked was a home of their own. Until that time, they made their base at Next Day Hill, the Morrow home at Englewood, New Jersey, which did not lack for comforts, since it had a staff of twenty-nine servants and stood in fifty acres of ground. In November 1930 they took a short lease on a house just outside Princeton, New Jersey; it was within easy driving distance of the site at Hopewell where they were building their home. But they still spent several days a week at Next Day Hill, for there Anne felt safe with her son from the trucial world outside.

It was at Next Day Hill on March 5, 1931, that something happened which cracked, though it did not shatter, their sense of peace, well-being, and security. The Lindberghs had acquired an Aberdeen terrier which they named Skeean, and attached to the Morrow household was a white terrier called Daffin, which had been the beloved pet of Anne and Constance for many years. March 5 was a Sunday, and it was at weekends that sight-seers were still inclined to drive out to the Morrow estate to see if they could catch a glimpse of the Lindberghs. (They were, in fact, at Princeton, but that of course was not common knowledge.) One car actually swung suddenly through the open Morrow gateway, drove down to the forecourt, and ran over Daffin as it bounded out to bark at the intruders. The car did not stop to find out what had happened to the terrier but left it lying on the forecourt and raced back to the road and away.

Daffin was still alive and in great pain when the servants carried it into the house and called the vet. He gave it a big enough dose of morphine to put it out of its misery.

Anne cried at first and then boiled with anger. Charles Lindbergh wandered around the house saying:

"If I'd been there, I would have shot them, I really would have shot them!"

They were back in the sordid world of oglers and pryers again, and their limited idyll was at an end, the truce broken.

On July 4, 1931, the whole Morrow family, plus Charles Lindbergh, gathered at Next Day Hill for their own private Independence Day celebration. There was a panel let into the wall which had come from one of their earlier houses, and on which it was their custom to sign their names and the date each year. That night Mrs. Elizabeth Morrow happily wrote in her diary:

"All the family and only the family. I wonder when that will happen again?" Not long afterward she added the word: "Never."

Three days later, Dwight and Elizabeth Morrow, plus Elisabeth, Constance, their dogs, and their staff, moved up to their island home, Deacon Brown's Point, in Maine. They were joined by Anne and their son-in-law for a brief visit on July 29, when their monoplane *Sirius* came down at North Haven on the first stage of the Great Circle flight to the Far East.

Anne Lindbergh has told the story of that remarkable voyage in her first and most famous book, *North to the Orient,* and it deserves its place in the annals of aviation, along with Lindbergh's lone flight across the Atlantic. The *Sirius* had been equipped with pontoons for landing on water and the wheels made retractable, and they wore flying suits heated by electricity to keep out the Arctic cold. For the first half of the journey they flew to places where no plane had ever been seen before.

Lindbergh was always a thorough planner and where possible he never left things to hazard, so he had made arrangements beforehand for fuel dumps at their stops en route. They flew across Hudson's Bay, over the ice packs to the Seward Peninsula, into Alaska, across the Bering Strait to Siberia, southward to Japan, and finally landed on the flooded Yangtze River at Nanking. They had their fair share of difficulties with the weather, and sometimes failed to make their expected rendezvous. It was Anne Lindbergh's job as radio operator to keep the outside world in touch with their progress—or lack of it—and sometimes it was a desperate struggle to locate a station, get a dot-and-dash message over, and haul her aerial in before her husband found a hole in the clouds and plunged them down onto the icy sea.

It has possibly become apparent from this narrative that Anne Lindbergh was no women's liberationist, and the greatest compliment she considered she had received during the journey was when a radio operator congratulated her on the skill with which she took and received messages.

"No man could have done better," he said.

The Yangtze had broken its banks, not for the first time in its history, and great tracts of Chinese countryside were flooded, villages engulfed, crops destroyed, livestock drowned, and hordes of refugees starving. Charles Lindbergh willingly offered his plane for service in famine relief flights, and almost lost it—and probably his own life—as a result. He was carrying a doctor and medical supplies to the flooded city of

Hinghwa and landed on a stretch of water, when starving Chinese saw the bags of medicine being loaded into sampans and decided that this was food—and food they needed and must have. They scrambled onto one sampan and sank it, then another, and finally approached the plane. When a number of them clambered over the pontoons of the *Sirius* and threatened to damage or sink it, Lindbergh hauled out a revolver and fired over the heads of the frantic coolies and succeeded in scaring them away long enough to get the plane aloft again.

Off Shanghai, the British airplane carrier *Hermes* was parked in the Yangtze and her captain not only offered hospitality to the Lindberghs —the first time a woman had ever slept aboard the ship—but hauled their plane aboard each night to protect it from the racing river current.

But putting it back in the water ended in disaster. The plane strained against the pulleys as it touched the water, was swung around by the current, tipped, and began to turn over. Both the Lindberghs were in their cockpits.

"Jump. Jump quickly!" cried Charles.

Obedient as a Chinese wife, without hesitation Anne went overboard. Her husband waited long enough to see her into the water, then jumped too, and came up to see, as he described it later, "Little Anne Pan, perfectly happy paddling along like a little mud turtle." They swam around until a tender picked them up and took them aboard the *Hermes*, where she was hurried down to drink Bovril and hot brandy and castor oil against the Yangtze's germs. Charles Lindbergh remained on deck to supervise the rescue of the craft. But *Sirius* had been badly damaged, and would fly no more until repair work could be done. "How long will it take, and *when* will we get home?" was Anne Lindbergh's reaction. She had begun to be very homesick for her baby son, and wished their journey could end there and then.

She was granted her wish, but not without paying for it. A telegram arrived in Shanghai on October 5, 1931, from her mother informing her that Dwight Morrow had died from a cerebral hemorrhage. The news of his death had caused something of a shock in the United States, where his stature had been building over the years. Many thought he would be the Republican presidential nominee at the next election in 1932, and that he would win. Radio programs throughout the United States were interrupted to announce his death, and it was a large front-page news item in the New York *Times*.

Morrow's passing seemed to take the heart out of Anne Lindbergh, and her husband sensed that she would be a burden rather than a help-mate if the journey continued. He told her he was canceling the rest of the voyage. He ordered the *Sirius* shipped back to San Francisco, and booked passages for themselves on the first, and fastest, ship sailing back to the United States.

"Oh, my fat lamb!" cried Anne Lindbergh when she saw her son, Charles, for the first time since leaving him in his nurse's arms the previous July.

He had grown twice as big, had developed a gibberish language of his own, and said "Den!" ("Again!") when his father flung him into the air and caught him. Charles Lindbergh was a very Swedish father in his reluctance to talk about his son, and he took some coaxing before he would admit even to his wife that he was "good-looking" or "a pretty interesting kid." It was almost as if he felt he would be tempting fate by acknowledging out loud the pleasure and pride he felt in him.

He called him Buster.

The Lindberghs had moved into their new home near Hopewell, in South Jersey, early in February 1932. Charles Lindbergh had found the site after examining it closely from the air, and had picked it for its isolation and the nature of its terrain. There were swamps and scant, infertile grassland to the south, difficult hill country to the north, and a single access-road, part of the estate, to the spot on Sourland Mountain where he decided to build. Yet Trenton, the New Jersey capital, was only fourteen miles away, Princeton was a twenty-minute drive, and New York a little over an hour and a half by car. Downhill, just short of the woods, was a field long enough to be used as a landing ground for his plane.

The house was not up to Guggenheim or Morrow standards, but it was large enough: a brick, white-painted villa with ten rooms and a separate wing to house the servants. These consisted of an English couple, Oliver and Elsie Whately, who acted as butler and cook-housekeeper, and a Scots nursemaid, Betty Gow, all three of whom had been carefully vetted for character, temperament, and reliability before being given employment.

She never said so, but one suspects that Anne Lindbergh never really liked the house or its situation, even before the blight of tragedy struck it. In appearance it was charmless, and there was nothing in the setting to lift the heart. Its chief merit seemed to be that it sat in five hundred acres of countryside whose nature repelled intruders, and therefore felt safe. She was in psychological need of a haven at this time, because she had passed a trying winter suffering from off-and-on bouts of a kind of ptomaine poisoning which had brought her physically and spiritually low. The sudden death of her beloved father had dealt her a heavy blow, and she was troubled by the melancholy condition of her mother, for whom Dwight Morrow's death was proving a profoundly distressing loss.

The doctors had confirmed that Anne Lindbergh was pregnant again, but for the time being the knowledge of it did nothing to cheer her up, only to make her glad that they had found a safe-feeling nest in which to await the baby's arrival. Again, she never said so, but again one suspects that she would have preferred to stay on in the old nest—the Morrow house at Englewood—for she still regarded it as her real home.

As it was, the Lindberghs spent their weekdays at Englewood and left their nursemaid, Betty Gow, in permanent residence there. Only at weekends did they go down to the new house at Hopewell, leaving Betty Gow behind. Anne Lindbergh looked after her fat lamb herself, and Oliver and Elsie Whately looked after the cooking and household chores. It was a regular routine—weekdays at the Morrow house, weekends at Hopewell—and it was one which anyone watching the Lindberghs' movements would or should have known about.

On the last weekend in February 1932, however, the Lindberghs decided to make a last-moment change in their routine, which was to have tragic consequences. All three, father, mother, and son, were suffering from colds, and though Charles Lindbergh laughed off his own and went off to New York as usual on Monday morning, February 29, he gestured at the rain sheeting across Sourland Mountain and suggested that it was no day for a sniffly mother and child to take to the road.

Anne Lindbergh agreed to put off for a day their departure for Englewood, and telephoned her mother and Betty Gow to tell them so. On Tuesday morning, March 1, the weather was still cold, wet, and blustery, and though the fat lamb's temperature had gone down, once more Charles Lindbergh advised against moving.

"Let's give Buster another day indoors," he said.

This time, when Anne Lindbergh telephoned, she suggested that Betty Gow come over to Hopewell to join her and help with the child, and the nursemaid arrived later in the morning, having been driven over by one of the Morrow chauffeurs. By that time, the baby was completely recovered and they decided that they would all go over to Englewood the following morning, Wednesday, March 2.

At 7:30 on the Tuesday evening, Anne Lindbergh and Betty Gow helped to put the baby to bed in his crib in the nursery on the southeast second-floor corner of the house, and closed and bolted all the shutters except on one window, where they were warped and refused to close. Then the mother went downstairs to await Charles Lindbergh's return from New York, while the nursemaid stayed upstairs to clean the bathroom and wait until she was sure the child had gone to sleep. She went down to supper just before eight o'clock with the Whatelys in the kitchen, on the opposite side of the house.

It was not until 8:20 that the honk of a horn announced that Charles Lindbergh was on his way up the private lane to the house. He went upstairs to wash his hands in the bathroom next to the baby's room, but, probably because he was late and supper was waiting, he did not look in on his son. Instead, he came downstairs again and they ate until 9:10 before a blazing fire. The wind was still blowing hard outside, but at one moment Lindbergh's head went up like a hunting dog's and he said:

"What was that?"

It was a sound, he afterward said, like an orange crate smashing. But there was no other strange noise, and it went out of his mind.

At 9:10 both Lindberghs went upstairs and Charles went into the bathroom and took a quick bath, afterward going down to his study, which was directly under the child's nursery. Anne Lindbergh stayed in her room. At ten o'clock Betty Gow went to the nursery. She did not put on the light, but instead left the door to the corridor open to enable her to see. She plugged in the electric heater to warm the room and her hands, because she intended to pick the child up and take him to his mother, and didn't want to startle him with her cold fingers.

Waiting there in the semidarkness, she became conscious of something missing about the atmosphere of the room, and gradually realized that she could not hear the child's breathing. She went to the crib. It was empty.

She was not alarmed so far. She walked down the corridor to the Lindberghs' bedroom and, knocking on the door, entered.

"Mrs. Lindbergh, do you have the baby?" Betty Gow asked.

"Why, no," said Anne Lindbergh, with some surprise. "I don't have him."

"Where is the colonel?" asked the nurse. "He may have him. Where is he?"

"Downstairs in the library," said Anne.

Had Lindbergh taken the baby away without telling them, one of his practical jokes? Betty Gow raced downstairs and burst into the study, where she found him at his desk.

"Colonel," she said out of breath, "do you have the baby?"

He looked up, startled. "No. Isn't he in his crib?"

"No," said Betty Gow.

He rushed past her and bounded upstairs to the nursery. Anne Lindbergh had already been there, made a hasty search, and then returned to her bedroom. Now Lindbergh himself looked in the crib. The imprint of the child's body was still on the bedclothes and pillow. The sheets with two large safety pins to fasten him in were undisturbed, which meant that he could not have left the crib by crawling out himself.

They hurried into the other rooms, just in case. He was not there.

Lindbergh went into his bedroom and took a Springfield rifle out of the closet, and went back to the nursery, his wife nervously following. There was a note on the window sill in an envelope, but he did not see it for the moment; and even when he did, he did not open it, preferring to leave it for police experts to examine for fingerprints.

In any case, he did not need to know what was in it, for he could guess. The Lindberghs had sometimes talked about the worst thing that could happen to them, and knew that they were most vulnerable through their child. Now it had come to pass.

"Anne," Charles Lindbergh said, "they have stolen our baby."

"It *isn't possible,*" Anne Lindbergh said.

"It seems to be," Lindbergh said bitterly.

In fact, "they" had done worse than steal the child. "They" had murdered him. At that moment the naked body of Buster, the fat lamb, was lying in a wood a mile down the mountainside, his head crushed in. He would lie there for another seventy-two days before anyone found him.

"Now you will face a reality," Anne Lindbergh said to herself that night. "You've lived in a smooth world of unrealities so far, but you've come up against it now."

But neither she nor her husband could have guessed just how bad it was going to be.

This book is the study of the lives of two people and not a rehash of the Lindbergh kidnaping, and it will be dealt with here only insofar as it made its impact upon them. Those who wish to read a detailed account of the crime will find a dozen books which deal with it—and there will be more.

My interest is what it did to Charles and Anne Lindbergh, how the pain of it changed their natures, shaped their future attitudes, explained the people they became from now on.

We live in a world which has become inured to the cruelty of man to man, but some of the degradations and deliberate tortures which the Lindberghs had to suffer in the aftermath of their son's disappearance are of a particularity. They pierce the protective skin we have all grown and make one wince with retrospective shame, for the way in which men can behave.

It was not the press this time against which Charles Lindbergh had cause for complaint. The kidnaping was the biggest story American newspapers have ever had to handle, and on the whole they acquitted themselves well. The fame of the parents of the victim was such that readers demanded news of the search for the missing child even when there was none to be had, and there were times when some of the tabloid newspapers in New York, Chicago, and other big cities came out with accounts (usually under the headlines: LINDY'S BABE FOUND or BLOOD MONEY PAID, TOT RELEASED) which were patently manufactured solely to sell newspapers.† But Charles Lindbergh discovered that when he asked for the help of reporters or newspapers in withholding items which might have hampered negotiations with the men he believed were holding his child, they co-operated willingly. He invited them into the Hopewell house in the first few hours after the kidnaping and talked freely to them, and they respected his confidence when he told them that this or that was off the record. At one point, when their constant presence in the house and grounds threatened to interfere with police operations, he asked them to retire to Trenton and get their information from headquarters there, and they withdrew without complaint. It was as if the very dreadfulness of the crime had effected a reconciliation between the hero and the media, as a war unites a nation and a death heals rifts in families. It would not last, but for a time they worked together.

The villains on this occasion were not newspapers but people, and not just the perpetrator or perpetrators of the crime, either. The envelope on the window sill of the nursery which Lindbergh had refrained from opening because of fingerprints‡ contained a ransom note, and it was followed by others. A go-between in the person of a redoubtable character named John F. Condon was appointed to contact the kidnaper and make arrangements for paying the ransom, and he soon had good reason to believe he was in touch with the criminal. A young man who talked with a heavy German accent kept a rendezvous with him, and finally produced Charles Lindbergh, Jr.'s, sleep suit which he had worn on the night of the kidnaping. It had been freshly laundered, which might have warned the Lindberghs of what was coming.

With this and other evidence to convince them, and with assurances from the kidnaper that the child would be delivered the moment the

† Circulations of U.S. newspapers went up an average of 20 per cent in the three weeks after the kidnaping.
‡ There were none. The kidnaper wore gloves.

money was handed over, $50,000 was collected and delivered by Condon to a man waiting behind a tombstone in St. Raymond's Cemetery in the Bronx, while Charles Lindbergh waited in the car and listened to the kidnaper calling out to the go-between. "Hey, Doktor," the man shouted, and Lindbergh would never forget the voice.

They received in return a handwritten note saying:

> the boy is on Boad Nelly. it is a small Boad 28 feet long. two persons are on the Boad. they are innocent. you will find the Boad between Horseneck Beach and Gay Head near Elizabeth Island.*

Overjoyed, certain that the baby would soon be released, Lindbergh flew a plane over the areas off Long Island mentioned in the note in search of the *Boad Nelly*. Of course there was no such boat and the child was already dead.

This was cruel enough, but at least the kidnaper was covering up his traces, trying to throw them off the scent.

There were others with not even this motivation. Of the 38,000 letters which were written to the Lindberghs after the kidnaping, just over half offered their sympathy or sympathetic suggestions. Twelve thousand used the occasion to send in long scrawls about their dreams and nightmares. Five thousand were from cranks who wrote in to crow over the misery of the Lindberghs and say that it was the wrath of God and a just punishment for the sins of pride, arrogance, and affluence. They were supplemented by others who sometimes found the private number of their telephone, who called in the night to say they had the child, or knew where it was, and then would jeer and cackle and mouth obscenities.

Some quite well known politicians and film stars decided that there was good publicity to be made out of the crime, and announced that they were coming to Hopewell with important clues. Then they would pronounce empty nonsense in front of the reporters and demand to be photographed with "those poor unfortunate Lindberghs, just to show the world how much we sympathize."

There were the gangsters who persuaded both Lindbergh and his friend and attorney, Colonel Henry Breckenridge, that they knew which mob was holding the stolen child, and were brought into the household to talk to Anne Lindbergh about their "negotiations." Their glibness fooled her by their seeming genuineness. ("Isn't it strange,"

---

* This was typical of the poor English in which all the ransom notes were written. It was to be a principal point of evidence at the trial of the kidnaper.

she wrote to her mother-in-law, "they showed more sincerity in their sympathy than a lot of politicians who've been here.") In Leavenworth Prison, where he was serving a sentence for income tax evasion, the Chicago gangster Al Capone announced that he could get the baby back from the mobsters, at a price. Lindbergh was tempted to go to Washington to argue for Capone's pardon in return for his child.

There was an ex-operator from the Department of Justice who, because of his background, aroused high hopes when he announced that he could retrieve the baby. His name was Gaston B. Means and what did not emerge until too late was that his background also included a long list of convictions for fraud. He had got his hands on $100,000 from gullible sympathizers before it was realized that he was a trickster.

But the worst pain of all was caused by a Virginia boat-builder called John Hughes Curtis who seemed public-spirited, sympathetic, high-minded enough to be genuinely eager to help. He succeeded in convincing Charles Lindbergh that through his rum-running connections—Prohibition was still in force in the United States—he had come across the seaman of a vessel where Charles Lindbergh, Jr., was being held. His stories were so sincere-sounding that for three whole weeks he kept Anne and Charles Lindbergh feverish with hope. Every day, Lindbergh would set off to sea with Curtis in a hired boat for a rendezvous with the ship holding his child, and every night Curtis would convince him that because of bad weather or crossed signals, something had gone wrong and they must wait until the morrow.

He was still at sea, still searching for the mythical kidnap ship, when a message came through that Charles Lindbergh, Jr.'s, body had been found, in the woods near Hopewell. The egregious Curtis broke down into floods of tears and confessed that his story had been a tissue of lies from start to finish. He had done it because he wanted to "become famous," he said, and threw himself on Lindbergh's mercy.

"Filth," said Lindbergh, and backed away when he tried to take his hand.

Early on the morning of May 12, 1932, a truck driver stopped on the Hopewell-Princeton road and went into the woods to relieve himself. As he was standing he noticed what seemed to be a shallow grave, and stirred it with his foot. A child's hand was laid bare. He removed enough earth to reveal the body.

The dead child was taken to a funeral home at Trenton which also served as the county morgue, and that afternoon Betty Gow was driven over and identified the remains as those of Charles Augustus Lindbergh,

Jr. (Anne Lindbergh and her mother-in-law, Evangeline, who was now with her, were called by the police but told they need not come.)

Charles Lindbergh arrived back at Hopewell the next day after the last of his agonizing journeys out to sea with the unspeakable Curtis. With his attorney, Henry Breckenridge, he drove into Trenton and went into the morgue. Newspapermen earlier in the day had been told that he would not look at the body of his son, but when the time came he said to the policeman on duty:

"Take that off."

He gestured to the sheet covering the body.

He had already told Colonel Norman Schwarzkopf, the New Jersey State Police chief who was in charge of the investigations, that he could identify his child no matter what the condition of the body by studying its teeth.

"He stood silent, his head bowed, and a flush of reddening color climbed into his face," the New York *Times* reported next day.

" 'He examined the teeth carefully,' said Mr. Marshall [the policeman]. 'He also looked at the foot with the overlapping toes but expressed no opinion on that.'

"Marshall asked: 'Colonel Lindbergh, are you certain this is the body of your baby?'

" 'I'm perfectly satisfied this is my child,' Colonel Lindbergh replied.

"He turned and walked from the room in silence."

A gray hearse was waiting outside, and a few moments later the body was loaded into it and driven to the crematorium at Linden. Lindbergh and Breckenridge followed in their own car. A police car and reporters tagged on behind. Schwarzkopf was waiting for them at the crematorium, and he went in when the body was consigned to the flames at 6:15 P.M. But Lindbergh and Breckenridge remained behind in the superintendent's house, and did not emerge until it was over.

Then they were rejoined by Schwarzkopf, and in the gathering darkness they drove across the rolling South Jersey countryside back to Hopewell and Anne and Evangeline Lindbergh. It was several nights since Charles Lindbergh had slept, and Breckenridge was troubled by the unnatural brightness of his color and the fact that there was otherwise no sign of emotion. He was suppressing things, Breckenridge decided. His hands were steady and so was his voice when he spoke. He talked dispassionately about the crime to Schwarzkopf, and did not react when the police chief hazarded a guess that something had gone wrong, that the baby had not been intentionally murdered.

With Anne Lindbergh he was gentle and understanding, and afterward she described him as "a wall to lean on." He talked "beautifully of death" to her and tried to persuade her that not every trace of their child was gone, that somewhere around them a spark of him remained.

"Immortality perhaps for the spark of life," she wrote bitterly in her diary, "but not for what made up my little boy."

Through the torpid, cushioning effect of her pregnancy, she was troubled about her husband's mental and emotional condition. She sensed the difference between her grief and his, for she had the fat lamb's physical attributes to remember, whereas Charles Lindbergh's was a deeper feeling for his son, "it reaches further into the future." How could the terrible void be filled? He urged her to think of nothing but the baby she was soon to bear, while at the same time *his* thoughts seemed now to be filled with nothing except helping the police track down the killer or killers of his son.

Ever since the first day of the kidnaping, the place had been filled with policemen. They had made their headquarters in the garage and wandered in and out of the house. Now that they knew the child was dead, Anne Lindbergh was more aware of their presence than ever. There were conferences at all hours of the day and night, in all of which Charles Lindbergh took part—as if he had become part of the team.

She could not see why they went on talking so much. What difference did it make now? The baby was dead.

Well, yes, she did see that there were the criminals to be apprehended, but what had that to do with Charles and herself? Why was Charles so anxious to reconstruct exactly how it had happened, to track down the murderers? If she didn't want to get any nearer to his killers, to see their terrible faces, the weapon they killed him with, the place where he was killed, why must her husband be gripped by the obsession?

It was true that Charles Lindbergh was now obsessed with knowing.

"A few days after the discovery of the baby's body, we decided to do a reconstruction of the kidnaping," said Colonel Schwarzkopf. "We had had an exact duplicate of the kidnap ladder made and this we placed up against the nursery window at Hopewell, and sent a cop up it to simulate the kidnaper. We put a bundle about the same weight as the baby in the crib, and our man carried the burlap bag we had found near the grave in the woods. He went up the ladder, put the bundle from the crib in the bag, came out again—and dropped the bag as he slipped on the ladder. After about three attempts, we had a discussion to try to work out what had happened."

They figured out that the kidnaper gagged or chloroformed the baby before he slipped it out of the crib and put it into the burlap bag, and that when he was climbing back onto the ladder a rung broke and he slipped. The man dropped the bag, and the baby's head struck the cement window ledge. He did not know at first how serious the injury was, because the child, being gagged or unconscious, could not cry out. When he saw blood seeping through the bag, however, he stopped at a place where there was water (this was where the child's thumb guard was found) and used the child's sleeping suit to bathe away the blood (which was why it was presented freshly laundered to the go-between, John F. Condon). When the kidnaper found the baby was dead, he buried it in the first remote place he could find.

Schwarzkopf said that Lindbergh not only watched the reconstruction with riveted attention but took an active part in the discussion afterward. He was full of it when he talked to his wife later. His mind "works on it incessantly," she wrote worriedly in her diary later. But she was nauseated by this grisly post-mortem activity. Surely decent grief, no matter how great, was better than this twisted, continuous wallowing in horror. With the baby stirring in her belly, she felt the need to build forward instead of backward.

"I feel as if it were a poison working in my system, this idea of the crime," she wrote. "How deep will it eat into our lives?"

CHAPTER

FOURTEEN

LOST FAITH

On August 16, 1932, Anne Morrow Lindbergh gave birth to her second child in her mother's apartment at 4 East Sixty-sixth Street, in New York City. The baby was a healthy boy weighing seven pounds fourteen ounces, and those—including his parents—who had feared the ordeal of the past few months might have harmed him were relieved to hear the doctor pronounce him perfect in every way.

Charles Lindbergh had hoped for a girl this time and had already chosen Anne for the baby's name. In the circumstances, should they now call him Andy? In the end they called him Jon,* though for the moment Anne Lindbergh preferred to refer to him as "my rabbit" and had to be chided by her husband that she would wear him out by looking at him so much.

The question was where to live and bring him up. Immediately after the birth, Charles Lindbergh issued a statement to the newspapers with which he hoped to persuade press and public to douse, at least for the time being, the blaze of publicity in which they had been living ever since their kidnaped child's body had been discovered:

> Mrs. Lindbergh and I have made our home in New Jersey. It is natural that we should wish to continue to live there near our friends and interests. Obviously, however, it is impossible for us to subject the life of our second son to the publicity which we feel was in large measure responsible for the death of our first. We feel that our children have the right to

---

* Though not until two months after his birth. The child was first registered without a name.

grow up normally with other children. Continued publicity will make this impossible. I am appealing to the Press to permit our children to live the lives of normal Americans.

By this time the whole nation (and, it might be said, most of the civilized world) felt the deepest sympathy for the Lindberghs, and were eager and anxious to let them know how deeply they felt for them in their sorrow. Americans are not a silent or a discreet people, and when they feel they show. The letters that poured into the newspapers, and into Hopewell post office, were almost entirely from people who wished them well. The visitors who came to gawk at the house quite often had tears in their eyes as they gazed at the place where the dead baby had lived. The newspaper articles were mawkish and sentimental, but they answered a need.

In their condition, the Lindberghs were in no mood to appreciate this. To them, sight-seers were a menace, publicity killed babies. That summer they were hurt when one of their best friends, Harry Guggenheim, gently suggested to them that they must learn to live with the press and public fame.

"As long as you do anything constructive all your life, you will have to meet it, you can't get away from it," he said. "The only thing to do is to change your whole attitude. Conquer it *inside* of you, get so you don't mind. You've got to stop fighting it, stop trying to get away from it."

Charles Lindbergh blurted out that he didn't mind what the newspapers said about him; it was their reporters and photographers, the physical presence of them on his doorstep, the flash bulbs exploding in his face, which shredded his nerves.

All right, said Anne Lindbergh, let's say we do give in and allow them to intrude into our private lives—open our doors to them. *Will we have peace then?*

Guggenheim tried to explain that peace of the kind she was contemplating just wasn't possible for them. They were not that kind of people. So long as they led lives of achievement, people (and the press) would always be fascinated with them. The only way they could retire from the public eye was by becoming vegetables—and that they would never be able to do. They must learn to live with things as they were, newspapers as they functioned, people as they behaved.

They shook their heads angrily at him. They were "too sore and hurt" to argue, and even sage advice from a friend made them wince.

In the circumstances, it seemed to them that their only solution was to live in a state of siege. Charles Lindbergh was angry and resentful that such a thing should have to be. Anne Lindbergh sadly realized that, since the fat lamb's death, they had lost their faith in the world. Other people who had had dreadful things happen to them had come to terms with life as it had treated them, and still felt the ground beneath to be solid enough to tread without fear. But she and her husband would never feel secure again. They were no longer in the world but surrounded by it, and it was menacing.

Some weeks before Jon's birth, Charles Lindbergh went to see a well-known breeder and trainer of German shepherd dogs, named Joseph Weber. He produced a handsome and enormous German shepherd which was partly trained, and said that the Lindberghs could turn him into an obedient guard dog within a couple of weeks. So Thor came into their lives. He proved to be a one-man palace guard on four legs, and a light in their lives.

Lindbergh trained Thor to open and close doors on command, to take Anne by the wrist and lead her upstairs or into the kitchen to get milk, to take the terriers for a walk on a leash, to take messages between master and mistress, to retrieve objects, leap mighty fences, to watch over them while walking, swimming, eating, or sleeping, to take his orders in a whisper.

"Thor is as different from most dogs," Harold Nicolson wrote later, "as a turbot is from a performing sealion."

He soon came to adore Anne Lindbergh and she came first for him always before her husband. It was soon one of the sights to watch him on shore when she was swimming in the sea. Thor would wait until he considered she had swum long enough, and then he would plunge into the water, swim out to her, brandish his tail in her face until she grabbed it, and then drag her by it back to the shore. He was ready to maul anyone who was not approved by his owners, and he became fiercely protective of the baby.

It had been intended originally that Thor would be their bodyguard when they took up residence once again in the house at Hopewell, but in fact the Lindberghs never went back to it for more than odd visits after the birth of Jon. They told themselves that it was because of the ghoulish sight-seers who came around at weekends, but the truth was that for Anne Lindbergh the house was blighted, and she shivered at the thought of passing another winter in it. Instead, they went back to Mother, and moved into Next Day Hill at Englewood, where there were guards on the gate, plenty of servants, and Thor ready to rend intruders.†

† The Hopewell property was donated to the state of New Jersey as a children's home.

Nevertheless, it was a mistaken move, as Anne Lindbergh soon discovered. Her husband had been deeply scarred by the kidnaping and its concomitant horrors, and the last vestige of boyishness had gone out of him. One day when he was playing tennis at the Guggenheims, she caught a smile crossing his sunburned face and realized that it was the first time he had looked like that, happy, relaxed, youthful, since their honeymoon. And it did not last.

Now that the search for his baby's kidnaper seemed for the moment to have run into the ground, Lindbergh had abandoned his feverish zeal for the hunt and turned back to his normal preoccupations. He was working at the Rockefeller Institute with Dr. Alexis Carrel on a blood pump for an artificial heart. He was plotting new routes for Transcontinental Air Transport and Pan American Airways.

But in between, as she soon realized, but from apathy did nothing about, he needed desperately the healing balm of a private life where he could relax with her and the baby and feel easy again. This was denied him. At Next Day Hill this was impossible.

The house at Englewood had been built as the home and headquarters of a national statesman. It was created to further Dwight Morrow's career as a senator and (if he had not died too soon) potential President, a place where the highest in the land could come and talk politics and high finance. With Morrow's death, it was in danger of becoming something of an anachronism, with its vast grounds, its salons, its huge staff, especially in the austerity regime which had come into being with the advent of Franklin D. Roosevelt to his first presidential term.

But Dwight Morrow's widow, Elizabeth, was determined that the house should live on, though its raison d'être had died. She was a gregarious and indefatigable woman, and she needed life and movement around her to give her something to comfort her in the aftermath of her husband's death. So she filled the house every day and every evening with visitors, women's committees, charities, children's programs, refugee projects, bridge parties.

More important than that, she drew Anne Lindbergh into her orbit and seemed to assume that it was just like it had been in the old days, when she was an unmarried daughter living at home. Her daughter had come back. Though she resisted, it was impossible for her not to get involved to some extent, and in her moral and physical weakness, Anne Lindbergh could not entirely fight her mother's influence though resenting it. It was too difficult and too hurting to explain to her mother that she was now a married woman and emancipated.

So there were inevitably times when Charles Lindbergh felt himself frozen out by the family circle, apt to come home and find his wife in another part of the house, instead of in their quarters waiting for him. And when he went in search of her, he was always running into blue-rinsed ladies who dimpled at the sight of him and drove him crazy with their cooing shouts of "Oh, Colonel Lindbergh!" It was soon for him what Anne Lindbergh later described as "an exacerbating situation," and the environment brought him no peace at the very time when he was most in need of it.

Fortunately for their relationship, and for Anne Lindbergh's mental stability—for she came close to a nervous breakdown around this time—there was the air through which they could fly, alone together, free from outside interference. In the spring of 1933, they took off in the *Sirius* for a transcontinental flight to Los Angeles and back to check a route for Transcontinental Air Transport's new cargo plane service.

That summer they embarked on their most elaborate and important survey flight of all. For Pan American Airways they left in the same plane for Greenland, Iceland, Scandinavia, Russia, and Britain to plot a new transatlantic passenger route, and then flew south to Spain, down to West Africa, back across the Atlantic to Brazil, and then by way of the Caribbean to Miami and New York. It was a fantastic voyage for those days, and it included every kind of hazard from ice floes and blizzards to sandstorms and tropical hurricanes. Anne Lindbergh's skill as a navigator and radio operator was taxed to the utmost, and her proudest moment was hearing the comment of a Pan American radio operator who, "after sending me a 150 word code through heavy static, made the astonished remark: 'My God, she got it!' "

Their voyage opened up the Atlantic to the prospect of a regular passenger service and provided the scientific data upon which Pan American Airways could plan one. It was one more "first" in the history of aviation associated with the Lindbergh name. When their plane, now named *Tingmassartoq*,‡ touched down at Miami on December 16, 1933, they found a message awaiting them from the White House:

COLONEL AND MRS C A LINDBERGH
WELCOME HOME AND CONGRATULATIONS UPON THE SUCCESSFUL
COMPLETION OF THIS ANOTHER FLIGHT MADE BY YOU IN THE IN-
TEREST AND FOR THE PROMOTION OF AMERICAN AVIATION STOP I
HOPE THAT OUT OF THE SURVEY YOU HAVE MADE NEW AND VALUA-

‡ Eskimo for "the one who flies like a big bird." An Eskimo boy had painted the name on the *Sirius* at an Arctic stop and they kept it.

BLE PRACTICAL AIDS TO AIR TRANSPORTATION WILL COME STOP
FRANKLIN D ROOSEVELT

They replied:

THE PRESIDENT
THANK YOU VERY MUCH FOR YOUR MESSAGE STOP OUR TRIP HAS
MADE US MORE CONFIDENT THAN EVER OF THE FEASIBILITY OF
ESTABLISHING REGULAR TRANSATLANTIC AIRLINES IN THE NEAR
FUTURE STOP ANNE LINDBERGH CHARLES LINDBERGH

It was to be the last time President Roosevelt and the Lindberghs
would exchange cordialities. Soon they would be involved in an acerbic
controversy that would initiate a lifelong enmity between them.

They had been away for five and a half months, and though the
sheer concentration of it, the daily fears and strains, the living from
hour to hour, had been good for Anne Lindbergh, the voyage had also
deprived her of her baby and she was desperate to get back to him. The
idea was to find an apartment in New York, spend less time at Englewood, have the courage to resist maternal pressures, and "keep a peaceful home for C."

But almost at once C. was involved in his first clash with the
Roosevelt Administration, and that took them to Washington. Charles
Lindbergh was concerned about what the President was doing to the
U.S. airmail service, which, because of his pioneer days flying the mail
between St. Louis and Chicago, would always be something dear to his
heart. He was prepared to take on Franklin D. Roosevelt himself in defense of it; and his eagerness was not lessened by the fact that in doing
so he would also be defending the Hoover Republicans he had helped
to get elected in 1928 and the big aviation interests for whom he
worked.

It so happened that during the lame-duck session of Congress which
had preceded President Roosevelt's inauguration in 1933 a senatorial
committee had been set up under the chairmanship of Senator Hugo
Black to investigate government subsidies paid to the merchant marine
for mail contracts. This did not reveal much headline-making material,
but when it was suggested that the investigation should be broadened
to include airmail contracts, Senator Black discovered a rich seam to
mine. Preliminary work had already been done for him, it turned out,

by a Hearst reporter named Fulton Lewis, Jr., who had uncovered some suspicious dealings between the government and the big air companies under the Hoover Administration, designed to squeeze small companies out of the airmail business. He had, for instance, discovered that the Post Office Department under Hoover's right-hand man, Postmaster General Walter F. Brown, had awarded a contract for the transport of airmail between New York and Washington to a big company at a rate three times as high as that proposed in a rejected bid from a much smaller company.

Fulton Lewis, Jr.'s, material had, so far, been suppressed by the Hearst organization, and it was handed on to Senator Black. He soon collected from the small air companies, smarting about the way they had been cut out of the mail business, additional material of a damaging nature.

"As Black patiently reconstructed the story," writes Arthur M. Schlesinger, Jr., "a dismally familiar picture emerged—immense salaries, bonuses, and speculative profits; dubious relations between the industry and the government officials who dealt with it; the avoidance of competitive bidding; the covert destruction of official records—all in all, an exceptionally blatant case it seemed, of an industry using government to exploit the public."*

The Black committee was soon making the headlines it had missed during the maritime mail investigations. There was evidence of a secret meeting in the Post Office Department in 1930 between Postmaster General Brown and the big aviation holding companies—all small companies were excluded—from which three big companies emerged with twenty-four out of twenty-seven federal airmail contracts. Brown himself was discovered to have destroyed several documents relating to other government-big business deals.

And soon the names of well-known people began to be mentioned at the hearings as those who seemed to have benefited unduly from the generosity of the big aviation interests. One of them was Charles Lindbergh. It was claimed that he had received a "gift" of $250,000 from Transcontinental Air Transport (which was vitally interested in airmail contracts) on joining the company, and it was inferred that his friendship with President Herbert Hoover could have been of great use to a company seeking contracts.

Lindbergh reacted to these insinuations with indignation. After consulting his friend and attorney, Henry Breckenridge, he sent a telegram

* *The Coming of the New Deal* (Boston: Houghton Mifflin, 1958).

to the Black committee on January 10, 1934, saying that his financial records had been placed at their disposal:

YOU ARE NOW IN POSSESSION OF A COMPLETE RECORD OF MY FI-
NANCIAL TRANSACTIONS IN REGARD TO AVIATION STOP IF THERE IS
ANY QUESTION REGARDING THESE TRANSACTIONS I AM AVAILABLE
AT ANY TIME TO CLARIFY THEM.

The New York *Times* reported next morning:

The colonel is known to resent an interpretation which grew out of a hearing Wednesday that he had received a "gift" of 25,000 shares in Transcontinental then worth $250,000. Stock which he received from Transcontinental should in no sense be considered as a gift, but as part of the payment to Colonel Lindbergh for accepting the post of technical adviser to the airline, which at that time held no airmail contract with the government."

The following day, the Black committee formally read into the record two letters which threw some interesting light on Lindbergh's financial status in the months following his transatlantic flight. Both came from C. M. Keys, president of Transcontinental Air Transport. They were both addressed to Colonel Charles A. Lindbergh care of the Daniel Guggenheim Fund for the Promotion of Aeronautics, 598 Madison Avenue, New York City. The first, dated June 6, 1928, read:

Dear Colonel Lindbergh:
Carrying out the Memorandum of Agreement, I have tied up for your account twenty-five thousand shares of stock of the Transcontinental Air Transport Inc. at ten dollars a share, and will deliver to you a check of the Transcontinental Air Transport Inc. for two hundred and fifty thousand dollars cash upon your request. All the records shall be clear for income tax purposes. Please consult Colonel Breckenridge and see if he agrees with the following procedure:
1) I will deliver to you the check for two hundred and fifty thousand dollars cash together with a brief memorandum showing exactly what it is for, which memorandum Mr. Couthell [TAT's accountant] and Colonel Breckenridge should prepare.
2) I will deliver to you certificate for twenty-five thousand

shares of stock and receive back either the Transcontinental Air Transport check or your personal check as Colonel Breckenridge and Mr. Couthell may advise.

3) This will complete the first part of our trade and will leave you with the stock in your possession.

I suggest you do not put very much of this stock in your own name because when you sell it—and I hope you will sell part of it on the first favorable opportunity—either the delivery of the stock in your own name or the transfer of it on the books would excite a lot of attention, which is quite unnecessary.

Colonel Breckenridge will no doubt agree to this advice.

Sincerely, C. M. Keys, President, Transcontinental Air Transport.

This was followed by a letter dated June 7, 1928:

My dear Colonel Lindbergh:

This will confirm agreement with you of yesterday as follows:

The Transcontinental Air Transport Inc. will pay you in cash the sum of two hundred and fifty thousand dollars. As a member of the underwriting committee of this company, I will forthwith sell to you twenty-five thousand dollars worth of shares of this company at ten dollars a share.

Both the cash payment above referred to and the delivery of the stock will be made immediately after June 1 when the company's stock is delivered. In addition, the Transcontinental Air Transport Inc. will give you a firm option on twenty-five thousand additional shares of the stock of the company at ten dollars a share as follows: 5,000 shares on June 1, 1929, 10,000 shares on June 1, 1930, 10,000 shares on June 1, 1931. All these options will expire on June 1, 1931. The only condition of these options is that you are engaged in the business of the company at the time the options begin.

In addition, the company will pay you beginning June 1, 1928, 10,000 dollars a year in monthly payments. Your work for the company will be of a technical and advisory character. You will act as chairman of the Technical Committee, which will have under its immediate authority all matters concerning the choice of equipment.

You will not, until you express a desire to do so, become a director of the company. It is not my desire or intention, nor is it yours, that this work shall prevent you from carrying on other activities for the general advancement of aviation in which you have so deep an interest. Nor will it prevent you from carrying on other business activities not competitive with those of Transcontinental Air Transport Inc.

I think the above letter defines the subject matter of our agreement. If so, please let me know so that I can use a copy of this letter as a memorandum in the Board meetings of the Transcontinental Air Transport Inc. on Friday. Sincerely, C. M. Keys, President.

Neither of these letters, of course, constituted evidence of any kind of fraud, and so long as Charles Lindbergh could prove he had paid income tax on the considerable profits he had made out of the transaction,† there was nothing with which anyone could rebuke him. He had cashed in on his reputation to make the maximum possible amount of money from those who wished to employ his services, and no one would blame him for that.

But the correspondence and the publicity did tie in his interests with those of the big air combines, and there were many who now expected him to come forward to testify on their behalf. Lindbergh was too sage to fall into that trap. These were the days of the New Deal, when the Roosevelt regime was endeavoring through the National Recovery Administration to haul the nation out of the worst depression in its history. Millions of Americans were out of work and hungry, and big business was the villain of the day.

It was no time for a national hero to line himself up on the side of what Schlesinger called the "Wall Street escadrilles, formed less to fly planes than to kite securities." There was no doubt from the start that Charles Lindbergh was on their side against the Senate committee and the Administration, but for the moment they had no weapons with which to fight back against the charges against them. He must have known only too well that some of them had been guilty of racketeering, even if the culprits did not include his own company; and to appear as the industry spokesman at this stage would have tarred him with the same brush as the worst of them. So though he strongly resented the way in which his name had been introduced into the scandal, he had no wish to champion so compromised a cause.

And then President Roosevelt made an error.

By this time Senator Black had produced enough evidence for him to state:

† Which he did.

"The control of American aviation has been ruthlessly taken away from the men who fly and bestowed upon bankers, promoters and politicians, sitting in their inner offices, allotting among themselves the taxpayers' money."

He pleaded with the President to expose the racketeers to the people and bring the racket itself to an end. In the last week in January 1934 he went to the White House to lunch with the President, and Roosevelt asked him what the Administration could do. Black replied that the President and the Postmaster General had power to cancel contracts obtained by fraud or conspiracy. On February 8, Roosevelt asked Attorney General Homer Cummings to look into the matter. Next day Cummings reported that the evidence of fraud in the airmail contracts was sufficient to justify their cancellation.

Then the question of timing arose. In the opinion of the post office, cancellation of the contracts should be postponed until June 1, which would give them time to advertise for new bids. They would thus avoid an interruption of the airmail service. "As the President saw it, however," Schlesinger writes, "if the contracts were crooked, they ought to be cancelled forthwith. But what about the air mail service in the interim?"

This was where Roosevelt went wrong. An assistant postmaster general contacted General Benjamin D. Foulois, chief of the Army Air Corps, and asked him whether his pilots could take over the delivery of the mail. The Air Corps had not handled the mail since 1918, and a few inquiries would have made it clear that they were no longer equipped to do so. Nevertheless, Foulois gave a confident reply that his pilots could successfully take on the job.

Roosevelt was foolish enough to believe him. On February 9, 1934, he abruptly issued an order canceling the airmail contracts forthwith of all the aviation companies, and directing the Army Air Corps to carry the mail during the emergency.

He could not have chosen a worse time to do it. That February the weather was even worse than usual, and there were blizzards in the West, gales, sleet, fog, and intense cold in the Middle West and East. The army pilots were just not trained to cope with such conditions. Few of them had experience of night flying. None of them knew the transcontinental airmail routes. The planes were not equipped for blind flying.

Almost immediately, there was tragedy. One plane crashed in flames near Jerome, Idaho. Another, iced up, smashed into a mountain in Utah. An army seaplane tried to land in rough and freezing weather off

Rockaway Point and was smashed to pieces. At the end of the first week of operations, five pilots were dead, six were injured, and eight planes wrecked. There had never been such a sequence of airplane disasters in American history. Eddie Rickenbacker, the World War I ace, now chairman of Eastern Airlines, one of the disenfranchised lines, called the President's action "legalized murder."

Any experienced airline pilot could have told the President what was going to happen, and Charles Lindbergh had seen it from the start. He reacted immediately to the cancellation of the airmail contracts and sent off a telegram of protest to the President, on February 11, 1934, at the same time presenting a copy of it to the press.‡ He maintained from the start that he was acting solely as an individual and did not consult even his own air companies until his telegram was written; but whether he jumped forward of his own accord or was pushed by the aviation interests, they could not have asked for a better spokesman nor a better excuse for fighting back against their accusers. Lindbergh's telegram to the President read:

> YOUR ACTION YESTERDAY AFFECTS FUNDAMENTALLY THE IN-
> DUSTRY TO WHICH I HAVE DEVOTED THE LAST TWELVE YEARS OF
> MY LIFE. THEREFORE I RESPECTFULLY PRESENT TO YOU THE
> FOLLOWING: THE PERSONAL BUSINESS LIVES OF AMERICAN CITI-
> ZENS HAVE BEEN BUILT AROUND THE RIGHT TO JUST TRIAL BEFORE
> CONVICTION. YOUR ORDER OF CANCELLATION OF ALL AIRMAIL
> CONTRACTS CONDEMNS THE LARGEST PORTION OF OUR COMMER-
> CIAL AVIATION WITHOUT JUST TRIAL. . . . YOUR PRESENT
> ACTION DOES NOT DISCRIMINATE BETWEEN INNOCENCE AND GUILT
> AND PLACES NO PREMIUM ON HONEST BUSINESS. . . . THE CON-
> DEMNATION OF COMMERCIAL AVIATION BY CANCELLATION OF ALL
> AIRMAIL CONTRACTS AND THE USE OF THE ARMY ON COMMERCIAL
> AIRLINES WILL UNNECESSARILY AND GREATLY DAMAGE ALL
> AMERICAN AVIATION.

The entry of the popular hero into the arena immediately changed the controversy from a quarrel between the aviation companies and the Administration into a duel between Lindbergh and Roosevelt, and effectively drew the public's attention away from the racketeering aspects of the airmail contract situation.

Roosevelt made no formal reply to the Lindbergh telegram, but a

‡ As one editor said later: "He never has any objection to calling up the newspapers, he just doesn't like us calling up him."

Democratic senator, George Norris,* was quoted as saying: "Now Colonel Lindbergh is earning his $250,000." The President's secretary, Steve Early, complained that Lindbergh had released his telegram to the press without allowing the President the courtesy of seeing it first, and it was just a piece of publicity.†

It would have been an interesting fight between the two most famous men of their day. As Schlesinger remarked, it "might have presented many Americans with a hard choice," and even had the odds been equal the President could have been hard put to it to prevail against "Lindbergh's apparently invincible prestige."

In the event, the fight did not take place. Lindbergh had timed his intervention only too well, and, above all, knew that the Army Air Corps was simply not capable of taking the place of the aviation companies. As for Roosevelt, he quickly realized that he had made a serious error and took steps to get out of the hole he had dug for himself. He ordered Secretary of War George Dern to see that there were no more deaths in the Air Corps, and flights were cut back until the weather improved. Simultaneously, Roosevelt asked Congress to enact new legislation by which future airmail contracts would be awarded as a result of carefully scrutinized competitive bidding.

He also made a placatory move toward Lindbergh. He instructed Secretary Dern to invite him to serve on a War Department board to review the future training program of the Air Corps.

But Lindbergh refused to be mollified. He was antipathetic to the Administration's policies in general, as were most Republicans, and Roosevelt's activities in connection with the airmail contracts confirmed him in his suspicions of the architect of the New Deal. He consented to meet Dern for lunch in Washington and afterward had a conversation with one of his fellow-guests, General Douglas MacArthur. There is no record of the conversation, but it is not likely to have been friendly to Roosevelt. Afterward Lindbergh sent a telegram to Dern saying:

> I GREATLY APPRECIATE THE HONOR OF YOUR REQUEST I BECOME
> A MEMBER OF A SPECIAL COMMITTEE TO STUDY AND REPORT ON
> ARMY AVIATION IN RELATION TO NATIONAL DEFENSE. I WOULD OF
> COURSE BE GLAD TO CONTRIBUTE IN ANY WAY I CAN TO THE MAIN-
> TENANCE OF AN ADEQUATE NATIONAL DEFENSE. HOWEVER ACCORD-
> ING TO THE ANNOUNCEMENT BY THE WAR DEPARTMENT THIS COM-

---

* He was an old friend of Lindbergh's father and had fought with him to keep America out of World War I.

† "Of course it *was*—a public appeal for justice," commented Anne Lindbergh.

MITTEE IS TO STUDY AND REPORT ON THE PERFORMANCE OF THE
ARMY AIR CORPS IN ITS MISSION TO CARRY THE AIRMAIL BY
EXECUTIVE ORDER. I BELIEVE THAT THE USE OF THIS ARMY AIR
CORPS TO CARRY THE AIRMAIL WAS UNWARRANTED AND CON-
TRARY TO AMERICAN PRINCIPLES. THIS ACTION WAS UNJUST TO
THE AIRLINES WHOSE CONTRACTS WERE CANCELLED WITHOUT
TRIAL. IT WAS UNFAIR TO THE PERSONNEL OF THE ARMY AIR CORPS
WHO HAD NEITHER THE EQUIPMENT DESIGNED FOR THE PURPOSE
NOR ADEQUATE TIME FOR TRAINING IN A NEW FIELD. IT HAS UN-
NECESSARILY GREATLY DAMAGED ALL AMERICAN AVIATION. I DO
NOT FEEL I CAN SERVE ON A COMMITTEE WHOSE FUNCTION IT
IS TO ASSIST IN FOLLOWING OUT AN EXECUTIVE ORDER TO THE
ARMY TO TAKE OVER THE COMMERCIAL AIRMAIL SYSTEM WITHIN
THE UNITED STATES. CHARLES A. LINDBERGH.

It was a public slap in the face for the President, and Lindbergh gave
it an extra sting when he appeared a few days later before a post office
committee in Washington and once more attacked Roosevelt's action.
The room was packed with admirers, and, as the New York *Times* reported, "whenever his face flashed in the familiar, winsome smile a
murmur of approval ran through the hall."

Only one other flier of note came forward to rebut Lindbergh's
charges. General Billy Mitchell, a World War I ace who had campaigned over the years for a strengthening of U.S. air power, blamed
the private airlines rather than the Administration for the Air Corps'
failure.

"The United States could not use [the aviation companies'] radio
system nor their radio equipment nor their planes," he testified. "The
Army Air Corps, which was not properly equipped for any kind of duty,
due to the machinations of these aviation profiteers and servile politicians, undertook to carry the mail under these conditions."

He believed the right decision had been taken and that "although,
unfortunately, lives have been lost, I think we will be better for it in the
end," adding angrily: "If an army aviator can't fly a mail route in any
sort of weather, what would we do in a war?"

He lashed into the aviation companies and their spokesmen. "If the
Government spends money on aviation," he told the House committee,
"it should make sure that it gets the best results for that money, and
not allow that money to be handled principally for gambling on the
stock exchanges."

As for Lindbergh: "[He] has disclosed himself as the 'front man' of the Air Trust. . . . He is a commercial flier. His motive is principally profit."

It was good hard-hitting stuff, yet no match for Charles Lindbergh's personal prestige. No matter what evidence was produced, his standing with the public was so high that no one for a moment doubted the purity of his motives. As Schlesinger wrote:

"The fight dented the myth of Roosevelt's invulnerability and strengthened the business community's dislike of what it considered personal and arbitrary actions by the New Deal. It quickened the pace and intensity of criticism of the Administration. It had its effect too on personalities: it brought Hugo Black into new prominence . . . and uncovered in Charles Lindbergh a man who perhaps appealed to more American hearts than anyone save Franklin Roosevelt."

In a sense, though they did not know it yet, they were shaping up as rivals, and rivals who did not respect each other. Roosevelt considered that Lindbergh had unfairly used his fame to plead the cause of big business. Lindbergh (as he told Harold Nicolson shortly afterward) "loathes Roosevelt because of the latter's treatment of the airmail companies."

It was a mutual antipathy that would grow.

CHAPTER

FIFTEEN

ORDEAL BY

TRIAL

It was true that Charles Lindbergh had vested interests in the American aircraft industry, and they made him unabashedly in favor of private enterprise controlling the future of aeronautical developments in the nation. In the summer of 1934 he could more than justify his faith by what was happening in the air.

On August 1 he went aboard a new flying boat in the harbor at Bridgeport, Connecticut, and took over the controls. It was the first of several new "giant" Clippers which had been ordered by Pan American Airways for their Atlantic and South American air routes, and Lindbergh had helped draw up its specifications and sat in with its designer, Igor Sikorsky, from drawing board to launching. It was designed to carry thirty passengers and cruise for over a thousand miles, and that day he put it through its paces. Eight hours later all existing world records for transport seaplanes had been shattered, and Lindbergh had flown the Brazilian Clipper, as it had been named, 1,242.8 miles at an average speed of 157.5 miles an hour.

With a fleet of ships like this, the United States could at last begin to challenge the supremacy of its biggest competitor, Imperial Airways of Great Britain.

When he came ashore after the record-breaking flight, Lindbergh tried to slip away without speaking to the reporters who were waiting, insisting that all credit and publicity should go to Sikorsky, who had designed the Clipper, and F. W. Nielson, president of the company which had financed it. But the others insisted that he stay with them and talk. Since nearly all the reporters present were aviation writers, they confined their questions to planes and avoided personalities, and

Lindbergh was free and easy with them. He reminded them that not only had he broken records that day, but that the same evening a Douglas landplane would be flying the first of a regular overnight service between the Atlantic and Pacific oceans.

"These two developments," he said, "represent the greatest forward strides that have been made in aviation in any one period of time."

He had "got a big kick" out of ferrying the Clipper up and down the Atlantic coastline, but his day was really made when he was flying back in his own small plane to Englewood, New Jersey, and a fog rolled in over the Hudson Valley. It was too thick to hope to get through, so he came down low to look for a landing field. The only one that looked feasible was a patch of green pasture, and it was covered with browsing cattle. Lindbergh brought his craft down to treetop height and "buzzed" the nearby farmhouse until the farmer came out, and, with his hired man, drove the cows into the next field. The flier then slipped the plane down and brought it to a halt just short of a six-foot ditch.

"I thought the guy was going to kill himself," said the farmer, A. W. Douglas, "but when he hopped out of the cockpit he was grinning all over his face."

He liked running up against such emergencies in the air. As his wife had noticed, they seemed to rejuvenate and inspirit him, and it was as if they took him back to the days when he had been happiest, lolloping over the Middle Western plains in his old Jenny on a barnstorming tour. Aviation was growing up and becoming safe and dull, and flying was no longer an art. But occasionally the elements showed that they still had a bite left in them, and he relished the challenges they presented to his skill as a flier.

What made Anne Lindbergh marvel was that he was never afraid. They had been in some nasty situations together, and she confessed later that she was often miserably scared, whereas her husband emerged from them positively invigorated by the danger. One time, when he put down at last after getting them to their destination through a Wagnerian storm, he noticed that she was shaking with a mixture of fear and relief. He seemed surprised. He himself was positively radiant. He had grown stern and his face had a terrible maturity to it, though he was only thirty-three; but the battle with the elements seemed to have softened the lines and made him look boyish again.

He grinned at her. "You should have faith in me," he said. Then he paused and the grin and the boyish look disappeared. "I have faith in you," he added. "I just don't have any more faith in life."

17. After their first meeting and flight together, Henry Ford and Lindbergh became friends and mutual admirers. In 1942, after President Roosevelt refused to allow Lindbergh to rejoin USAAF and fight in World War II, Lindbergh went to work for Ford at his bomber plant at Willow Run. In this later picture, he is seen (second from left) when Igor Sikorsky presented his first helicopter to the Henry Ford Museum.

18. Lindbergh hated the attention of press photographers and refused to pose for them except in aid of causes in which he was interested. This one was taken by a long-distance lens at the end of a transcontinental flight.

19. During their courtship, Charles Lindbergh and Anne Morrow took secret flights together from the private airfield of a friend, Harry Guggenheim, at Falaise, Long Island. This, their engagement picture, was taken about this time. They were married on May 29, 1929.

20. Charles and Anne Morrow Lindbergh made many pioneering flights together, across the polar cap to China, across the Atlantic via Greenland, over the South Atlantic from Africa to Brazil. Here they are shown just before take-off on one of their flights together.

21. This picture of Charles Augustus Lindbergh, Jr., was taken on his first birthday, June 22, 1931, at the home of his grandmother, Mrs. Elizabeth Dwight Morrow, at Next Day Hill, Englewood, New Jersey. June 22 was also the birthday of Anne Morrow Lindbergh, the child's mother.

22. The Lindberghs moved into their new home, on Sourland Mountain, near Hopewell, New Jersey, in February 1932. They had chosen it for its isolation and difficulty of access for strangers. It was here, a month later, that their first child, Charles Augustus, Jr., was kidnaped.

In the fall of 1934 Anne Lindbergh thought she was pregnant again, and was disappointed when it proved to be a false alarm. Once upon a time she had been startled and somewhat dismayed when her husband had announced that he wanted a *large* family, and she confessed later that she had a sudden picture of herself as an Earth Mother, sitting on the porch of some Minnesotan log cabin and contemplating her flock, busily chopping down trees.

But now it was she who wanted to breed, to produce hostages to fortune, to prove through her own fecundity that the brutal death of one child could not scare her from producing more. In addition to which, she was afraid that just having one child would make him too precious. She tried to restrain herself, but "both losing a child and not having another tend to make me overloving." She did not despair. Better luck next time.

In September they flew out to California to stay with her sister Elisabeth and her new husband, at the ranch in Beverly Hills which Will Rogers* had lent them. The glowingly beautiful but doomed Elisabeth had met and fallen in love with a Welshman named Aubrey Morgan on a trip to Britain the previous year and had settled down to the life of a country hostess on his small estate near Cardiff (where his family owned a department store). But her physical condition rapidly deteriorated in the damp Welsh climate and she had been advised by her doctors to seek sunshine in California. Everyone pretended that she was getting along marvelously, but as she sat listlessly in the shade while they walked or played in the hot sunshine, it was obvious that fate had put a finger on her, and the appointment it signified was not very far away.

The Lindberghs had four days of perfect peace and privacy, and then the telephone rang. Colonel Norman Schwarzkopf was on the line. New York police had arrested a German-born Bronx carpenter named Bruno Richard Hauptmann for the kidnaping and murder of their baby. Proceedings would be begun at once in order to have him extradited to New Jersey and put on trial.† Colonel Lindbergh's testimony would be necessary at the extradition proceedings.

Charles Lindbergh broke the news to his wife and she said: "Oh, God, it's starting again."

"Yes," said Lindbergh grimly. "But they've got him at last."

* Will Rogers, the famous "cowboy philosopher," was an old Morrow friend and admirer of Lindbergh.

† At that time extradition proceedings were necessary between states even for federal crimes. But as a result of this case, Congress passed the so-called Lindbergh Law making them no longer necessary for kidnap and murder.

They started back at once and landed at West Trenton Airport, New Jersey, on September 5, and Schwarzkopf was waiting for them. Charles Lindbergh and the New Jersey police chief drove to the Bronx Courthouse together next morning for the extradition proceedings. Anne Lindbergh stayed at home at Englewood. Their names were in the headlines again and reporters were once more knocking at their door. In the circumstances, there was only one place where they could be sure of being safe and undisturbed, at Next Day Hill with her mother.

But Anne Lindbergh was dismally aware that it was very much like going back to the womb. A very busy womb, too.

This writer became aware during his researches into the background of Anne and Charles Lindbergh that there are many people who still believe that Bruno Richard Hauptmann, who was executed in the electric chair for the murder of their baby, did not in fact kill him. Books have been written and will go on being written to charge that the state executed the wrong man, that the crime was the work of a gang rather than a single individual, that there was conspiracy rather than pure chance behind the chain of events which led to the death of Charles Augustus Lindbergh, Jr.

It is no part of the purpose of this book to pursue these contentions, except insofar as they concern the Lindberghs. This is their story, not that of a crime or a trial.‡ It must be admitted, however, that for some time they also shared doubts about some aspects of Bruno Richard Hauptmann's guilt, or rather the exact nature of his involvement in the crime. From the beginning they found it difficult to believe that one man could have been responsible for the planning and execution of the kidnap, and assumed that it was a carefully plotted and well-rehearsed crime which went wrong at the last moment.

There were strong elements to bolster this belief, and the chief of these was timing. How could a German carpenter like Bruno Richard Hauptmann, living and working in the Bronx, with no apparent access to news of the movements of the Lindberghs, have possibly discovered that they were going to be in Hopewell on the night of the crime? Had they kept to their normal routine, they would have left for the Morrow home at Englewood thirty-six hours earlier. On Monday, because of the baby's cold, Anne Lindbergh postponed their departure until Tuesday. On Tuesday morning, and not until then, she put back their departure

‡ For those who are interested in these aspects, I would strongly recommend *Kidnap*, by George Waller (New York: Dial Press; London: Hamish Hamilton, 1961), for the narrative of the crime, and *The Trial of Bruno Richard Hauptmann*, ed. by Sidney B. Whipple (New York: Doubleday, Doran & Company, Inc., 1937), for a transcript of the proceedings.

for yet another twenty-four hours. How could a potential kidnaper find out about these last-minute decisions and plan his crime accordingly for Tuesday night, unless he had associates close to Anne Lindbergh who were keeping him in touch with her momentary decisions?

How could he have known that the Lindberghs and the baby would be there on Tuesday night when he arrived? How could he have known that there was a window in the nursery that would not close, that Charles Lindbergh would be late home from New York, that Anne Lindbergh would not go into the nursery to say good night to her son (as she usually did) just about the time when the kidnaper's ladder was placed against the nursery window?

As Anne Lindbergh remarked, it looked like "a well-made plan," and for a time both she and her husband had comforted themselves by thinking that it was a *professional* job and that the kidnapers would "want only the money and will not maliciously hurt the baby." That hope was shattered with the discovery of the body.

And then, as the evidence piled up against Hauptmann, they slowly began to accept that there really had been only one man concerned in the kidnaping and killing of their child. That made it harder to bear, because then *chance* came into it, and for the rest of their life they would be confronted by that most sterile occupation, saying to themselves: "If only. . . ."

"I feel as though I could hardly bear it," Anne Lindbergh told herself, as the realization flooded in on her. "I would rather believe in crueler mankind than in such a cruel god of chance—chance that we came down that weekend and without Skeean [their Scottie dog], chance that the baby caught cold and had to stay over, chance that I was not taking care of him alone, being overcareful as I usually was without Betty [Gow], chance that I didn't send Elsie [Whately] upstairs as I had the night before—and then finally chance that the baby was hurt or killed being taken out of the window."*

It was almost too terrible to bear, and her husband said sadly to her:

"Everything is chance. You can guard against the high percentage of chance, but not against chance itself."

The police had kept him in close touch with their investigations in the two and a half years since the kidnaping, and after Bruno Richard Hauptmann's arrest Schwarzkopf saw to it that all the evidence the state planned to present in court was placed before him. He studied it with great care. On October 8, 1934, he dyed his hair and put on an old cap and went to the Bronx Courthouse, where he lurked in the back-

* Anne Morrow Lindbergh, *Hour of Gold, Hour of Lead* (New York: Harcourt Brace Jovanovich, 1973).

ground and listened to Hauptmann calling out: "Hey, Doktor! Hey, Doktor!" He had no doubt whatsoever that it was the voice of the man who had collected the ransom money, and that unforgettable voice, combined with all the evidence he had digested, convinced him that this was the man who had killed his son, and equally certain that he had done it alone. Slowly, point by point, he went over the evidence with Anne Lindbergh and made her see that it must be so.

Once she accepted it, she lost all interest. She put the thought of Hauptmann and his trial out of her mind, and concentrated on the book she was writing (*North to the Orient*) and her baby. Only when the time came for her to be summoned into court did she drag her mind back. Otherwise, Hauptmann was simply the grisly instrument of an evil coincidence, to be pumice-stoned out of the memory.

Charles Lindbergh did not feel that way. He had to be there.

The trial of Bruno Richard Hauptmann opened in the Hunterdon County Courthouse at Flemington, New Jersey, on Thursday, January 3, 1935, and almost at once became, in the parlance of the day, a three-ring circus, and in my memory an obscene spectacle.† Pictures float back into the mind of that small, clean Andrew Wyeth town of painted houses and churches reeling before the invasion of people who didn't belong. Continuous publicity in the press had whipped interest to a per-fervid pitch, and everyone wanted to be there. Three hundred reporters, sketch writers, and sob sisters had flocked into Flemington and had taken over the Union Hotel, across the street from the courthouse, and every rooming house in town was bulging at the seams. Not all of the newsmen had tickets for the proceedings and were avid for ancillary and off-beat stories; and once more the flacks were there to cater to them, as they had done after the kidnaping. They shipped their clients, starlets, strip teaseuses, politicians, café society debutantes, across the river and set them loose among the reporters and photographers, and any marginal comment about the crime was good for a story and a picture. The pages of the newspapers were open, and everything else happening in the world took second place.

Main Street, Flemington, was jammed with cars, sight-seers, candy-barkers, mendicants, and pickpockets. One of my fellow copyboys bought a stack of small envelopes of translucent paper and typed on them, "Certified veritable lock of hair from Baby Lindbergh," and surreptitiously sold the small curls they contained at five dollars each. It was noticed that his own luxuriant crop of hair grew sparser as the trial

† The author attended the trial as a youthful copy runner and dogs-body for reporters covering the proceedings for a New York newspaper group.

proceeded. There were autographed photographs of Colonel Lindbergh (forged) going for two dollars apiece. Two Polish prostitutes from Philadelphia arrived in town and spread the word around that they offered something over and above the usual wares of their profession; and it seemed that one had a transfer picture of the *Spirit of St. Louis* flying over Manhattan on an intimate part of her anatomy, while the other had a transfer picture of the *Spirit* flying over the Eiffel Tower. You could ride from New York to Paris with Lindy at a special cut rate.

Thanks to the judge who conducted the trial, Justice Thomas Whitaker Trenchard, the carnival atmosphere was sedulously excluded from the courtroom, but each evening the chief prosecutor and the chief defense attorney would cross the road to the Union Hotel to give highly colorful interpretations of what they had achieved during the day, and wildly exaggerated forecasts of what they would elicit on the morrow. The defense attorney, Edward J. Reilly, beneath whose air of false bonhomie beat a heart of seven-carat gold, was particularly prone to make snide charges against the prosecution's witnesses which he was never able—and sometimes didn't even try—to justify in court. But he made the headlines with them, and that, it soon became apparent, was the principal reason for his appearance in the case. His interest in getting his client acquitted was peripheral.

Anne Lindbergh made only two appearances in court, and found both of them an ordeal. "Not to disappoint C. at the Trial" was her chief worry, and in order not to break down while she gave her evidence she gazed at a patch of blue sky through a courtroom window and resolutely kept her eyes away from Hauptmann. Her second appearance was when she accompanied her mother, who had been called to testify about one of her servants, and this time she had more control of herself and later wrote down in her diary how it had been: the "sad eyed Sob Sister" watching her, the "pale profile of Hauptmann startling one through a gap in the heads," the "pathetically bedraggled thin face, tired and bewildered" of the accused man's wife, Mrs. Anna Hauptmann, the "smart stenographer" taking it all down, the judge "dignified, unruffled." It was "a far worse day emotionally" than when she had testified, because she was "freer to feel." She listened to a long, technical discussion about the kind of wood which had been used for the kidnap ladder and thought, with a stab in the heart, how "incredible" that her baby "had any connection with this!"

Charles Lindbergh went from Englewood to Flemington every day of the six-week trial and sat in court whether his presence was necessary or not. His evidence was concise, positive, and convincing, and he showed absolutely no emotion, whether he was talking about the night he discovered his son was missing or hearing the voice call out "Hey, Doktor" from a Bronx cemetery on the night the ransom money was handed over.

"Since that time have you heard the same voice?" asked the prosecutor, David Wilentz.

"Yes, I have."

"Whose voice was it, Colonel, that you heard calling 'Hey, Doktor'?"

Lindbergh looked steadily in the direction of the accused man. "It was Hauptmann's voice," he said. There was conviction in his tone.

The prosecution had a good circumstantial case and they presented it effectively. Wood experts had traced the ladder used to reach Charles Lindbergh, Jr.'s, nursery window from a pine forest in South Carolina by way of a Bronx lumberyard to Hauptmann's workshop. Police had discovered a cache of the ransom money in Hauptmann's garage. The weakest part of their case was the *pure chance* by which the kidnaper had found the Lindberghs at Hopewell when he called, instead of in Englewood. But Reilly, the defense attorney, was too busy scattering red herrings and casting aspersions on witnesses to drive home the reasonable doubts the jury might have had in Hauptmann's sole responsibility, and the prosecution kept their attention concentrated upon the positiveness of his involvement in the crime.

A quieter, cleverer, more dedicated defender would probably not have saved him from prison but very probably from the electric chair.

On February 13, 1935, Judge Trenchard began his summing up in the trial, and as word of it spread great crowds began to converge on the Flemington Courthouse and had to be bodily cleared from the road and the courthouse steps by the police. They crammed the opposite sidewalk and the porch of the Union Hotel, staring across at the old colonial building with its fake-Greek colonnade, watching for the light to go on in the window on the first floor right, which would tell them that the jury was about to enter their room and begin deliberations. Everyone knew that the trial had gone into its terminal phase, and a sort of deathwatch had begun. But in no sense was the crowd subdued by the drama of the occasion; there was, if anything, rather more a festive, Kentucky Derby atmosphere, and as if to add to the track-meeting impression, men were moving among the throng offering odds against Hauptmann's chances of acquittal, but getting few takers. The reporters had already decided that Hauptmann hadn't a chance and had begun sending "hold" stories to New York and "color" pieces beginning: "The butcher of Lindy's baby waits in the death cell / faces a life term / tonight / while outside a heartbroken mother and child sob for a missing father. Anna Hauptmann and her son . . ." My voice was hoarse from dictating them over the line, and my stomach was turning at some of the phraseology, but they were going to sell newspapers in the morning. All they were waiting for was the verdict: death sentence or a life term.

Charles Lindbergh slipped out of the courtroom the moment Judge Trenchard's summing up was done and was smuggled into a car by the side door of the courthouse. No one in the joky crowd noticed him as the car swept past.

When he reached Next Day Hill, he found that Harold Nicolson, the English writer who was doing Dwight Morrow's biography, had arrived that morning and was waiting with Anne Lindbergh, her mother, and a brother-in-law. He told them that the jury was out and deliberating, but they already knew it from the radio. Nicolson was impressed by the calm, detached way in which they were taking what must be a momentous and sickening moment in their lives.

Their attitude, he wrote in his diary that night, was "as usual exactly right in balance and sincerity, not a trace of a false note. It is that, I think, which makes me like these people so much—the absolute purity of their judgment."

He had stayed for long periods in the Morrow household over the past few months, but this was the first time the Lindberghs talked to him about Hauptmann. Charles said he had been studying him in court and he told Nicolson he was "a magnificent looking man. Splendidly built. But that his little eyes were like the eyes of a wild boar. Mean, shifty, small and cruel."

The Englishman mentioned that he had been impressed with the account he had heard on the radio of Trenchard's summing up. The greatest praise he could find for it was that it was one with which even an English judge would not have been ashamed. Lindbergh quietly pointed out that the judge had not been quite so impartial as second-hand accounts had made him seem. For instance, he kept on saying to the jury, in going over Hauptmann's evidence: "Do you believe that?" It sounded all right when read later. But what he had actually said was: "Do *you* believe THAT?"

For the first time since he had got to know him, Nicolson was worried about Lindbergh's physical condition. He looked to be under an enormous load. He had also developed a terrible cold, which made his eyes red and running and provoked bouts of sneezing and coughing.

The jury had been out for five hours when they sat down for dinner that evening, and the broadcasters forecast that the verdict was imminent. They were now very touchy. Lindbergh was sneezing.

"They [the family] knew that the first news would come over the wireless," Nicolson wrote, "so that there were two wirelesses turned on —one in the pantry next to the dining room and one in the drawing room. Thus there were jazz and jokes while we had dinner, and one ear was strained the whole time for the announcer from the courthouse." After dinner they retired to the library, the radio blaring at them from the drawing room next door. Mrs. Morrow took out an album of family pictures, and they all made a show of studying them. Then Nicolson was called away to talk to a Morrow relative in another room about his biography, and while they were talking "suddenly Betty [Morrow] put her head round the huge Coromandel screen. She looked very white. 'Hauptmann,' she said, 'has been condemned to death without mercy.' "

Nicolson went into the drawing room. "The wireless had been turned on to the scene outside the courthouse. One could almost hear the diabolic yelling of the crowd. ('A-tishoo! A-tishoo!' from Lindbergh.) They were all sitting round . . . Anne looking very white and still. 'You have now heard,' broke in the voice of the announcer, 'the verdict in the most famous trial in all history. Bruno Hauptmann now stands guilty of the foulest . . .' ('A-tishoo! A-tishoo! A-tishoo!') 'Turn that off, Charles, turn that off.' "

They all went into the pantry, and glasses of ginger beer were poured out. Charles Lindbergh sat on the kitchen dresser looking very pink about the nose.

"I don't know," he said to Nicholson, "whether you have followed this case very carefully. There is no doubt at all that Hauptmann did the thing. My one dread all these years has been that they would get hold of someone as a victim about whom I wasn't sure. I am sure about this—quite sure. It is this way . . ."

And then quite quietly, while they all sat in the pantry sipping their ginger beer, he went through the case point by point.

"It seemed to relieve all of them," wrote Nicolson. "He did it very quietly, very simply. He pretended to address his remarks to me only. But I could see that he was really trying to ease the agonized tension through which Betty and Anne had passed. It was very well done. It made one feel that here was no personal desire for vengeance or justification; here was the solemn process of law inexorably and impersonally punishing a culprit."

Nicolson added:

"Poor Anne—she looked so white and horrified. The yells of the crowd [on the radio] were really terrifying. 'That,' said Lindbergh, 'was (A-tishoo!) a lynching crowd.' "

It was nearly midnight and they went up to bed. "I feel that they are all relieved," Nicolson commented.‡

Anne Lindbergh wrote in her diary:

"The trial is over. We must start our life again, try to build it securely—C. and Jon and I."

It was not as easy as that to forget about the Hauptmann case and start a new life, because there was their living son to think about. What Hauptmann had done to Charles Augustus, Jr., someone might now do to Jon, and the thought of it was ever present in their minds.

"Jon plays in a wire entanglement like a tennis court," wrote Harold Nicolson. "I suppose they think that people may creep through the trees and snatch him while his nurse's back is turned. I do feel sorry for them. . . . It is so difficult to think of tragedy associated with a little thing in overalls who toddles about picking up chestnuts and stuffing them in his pockets. Charles Lindbergh adores the baby, and is so attractive with him."

Nicolson had arrived at Next Day Hill prepared to be very cool, English, and snob toward Charles Lindbergh, about whom he had not heard very promising prior reports. One of Anne Lindbergh's close friends had dined with him before he set out for New Jersey, and filled his ear with mischief.

"She says [Lindbergh] is no more than a mechanic," he wrote in a letter to his wife, "and that had it not been for the Lone Eagle flight he would now be in charge of a gasoline station on the outskirts of St. Louis. Although the Morrows are themselves of humble origin, yet they were always cultured people and distinguished. Thus Lindbergh is really of a lower social stratum and they treat him with aloof politeness, as one treats a tenant's niece. He is himself 'not easy.' Anne has a difficult task."

He soon (or rather Lindbergh soon) changed his mind. A few days after meeting him for the first time he was writing: "It is all nonsense people saying that Lindbergh is disagreeable. He is as nice as can be."

Shortly afterward, he wrote:

"Lindbergh himself talks to me a great deal. Though he is reputed to be silent, I think he likes me. He sits on at breakfast—chatter, chatter, chatter—so that I have to break off and go. . . . I find him, apart from his actual physical charm, really a delightful companion. She is an absolute angel."

And then:

‡ These comments are as Harold Nicolson originally wrote them. They were slightly abridged in the published edition of his *Diaries and Letters*.

"I find it very useful to talk to Lindbergh about American political conditions. He is a Democrat by instinct but a Republican in practise. He loathes Roosevelt because of the latter's treatment of the airmail companies. But he is a sensible man without unthoughtful prejudices and with a direct approach to things. He is interested in England with our class distinctions and privileges. He thinks them ghastly and I'm not sure he's not right. . . . Lindbergh has been so famous in his life that he has no inferiority complex and is able to discuss all this with complete detachment. He is a very decent man. His reputation for sulkiness and bad manners is entirely due to his loathing of society. 'What I loathe most,' he says, 'are the silly women who bring their kids up to shake hands with me at railway stations. It is embarrassing for me and embarrassing for the kids. It fair makes me sick.' "

Soon Nicolson was "under the glamor of that mouse-like modesty of Anne and that stag-like modesty of Charles. But oh my God, what charming people."

Yet he was aware that the horror of their son's murder had "given them a twist about the intrusion of strangers. They are not normal on that point." More than ever, during the trial and afterward, Next Day Hill was a house under siege. Crowds had come back to clog the roads and peer and peek through the gates. Mail, which had dropped to a few score a day, began to flood once more into Englewood Post Office at the rate of thousands, to sympathize, to console, to chide, to gloat, or to threaten the Lindberghs.

"Even Mrs. Morrow has to have all her letters opened for her," Nicolson wrote, "ever since she came here one night at midnight. Being all alone in the house she took her letters to read in bed. The first one was: 'You will be the next to go—so be careful and prepare yourself—it will come at night.' She got up and fetched Skeean. Skeean is the Aberdeen terrier aged between 43 and 46, but he was *some* help. Since then she has her letters opened by her private secretaries."

Thor, the German shepherd, was now installed at Next Day Hill to protect the Lindberghs and the Morrows. He could be a terrifying menace to strangers and refused to take his eyes off anyone of whom the Lindberghs had not yet said, "This is a friend," ready to leap at the slightest wrong move. Nicolson could not resist writing his wife a comic account of his introduction to him:

" 'What a nice dog!' I said.

" 'You will have to be a little careful at first, Mr. Nicolson,' he [Lindbergh] answered.

" 'Is he very fierce?'

" 'He's all that. But he will get used to you in time. . . .'

" 'Thor is his name, is it not? I read about him in the newspapers.' I stretched out a hand towards him. 'Thor!' I said, throwing into the word an appeal for friendship that was profoundly sincere. He then made a noise in his throat such as only tigers make when waiting for their food. It was not a growl. It was not a bark. It was a deep pectoral regurgitation—predatory, savage, hungry. Lindbergh smiled a little uneasily. 'It will take him a week or so,' he said, 'to become accustomed to you.' He then released his hold upon the collar. I retreated rapidly to the fireplace, as if to flick my ash from my cigarette. Thor stalked towards me. I thought of you and my two sons and Gwen and Rebecca, and my past life and England's honour. 'Thor!' I exclaimed. 'Good old man!' The tremor in my voice was very tremulous. Lindbergh watched the scene with alert, but aloof, interest. 'If he wags his tail, Mr. Nicolson, you need have no fear.' He wagged his tail and lay down. . . . I turned to Lindbergh.

" 'What happens,' I asked, 'if Thor does not wag his tail?' 'Well,' he said, 'you must be careful not to pass him. He might get hold of you.' 'By the throat?' I asked—trying, but not with marked success, to throw a reckless jollity into my tone. 'Not necessarily,' he answered. 'If he does that, you must stay still and holler all you can.' "

Soon, however, Nicolson had turned Thor into a friend, and was taking him out for a morning walk, but he was "always afraid he will eat someone on the way." The household had accepted Nicolson to such an extent that they began to relax and not feel too self-conscious of his presence. He moved among them with the air of a superior, but amiably inclined, being on a visit from another planet, and aroused in Anne Lindbergh a mixture of amused exasperation. Why was he so *English* and such a snob? Yet when he praised her writing and gently but firmly insisted that she must continue, because she was a *real writer*, she was uplifted and made airborne by his praise, because she had sensed the sincerity in his voice and knew that for once he was not being patronizing.

Every night he put down in his diaries or his letters the wry comments about them that pinned them down like butterflies in a collection. Anne was "a shy little thing with a touch of tragedy at the mouth." At a dinner "Lindbergh had said not a word all evening, just fiddling with a piece of string. 'Well,' he said (as the guest's car crunched over the gravel on its way out), 'I taught myself three new kinds of knots this evening.' " Sometimes, when he was feeling homesick for England, his worst snobbishness came out, and though he felt "rather ashamed" of putting his feelings down on paper even to his wife, he wrote:

"Mrs. Morrow is . . . a really educated, intelligent and wise woman. I like her very much indeed, but one feels even with her there is a housekeeper's-room atmosphere. She is like the very best type of retired upper servant. (How Gwen will squirm at this snobbishness.) Anne is like Emily Booth.* Charles Lindbergh is like a bright young chauffeur."

Only with the youngest daughter, Constance, did he feel in the presence of someone completely free, relaxed, happy-go-lucky, self-confident, and cosmopolitan.

"She is a pearl," he wrote. "She is the only one of the family who teases Lindbergh. She asks him questions. She rags him about his fame complex. He just grins at her. 'Well, Colonel Lindbergh, it's no use turning on the Lindbergh smile famous in two continents in order to impress your little sister-in-law. It doesn't work.' "

She delighted him. But oh what a family touched with tragedy! While he was in the household, the eldest sister, Elisabeth, collapsed into her final illness, in California. Betty Morrow at once decided she must fly out to her from Englewood, despite the fact that storms were raging across the nation. After some difficulty, Charles Lindbergh found a plane seat for her, and they all went out to the front door of Next Day Hill to bid her godspeed.

"She really looked exactly like the perfect edition of the lady's maid out there on the porch with the wind howling and the rain buffeting across the night," Nicolson wrote to his wife. "Charles, obviously uneasy, muttering to me: 'It's a hell of a risk in this weather.' (His own company has refused to fly her.) She said goodbye with such calm dignity—a defiant dignity, Promethean it was. . . . She is an ugly little woman of 65 with a disagreeable mouth, but there's something about her which is inspiring. She's not brilliant, not amusing, and her poetry is very poor. There is something about her that is so impressive and so perplexing that I long for you to be with me so that we can discuss it together."†

Elisabeth died. "Some curse of the Atreids seems to cling to this family," he sighed.

It was almost as if Charles Lindbergh were training his second son, Jon, to fight back singlehanded should a kidnaper dare to come for him.

---

* Of the Salvation Army.

† The comments were not entirely one-sided. Though Anne Lindbergh's were not quite so snobbish, she about this time was writing in *her* diary about *him:* "H.N. talked all through lunch, was amusing and entertaining (that's the word, that's what the British are—'entertaining'). It baffles me like sitting in a theater and looking always at a beautifully painted curtain. I keep waiting and waiting for the curtain to rise and show the real play."

He was an attractive curly-haired boy not quite three years old, but already he was being taught to swim, climb, fend for himself. Anne Lindbergh could not bear to watch when her husband flung their child into the pool and watched him struggling in the water, but beamed proudly enough when, after a few days of such baptisms, Jon came dripping toward her to announce: "Mummy, I can thwim!"

At North Haven, the Morrow island home in Maine, she cringed when Lindbergh coaxed, badgered, and goaded Jon up a steep cliff, catching him when he fell, but laughing at his bruises and taking no notice when the child wailed: "I want to come down." His father shook his head. "No, you want to go up." And up he went.

She was amazed, as were all the others, when Jon displayed no ill effects from this toughening-up process. Even his father was soon admitting that he was shaping well.

"He certainly is a game little youngster," he said.

Jon was one of the compensations of that black year of 1935, and there were others. Harold Nicolson had urged Anne Lindbergh to take up writing seriously, and she had imbibed encouragement from his words. Now *North to the Orient* was delivered to the publishers, and their praise of it seemed genuine. Lindbergh's work on the perfusion pump with Dr. Alexis Carrel leaked into the newspapers and his contribution to science was generously acknowledged.

But their achievements and their domestic joys and fulfillments were constantly overshadowed by preoccupations with the outside world, and worries about their future. The Hauptmann case was over, but public interest in him (and in the Lindberghs) did not die. Governor Harold G. Hoffmann of New Jersey, for what seemed like political reasons, had visited the convicted kidnaper in his condemned cell and announced that he had "serious doubts" about the case. Public curiosity about the Lindberghs flared up once more, and induced in Anne Lindbergh a despair which showed itself in an apathy, a torpor, out of which she could not shake herself. She knew that Charles Lindbergh was restless and frustrated with life in the bosom of the Morrow family, and that her urgent priority was to give him "a home and a sense of freedom and power and fulfilment." But somehow the urgency of it filled her with helpless inadequacy, and aroused in her an increasing resentment of her mother, because her tremendous verve and energy was in such contrast to her own pale exhaustion.

The worst moments came when Charles Lindbergh was driven upstairs to take refuge in their bedroom, because the house was so full of people, and he sat there, tight-lipped, cloaked in gloom and unhap-

piness. He never said anything, but she could hear what he was thinking: *We've got to get away. We must have a home of our own.*

But where? They considered for a time buying a plot of land on one
of the Maine islands and building there, but abandoned the idea when
they saw a family moving in to a plot next to the tract of headland on
which they had set their heart. Harry Guggenheim offered them some
land on his estate at Port Washington, on Long Island, but they had a
revulsion of feeling against it when some men firing the brushwood to
clear the land wantonly burned and gravely damaged many of the old
trees on the estate. It was as if they felt the trees, until their premature
death, would reproach them for what man had wrought against them
just to provide them with a space to live.

That summer they flew to Minnesota to visit Little Falls. It was the
first time Anne Lindbergh had seen her husband's childhood home, and
one does not get the feeling from her writings afterward that the countryside called to her. The people were hospitable, pleasant, welcoming,
and they stayed while in Little Falls with Martin Engstrom, who still
ran the hardware store and soft-drink parlor which Charles Lindbergh
had patronized as a boy. The bedroom had, Anne Lindbergh noticed, a
framed poem by Edgar Guest on the bureau, a heavy red crocheted
cover on the bed box, a large leather rocking chair, shell and bead caps
for the lights.

As she followed her husband around the old Lindbergh farm on the
Mississippi banks, she saw the zeal in his face, and felt that she mustn't
complain. She must "see it Charles's way, I must try and feel it with
him." But it just wasn't her. And if Lindbergh had had any idea when
they first arrived of finding a home here, he must have realized soon
enough that it wouldn't work, that here his wife would droop and fade
away. They must look elsewhere.

But where, where, where?

Once more they began to toy with an idea which had occurred to
them ever since Harold Nicolson had come into the house. Whatever
else you could say about the English, at least they had peace and security over there. How about England, then, for a home and a refuge?

Or even for a visit? Just to get away from the guards on the gate, the
constant bustle of people in the house, her strong-minded, omnipresent
mother, the headlines in the newspapers, this terribly sapping sense of
insecurity? They talked about it for hours on end.

And then things began to happen which made up Charles Lindbergh's mind.

During her lifetime, Anne Lindbergh's sister, Elisabeth, had started a nursery school at Englewood with a friend, and the friend, Constance Chilton, continued it after her death. It was known as the Little School, and Jon Lindbergh was enrolled in it in 1935. One of the teachers drove him back and forth from Next Day Hill each day.

Colonel Henry Breckenridge, Lindbergh's attorney and friend, had been around to the newspapers and news syndicates and succeeded in convincing them that if Jon Lindbergh was to have a reasonably normal life (not to say a safe one), the less publicity about him the better. It was tacitly agreed that there would be no photographs given out of him, and no newspapers would try to snatch one. But one day while Jon was being taken into school his teacher noticed a truck parked nearby and what looked like rifles or guns of some sort poking out of the back. She dragged the boy into the school and raised the alarm. The truck raced away but was intercepted by the police. The guns were camera lenses. A news syndicate was trying to snatch pictures, but the alarm had been given too soon for them to get any.

A few weeks later they tried again, and this time their tactics were even more alarming. A car passed the one driven by Jon's teacher, with the boy beside her, and suddenly swerved and forced her to swing into the curb. Men spilled out of it and dashed across. The teacher cringed in terror. The boy began to cry. The photographers moved in, took some dramatic pictures, and decamped. They made the front page of one newspaper the following morning. Jon was withdrawn from the Little School that day, and henceforward stayed at home.

Was it always going to be like this, until he grew up? If so, the future looked bleak indeed.

It looked even bleaker on December 5, 1935, when Governor Hoffmann got himself back into the headlines over the Hauptmann case. The justices of the Supreme Court of the United States had just completed their hearing into Hauptmann's appeal against his sentence, and would hand down their verdict on December 9. Now Hoffmann announced that no matter what their decision,‡ he proposed to ask the New Jersey Court of Pardons to grant Bruno Richard Hauptmann a personal interview should he wish to plead for a commutation of his death sentence. His political motivations (he was a Republican) became apparent when the news spread that he had tried to sack the attorney general who had prosecuted Hauptmann, David Wilentz (a Democrat), but had been thwarted by the nature of Wilentz's term of office. So instead he planned to dismiss the police chief involved in the case, Colonel Norman Schwarzkopf (also a Democrat).

‡ They rejected the appeal.

All this exploded in a *feu d'artifice* of sensational headlines. Lindbergh was both appalled and angry. The way in which Hoffmann had announced his intention to interfere in the case had raised public doubts that were bound to have repercussions on their lives. Moreover, Schwarzkopf, whom he considered a good and conscientious policeman, had become his friend, and he deeply resented his usurpation.*

On the morning of Saturday December 7, he told Anne Lindbergh that she had better start packing. She must be ready to leave at twenty-four hours' notice. They were going to spend the winter—all three of them—in England or Sweden. Maybe they would stay longer. It all depended.

Leaving her making lists of clothing, books, baggage, things for Jon, he took off for Washington to see friends and make arrangements. He had reached the end of his tether, and must break it once and for all. Life in America wasn't possible any more.

Jon, Anne, and Charles Lindbergh sailed from New York for Liverpool, England, in the early hours of December 22, 1935, aboard the U.S. passenger-freighter *American Importer*, 7,590 tons. They were well out into the Atlantic before the American public learned that their hero had left them.

It was, as the New York *Times* remarked when the news became known, as if America had decreed exile for her own son.

* Schwarzkopf went on to become an intelligence officer in the U. S. Army in World War II, and is generally believed to have masterminded the countercoup which restored the present Shah-in-Shah to the Iranian throne in 1954.

Part
Four

Innocents
Abroad

CHAPTER

SIXTEEN

SURCEASE

It was just like old times. In fact, it was better. Here he was, back in
Europe again, once more everybody's hero. Only this time, after the
first flurry of publicity, they let him alone, and there were no more flash
bulbs in his face, no more badgering reporters, no enormous receptions,
and, best of all, no more crowds.

Not only could he go where he liked in freedom and comfort, but he
was able to taste the fruits of his fame where and how he wished, picking out from the stacks of invitations those he wished to see, where he
wanted to go, what functions or institutions he should honor with his
presence, without anyone but himself influencing his choice. It was
wonderful. It was peace. It was a holiday (and perhaps something even
more permanent than that) from fear.

THE LINDBERGHS: LEAVE THEM ALONE was the headline in the London
Daily Mirror, and politely the British people did so.

Aubrey Neil Morgan, widower of Anne Lindbergh's sister Elisabeth,
had come on ahead of them to England in a faster ship, and he was on
the dock at Liverpool to greet them when they came ashore on the last
day of 1935. They drove to the Adelphi Hotel and read the editorials in
the New York papers voicing the shame of the American people over
the circumstances of their departure. The New York *Herald Tribune*
had written:

> The departure of Colonel and Mrs. Lindbergh for England,
> to find a tolerable home there in a safer and more civilized
> land than ours has shown itself to be is its own commentary
> upon the American social scene. Nations have exiled their he-

roes before; they have broken them with meanness. But when
has a nation made life unbearable to one of its most distinguished men through a sheer inability to protect him from its
criminals and lunatics and the vast vulgarity of its sensa-
tionalists, publicity-seekers, petty politicians and yellow newspapers? It seems as incredible as it is shocking. Yet everyone
knows that this is exactly what has happened. . . .

Anne Lindbergh looked through the rain-pocked windows of the
hotel down to the Liverpool streets with their trams, buses, chimney
pots, red-cheeked children, women with shawls, nursemaids wheeling
prams, brick houses, raincoats, drably dressed women, and a wave of
homesickness swept over her. It was all so *terribly* English.

Then she glanced across at her husband playing in the corner with
Jon, and her spirits lifted. He looked relaxed for the first time in
months.

When they woke up next morning, it was 1936, and the black year
was over.

Harold Nicolson was one of the first to greet them when they arrived
in England, and in March he offered the Lindberghs a place to live in
pleasant countryside yet convenient for London. Nicolson, his wife,
Vita Sackville-West, the writer, and their two sons, Ben and Nigel,
lived in an old Tudor manor-castle near Sissinghurst, Kent, in the
southeast corner of England. They also owned a large cottage nearby
called Long Barn, which they had reluctantly decided to sell to pay for
the alterations they were making to the castle and for the garden which
Nicolson had designed and his wife was planting in the grounds. (It
would soon become one of the most famous gardens in England.) But
at the beginning of 1936, Vita's mother, Lady Sackville, died and left
her daughter a small fortune as well as two legacies for her sons.

There was therefore no longer any need to sell Long Barn, and
Nicolson suggested to the Lindberghs that it might suit them. They
looked it over, found it perfect for their needs, and took a year's lease at
two hundred dollars a month, with an option to renew at the end of
the first year.

Before their arrival, Nicolson telephoned "dear old Mrs. Woods" who
ran the Weald Post Office and asked her to use her influence in the
village to see that the newcomers were not bothered at Long Barn. She
was "very flattered at being roped in as an ally" and promised that "no,
sir, we shall not stare at the poor people."

Soon they were a familiar sight in Sissinghurst, where Anne Lindbergh often went shopping with Jon hanging on her arm. Charles Lindbergh knew the luxury of being able to stretch his long legs in a first-class carriage of a train to London and read his *Times* or his private papers without anything more than a friendly nod from his fellow commuters. Nigel Nicolson, who was nineteen at the time, would often go over to Long Barn to see the famous new tenants and marveled at the boisterous games in which father and son would engage. One time he was startled to see Lindbergh take Jon by the ankle—he was now three and a half years old—and swing him round and round his head. "Not that Jon seemed to mind much," he remembered.

Shortly after they arrived at Long Barn the Hauptmann case flared up in a last baleful blaze of publicity. Governor Hoffmann had temporarily reprieved the convicted killer, but his time had now run out. On April 3, 1936, stunned by the failure of the false hopes Hoffmann had aroused in him, Hauptmann was taken to the execution chamber and placed in the electric chair at 8:44 P.M. He was pronounced dead three and a half minutes later.

Even the British newspapers were full of the story, and for the next few days the Lindberghs locked themselves away at Long Barn and did not see anyone. But on April 12, they accepted an invitation from the Nicolsons to come over for lunch. They arrived with Minna Curtis, an old friend of Anne Lindbergh's, who had just come over from New York; a neighbor and fellow-politician of the Nicolsons called Victor Cazalet was the other guest. Nicolson thought Lindbergh looked well but subdued, but when the talk turned to American politics, he suddenly became talkative and launched into a tirade against the lying, cheating, and corruption of the American political scene. Recalling the conversation in his diary that night, Nicolson wrote:

"Charles says he has to make up his mind whether to devote himself to science and mechanics or whether to use his own legend to clean up American politics. He has evidently thought about it a great deal, and thought that on the whole he must follow 'the bent of my mother's family rather than the bent of my father, and follow mechanics and not politics.' "

Nicolson was fascinated. It was the first time he had realized that Lindbergh was interested enough in politics to announce that he was not going in for them.

A few days afterward a strange thing happened. Lindbergh arrived at the castle and asked for Nicolson. When he was shown into the study, he said, in his usual straightforward way:

"I have been doing some study into psychic research. Would you know of a medium here or in London whom we could visit, so that we could attend a séance?"

Nicolson regretted that such esoteric matters were outside his ken, and Lindbergh thanked him and left. The subject was never brought up again.

King George V had died earlier in the year (the Lindberghs and Mrs. Morrow had watched his funeral from the windows of the Ritz Hotel), and now Edward VIII was King of England, though not yet ceremoniously crowned. In political circles in Britain the leaders were rather more concerned with Edward's private life than with what was happening in Europe. The Italian dictator Benito Mussolini had shown his contempt of the democracies by defying Britain, France, and the League of Nations and marching his armies into Ethiopia, whose monarch, Haile Selassie, was now in flight. The German dictator Adolf Hitler, encouraged by the success of Mussolini's bluff, decided that the time was ripe for some saber-rattling of his own, and he sent his armies into the demilitarized zones along the Rhine and declared them an integral part of the National Socialist Reich.

The democracies in Europe were being defied and threatened, but they preferred not to know. The period of appeasement, of look-the-other-way-and-pretend-it-isn't-happening, was beginning in Britain, and it was the policy of His Majesty's Government to ignore the dictators and hope they would go away. In the meantime, the Tory Prime Minister, Stanley Baldwin, had a domestic problem on his hands which he considered much more disquieting. The King had got himself involved with a married woman. Worse than that, she was an American, Mrs. Wallis Simpson.*

Harold Nicolson was a friend of the new King's, but even he was rather shocked by Edward's choice of a female companion. He accepted a dinner invitation from Mrs. Simpson on April 2, 1936, and when he got there found that the King was the chief guest, together with Lady Oxford, Lady Cunard, Lady Colefax, Alexander Woollcott, and Mrs. Simpson's husband, Ernest. That night Nicolson wrote:

"Something snobbish in me is rather saddened by all this. Mrs. Simpson is a perfectly harmless type of American, but the whole setting is slightly second-rate. I do not wonder that the Sutherlands and the Stanleys are sniffy about it all."†

---

* Who subsequently divorced her husband and married Edward after his abdication. She is now the Duchess of Windsor.

† The Duke of Sutherland and Lord Stanley. The American-born Lady Astor was stuffy too. To Nicolson she deplored "the fact that any but the best Virginian families should be received at Court."

But when he saw Lindbergh at lunch a few days later, Nicolson mentioned that the King had particularly asked to see him. He and Anne had tea with Edward early in May, and on May 27 they were invited to the first big banquet given by the monarch since his succession. It made all the newspapers in the United States as well as in Britain, although not simply because of the presence of the Lindberghs. The Associated Press reported:

> Colonel and Mrs. Charles A. Lindbergh were King Edward's guests at a royal dinner this evening at St. James's Palace, where a notable party was assembled. The Court Circular listed those who attended as Commander Lord Louis Mountbatten, R.N., and Lady Mountbatten, the Rt. Hon. Stanley Baldwin and Mrs. Baldwin, Colonel Lord Wigram and Lady Wigram, Mr. Alfred Duff Cooper and Lady Diana Cooper, Lieut. Col. the Hon. Piers Leigh and Mrs. Leigh, Lady Cunard, Admiral of the Fleet Sir Ernle Chatfield and Lady Chatfield, Colonel Charles Lindbergh and Mrs. Lindbergh, and Mr. and Mrs. Ernest Simpson. This issue of the Court Circular is notable not only for the inclusion of the Lindberghs as royal guests, but also for the first mention of Mr. and Mrs. Simpson, who have long been known as intimate personal friends of the King before and after his accession.

Charles Lindbergh was blithefully unaware that the "official" presence of the Simpsons was going to cause a scandal in Britain the next day, and that Prime Minister Baldwin was profoundly shocked at having to sit at the same table as "that woman." He talked to the Prime Minister about aviation and the need for Britain to be strong in the air in order to cope with the threats from the dictatorial powers, but decided from Baldwin's expression that he preferred not to pursue the subject. Lindbergh felt snubbed. He could not know that the British premier was worrying about how to get Wally Simpson out of King Edward's life, and could not care less about Lindbergh's opinions about air power.

Anne Lindbergh had a much better time with the King himself. He was delighted with her. She had been rather shy at first, he told Nicolson later, "but with my well known charm I put her at her ease and liked her very much."

In some ways, the first six months of their stay in England was like a second honeymoon, and better in many ways, because no one harassed them. They were welcome everywhere, and all doors were open to them, and they loved the peace and seclusion of Long Barn. True, both of them were somewhat baffled by what seemed to them the strangeness, the indifference, of the English, their lack of "give." Charles Lindbergh would come back from a meeting and tell Anne he had, he felt, impressed and interested his companions by what he had told them, but then add to himself: ". . . *impressed and interested* (if an American is able to judge and recognize such qualities in Englishmen, which I sometimes doubt)." Anne would feel a sudden estrangement that worried her. "What *is* there about the English?" she would ask herself. One moment she seemed to be talking perfectly openly with them, an easy, natural conversation, and then—*snap*—the blind would slam down in her face and she was shut out from them. "I sit in terror waiting for the moment—no warning—just *snap!* And you're left staring at the shutters."

But for the moment they were no more than mildly critical and still grateful above all to the British for having provided them with such a secure sanctuary from outside pressures. In this environment they could relax and know that their child was safe and thriving. They could even begin planning again to increase their family. Thank God for the English—infuriatingly complacent, class-ridden, old-fashioned, so stubbornly aware of their superiority, so convinced that the Almighty was on their side, yet so friendly and so secure. They gave them a cosy feeling of living inside a cocoon, and for the time being that was what they wanted.

And then, at the beginning of June 1936, a letter arrived at Long Barn, and it was to have a profound effect upon their future. It came from the United States Embassy in Germany and it was signed by a certain Truman Smith.

Major Truman Smith was a career officer in the U. S. Army and at that time he was military attaché, in charge of Army and Air Intelligence, in Berlin. He had little or no technical knowledge of aviation or aeronautics, and his activities since the advent of the National Socialist regime in Germany had been mainly to chronicle the expansion of the land forces of the Reich. But he was well aware that under Hermann Göring the German Air Force (the Luftwaffe) was emerging from its interwar hibernation and burgeoning into the most powerful air arm in Europe. His budget was too small to employ spies or more than one (untrained) assistant, yet he felt that he was being inadequate in his job if he did not keep Washington closely informed of the tremendous strides the Nazis were making in their aviation armament. But when he wrote to the War Department and pleaded for an assistant who would be capable of assessing these developments, he was informed that one would not be available at the very earliest before 1937.

It was just about this time that his wife, Kay, reading a copy of the New York *Herald*, Paris Edition, at their breakfast table in Berlin, noticed an item recounting a visit Charles Lindbergh had made to an aircraft factory in France. She pointed it out to her husband, and an idea was born in his mind. If Lindbergh was willing to look at French aircraft factories, why should he not examine German ones as well? Why not invite him to come over, and ask him to make a tour of German aviation centers, without, of course, making it too explicit that he would be acting as an unpaid informant for the U. S. Army?

"Colonel Lindbergh was at this time a mere name to the military attaché," wrote Truman Smith in a report he made later.‡ "He had never met him, but he knew that Lindbergh was not just a daring flier; he was also highly qualified in various phases of aeronautical science. . . . It was likewise his impression that the German Air Ministry would like nothing better than to curry favor with Hitler by presenting the world-famous flier as the special guest of the Luftwaffe."

Smith was an ambitious officer and he was not unaware of the kudos that would accrue to him and his office if he succeeded in snaring such a highly qualified celebrity as his assistant. Accordingly, he first approached a close friend attached to the German Air Ministry and from him obtained confirmation that the Luftwaffe chief, Hermann Göring, would indeed be delighted to welcome Colonel Lindbergh. Then he sat down to write a letter.

AMERICAN EMBASSY
Office of the Military Attaché
Tiergartenstrasse 30
Berlin

May 25, 1936

My dear Colonel Lindbergh:
Although I have not had the pleasure of your personal acquaintance, I feel free on account of my position in corresponding with you with respect to a possible desire on your part to visit Germany during your stay in Great Britain.
In a recent discussion with high officials of the German Air

‡ *Air Intelligence Activities, with Special Reference to the Services of Colonel Charles A. Lindbergh, Air Corps Reserve.* A record prepared by Colonel Truman Smith, USA (retired), between September 1954 and September 1956. Yale University Library.

Ministry, I was requested to extend to you in the name of General Göring and the German Air Ministry an invitation to visit Germany and inspect the new German civil and military air establishments.

I was further instructed by General Göring to inform you that the strictest censorship would be imposed by the German Air Ministry with respect to your visit and that they would not allow even the slightest notice to appear in connection therewith except with your distinct approval and in case such should be your wish.

General Göring and the Air Ministry believe that the present air development in Germany would prove of particular interest to you and they would be highly honored in case you would give them the opportunity to be your hosts for a week or for whatever time seemed to you appropriate. . . .

I need hardly tell you that the present German air development is very imposing and on a scale which I believe is unmatched in the world. Up until very recently this development was highly secretive, but in recent months they have become extraordinarily friendly to the American representatives and have shown us far more than to the representatives of other powers. General Göring has particularly exerted himself for friendly relations with the United States.

From a purely American point of view, I consider that your visit here would be of high patriotic benefit. I am certain they will go out of their way to show you even more than they show us.

I do not wish, however, to stress merely the patriotic side of a visit by you to Germany. I am of the opinion that you will be both greatly interested and impressed by the air developments in this country and that a visit by you to Germany can be carried out with more privacy to your person than can a visit anywhere else in the world. . . .

With very best wishes, and with those of my wife added, who is extremely hopeful that Mrs. Lindbergh will come with you, I am

                                        Yours very sincerely

                                        Truman Smith
                                        Major, G.S.
                                        Military Attaché

At that time Truman Smith did not know Lindbergh's address in England and had sent his missive by way of the American military attaché in London, and it was not until two weeks later that he received a reply, written on the cross-channel boat from Boulogne to Folkestone as Lindbergh was returning from his visit to France.

LONG BARN—WEALD—SEVENOAKS
France
June 5, 1936

Dear Major Smith:
I have just received your letter of May 25th forwarded by Colonel Scanlon. Thank you very much for writing.
I would be extremely interested in seeing some of the German developments in both civil and military aviation. I wish you would transmit my thanks and sincere appreciation to General Göring and the German Air Ministry for inviting me to visit Germany and to inspect the new German air establishments. I would like very much to accept the invitation, but it is very difficult to come at the time suggested in your letter (June 28). . . . [There would be] an advantage, from my standpoint, in coming after July 21st in that the plane which we are now building in England will be completed. . . . Please let me know what the exact situation is. I will be glad to make every effort to come at a time which will be convenient to General Göring and the Air Ministry.
One of the things I appreciate most about the invitation is the fact that General Göring has been so considerate in realizing the impossibility of doing anything properly, or of concentrating on a problem intelligently if one is always surrounded by pressmen and the values which most of them represent. I do not think it will be possible for me to come to Germany and go to various German air establishments without the fact being known. However, I can see no objection to that. What I am most anxious to avoid is the sensational and stupid publicity which we have so frequently encountered in the past; and the difficulty and unpleasantness which invariably accompany it. . . .
I hope that General Göring does not feel that it is necessary to provide any special entertainment as far as I am con-

cerned. . . . As a matter of fact, I thoroughly dislike formal functions and have not attended one for several years.*

It is extremely kind of you and Mr. Mayer [the chargé d'affaires] to invite us to stay at your homes. My wife would like very much to visit Germany, and we will plan on coming together. . . . We shall wait to hear from you before making any definite plans. . . .

Sincerely,
Charles A. Lindbergh.

When the Lindberghs came across to Sissinghurst Castle at the beginning of July to tell their landlords they would shortly be leaving for Germany as guests of the Nazi Government, they must have wondered why Harold Nicolson eyed them slightly askance. Until Hitler's advent, Nicolson had been a frequent visitor to Germany, where he had many friends. He spoke German well and was a student of German art and literature. One of the great regrets of his life was that he was tone-deaf, and therefore unable to appreciate the great German composers. But only a few days before he had been involved in an incident which was now the talk of diplomatic and political circles in London, and succinctly summed up his attitude to the Nazi regime.

Invited to lunch by Mrs. Margaret Greville, one of the society hostesses of the day, he found himself sitting next to a German woman who turned out to be an ardent Nazi.

"Do you know my country, sir?" she asked Nicolson.

"Yes, I have often visited Germany."

"Have you been there recently, since our Movement?"

"No, except for an hour at Munich, I have not visited Germany since 1930."

"Oh," said the woman fervently, "you should come now. You will find it all so changed."

"Yes," replied Nicolson grimly, "I should find all my old friends either in prison, or exiled or murdered."

Nicolson had once summed up Charles Lindbergh as "not a stupid man in the very least, but I doubt if he knows who Goethe was." Their conversations in Britain had revealed that he did not know much history, either, and so far as postwar Europe was concerned his mind was an empty void. He must have hoped that Lindbergh's mental digestive processes would be able to balance the rich ideological diet with which they would inevitably be fed in the next week or two.

* This was written a few days after he had dined with King Edward at St. James's Palace, which the Germans would have known about.

Early in July the Lindberghs went to Reading and took delivery of a new plane which had been built for them by F. G. ("Freddy") Miles, a well-known English aircraft manufacturer. It had been constructed to Lindbergh's own specifications, and he was pleased with the result. It was small, comfortable, highly maneuverable, and had a range capable of taking them to most places in Europe. After putting it through its paces, he told Anne they were ready to go. They left Jon behind with his nurse, asked the local Kent County Police to keep an eye on Long Barn, and took off for Germany on July 22, 1936.

When they landed in Berlin later that day, there was quite a lineup waiting to greet them on the airport. All American naval and military attachés in Berlin had been summoned to attend. There were officials from the Air Ministry and Germany's civil airline, the Lufthansa. Wolfgang von Gronau, president of the Air Clubs of Germany, extended the greetings of the German aviation community. And Colonel Gustav Kastner stepped forward smartly, snapped to attention and raised his hand in the Nazi salute, and announced that henceforward he would be the personal representative of the Lindberghs during their tour. He extended the cordial greetings of his chief, General Hermann Göring.

Then they drove with Truman and Kay Smith to the military attaché's house, there to work out the schedule for their visit. Though they did not realize it then, it was to prove a watershed in their lives.

CHAPTER

SEVENTEEN

HOOKED

The United States Ambassador to Germany in 1936 was Dr. William Edward Dodd, a historian and German scholar (Ph.D. Leipzig, 1900), a liberal in outlook, an anti-isolationist, and a firm advocate of American participation in international affairs. Truman Smith, in the report which he later wrote for the War Department, described Ambassador Dodd as "a pacifist" and questioned "his fitness for the ambassadorial post at this particular period in history" owing to "his marked distaste for military matters."

Truman Smith misread his man. Dodd's distaste was for the brutish National Socialists who had taken over Germany and were in process of destroying the values he had come to love in German life and the German people. It is too strong a word to say that he also had a "distaste" for Truman Smith—he probably never impinged upon his life to a sufficient extent—but he and his military attaché were certainly antipathetic. This is not perhaps surprising in view of the fact that Major Truman Smith rather admired many aspects of the Nazi regime which Dodd so much loathed. Smith was not by any means isolated at the American Embassy in those days in his approval of Adolf Hitler, as many a correspondent remembers. There were some attachés who believed that a good day had arrived for Germany when the swastika had taken over, and their prototype was portrayed by Herman Wouk in his novel *The Winds of War*, in the character of Kip Tollever. Tollever, just back from being naval attaché in Berlin in the years before the outbreak of World War II, is talking to the man destined to be his successor:

When Victor Henry probed a bit about the Nazis and how to deal with them, Kip Tollever sat up very erect, his curled fingers stiffened as he gestured, and his tone grew firm. The National Socialists were *in*, he said, and the other parties were out, just as in the United States the Democrats were in and the Republicans out. That was one way to look at it. The Germans admired the United States and desperately wanted our friendship. Pug [Henry] would find the latch off, and the channels of information open, if he simply treated these people as human beings. The press coverage of the new Germany was distorted. When Pug got to know the newspapermen, he would understand why—disgruntled pinkos and drunks, most of them.

Then the attaché went on:

"Hitler's a damned remarkable man," said Tollever, poised on his elbows, one scrubbed hand to his chin, one negligently dangling, his face flushed bright pink. "I'm not saying that he, or Göring, or any of that bunch, wouldn't murder their own grandmothers to increase their power or to advance the interests of Germany. But that's politics in Germany nowadays. We Americans are far too naive. The Soviet Union is the one big reality Europe lives with, Pug—that Slav horde, seething in the east. We can hardly picture that feeling, but for them it's political bedrock. The Communist International is not playing mah-jongg, you know, those Bolos are out to rule Europe by fraud or force or both. Hitler isn't about to let them. That's the root of the matter. The Germans do things in politics that we wouldn't—like this stuff with the Jews—but that's just a passing phase, and anyway, it's not your business. Remember that. Your job is military information. You can get a hell of a lot from these people."*

Truman Smith "considered it fortunate" that Ambassador Dodd was in the United States when he had his idea of inviting Lindbergh, so that he did not have to ask his permission. Instead he obtained the approval of the chargé d'affaires, Ferdinand Mayer, whose attitudes he found more congenial. Smith may well have feared that had the ambassador been in Berlin he would have strongly objected to Lindbergh appearing on the scene as a guest of the Nazis, on the grounds that his propaganda value in building up the prestige of the party would far outweigh any aviation information he might pick up during his tour.

* Herman Wouk, *The Winds of War* (London: Collins, 1971).

This was the year of the Olympic Games in Germany, and on the orders of the Propaganda Ministerium under Joseph Goebbels a supreme effort was being made to make the Nazis seem "respectable." Anyone with a reputation or a famous name (provided it wasn't Jewish, of course) was being invited to come over as guests of the regime, and in London the Nazi envoy, the egregious Joachim von Ribbentrop, was doling out invitations with the eagerness of a theater press agent papering the house for an ailing play. Members of Parliament and scores of dead-beat peers were already on their way, to be wined, dined, entertained, and shown the sunny side of National Socialism.

It would, of course, be unfair to Truman Smith to suggest that he was aware of this. All he was aware of, as he continually insists in his subsequent report, was the necessity of getting information about German aviation. But his timing and his choice of man certainly played into Nazi hands. In the circumstances, it was laughable for Smith to promise Lindbergh "that a visit by you to Germany can be carried out with more privacy to your person than anywhere else in the world." Charles Lindbergh was far too big a prize for the Nazi propaganda machine to be allowed to wander around incognito. The moment Hermann Göring heard that he was coming, he announced gleefully:

"He will be my guest at the opening of the Games."

But that was only one of the engagements. On the second day of his arrival, he was guest of honor at a luncheon given by the Air Club in Berlin at which he was welcomed by General Erhard Milch and flanked by Hans Dieckhoff, German ambassador to the United States, who had flown in from Washington, and Duke Friedrich of Mecklenburg. He had been told that he would be expected to make a speech, and he prepared it carefully beforehand and submitted it to Truman Smith for his "approval" when it was finished.

It was a good speech. He had thought about it a great deal beforehand and treated his guests to a disquisition on time and air travel, astronomy, geology, and psychology.

"Our ideas of time and substance are entirely different from those our fathers held," he declared. "And unlike the builder of the dugout canoe, we have lived to see our wings of fabric turn into carriers of destruction even more dangerous than battleships and guns. . . . Aviation has, I believe, created the most fundamental change ever made in war. It has turned defense into attack. We can no longer protect our families with an army. Our libraries, our museums, every institution we value most is laid bare to bombardment. Aviation has brought a revolutionary change to a world already staggering from changes. It is our responsibility to make sure that in doing so, we do not destroy the very things which we wish to protect."

The speech had a good reception, and even though it was an implied attack on air bombing, which was the basis of Nazi military strategy, it was printed verbatim in the German newspapers next morning. Truman Smith expressed surprise, though he should have known that German propaganda tactics at this moment were to keep neighboring countries constantly aware that they possessed a bombing fleet capable of destroying them, and Lindbergh's speech had provided an extra reminder of it.

There was something in the German air which seemed to turn the usually taciturn Charles Lindbergh into a talker. He gave another speech the following day, while lunching with the Richthofen Squadron, a pursuit wing of the Luftwaffe. He coined a felicitous phrase when replying to the toast:

"Here's to bombers, may they get slower! And here's to pursuit planes, may they grow swifter!"

In the next days, he attended a reception given by the mayor of Berlin and signed the city's Golden Book, took tea with former Crown Prince Wilhelm, at the Cäcilien Palace, and duly took his place with his wife beside Hermann Göring in the Luftwaffe chief's box on the opening day of the Olympic Games. (As a teetotaler and something of a prude, he must have been somewhat disconcerted to find as a fellow guest in the Göring box none other than Eleanor Holm, the American champion swimmer who had been thrown off the U.S. team for drinking champagne and living it up on the voyage across the Atlantic.)

"By far the most important social event of the visit," reported Truman Smith, "was a formal luncheon given by Minister Göring on July 28 at his official residence on the Wilhelmstrasse. This was a large and elaborate affair for both gentlemen and ladies and could be termed rather accurately a 'state' luncheon."

All these affairs, Smith remarked, were reported "fully and inaccurately" in the American press.

"Despite the military attaché's effort to restrict Lindbergh's social obligations," he wrote, "the strictly intelligence visits and inspections consumed less time than the purely social activities."

By the time it was over, Lindbergh had visited several aircraft factories and been told by General Milch of Germany's plans to build an air force "second to none in the world." He did not gather any more information than was already known by most intelligence forces, and he came away with a much exaggerated idea of the Luftwaffe's potential, because Göring, well aware that his aviation program was seriously behind schedule, had ordered factories, airfields, and flying squadrons to pack their "shop windows" in order to impress the visitor and conceal from him the serious deficiencies on the shelves behind. His visit lasted nine days on this occasion, and he flew off again with his wife on August 1, 1936. But it had been nine days well spent—from the point of view of the National Socialist Government. So far as aviation was concerned, Charles Lindbergh had been tremendously impressed by developments which were not terribly impressive. More important, he had found the atmosphere fraternal: the people congenial, the press under control, officials deferential, discipline good, morals pure, and morale high. It was a refreshing change, he found, from the moral degradation into which he considered the United States had fallen, the apathy and indifference of the British, and the decadence of France. The German Government had vowed that they would show him everything he asked to see, and since he did not ask to see concentration camps, political prisoners, Jews, Communists, Socialists, Social-Democrats, or other opponents of the regime, his picture of the Nazi Reich was a decidedly favorable one.

He made it clear both to Truman Smith and to his Nazi hosts that he would like to come again. The American military attaché and his friends in the German Air Ministry put their heads together to find a suitable occasion for a return visit. As for Göring, he was aware that in Charles Lindbergh he and his fellow Nazis had found a particularly sympathetic means of explaining their aims and ideas to the West.

It was Göring himself who came forward with the next invitation.

Before returning to England from Germany, Anne and Charles Lindbergh flew to Copenhagen for a scientific congress, and there he met up with his old friend, Dr. Alexis Carrel. Carrel had brought Lindbergh's perfusion pump with him from New York, and while Lindbergh demonstrated it, the surgeon lectured on its uses.

So far in this narrative, Dr. Carrel has had only marginal mention as the biologist with whom Lindbergh had worked at the Rockefeller Institute in New York in his experiments on the transplant of bodily tissues and organs. His influence on Lindbergh, however, had gone far beyond encouraging him to collaborate in his scientific experiments. He had become Lindbergh's mentor in many spheres of thinking, and had filled his young, philosophically untrained mind with ideas and theories which were only peripherally associated with advanced surgery, but were to have an important bearing on his disciple's attitude to the National Socialists and their ideology.

Alexis Carrel was sixty-four years old in 1936. In 1912 he had won the

Nobel Prize for discovering a method of suturing blood vessels during surgery, and since that time had gone on to more daring work which had won him deserved fame, particularly in the United States. He was a tiny little man with a face whose precise features were made prim by the pince-nez which he wore instead of normal glasses. He was something of a dandy and in off-hours wore a black Nehru-type jacket (though it was not called that in those days) with brass buttons, and a white skullcap pulled down close over his ears. His surgery at the Rockefeller Center was decorated with black walls and black-hooded lights, and he and his assistants wore black monklike gowns which reached to the floor, though his hood was white to distinguish him from his subordinates.

Like many another little man, he had an outsize temper and was apt to develop tantrums when confronted by mistakes, and he could be insultingly rude to colleagues whose wits were not as sharp nor intelligence as acute as his own.

What kept him continually in the public eye was not so much his surgical discoveries as his theories about genetics, a subject on which he talked for long hours not only with Charles Lindbergh but also with any reporter prepared to listen.

"There is no escaping the fact that men were definitely not created equal, as democracy, invented in the eighteenth century, when there was no science to confront it, would have us believe," he declared in a shipboard interview aboard the *Île de France* in 1935.

A year later a book by him called *Man, the Unknown* was a national best seller in the United States. Its theories and suggestions caused something of a sensation. He advanced the idea that future generations might well consider killing off their worst types, as is done among pedigree dogs, in order to improve the race. He advocated the abolition of prisons and their replacement "by smaller and less expensive institutions" where criminals could be either disciplined or "dealt with."

"The conditioning of petty criminals with the whip," he wrote, ". . . followed by a short stay in hospital, would probably suffice to restore order."

He had more drastic solutions for more serious crimes or disabilities: "Those who have murdered, robbed while armed with automatic pistol or machinegun, kidnapped children, despoiled the poor of their savings, misled the public on important matters, should be humanely and economically disposed of in small euthanistic institutions supplied with proper gases. A similar treatment could be advantageously applied to the insane, guilty of criminal acts. Modern society should not hesitate to organize itself with reference to the normal individual. Philosophical systems and sentimental prejudices must give way before such a necessity."†

These ideas bore an uncanny resemblance to those which National Socialism was beginning to follow in Germany. He already shared with Nazi theorists the assumption of the superiority of the Nordic race, his explanation of this being that lesser races—blacks, Latins, Indians, and Asiatics—had been "burned" into inferiority by generations of too fierce light grilling down upon them.

"Excessive light is dangerous," he wrote. "We must not forget that the most highly civilized races—the Scandinavians, for example—are white and have lived for many generations in a country where the atmospheric luminosity is weak during a great part of the year. In France, the populations of the north are far superior to those of the Mediterranean shores. The lower races generally inhabit countries where light is violent and temperature equal and warm."

It was upon these northern, superior peoples, Carrel believed, that a new scientific organization must concentrate its efforts to bring about "the formation of men of superior quality." The work should be directed by intelligent men "entirely concerned with individuals belonging to the races who produced Western civilization." Instead of encouraging the survival of "the unfit and the defective," he wrote, "we must help the strong: only the elite makes the progress of the masses possible."

While he did not share all of Carrel's more way-out theories, there is little doubt that Charles Lindbergh was deeply impressed by many of them, by Carrel's "deep concern about the trends of modern civilization and their effect upon his fellow men," as he wrote shortly afterward. He agreed with Carrel that the Western democracies were in a phase of deterioration, and that they were being sapped morally and physically by loose living and lack of purpose. Carrel, a stanch Roman Catholic with a touch of fire and brimstone in his religious philosophy, believed that only a return to a form of Puritanism could restore the people of the democracies to their former glory; and not only would he have banned alcohol and cigarettes as drugs dangerous to the body but he would also have prohibited public dancing, "African" jazz, "immoral" films, and overt sexuality as being equally dangerous to the mind.

Except that being a Frenchman, he could not suppress his loathing for the Germans, he might have been a colleague of Rosenberg outlining the racial theories of the new National Socialist Reich. Or perhaps

† Alexis Carrel, *Man, the Unknown* (New York: Harper & Brothers, 1935).

that is going too far, because Alexis Carrel was never anti-Semitic, and could point out that some of his best friends were Jews, including Albert Einstein.

Charles Lindbergh loved and admired him, and imbibed much of what he said and thought. It can hardly fail to have an effect upon his thinking when confronted by the Nazis during his stay in Germany. Especially since, because of his hatred of the press, he did not believe a word that Western newspapermen in Berlin were saying about the brutish persecutions and evil motivations of the regime.

The Lindberghs were back in England by the beginning of September, and on the eighth of that month they came over from Long Barn to have tea with the Nicolsons at Sissinghurst. They brought Betty Morrow and her daughter, Constance, with them.‡ Harold Nicolson thought the Lindberghs looked splendidly invigorated from their trip, but he was profoundly depressed when Charles began to talk about Germany. The free-loaders were now flocking home from their visits to the Olympic Games as guests of the Nazis, and all of them seemed to have returned in the same euphoric mood over the Hitler regime and what it was doing for Germany. A fellow member of Parliament and his wife, Henry and Honor Channon,* were among those who (Nicolson wrote) seemed to "have fallen under the champagne-like influence of Ribbentrop and the youthful influence of the Brunswicks, the Wittelsbachs and the House of Hesse Cassel" (their aristocratic hosts during the Games).

> "They . . . had not been in the least disconcerted by Göring or Goebbels," Nicolson wrote in his diary. "They think Ribbentrop a fine man, and that we should let gallant little Germany glut her fill of the Reds in the East and keep decadent France quiet while she does so. Otherwise we shall have not only Reds in the West but bombs in London, Kelvedon [the Channon country home] and Southend. I say that this may be expedient but that it is wrong. We represent a certain type of civilized mind, and that we are sinning against the light if we betray that type. We stand for tolerance, truth, liberty and good humour. They stand for violence, oppression, untruthfulness and bitterness."

‡ Constance was now secretly engaged to Aubrey Neil Morgan, former husband of her dead sister, Elisabeth, and she would marry him the following spring.
* Henry (later Sir Henry) Channon, Tory M.P. for Southend, was an American by birth. He was married to Honor Guinness, daughter of Lord Iveagh.

Now here were the Lindberghs playing the same Gramophone record, with variations on the aviation theme. Noted Nicolson:

> [Lindbergh] has obviously been much impressed by Nazi Germany. He admires their energy, virility, spirit, organisation, architecture, planning, and physique. He considers that they possess the most powerful air force in the world with which they could do terrible damage to any other country. . . . He admits that they are a great menace but denies that they are a menace to us. He contends that the future will see a complete separation between Fascism and Communism, and he believes that if Great Britain supports the decadent French and the Red Russians against Germany, there will be an end to European civilization.

At Lindbergh's request, he promised to get in touch with some members of the British Government so that the flier could warn them about the growing strength of the German Air Force. As he explained to the Englishman, he felt happy at the fact that Germany was regaining strength, because he believed that a strong Germany (even a Nazi one) was essential to the welfare of Europe. But he went on to assure Nicolson that he did not like to see England fall so far behind in air strength, because he also regarded a strong British Empire as essential to world stability. So could he talk to someone?

Nicolson fixed up a lunch at the House of Commons a few weeks later with Sir Thomas Inskip, Minister of Defence, and sat back while Lindbergh, shyly at first, then with increasing confidence, poured out alarming statistics about Germany's air expansion. There could be no defense against the bomber fleets they were building, he said, and "all fortification is useless." Popeyed with alarm, Sir Thomas scribbled it all down in a notebook.

"It is a successful luncheon and for once I feel that I have done some real good," Nicolson wrote afterward.

Lindbergh did not agree with him. He considered that his hosts had simply listened to him and then forgot about it. "I was learning how difficult it was for a foreigner to contribute anything to English life," he noted later. He had expected, it seemed, to be called in and set up as some sort of an adviser, and felt he had been snubbed. "If it wasn't British, it simply wasn't 'best.' . . . Obviously, the British preferred to carry on in their own way."

In fact, he had done a quite considerable job at the luncheon party, though on behalf of Nazi Germany rather than Britain. He had scared

Sir Thomas Inskip rigid with his dire forecasts of Germany's might, and in the months to come he would scare the rest of His Majesty's Government, including the Prime Minister, Neville Chamberlain.

By the time the Lindberghs returned to England Anne Lindbergh knew that she was pregnant again. It did not prevent her from accompanying her husband on several of his expeditions, and during the sixth, seventh, and eighth months of her pregnancy she was with him on a strenuous flight to India and back. At the outset of the journey they were reported missing over the Alps while flying from France to Italy, but it was a false alarm, as it always was in Lindbergh's case. The journey was a rough one and he put down unexpectedly at Pisa Airport, forbidding local officials to report his arrival. It seemed now to have become one of Charles Lindbergh's favorite games, to persuade the newspapers to headline: LINDBERGH MISSING or LINDY LOST and then show them to Anne and his friends with the remark: "There, you see. Wrong again!"

Unlike American newspapers, the British press did not go in for "infanticipating," to use the word invented by the most famous American columnist of the day, Walter Winchell. But they did expect that when a famous couple had a baby, they would be informed of its arrival. They were disconcerted to discover that Lindbergh adopted exactly the same attitude toward them as to their American confreres, and concealed the birth of his third child until twelve days after the event. If he had chosen to do so because he wished to avoid publicity, exactly the opposite happened. Lindbergh's second living son was born on the evening of May 12, 1937, which was the day King George VI was crowned in Westminster Abbey, and British newspapers were full of the coronation ceremony. A Lindbergh baby would not have rated more than a paragraph. His mother-in-law, Mrs. Dwight Morrow, had come over from America to be with her daughter during the accouchement, and she could not understand why Lindbergh was being so secretive about it.

"If you want to avoid being bothered by the press," she said, "why don't you simply announce the birth of your child? After all, he's normal and born in wedlock."

But he was adamant, and did not allow the news to get out until May 25, when, of course, it got much more attention in the newspapers.

He was named Land, after Evangeline Lindbergh's family.

That fall, the Lindberghs flew back to Germany, this time as guests of honor of the German Government at the Lilienthal Aeronautical Congress in Munich.

The visit had once more been engineered by Truman Smith, the American military attaché in Berlin, who had by this time convinced himself (and some of the more credulous agents in the War Department in Washington) that he and Charles Lindbergh between them were cracking the secrets of the Luftwaffe wide open. This time the German World War I ace Ernst Udet took Lindbergh in hand and flew him around Germany, showing him new planes, aircraft factories, allowing him to handle the Messerschmitt 109, boasting of the superb technical and numerical superiority of the German Air Force over any other force or combination of forces in Europe.

Lindbergh believed him. How was he to know that at this moment Udet, as director of the Technical Department at the Air Ministry, was making a mess of Germany's aviation program? Everything was behindhand. Udet's lack of managerial and technical know-how, his habit of putting old flying pals in jobs they could not handle, his bad relations with the aircraft manufacturers, his falsification of records, his general unfitness for the job, were already starting the chain reaction in the Luftwaffe's building program that would eventually cost Germany the air war and Udet his life (by suicide).

The Germans were so obviously friendly and deferential to him that Lindbergh would have found it impossible to believe that Udet was lying to him,† and would have been even more incredulous had he been told that he was being deliberately used by the Luftwaffe to carry stories of their invincibility back to the democracies and terrorize them. It was a ploy they were to repeat shortly afterward, with devastating effect, on the chief of the French Air Force, General Joseph Vuillemin, for whom they also wheeled out their "secret" planes and demonstrated what they could do. He rushed back to Paris in a condition bordering on panic to tell the French Government about the might, the unbeatable might, of the Luftwaffe.

"The Germans set out to make a great impression on him," wrote Paul Stehlin, assistant French air attaché in Berlin, who accompanied Vuillemin on the tour. "They succeeded and Vuillemin's opinions had more effect than they deserved upon the decisions of our government."‡

---

† Just before he shot himself in 1941, Udet was called in and sacked by Hermann Göring, who called him "a liar, a big mouth and an incompetent." General Milch, who took over from him, said his principal accomplishments were "flying, drinking, womanising and fabrication, in that order."

‡ Paul Stehlin, *Témoinage pour l'Histoire* (Paris: Robert Laffont, 1964).

Lindbergh was by no means panicked by what he saw on this and a subsequent tour in 1938, but he was certainly impressed. He was so convinced of the sincerity of his hosts, so deceived by what he considered to be their frankness, friendliness, and respect for his reputation, that he accepted everything they told him, including production figures that were false and future plans that were never fulfilled. It was true that he saw some splendid planes, but there were never as many of them as the Germans indicated.

He came back to Truman Smith with the glint in his eye of a man who has found gold, and between them they sat down to enumerate his treasure trove of facts about the mighty armadas the Nazi Reich was building. He now genuinely believed that the Luftwaffe could outmatch any combination of air powers in the world, and that in consequence Western Europe was at Germany's mercy.

Off went the devastating report to Washington. Soon General H. H. (Hap) Arnold, chief of staff of the United States Air Force, was circulating an estimate of the Luftwaffe's strength at 10,000 planes. Lindbergh estimated that Germany was building between 500 and 800 planes a month. This was in 1938. In fact, as the figures now available from German military sources show,* the Luftwaffe's strength *two years later* was only 4,665 planes in all, consisting of 1,711 bombers, 414 dive bombers, 354 escort fighters, 1,356 pursuit planes, and 830 reconnaissance and other planes. At that moment (May 1940, when the attack on France began) Germany was turning out only 125 fighter planes a month, while Britain was producing 325. Bomber production in Germany in 1940 was around 300 a month, but in 1938 was considerably below that figure.

In fact, at the moment when Lindbergh and Truman Smith were lauding the might of the Luftwaffe, it was in no condition to fight a war—and certainly not against the combination of nations which faced it at that moment—namely, Britain, France, Czechoslovakia, and the Soviet Union.† But Hermann Göring was convinced that if he could only bluff the West into believing in his invincibility, a war would not be necessary. He knew from Lindbergh's conversations with Udet that the American flier was a firm believer in the Douhet theory of warfare, as, in fact, were most students of war at that time, including Göring himself. Giulio Douhet, an Italian expert on strategic air power, was the author of a book called *Command of the Air*, which maintained

---

* German Military History Research Bureau, Speciality Group 6: Air Force and Aerial Warfare History.

† Britain and France had a military alliance. France had a military alliance with Czechoslovakia, and so did Soviet Russia.

that all future wars would be won by the nation with the biggest bomber force, whose devastating attacks would completely destroy an enemy's capability of defense or riposte. Field marshals carried a copy of Douhet in their knapsacks. Statesmen in the West read him and had nightmares about death, destruction, and defeat.

All Göring had to do was persuade Lindbergh that the Luftwaffe was indeed capable of utterly destroying any nation or combination of nations, that its strength and readiness could not possibly be matched, and the battle would be half won. His prestige was such that he could convince the statesmen and military leaders of every nation which stood in Germany's way.

Göring had judged his man shrewdly. Once he believed what the Germans told him and showed him, Charles Lindbergh, with the utmost sincerity, fervently believing he was helping to save European civilization, set himself the job of persuading National Socialism's enemies to lay down their arms and give in without a fight.

By the summer of 1938, the Lindberghs were the most popular bringers of bad tidings on the London and Paris social scenes.

"Charles and Anne Lindbergh and Mrs. Morrow come over from Long Barn," noted Harold Nicolson on May 22. "Lindbergh is most pessimistic. He says we cannot possibly fight since we should certainly be beaten. The German Air Force is ten times superior to that of Russia, France and Great Britain put together.‡ Our defences are simply futile and the barrage-balloons a mere waste of money. He thinks we should just give way and then make an alliance with Germany. To a certain extent his views can be discounted, (a) because he naturally believes that aeroplanes will be the determinant factor in war; and (b) because he believes in the Nazi theology, all tied up with his hatred of degeneracy and his hatred of democracy as represented by the free Press and the American public. But even when one makes these discounts, the fact remains that he is probably right in saying that we are outmastered in the air."

In the discussion that followed, Nicolson gave a short, sharp description of exactly what he thought of the Nazis and indicated that he would rather die than make an alliance with them. It is indicative of Lindbergh's misreading of Nicolson's character, as well as his own feelings about the National Socialist regime, that he afterward described

‡ Nicolson was exaggerating. Lindbergh said the Luftwaffe was superior but not *ten* times so.

his host's anti-Nazi remarks in his own diary as "very anti-German,"* whereas Nicolson's feelings were much more accurately described in his own words:

"I love Germany and hate to see all that is worst in the German character being exploited [by the Nazis] at the expense of all that is best."

There were other hosts, however, who were much more willing to accept Lindbergh's policy of coming to an arrangement with the Nazis. Chief of them was the sharp-tongued and incisive Member of Parliament for Plymouth, the American-born Lady Nancy Astor. She was a famous society hostess and specialized in weekend parties for statesmen, politicians, diplomats, writers, and artists at her lavish country estate at Cliveden, in Berkshire. She had taken up the Lindberghs in a large way ever since their arrival in England, and she now encouraged him to disseminate his opinions among her influential guests. Violently anti-French, she shared Lindbergh's view that they should be abandoned by Britain in favor of a better understanding with Germany.

During one week in May she saw to it that Charles Lindbergh lunched, dined, or took tea with the Minister of Defence (Sir Thomas Inskip), the Minister for War (Leslie Hore-Belisha), the George Bernard Shaws, the American ambassador to London (Joseph P. Kennedy), and the American ambassador to Paris (William C. Bullitt). He talked "in detail" about England, America, the Soviet Union, France, Germany, and aviation. He assured Inskip that Germany's aircraft building program was so great that "the Germans can probably produce more military aircraft than the British Empire and the United States combined, with the facilities which now exist."

He came away from these meetings "encouraged" about the way these people around the Astors felt about Germany and reacted to his words. But he did not realize how closely his dire predictions of death and destruction had been listened to until Bullitt called him to invite him to Paris. There he dined with the American envoy at his home in Chantilly and lectured a fellow guest, Guy la Chambre, the French Minister for Air, on the folly of hoping to oppose the German Luftwaffe. Shortly afterward, he repeated it all again to Joseph Kennedy, who saw that the British Prime Minister, Neville Chamberlain, was informed.

It was a busy summer. The only prominent person in Britain whom he does not seem to have scared out of her wits by his saber-rattling line

* See *The Wartime Journals of Charles A. Lindbergh* (New York: Harcourt Brace Jovanovich, 1970), Sunday, May 22, 1938, p. 28.

was the Queen of England, whom he met twice at this time—once at the Astors, once (wearing knee breeches) at a ball at Buckingham Palace. She asked him to dance. He told her he had never danced in his life. So they talked and she "asked about the Hearst press and American newspapers," a subject on which he no doubt waxed extremely eloquent.

In August the Lindberghs flew to Russia at the invitation of the Soviet Government and were shown over a number of aircraft establishments and factories. He was not impressed. They traveled back by way of Czechoslovakia and were shown the Czech Air Force. He did not think much of it.

They arrived back in London when the Western democracies were facing the greatest crisis in their relations with the National Socialist Reich. Adolf Hitler had threatened to seize the Sudetenland from Czechoslovakia, and had been warned that if he did so there would be war. If Czechoslovakia were attacked by Germany, both the Soviet Union and France were pledged to go to her aid; and if France were involved, then, by treaty, so was Britain.

Lindbergh was appalled to discover when he returned from his trip that the British seemed determined to stand by their allies and were preparing for war. Gas masks were being issued, air raid trenches dug in Hyde Park. How could he stop this madness? Germany would wipe the floor with the lot of them. European civilization would be destroyed. And all because, as he saw it, Germany was seeking justice for the wrongs which had been done to her in the past.

He searched around desperately for a way of preventing the catastrophe which he now envisioned. It was at this moment that Joseph Kennedy, the American envoy in London, came to his aid. Kennedy, as strongly convinced as Lindbergh that Germany was insuperable and determined to keep Britain out of war even if it meant giving in to the Nazis, saw in Lindbergh's prestige a way to influence the British Government toward a policy of appeasement. He summoned Lindbergh to the embassy and asked him to assess for him the exact nature and strength of the Luftwaffe.

It was a moment when Prime Minister Chamberlain had begun personal negotiations with Adolf Hitler to avoid a war. He had been to Berchtesgaden to argue with the Führer, and was due to continue the discussion at Bad Godesberg on September 22. On the evening of September 21, Kennedy asked Lindbergh to put his views in writing. When Chamberlain left for Bad Godesberg on September 22, he had a summary of Lindbergh's views with him, and they were devastating. For Lindbergh had written as follows:

September 22, 1938

Dear Ambassador Kennedy:

This letter is to confirm and clarify the statements I made to you yesterday in regard to military aviation in Europe.

Without doubt the German air fleet is now stronger than that of any other country in the world. The rate of progress of German military aviation during the last several years is without parallel. I feel certain that German air strength is greater than that of all other European countries combined, and that she is constantly increasing her margin of leadership. I believe that German factories are capable of producing in the vicinity of 20,000 aircraft each year. Her actual production is difficult to estimate. The most reliable reports I have obtained vary from 500 to 800 planes per month. . . .

I do not believe civilization ever faced a greater crisis. Germany now has the means of destroying London, Paris and Prague if she wishes to do so. England and France together have not enough modern war planes for effective defense or counter-attack. France is in a pitiful condition in the air. England is better off, but her air fleet is not comparable with Germany's. . . . Czechoslovakia has no completely modern aircraft except those obtained from Russia. . . . Judging by the general conditions in Russia, I would not place great confidence in the Russian air fleet. . . .

It seems to me essential to avoid a general European war in the near future at almost any cost. I believe that a war now might easily result in the loss of European civilization. I am by no means convinced that England and France could win a war against Germany at the present time, but, whether they win or lose, all of the participating countries would probably be prostrated by their efforts. A general European war would, I believe, result in something akin to Communism running over Europe and, judging by Russia, anything seems preferable.

I am convinced that it is wiser to permit Germany's eastward expansion than to throw England and France, unprepared, into a war at this time.

We must recognize the fact that the Germans are a great and able people. Their military strength now makes them inseparable from the welfare of European civilization, for they have the power either to preserve or destroy it. For the first time in history, a nation has the power either to save or to ruin the great cities of Europe. Germany has such a preponderance of war planes that she can bomb any city in Europe with comparatively little resistance. England and France are too weak in the air to protect themselves.

Yours sincerely,
Charles A. Lindbergh

It should perhaps be emphasized once more that most of the assertions contained in this letter were untrue, and that Charles Lindbergh had been tricked into grossly overblowing the power of the Luftwaffe. But that was something which Neville Chamberlain did not realize. Confronted by an intransigent Adolf Hitler, terrified that if he did not give way to the Nazis over their demands on Czechoslovakia all Lindbergh's dire predictions of Teutonic fire and brimstone would come true, he became convinced that surrender was the only possible choice. He persuaded the French Prime Minister, Édouard Daladier, to act likewise. And at Munich on September 29, 1938, Britain and France sacrificed their Czechoslovakian ally and kissed the Soviet Union goodby as a potential ally.

It was quite a victory for the German Air Force considering the fact that it had not even needed to get airborne.

CHAPTER

EIGHTEEN

THE ALBATROSS

No one was more relieved than the Lindberghs when the British and French gave in to Adolf Hitler's threats at Munich and signed over their Czechoslovakian ally to the Nazis. Charles Lindbergh had no doubt whatsoever that Chamberlain and Daladier had made the right decision in surrendering, for he believed that in so doing they had saved the democracies from destruction and Europe from Communism. "It always seems that the Fascist group is better than the Communist group," he was writing at this time, adding that "Communism seems to draw the worst of men."

While the Munich Pact was being negotiated, he and Anne sweated it out, not inappropriately, with their friends Lord and Lady Astor at Cliveden. He kept waking up in the night, thinking of England being bombed. On September 29 he left Anne behind with Lady Astor and went into London to see Ambassador Joseph Kennedy at the American embassy, and he was with him when the "good news" came through that the democracies had given way to the dictators. He was inclined to give credit for the outcome of the conference to the American envoy, for "Kennedy has taken a large part in bringing about the conference between Hitler, Chamberlain, Mussolini and Daladier." In this, of course, he was being too modest. Without the devastating statistics and predictions with which Lindbergh had provided him, Kennedy would never have been able to convince Chamberlain of the need to appease Adolf Hitler. Moreover, Kennedy's influence had been solely upon the British Prime Minister, whereas Lindbergh had worked on the French as well. It is true that no one man, no matter how influential, could have brought about the state of fear and helplessness in which the leaders of the democracies groveled at Munich. It is probable that Neville Chamberlain would have submitted to Hitler whether Lindbergh had been on hand or not; and certainly, if Lindbergh had not existed, the Nazis would have found someone of equal prestige to do their propaganda for them. It is nonetheless valid to say, however, that at a crucial moment in the crisis year of 1938, Lindbergh's was the voice the leaders of the democracies listened to—and what he told them (though he did not realize it) was false. To him, therefore, goes much of the credit for Munich. And the blame.

Two weeks after the Munich Pact was signed, and at a moment when the German Army was still taking over the Sudetenland areas of Czechoslovakia, Anne and Charles Lindbergh arrived for their third visit to Berlin. In the circumstances it is hardly surprising that this time they were more warmly welcomed than ever by the National Socialist Government. One of the elements which persuaded the Nazis that Lindbergh was now firmly in their camp was a flurry of press publicity which had begun as he left Britain. Some of the highly critical remarks which Charles Lindbergh had made about the strength and qualities of the Soviet Air Force had been leaked to an influential underground newssheet called *The Week*, edited and published in London by a Left-inclined newspaperman named Claud Cockburn. Cockburn, when wearing his respectable hat, was diplomatic correspondent of Britain's most powerful newspaper, the *Times*, which at that time was following a pro-Chamberlain line and had supported the Munich Pact. He was therefore privy to much information circulating among the pro-appeasers, or Cliveden Set, as he had dubbed them (after Lady Astor's home, where they were apt to foregather).

He now announced in *The Week* that at a dinner party at Cliveden during the Munich crisis, Lindbergh had informed Lady Astor and her guests that (1) Russian aviation was in a chaotic condition; (2) he had been invited to become chief of the Russian civil air fleet; and (3) the German air fleet could whip the Russian, French, and British air fleets combined.* The story had been immediately cabled to Moscow, where the Soviet leaders, who had treated Lindbergh and his wife as honored guests during their visit, were astounded that he could repay them with

* Cockburn had got it slightly wrong. Lindbergh had accused the Red air force of being inefficient and badly organized; he had not said that Germany could *whip* the combined air forces, only that the Luftwaffe was stronger than all three; and he had never been offered the post of chief of Soviet aviation. Moreover, he had made his remarks to a group of M.P.s at a London club, and not at Cliveden.

23. In 1936, while living in England, Charles and Anne Morrow Lindbergh were invited to Germany as guests of the National Socialist Government. While there they stayed with the American military attaché in Berlin, Major Truman Smith, with whom Charles is seen here during an inspection of German aircraft factories.

24. Lindbergh made four trips to Germany between 1936 and 1938, and met most of the leaders of the German Air Force during that period. In this picture he is shown talking to Luftwaffe General Erhard Milch, Germany's second-ranking airman, at a ceremony at Potsdam.

25. During his German visits, Lindbergh several times met Field Marshal Hermann Göring, chief of the Luftwaffe. Later the Marshal decorated Lindbergh with the Service Cross of the German Eagle, a Nazi medal which the flier refused to return when World War II began. In this picture, with Anne Morrow Lindbergh (left) looking on, he is shown handling Göring's ceremonial sword.

26. Lindbergh was taken on several tours of German air stations and aircraft factories during his visits to Nazi Germany in 1936–38. He is here seen discussing air tactics with Willy Messerschmitt, builder of two famous World War II fighter planes, the Me109 and Me110.

27. Another picture of Lindbergh on a tour of the Messerschmitt aircraft factory at Augsburg with Willy Messerschmitt and a German Air Force officer.

28. Back from a Europe about to plunge into war, Charles Lindbergh returned to the United States in 1939 determined to persuade his fellow Americans to keep out of the conflict. Here he is seen making the first of a series of radio talks which soon rallied the nation's isolationists behind him.

such insults. *Pravda*, the official party newspaper, declared that he should be arrested if he ever set foot in the Soviet Union again, and a round-robin letter of rebuke to him was signed by the Soviets' most famous pilots, most of whom had been his hosts during the Lindbergh visit.

When Charles Lindbergh reached Berlin, he found waiting for him at the American embassy an anguished cable from the American military attaché in Moscow, Major Faymonville, saying that he had been personally compromised and American-Soviet relations damaged by Lindbergh's "insulting" remarks, and would he deny them. But despite pressure from other American sources, he refused to issue a statement of denial or explanation. "I never comment on stories in the press," he insisted. Nor would he agree to send a private message to the Soviet Government.†

Lindbergh's anti-Soviet comments (true or not) did nothing to diminish him in National Socialist eyes, of course, and nothing was henceforward too good for him. The Luftwaffe gave a dinner on the night of October 11, 1938, for visiting delegates to the Lilienthal Congress. It was held in the banqueting hall of the Neue Palast at Potsdam, lit by 3,000 candles. Charles Lindbergh had the place of honor beside the host, General Erhard Milch. Milch, who was State Secretary at the Air Ministry at this time, told his guest that his chief, Hermann Göring, was anxious to talk to him, and looked forward to doing so on the evening of October 18, when he would be coming to dine with the new ambassador, Hugh Wilson, at the American embassy.‡ He did not say any more than this at the time, and Lindbergh assured Milch that he would be there and looked forward to talking to Göring.

On the afternoon of October 18, the Attaché Section of the German Air Ministry telephoned Major Truman Smith, the American military attaché, at the embassy. Told that he was out of the office, the speaker said he would leave a message: *Would the military attaché please note that when Reich Minister Göring arrived at the embassy that evening*

---

† This was in marked contrast to his reaction a few weeks later, when the New York *Times* and other U.S. newspapers printed a story that he had sent a report about the Luftwaffe to Washington. He immediately telephoned the embassy in Berlin and asked someone to contact Udet and other German air chiefs and apologize for the publicity, which had not been of his doing. He pointed out that he was "very anxious" not to have any misunderstandings with the Germans. Truman Smith cabled back: UDET AS REQUESTED STOP THEY ARE NOT DISTURBED STOP [German] PRESS TOLD BY AIR NOT TO NOTICE STOP SMITH

‡ Wilson had replaced William Dodd in March 1938.

there would be a short ceremony. General Göring intended to present Colonel Charles Lindbergh with a decoration.

Truman Smith subsequently declared that since no American was in his office at the time, and since the message was therefore taken down by a German secretary, its significance was missed. The secretary did not bother to pass on the information. If true, this seems to be extraordinary. A German would surely have thought it even more important than an American that Colonel Lindbergh was going to receive a decoration from the second most important man in the Reich. However, Truman Smith maintains that he never received the message (or not, at least, until the following morning, when it was too late). So no one at the embassy knew what was going to happen later in the evening.

Göring was the last to arrive at the dinner party. He exchanged greetings with his host, shook hands with the other guests, and then, with Ambassador Wilson at his side, advanced on Charles Lindbergh. He had a red box in his hand which his aide, Karl Bodenschatz, had handed to him, and when he came face to face with the flier, he began to speak. Lindbergh, who knew no German, was nonplussed. The American consul general in Berlin, Raymond H. Geist, stepped forward to interpret.

"It was discovered, to the surprise of the military attaché," Truman Smith wrote later, "that Göring was decorating Lindbergh with the Verdienstkreuz der Deutscher Adler (Service Cross of the German Eagle), a high German decoration for civilians."

According to Smith's recollection, Göring said as he pinned on the cross that he was awarding it to Lindbergh for his "services to the aviation of the world and particularly for his historic 1927 solo flight across the Atlantic," and notes that Lindbergh confirmed this impression in the diary entry he made on the night in question. This is not quite correct. What Lindbergh says in his entry for October 18 is:

"I found that he had presented me with the German Eagle, one of the highest German decorations, 'by order of der Führer.' "

It was an awkward moment for a non-German (or a non-Nazi German, for that matter) to receive a high award from the National Socialist regime. Even if it was a belated recognition of his transatlantic flight (most nations had decorated him ten years earlier), it could only be confirmation that the Nazis regarded him as their friend, at a moment when the world was beginning to recognize the grim implications of Munich.

Ambassador Wilson, who realized only too well what Munich had wrought, was sufficiently aware of the tainted nature of the decoration to wonder whether Lindbergh would refuse it. He breathed a sigh of relief when he did not. As he said in a letter he wrote to Lindbergh later:

> Neither you nor I nor any other American present had any previous hint that the presentation would be made.
> I have always felt that if you had refused the decoration presented under these circumstances, you would have been guilty of a breach of good taste. It would have been an act offensive to a guest of the Ambassador of your country, in the house of the Ambassador. . . .

In fact, Charles Lindbergh never had any idea of refusing the medal. It came from the head of a government he respected and a people he admired, and he was pleased with the gesture. Three weeks later, the regime showed its true face by sending storm troopers into the streets of Berlin to round up the Jews, smash their shops, and seize their property. Lindbergh's reaction to this orgy of hate and destruction was:

"They have undoubtedly had a difficult Jewish problem, but why is it necessary to handle it so unreasonably?"

But he certainly did not feel it justified sending back his decoration, and he never did so.

It was a medal that would hang heavy round his neck in the years to come, and if Charles Lindbergh did not realize this, his wife certainly did. Truman Smith wrote later:

"When Colonel Lindbergh and the military attaché reached home late that evening, they found their wives had not yet retired. Colonel Lindbergh without comment drew the medal box from his pocket and handed it to Mrs. Lindbergh. She gave it but a fleeting glance and then —without the slightest trace of emotion—remarked: 'The Albatross.' "*

It was in a mood of disenchantment with England that Charles Lindbergh began making his plans in the winter of 1938–39. His love affair with the English people (he very rarely used the words "Britain" or "British") was petering out in a succession of minor irritations and major disappointments.

Why were the English so inefficient? He was always running around London trying to get replacements which he could have obtained in ten

---

* Lindbergh's own feelings were summed up in a letter he wrote on May 31, 1955: "The decoration Göring gave me that night never caused me any worry, and I doubt that it caused me much additional difficulty. It turned out to be a convenient object of attack for our political opposition, but if there had been no decoration they would have found something else. I always regarded the fuss about it as a sort of teapot tempest."

minutes in New York. The telephone did not work. The people were always stopping for tea "which seems a little effeminate to me" and only for "society women and Eastern dudes." There was a combination of "bluff and vanity" about the English which made them infuriatingly opinionated, so that "anything you say [to them] has about as much effect as spray on a rock."

He had had a quarrel with the English obstetrician just before Anne had given birth to Land Lindbergh in a London clinic. The doctor had insisted that final labor pains had not yet begun, and had been crisply informed that he (Lindbergh) knew better, because he had closely observed his wife's behavior throughout at her previous two accouchements.

He was angry when "Anne failed her driving test!!!! After fifteen years of driving without an accident!" He searched for an ulterior motive in the fact that the English examiner had refused to pass her. Either he "wanted to be smart" or he was "so stupid that he mistook experience and ability for incompetence."

But these were minor annoyances compared with the fundamental faults in the English character. They had confidence rather than ability, tenacity rather than strength, and determination rather than intelligence. It was a land made up of a great mass "of slow, somewhat stupid and indifferent people" and a few geniuses, and the geniuses were becoming increasingly hard to find.

In the summer of 1938 they gave up their lease of Long Barn and moved across the Channel to an island off the Brittany coast. Its name was Illiec and the small strip of rock, beach, a small wood, three houses, and a chapel had been bought for the Lindberghs by Dr. and Mme. Alexis Carrel, who owned the slightly larger neighboring isle of St. Gildas. It was a storm-tossed spit of land, but the Lindberghs and their children loved it for its wild beauty, its wildlife, and its remoteness. Charles Lindbergh found it the most satisfying place he had ever lived in since leaving the farm at Little Falls. Here Lindbergh could work and talk with Carrel, relax with Anne and the children knowing they were completely free from molestation, and also be reunited with the two dogs, Thor and Skeean.

But Illiec would be too rough and movement difficult once the fall storms began, and they had to settle for somewhere to stay for the winter. Their enthusiasm for England was gone. Paris brought them too close to the machinations of the corrupt and "decadent" French political machine. But on the same night that Hermann Göring gave him his medal, General Milch talked to Charles Lindbergh about finding a home in Berlin. He nodded agreement. He and Anne had already talked about it, he said—it would make an excellent base.

From the point of view of watching Europe slide inexorably into war, it certainly was. By this time, every foreign correspondent in Berlin, including the author, and the shrewder diplomats knew that the die had been cast and war was inevitable; and the German capital was a fascinating (if grim) vantage point from which to see it happen. But the extraordinary thing is that Charles and Anne Lindbergh were not thinking of it in that way at all. They planned to make a home there, not only for themselves but for their children as well.

On October 28, 1938, they went to look at a house near Wannsee, on the outskirts of Berlin, which was well if heavily furnished, and had a large garden, well planted and shrubbed, running down to a river, with swans. Charles Lindbergh thought it would be "an excellent place for Jon and Land," and they decided to take it provided they could get a satisfactory lease.

Next day they went to the German Air Ministry to ask one of the Luftwaffe billeting officers there, Colonel Wendland, about the lease. He made some inquiries about it and then advised them against it, on the grounds that the owner wanted foreign currency and a high rent.†

Instead, he suggested they go and see Herr Albert Speer, then city planning chief for Berlin,‡ who would willingly build the Lindberghs a house "at almost any location we wished in Berlin."

While they were considering this prospect, and while Colonel Wendland was having further houses inspected for possible lease, they returned to Illiec. It was while they were there that anti-Jewish riots broke out in Germany, after a rabble-rousing speech by Propaganda Minister Joseph Goebbels at a dinner commemorating the Nazis' so-called Beer Hall Putsch of 1923. Charles Lindbergh was surprised and skeptical of reports of the violence done to Jews and their property and confessed that "my admiration for the Germans" was constantly being "dashed against some rock such as this." By this time he was so deep an admirer of the Germans ("They are so like our own people. We should be working with them and not constantly crossing swords") that he was

---

† It was, in fact, a Jewish-owned house. Many Jews in Berlin at this time were trying to let their houses to foreigners, knowing that they would thus be safe from seizure by the Nazis.

‡ He later became Minister of Armaments and War Production in the Nazi Government, and was sentenced as a war criminal to twenty years imprisonment at the Nuremberg trials.

reluctant to believe that a regime which had made him feel so much at home could be responsible for brutalities of this kind.*

Anne Lindbergh, on the other hand, was profoundly shocked by the German excesses, and her mother, writing to her from America, left her in no doubt about what *she* thought about the Nazis. Anne told her husband that in the circumstances she did not think she could comfortably accept the idea of making a home in Berlin with her children. Her opinion was reinforced by a cable which arrived from Alexis Carrel— who was in New York at the time—saying that "anti-German feeling" in America was "now very strong," and advising them to cancel their plans. He had, in fact, already promised Anne Lindbergh that they could stay in Paris for the winter, and no more was heard of his hope of setting up a home in Berlin.

He did, however, pay two more visits to Berlin during the next few months, and the reason behind them throws more light on Charles Lindbergh's curiously naïve attitude to the Nazi regime. During his trip to Germany in October he had talked to General Milch and Ernst Udet about his hopes for seeing a rapprochement in Europe between France and Germany, and when they replied that they shared these hopes, he said he knew one way of bringing them together: through aircraft. The French were short of engines for their planes. Why not allow them to buy them from the Germans? On the other hand, they had a prototype of a promising new fighter. Why shouldn't the Germans buy it from the French? In other words, a joint Franco-German plane with a French Dewoitine 520 body and a German Daimler-Benz 601 engine.

The Germans heartily agreed that it was a good idea, and Lindbergh thereupon rushed back to Paris and immediately went into conference with the American ambassador, William C. Bullitt, and Guy la Chambre, the French Air Minister. He said as a start the Germans would be willing to begin selling aircraft engines to the French.

It seems incredible that at this period in time, when every intelligence agency in Europe was forecasting that the Nazi armies were about to march again,† that anyone could have taken the proposition seriously. But Lindbergh was convincing. Once more he clearly believed

---

* He later put it down to the fact that the Germans hated the Jews for being responsible for internal collapse and revolution after World War I: "They lived in the best houses, drove the best automobiles, and mixed with the prettiest German girls."

† They marched in Prague on March 15, 1939, and occupied the remainder of Czechoslovakia in the next thirty-six hours.

in the sincerity of the Germans, and succeeded in making the ambassador and the French minister believe in them, too.

On February 21, 1939, Bullitt cabled to Franklin D. Roosevelt at the White House:

THIS LETTER IS FOR YOU ALONE AND I HOPE YOU WILL ANSWER IT BY CABLE IMMEDIATELY. ABOUT THE FIFTH OF FEBRUARY GUY LA CHAMBRE SAID TO ME LINDBERGH HAD INFORMED HIM THAT ON A RECENT TRIP TO GERMANY HE HAD ASCERTAINED THAT THE GERMAN GOVERNMENT WOULD BE GLAD TO SELL BENZ MOTORS OF ABOUT 1050 HORSEPOWER TO FRANCE. . . . HE ASKED IF I THOUGHT THERE WOULD BE ANY HOSTILE REACTION IN THE UNITED STATES IF IT SHOULD BECOME KNOWN THAT THE FRENCH GOVERNMENT HAD PURCHASED THREE BENZ MOTORS IN GERMANY. I REPLIED THAT I DID NOT THINK THERE WOULD BE ANY HOSTILE REACTIONS. IN FACT PEOPLE WOULD THINK IT RATHER CLEVER OF THE FRENCH TO HAVE GOT HOLD OF EXAMPLES OF THE BEST GERMAN MOTORS FOR THOROUGH INSPECTION.

At the same time, Guy la Chambre summoned his assistant air attaché back from the French embassy in Berlin, and instructed him to help Lindbergh with the project. The attaché, Paul Stehlin, was himself on close terms with Göring's sister and knew much of what was going on in Nazi aviation circles. He was "both stunned and paralyzed" that anyone could believe that the Germans would go through with such a project.

Stehlin waited until Lindbergh had completed two visits to Germany, during which he talked to Udet and General Milch, before embarking on practical negotiations. Then he called up Ernst Udet and asked for a meeting. He was an old friend of the Luftwaffe's technical director, and he was invited to come round to talk to him.

A few days later Stehlin arrived at Udet's Berlin apartment and found him there with three colleagues from the Luftwaffe.

"A couple of bottles of brandy were on the table and it was obvious that all of them had been drinking for some time," Stehlin said.‡ "Udet greeted me with his usual bear hug and poured me a large cognac. I drained it down."

A code name for the project for purchasing the engines had been given, and it was Fieseler Storch. This happened to be the *real* name of a small reconnaissance plane which everyone knew about. So when

‡ In a conversation with the author.

Stehlin said that he had come to discuss Fiesler Storch, Udet deliberately chose to misunderstand him.

"We've built scores of them," he said. "How many is France interested in buying?"

Stehlin said: "I'm not talking about aircraft, I'm talking about *Project* Fiesler Storch."

Udet poured out more drinks, and urged his guests to put them down, then recharged them. He was very drunk. Finally, he said: "All right, I know. You're interested in the Daimler-Benz engine. Well, what are you going to do?"

Then he began to laugh, and his Luftwaffe friends joined in. "Finally, I laughed, too," said Stehlin. "It was the only thing to do. I realized that the Germans had been bluffing all along. They were amazed that Colonel Lindbergh had fallen for the idea, and they were even more surprised that it had been taken seriously by the French. Nothing came of it, of course."

By this time, even Charles Lindbergh must have begun to suspect that the Germans were not being quite as sincere with him as he wished to believe. But in conversation, he insisted that they could not possibly not be genuine in their peace efforts.

"I met him in Paris shortly after my session with Udet," Paul Stehlin said later, "and I told him what had taken place. He was quite angry and flared up at me. General Milch had personally assured him of his good will, he said; he trusted him. I told him to beware of Milch. 'You know what they say about him in Germany. *When Milch pisses, ice water comes out.*' He looked very offended, and his eyes blazed at me as if I was both a warmonger and a dirty talker. 'It all depends to whom he gives his word,' he said very coldly."

But just about this time, he was certainly beginning to wonder whether Milch was stalling him—as, it turned out, he certainly was. He was reluctant to believe that he was not being honest. "In the contacts I have made up to date," he wrote in his diary about his meetings with the Nazis, "no officer has lied to me or attempted to mislead me."

But now he had to consider that possibility. (Stehlin had long since decided that "they were leading him by the nose.") It was only weeks later that he admitted to himself that Project Fiesler Storch had collapsed.

"The remarkable thing is," said Stehlin, "that anyone who knew the Nazis could ever have believed the project was on. But then, of course, Lindbergh didn't know the Nazis—or Germany either."

Shortly after the failure of the Lindbergh effort, rumors about it swept Berlin and surfaced at a famous cabaret, where the resident comedian, Werner Finck, regularly made fun of the Nazis (when he wasn't in jail, that is).

"Have you heard about the new Franco-German bird they have hatched in the aviary at Frankfurt?" Finck asked his audience. "It's the result of mating a German eagle with a Strasbourg goose. The first thing it did when it was hatched was try to give a German salute with its right foot, and fell flat on its face, squawking. 'What's that you're saying?' asked the keeper, helping it up. '*Heil Hitler!*' replied the bird, between mouthfuls of mud. 'It may have been *Heil Hitler!* to you,' said the keeper, 'but it sounded more like *Merde!* to me.'"

The spring of 1939 was a frustrating one for Charles Lindbergh. Nothing seemed to be going the way he predicted. He grew increasingly angry at the manner in which Neville Chamberlain was now being criticized, in the letters he received from America ("a complete lack of understanding of the situation in Europe"), and in conversations with Britons and Frenchmen. He stoutly defended Chamberlain for concluding the Munich agreement and considered he had "done a good job with the materials and conditions he had to work with." He bridled when people suggested that Hitler and the rest of the Nazis were mad, and crisply told Lord Lothian during a dinner at Cliveden that "I have a little more confidence in the sanity of German leadership" than he had.

He stayed at Cliveden while on a trip to England to pass a medical test and get his pilot's certificate renewed, and the only good news he got out of his stay was the RAF doctor's verdict that he was in superb health. He held his breath for three minutes and thirty seconds during the test, and was told that this was a record. He was pleased. He had inherited his father's "exceptionally good lungs." But he was depressed by his conversations with his fellow guests at Cliveden and with Joseph Kennedy at the American embassy in London. He saw so little sign of life or virility about the English, and he concluded that the people were just not attuned to the modern world.

"The more I see of modern England and the English people, the less confidence I have in them," he decided. They had no long-range vision, no steadiness, no strength. He felt sorry for them. Once they had been great, but now were in decline, refusing to look facts in the face and recognize the realities of their situation, which was desperate.

It was an important period in his mental development. Already he was beginning to write off Britain as a power in the world and think of Germany as the master of Europe and maybe much more. It would be untrue to say that this caused him any qualms. He still regarded the Nazi regime as one basically good for the German people, and possibly for the world (though not, of course, for the Jews). He flew back to Paris on March 11, 1939, to keep an appointment with the American sculptor, Jo Davidson, who was doing a head of him. During the sitting, Davidson began railing against Neville Chamberlain and the sellout at Munich, and said he could not understand why Lindbergh was in favor of both.

Lindbergh, in turn, couldn't understand why Jo Davidson felt so bitter about it, although he recognized that "being Jewish" Davidson had every reason to be against the trends which were now going on in the world. Still, he hoped that Jo's mood wouldn't show up in the sculpture! Why was he such an idealist? Why should he and "other fine and able men like him" keep trying to build up a sort of Platonic utopia? Why didn't they accept things as they were? Lindbergh did not seem to see the irony of asking an artist (though "far more broadminded than most") and a Jew to accept a regime headed by a philistine and an anti-Semite.

Four days after this conversation took place, Hitler occupied Czechoslovakia and ripped Chamberlain's policy of appeasement into shreds. The Nazis had promised at Munich to have no further territorial ambitions in Europe, and now they had broken their pledge. It made even the appeasers realize at last that war was inevitable.

Charles Lindbergh was not one of those who were shocked by Germany's action. He studied Hitler's speech of justification in the newspapers on April 2, 1939, and thought it one of the best-written political speeches he had ever read. He was now convinced that Adolf Hitler, despite the fact that he was damned everywhere save in his own country, despite the fact that his critics called him a fanatic and a madman, held the future of Europe in his hands, and maybe of civilization, too.

He just could not understand why the leaders of the Western democracies were so opposed to him. His policy had been consistent. While disapproving of "many things" he had done and promises he had broken, Lindbergh could not see why democratic statesmen could not come to terms with him. After all, he had only been a little faster than other countries in breaking promises.

What had to be faced, however, was the possibility that Britain and France, having now given a guarantee to Poland, might stand by their pledges in the event of a German march eastward. In that case, there would be war. His feelings about that were beginning to crystallize. He did not believe that such a war would be justified, for he sympathized with Germany's *Drang nach Osten*, her eastward drive toward Russia, for that would build a wall against Communism, or possibly even de-

stroy it. And it was Communism he feared, not Fascism or National Socialism.

But what if the British and French were foolish enough to insist on a
war? What would he do? How would he stand? In what way would the
United States be affected?

He spent long hours talking it over with Anne Lindbergh, and could
not escape the feeling that he needed to go back to the United States,
to find out the mood of the American people, to tell them how it really
was in Europe, and rinse their minds clean of the distorted facts the
newspapers printed about the situation. His main concern was whether
he dare risk taking his wife and their two children back with him, because he feared it would be the same old story of harassment and persecution. How could the United States claim to be a proud democracy,
he asked himself, when there was no freedom there for anyone like himself, in whom the public and press were interested? And then, in a
strange revelation of his feelings, he wrote:

"I did not feel real freedom until I came to Europe. The strange
thing is that of all European countries, I found most personal freedom
in Germany, with England next, and then France."

It was an extraordinary statement to make in view of the facts. He
had been to Germany only five times in his life, and they were visits
which never lasted more than ten days at a time. He spoke no German,
and wherever he went he had been accompanied either by a Luftwaffe
or a Nazi interpreter. There is no record that either he or Anne ever
spoke to a German civilian during their visits, except to servants. His
only contacts were with air force officers or party officials. He had never
been in a *Weinstube*, a beer hall, or a café in Germany. He went only
once by himself to the cinema (where he saw an official anti-Jewish
propaganda film).

What could he possibly mean by "personal freedom" if these closely
controlled VIP visits to the German Reich meant more to him than his
years in America, and his homes with his children in the Kent countryside and on the island of Illiec?

Anne and Charles Lindbergh eventually decided that, to begin with,
he would go back to the United States alone. Like a pioneer looking for
a place to settle in hostile territory, he would look the situation over
and decide whether it was safe to bring in his family. Anne, the two
boys, and the dogs would wait in Paris until he cabled them.

He sailed aboard the *Aquitania* for New York on April 8, 1939. He
had asked the shipping line to find him a separate table in the dining
saloon, but the first night out he found himself sitting next to a very

pretty Romanian girl on her way to join her American husband in Ohio. At the end of the meal, he called the steward and insisted that he be given a place alone in future. He suspected that the girl's feelings would be hurt when she realized he had changed tables, and as "I think she is partly Jewish" he decided that she would probably think it was on that account. (Why? He did not explain.) He maintained that his real reason for leaving her was that "if I don't, the newspapers in America will grab her, photograph her, interview her, and then throw her in the gutter according to their usual procedure."

It was in this bitter mood that he left crisis-ridden Europe behind to return to his homeland. His reading on the voyage was W. G. Phelps's *The Glory That Was Greece.*

In New York, when the *Aquitania* docked on April 14, the reporters and photographers were more exigent than ever, and he made what he called "a barbaric entry into a civilized country." Where did freedom end and disorder begin? he angrily demanded. How long must he put up with the "lies and insults" of the press?

It was just like old times, and his feud with the public and newspapers flared up as fiercely as ever. He was called to Washington and was appalled at the scene which greeted him on the White House steps —cameramen, inane women screeching. Why, African savages had more dignity and self-respect. His face was red with anger as he roughly pushed past them.

But it was later on the same day that his fury burst bounds. He had an appointment at a meeting of the National Advisory Committee for Aeronautics, on whose committee he sat, and when he reached the council room he found it packed with newspaper and newsreel cameramen. He said he would wait in an anteroom while they took their pictures, but was told that they would refuse to take any unless he appeared in them. In that case, he replied tartly, there wouldn't be any pictures. Then the photographers came back with a proposition: They would leave him alone in future, they said, provided he posed for one picture, and they gave their word of honor.

"What?" cried Lindbergh. "Do you mean to tell me that *press photographers* are talking to me about their *word of honor?* The type of men who broke through the window of a Trenton morgue to open my baby's casket and photograph its body—they talk to me of *honor?* I refuse to come to the meeting until you get them out!"

They were put out of the room, and the meeting started.

He had been summoned to Washington for his first (and only) meeting with the President. Franklin Roosevelt has left behind no record of how Charles Lindbergh impressed him, although one suspects that even at this stage he disliked him, suspected his motives, saw in him a potential threat to his political supremacy. Lindbergh's own impression of the President was curiously confused. "I liked him and feel that I could get along with him well," he wrote, but then went on to say that he was accomplished (but too pleasant), suave (but too suave), an interesting conversationalist (but too easy), and he did not trust him.

Roosevelt welcomed him back to America and said the United States would be glad to have his help and advice in the difficult days to come. Lindbergh replied that he had agreed to be called back into the Army Air Force for temporary service, and would do the best he could. They shook hands and parted after fifteen minutes of "too easy" conversation.

"It is better to work together as long as we can," Lindbergh decided, adding: "Yet somehow I have a feeling that it may not be for long."

The situation in America had not improved, and "personal freedom" was obviously still unobtainable, but he had now made up his mind that he was needed. He cabled to Anne to book her passage. She and the family arrived in New York aboard the *Champlain* on April 28, 1939, and three weeks later father, mother, and two sons stood on the landing stage at Long Beach, Long Island, and watched a Pan American Clipper take off with the first airmail for Europe. It would be following the route Anne and Charles Lindbergh had pioneered, and it was a moment for quiet pride.

On June 2, they signed a lease on a house at Lloyd Neck, a secluded spit of land on the North Shore of Long Island. By that time Charles Lindbergh knew exactly why he had decided to stay in America: to keep his country from getting involved in the war in Europe that he was now convinced was coming. For the moment, however, he had not quite decided how he was going to go about it.

Part
Five
Peacenik

CHAPTER

NINETEEN

PORTRAIT OF AN

ISOLATIONIST

His new army uniform was ready. He had been fitted for his parachute. He had talked with Roosevelt, Secretary of War Harry Hines Woodring, and General "Hap" Arnold, chief of the Air Corps. He had been assigned a single-seater P-36A fighter plane to keep him mobile. He was back on temporary active duty as a colonel in the Army Air Corps, with the job of looking over new air bases, new planes, the recruitment of more air cadets, and finding a site for a new air force research institute.

Charles Lindbergh was now thirty-nine years old, but there was a tenseness about his facial muscles that somehow made him look older. The famous smile was not a feature that many people noticed these days, because he rarely flashed it in public. He had the air of a man with problems on his mind, and most of the problems were concerned with the future of his country. He did not like "the trend of recent years," and was apprehensive.

Shortly after he reported for service, he flew out to Wright Field, at Dayton, Ohio, to inspect new types of aircraft. The air force major who took him around the field asked him about his sojourn in Europe, and remembered that Lindbergh "lashed out" against the effeteness of the British and the French, and spoke in glowing terms about the German Air Force and the Nazi Government.

"Don't believe anything you read about them in the press," he said. "It's lies—all lies."

He stayed that night with General George H. Brett, the station commander, and that evening they went across to one of the officers' houses for supper. A cocktail party was in progress when they got there, and Lindbergh hated cocktail parties.

"He was offered a Coke, and, when he refused this, a cup of coffee," said the major who had escorted him earlier in the day. "He had to be pressed before he finally accepted a glass of water. It was a mixed company of officers, their wives and a couple of visiting friends, and one of the girls had had too many martinis and was flying. She took one look at Lindbergh and zoomed in, tried to clasp him in her arms, crying out: 'My hero! The Lone Eagle!' We were all a bit embarrassed and tried to head her off, but she kept coming back at him. Finally, he turned on his host and said: 'That woman is in a disgraceful condition. Such people shouldn't be allowed to drink. She is a shame to American womanhood.' A lot of the folks there began laughing, until they saw that he was serious. They got the woman out, and we sat down to a very sober supper. We *all* drank water."

Lindbergh had always been contemptuous of people who drank, but now it began to be a serious preoccupation with him, particularly drinking by women. He had come back from Germany imbued with many of the National Socialist ideals about the role of the female in society, and it troubled him to find so many American women of marriageable age mixing and working on equal terms with men, and only too often matching them drink for drink. It was encouraging loose living, and loose living led to the deterioration of the race. One of his objections to the Soviet Union had been the way it was trying to eradicate "the God-made difference between men and women." How could a civilization count itself a superior one if its women were encouraged to leave home and work, and "material efficiency" was considered "first and the bearing of children second, if not third"? Whereas in Germany they ordered it better. *Kinder, Kirche, Küche* (children, church, and kitchen) were what women under National Socialism were told to consider their principal spheres of interest, and it seemed to him that such dedicated, God-fearing mothers and housewives were as essential to America if it was to preserve the purity of its people and the strength of its ideals.

It is fascinating to study his diary during this formative period of what became his isolationist stance and discover the bugs that were biting him, the bogeys which haunted his brain as he sat down to pen his doings and his thoughts at the end of each day. He seemed to feel that the survival of the white race was being threatened by what was happening not only in Europe but also in the United States. In the outside world, the heritage of white civilization was being challenged by Asiatic hordes consisting of "Mongol, Persian and Moor." (He really meant the Russians and Japanese, and was surprised when the Persian ambassador complained when he expressed the same thoughts in a *Reader's*

Digest article.) Inside the United States, he warned about the "infiltration of inferior blood."

What did he mean by "inferior blood"? The fruits of the wombs of drinking mothers? It was a period when, with regard to air force cadet recruitment, he was suggesting a prior study of the antecedents of all candidates, and recommending tests of their future spouses before permission to marry was given.

But, at the same time, he may have been afraid of a menace to white supremacy and racial purity from the Negroes, about whom he also frequently expressed concern. "We have this race problem which is bound to cause the most serious trouble," he was writing. "The Civil War did not settle the Negro problem by any means." How he wished all blacks were like the "old Negress, chockful of character and that mixture of friendliness and respect" whom he met on a trip to Florida, full of the qualities that made "the Southern Negro so lovable." There was "nothing fawning or antagonistic about her" and she knew nothing of "the problems nor the unhappiness of the Northern Negro."

One afternoon in July 1939 he went to lunch with a couple of army officers, one of whom had never been outside the United States, the other a former military attaché at the American embassy in London. The homebody officer asked them how the British felt about the United States. The former military attaché (a Colonel Davidson) replied, and Lindbergh printed his statement with no comment:

"Well, I'll tell you," said Davidson. "The English feel about us the way we feel about a prosperous nigger."

He was busy writing an article called "Aviation, Geography and Race"* in which he set out to warn his fellow Americans of the alien hordes battering at their gates, and beseeching them to "build our White ramparts again" and create a defensive strength based on "an English fleet, a German air force, a French army, an American nation" capable of throwing back a Genghis Khan and saving "our common heritage." He made it clear that the most important of these was Germany's air force, "a tool specially adapted for western hands" which could provide the barrier between "the teeming millions of Asia and the Grecian inheritance of Europe." The inference was that if America had to choose its ally from between Britain and its ships, Germany and its planes, or France and its troops, the Luftwaffe was the one to pick.

Each time he came back from one of his air corps inspection tours he would foregather in Washington or New York with Kay and Truman Smith, to discuss the sad state of the nation and the machinations of

---

* It eventually appeared in *Reader's Digest* (November 1939).

the man in the White House. The Truman Smiths had been called back from Berlin about the same time as Lindbergh's return, and they were badly missing Germany, where life had been so much more orderly. They made no secret of their antipathy to Franklin Roosevelt and his "pro-English" policy and were busy building up a following in the Army of those who believed (or could be convinced) that the United States was in danger of backing the wrong horse.

Both they and Charles Lindbergh were keeping in touch with Hugh Wilson, the American ambassador to Germany, now back in the United States. He had been recalled by President Roosevelt as a protest against the anti-Jewish riots in Berlin in November 1938, and Wilson was convinced that the President had acted under the influence of the "Jewish lobby" in America. They all agreed that though they did not approve of violence, anti-Semitism in Germany was understandable because, before the advent of the Nazis, in Wilson's words, "the stage, the press, medicine and law [were] crowded with Jews . . . among the few with money to splurge a high proportion [were] Jews . . . the leaders of the Bolshevist movement in Russia, a movement desperately feared in Germany, were Jews. One could sense the spreading resentment and hatred."†

It must not be allowed to happen here, and that meant getting rid of the elements around Roosevelt who were influencing his policy. Or, if that was not possible, getting rid of Roosevelt himself. That, at least, was how the Smiths and Wilson felt about it, and were trying hard to turn Charles Lindbergh's growing suspicions of his President into a solid conviction. Kay and Truman Smith had by this time consolidated their friendship with the Lindberghs to the extent that they were now regular companions, and Smith was beginning to be accepted by his friend as a trusted military and political adviser.

As if they already sensed something conspiratorial in their association and were afraid the Administration was watching them—as, indeed, it soon would be—they agreed that when they were traveling and wished to communicate political or military information, they would do so in a simple code, deliberately chosen to seem innocuous. Every week in the months leading up to the beginning of hostilities in Europe, Smith would send Lindbergh a telegram saying: THIRTY (or twenty or forty) PER CENT. This meant his assessment of the likelihood of war.

The former military attaché was now working in Army Intelligence in Washington and he had access to confidential files on many of his senior officers, and knew pretty well how they stood with regard to the

_____
† Hugh Wilson, *Diplomat Between Wars* (New York: Longmans, Green, 1941).

Administration. A member of the anti-Roosevelt faction was known as FRIEND. Anti-Roosevelt congressmen and senators, with many of whom Smith was in close contact, were respectively referred to as SIX and EIGHT, so that a telegram reading, CAN YOU DINE SEPTEMBER 10 WITH SELF AND FRIEND SIX COMING, would mean: *Can you come to dinner September 10 when army general and congressman, both anti-Roosevelt, will be coming.* Certain famous members of both Houses had their own code names, but there seems to be no record of them except that Representative George H. Tinkham (R., Mass.) was known as BEARD. This is hardly surprising, since a long flowing beard was one of the three most striking features of this enemy of the Administration. (The others were his bald head and his huge Roman nose.)

But as late as June 1939, as the war clouds curdled over Europe, Charles Lindbergh had still not decided what exactly he would do if war came. His commanding officer, General "Hap" Arnold, suspected that his mind was running along political rather than military lines. He had been getting reports from the Walter Reed Hospital, where Truman Smith was having treatment, that Smith's most frequent visitor was Charles Lindbergh, and that they spent hours in earnest colloquy.

On the afternoon of June 7, Arnold called Lindbergh into his office and, after some hesitation, said:

"Do you mind if I ask you a personal question?" Lindbergh shook his head, and the general went on: "Say, what are you shooting at? Have you set a goal for yourself, or do you take life as it comes?"

Lindbergh replied that life was too complex at the moment to be shooting at anything. Arnold seems to have asked him whether he had thought of going into politics, because he went on to say that he did not want any political office "or any special reward for what I did," and that he liked to feel his way along and allow events to govern the way in which he moved.

At the end of the month, however, his attitude had become more purposeful. On June 30 he changed from his army uniform into civilian clothes (always a signal that he was going to talk politics) and drove to the Capitol for an appointment with Senator Harry Byrd, an anti-Roosevelt Democrat from Virginia, who took him along to see John Nance Garner. Garner was not only a Democrat but also Vice-president of the United States. Despite that fact he was a stern opponent of the New Deal's "socialistic" policies and highly suspicious of the President's foreign policy. He and Lindbergh both agreed that "the British and the Jews" were trying to push the United States into a European war, and that there was far too much pro-British, pro-Jewish propaganda going around. America was in danger of being involved in European problems which did not concern her, and which could not be solved by "American good will and idealism."

He came away from this conversation convinced that he must make a decision about his future, and with the growing belief that it would be on the ground rather than in the air from now on. Almost in a symbolic act of renunciation, he flew some days later from Denver for an appointment in Salt Lake City and said a sort of temporary good-by to the skies on the way. There were heavy clouds sitting on the snow-capped peaks around Denver and they rose up as high as twenty thousand feet. He climbed through them and felt like a god as he rode on top of them, a mystical feeling of becoming an extraterrestrial being freed from the earth and its problems down below. "I owned the world that hour as I rode over it," he wrote. "This hour was mine, free of the earth, free of the mountains, free of the clouds—yet how inseparably I was bound to them, how void my space would be if they were gone. Everything—life, love, happiness—depended on their being there when I returned."

He threw his plane around the sky in a sort of ecstasy, and then put it into a glide, "to go back to earth and live among men." And their political problems.

On August 28, 1939, Truman Smith sent him a telegram: YES EIGHTY PER CENT, which meant that he considered war in Europe was practically certain. Three days later, Nazi troops marched into Poland, and the world held its breath while waiting to see what Britain and France would do. When a day passed and there had been no announcement from London or Paris, Charles Lindbergh remarked to Anne that the Allies "seemed hesitant" about declaring war "in spite of their promises to Poland."

"Maybe they've talked to a general," she said.

But on September 3 the declaration came and that night they tuned in the radio to listen to Roosevelt's speech. Lindbergh was one of the few people around who hated the sound of the President's voice and disliked the quality of his speeches. But in this one, he promised to keep the United States neutral and told the people to beware of propaganda, and since this accorded with Lindbergh's views "it was a better talk than he usually gives." He added: "I wish I trusted him more."

The next day he shut himself in his study at Lloyd Neck and two days later had written a long article and two radio talks, all of them designed to "clarify the issues" for the American people about the war in

Europe, and make them understand why they shouldn't take sides—or get involved.

He had made up his mind at last. "I do not intend to stand by and see this country pushed into war," he said. "Much as I dislike taking part in politics and public life, I intend to do so if necessary to stop the trend which is now going on in this country."

While he waited to make his first broadcast, he foregathered with Truman Smith and a map of Poland, and plotted the course of the Nazi forces as they crushed the Polish armies and bombed Polish cities. It was all going as they had predicted. The German Army and Air Force were invincible.

Franklin D. Roosevelt was alarmed when he heard that Charles Lindbergh was going to give a radio talk about the war in Europe, and not entirely because he knew he would be advocating America's noninvolvement in the conflict. He was against involvement himself, insofar as that meant military intervention, as he made clear in his fireside talk after Britain and France had gone to war. He was only too aware that 70 per cent of the American people, according to a Gallup poll taken in September 1939, were in favor of neutrality, and he was too much of a politician to fight that. The difference between the President and Lindbergh was that Roosevelt's sympathies were with the Allies and he wanted them to win, and he would like to help them in every way short of actually opening fire; whereas Lindbergh didn't care, and believed Germany would win, anyway. Lindbergh saw it as a sort of private fight between Germany on the one side and Britain and France on the other in which no great principles were involved, in which the goals were territory and power rather than morality and justice, and in which Germany had possibly more right on her side than the two countries which had declared war on her. It was up to America to sit it out and then offer congratulations and the hand of friendship, plus a treaty, to the winner.

With rather more percipience, Roosevelt saw the war in global terms, as the first battle in a struggle for the ideological control of men's minds and ideals. Unlike Lindbergh (or most Americans) he had read *Mein Kampf* and realized the true nature of Hitlerism, the Führer's ambitions for world hegemony, the evil basis of racial hate and "blood supremacy" by which they were motivated. Contrary to Lindbergh's predictions, he believed the good guys were going to win, and he wanted to be behind them, cheering, helping a little, while they did so.

This was how he viewed the situation as a statesman. But he was a politician, too, and in that role he was well aware of Charles Lindbergh's challenge to his prestige. Having tangled with him and suffered damage during the airmail controversy in 1933, he was anxious not to have him in the opposition camp again. He was particularly concerned at Lindbergh's decision to launch what was obviously going to be an isolationist campaign by way of the radio, which Roosevelt considered his very own medium. It was his invention of radio "fireside chats" which had familiarized the nation with his ideas and his personality, and brought the American President for the first time into the homes of all American citizens. He regarded Lindbergh's announced intention to visit in the same homes as a positive intrusion, and one to be circumvented if possible.

But how to head him off?

Roosevelt, who loved power himself and had no doubt in his mind that Lindbergh also nourished political ambitions, despite any protestations to the contrary, decided that the only way was to entice him into the Administration. It would have to be a post in the Cabinet, and an important one. He squirmed at the prospect of having a self-righteous, teetotal, reputedly puritanical Minnesotan sitting in on some of the free-and-easy sessions which often took place at the White House, and he could imagine the apopleptic wrath with which Lindbergh's advent would be greeted by his Secretary of the Interior, Harold L. Ickes, who loathed him and called him "that tarnished hero." But he would have to put up with it, just as they all had to put up with John Nance Garner.

Somewhere around September 14, 1939 (the date cannot be firmly established), Secretary Woodring called General Arnold, the air corps chief in to see him. He told him that the President wanted Charles Lindbergh to join the Cabinet, and that he was prepared to offer him an entirely new and important post as Secretary for Air. Could he sound out Lindbergh to see if he would accept—*and do it as urgently as possible?*

Now this is where the mystery begins. One would have thought that Hap Arnold would have welcomed the President's move, despite the obvious politics involved in it. He admired Lindbergh as a man and as an aviation expert—even to the extent of swallowing his erroneous figures about the state of the Luftwaffe—and must surely have realized that there couldn't have been a better appointment. For one thing, it would mean a separate Air Force under the control of a man who understood its purpose, its function, and its needs. Every flier in the service would welcome him, and feel better about things. Hap Arnold himself would benefit by becoming Commander in Chief of a separate Air Force instead of head of an Air Corps. It was a moment in history when the air arm of the United States badly needed a man at the top with influence, drive, and know-how to build up its strength and morale in readiness for the emergencies which seemed to be looming.

So why didn't Arnold welcome the offer and say that he would see Lindbergh at once and offer him the post? Not only offer it, but strongly advise him to take it, for America's sake.

Of course implicit in the offer was the proviso that Lindbergh in his radio broadcast must not attack the Administration. But General Arnold had already seen the text of Lindbergh's speech (Lindbergh himself had shown it to him), and he knew that it did not attack either Roosevelt or the Administration. It simply urged the nation to "stand clear" of the conflict, which was, Lindbergh declared, a mistaken squabble between "white races" who would be better occupied uniting to do battle against Mongol hordes and Asiatic intruders. The President was not even asking him to cancel his talk, only tone it down—which he didn't need to, anyway.

In the circumstances what happened next is all the more mysterious.

On the afternoon of Thursday, September 14, 1939, the day before the radio broadcast, Lindbergh came into General Arnold's office with a report for signature. According to Lindbergh's own account of this meeting, Arnold said he had seen Secretary Woodring and told him that Lindbergh had asked to be relieved of his "active-inactive" status in the Air Corps and that he was planning to speak on the radio the following evening against the United States entering a European war. "Woodring was very much displeased, Arnold said." But displeased about *what*? About Lindbergh's plan to speak in favor of American neutrality? It hardly seems likely, since Woodring was a well-known noninterventionist himself, and the policy of the Administration at this time was also noninterventionist.

Could it have been that Woodring was displeased that Lindbergh was leaving the Air Force, at just the moment when he was needed? Lindbergh does not say so. He leaves readers of his diary to infer that Woodring's motives were much more political, but carefully does not say so directly. The passage in his diary can be read to refer either to his leaving the Air Corps *or* to his radio talk:

"He asked Arnold if he (Arnold) couldn't find some way of stopping me. Arnold replied that he did not think so. Woodring then said he was very sorry because he had hoped to make use of me in future, but didn't see how he could do so if I followed out my plans. (There was obviously something behind that statement.)

Now, why didn't General Arnold go on to explain what Woodring meant when he said "he had hoped to make use of me in future" was that the President was hoping he would accept the post of Secretary for Air? What stopped him? Why, instead, did he let Lindbergh go without mentioning it?

For that is what he did. After Lindbergh had gone, he called in Lieutenant Colonel Truman Smith, Lindbergh's passionately anti-Administration adviser, and it was to him that he gave the mission of telling his friend that a cabinet post was being offered to him.

Truman Smith, by accident or design, made a mess of it.

Charles Lindbergh spent Thursday evening in Washington at a meeting of the National Advisory Committee for Aeronautics (NACA), but was called away several times to make telephone calls about his radio talk the following evening. It was 11 P.M. when he got back to his apartment.

There was a telephone message waiting for him. It was from Truman Smith. It was marked *important*. But it was obviously not urgent, because Smith had only asked Lindbergh to call him on Friday morning. When he did so, Truman Smith simply said he had something important to tell his friend, and they made an arrangement to meet at lunchtime.‡

Now, this is pretty extraordinary behavior on Truman Smith's part. He is given the job of telling Charles Lindbergh that he is being offered a post in the Roosevelt Cabinet. No matter what his opinion about it, he could hardly have considered it a trivial matter. One would have thought that immediately he had been assigned the mission, he would have searched out his friend at once. Why did he wait twenty-four hours?

Lindbergh spent all Friday morning once more at a NACA meeting, and it did not end until 2 P.M. He took a taxi back to his apartment, where Anne Lindbergh and a friend named Jim Newton (an ardent Oxford Grouper) were waiting to have lunch with him. They were joined by a well-known anti-Roosevelt radio commentator named Fulton Lewis, on whose program Lindbergh would appear that evening.

Truman Smith finally arrived for coffee, and at once told Lindbergh that he had "something very important" to talk to him about. Lindbergh wrote in his diary:

> Truman and I went into the bedroom, where we could talk alone. He told me he had a message which he must deliver, *al-*

‡ Lindbergh suggested before 10 A.M., but Smith said he had "other engagements."

though he knew in advance what my answer would be. [My italics. L.M.] He said the Administration was very much worried by my intention of speaking over the radio and opposing actively this country's entry into a European war. Smith said that if I would not do this, a Secretaryship for Air would be created in the Cabinet and given to me! Truman laughed and said, "So you see, they're worried."*

According to Lindbergh, Smith then went on to say that he had asked General Arnold if he "thought for a minute" that Lindbergh would accept. Arnold had replied, Smith said: "Of course not." *But why not?* As mentioned earlier, this offer was a breakthrough. Lindbergh's acceptance of such a post would have meant a radical change in the status of the Air Corps, and a great boost for the morale of every army flier. What could Arnold possibly have had against it?†

As for Truman Smith: If he had carried out such an important mission (even while loathing it) in such a fashion for any other country's army, he would undoubtedly have been drummed out of the service. If he had acted that way while under the orders of his favorite armed force, the German Army, they would almost certainly have shot him.

On the evening of Friday September 15, 1939, Charles Lindbergh spoke to the American people over all the national networks and appealed to them to stand aside from the conflict in Europe. It was a speech which gained a good deal of support from those who, in the words of the Chicago *Tribune,* were prepared to take "a cold, hard look at the situation." The New York *Times* and *Herald Tribune* both printed it in full, and all other papers gave long extracts. For once, Charles Lindbergh carefully read all the newspapers, and on September 16 he and Anne even drove from Lloyd Neck to Oyster Bay to pick up the evening papers and read what they were saying about him. The passage in his speech which seemed to have gained most attention was the one in which he said:

> These wars in Europe are not wars in which our civilization is defending itself against some Asiatic intruder. There is no Genghis Khan marching against our Western nations. This is not a question of banding together to defend our White race

---

* *The Wartime Journals of Charles A. Lindbergh* (New York: Harcourt Brace Jovanovich, 1970), p. 257.

† The incident is not mentioned at all in Arnold's own book on the period, *Global Mission* (New York: Harper & Brothers, 1949).

against foreign invasions. This is simply one more of those age old quarrels among our own family of nations. . . . We must not permit our sentiment, our pity, or our personal feelings of sympathy to obscure the issue, to affect our children's lives. We must be as impersonal as a surgeon with his knife.

It was probably not this speech which made President Roosevelt henceforward regard him as the Administration's enemy so much as the manner in which Charles Lindbergh responded (or rather, did not respond) to his overture. It is true that it had been a political gesture, but Lindbergh was normally meticulously polite to officialdom. In this case, there was not even an acknowledgment or a polite refusal. Roosevelt was not to know that this was almost certainly due to Truman Smith's maladroitness in presenting his offer.

The speech did, however, for all the Administration's attempts to diminish its importance, strike a chord in the great mass of Americans, most of whom were apprehensive about involvement in the war, and welcomed the assurance of a man so prestigious as Charles Lindbergh that it was okay if they looked the other way. It also rang a loud bell in the heads of every isolationist and anti-Roosevelt senator and congressman in Washington, and from this moment they came buzzing around him like bees. Ex-President Hoover sent for him to congratulate him and spur him on to the good work. He had a long private session with Senator William E. Borah, the die-hard, last-ditch Republican from Idaho, who was already speculating about presidential prospects for 1940. There were strong indications that the Democrats would nominate Franklin Roosevelt for a third term. Only a super-strong Republican could defeat him. Had Lindbergh ever thought of setting his cap at the White House? He would make a good candidate (Republican, of course). Lindbergh replied that he would consider it a great honor, but did not believe he was ideally suited for political office. But he was pleased.

Encouraged by the support he was getting, he wrote new radio scripts, planned articles, went to endless meetings at the House. His right-hand man now was Truman Smith, who was so busy doing chores for him that one wonders how he found time to look after his job in Military Intelligence. He scurried around gathering in anti-Roosevelt politicians with whom Lindbergh could concert his isolationist campaign. One meeting with Representative Tinkham (BEARD) took place at midnight in Smith's apartment in great secrecy, and they conferred on plans for preventing Roosevelt from repealing the arms embargo to Europe, which would inevitably favor Britain and France.

Smith did a daily sitrep on the war situation for Lindbergh and marked up his map for him. Smith opened his fan mail and tallied the fors and againsts.‡ Smith clipped the newspapers with mentions of him. This constant *va-et-vient* on Lindbergh's behalf seems to have attracted no particular attention from his military superiors, and it was several months before anyone mentioned to the White House that Smith was spending more time with Lindbergh than he was at the office.

Meanwhile, the blitzkrieg in Poland was over, and all Charles Lindbergh's predictions about the might of the German Luftwaffe had been fulfilled. The air arm had won the war against Poland, and Britain and France had stood helplessly by while their ally was bombed and strafed into defeat, its troops panicked and put to flight by screaming Stukas, its ancient cities rubbled by Göring's bomber fleets. Poland was divided up between Germany and the Soviet Union, and the mighty Reich was now free to turn its armadas against the West.

It was at this point that Anne Lindbergh told her husband that she was writing an article, too. It was called "A Prayer for Peace," but the title was misleading.

‡ Most were "for" at this stage.

CHAPTER

TWENTY

THE BATTLE THE WRONG

SIDE WON

One of the sentences in Lindbergh's first radio talk had attracted particular attention among his listeners. In telling the American people to forget their sympathies and keep an unsentimental attitude toward the war, he added:

"We must be as impersonal as a surgeon with his knife."

It was suggested that Anne Lindbergh had written this sentence into her husband's speech, and she did not deny it at the time. It was a chilling line to use at a moment when Polish children were dying under Nazi bombs in Warsaw and Cracow, and Göring's minions were rounding up the first slave laborers. The sentiment behind it seemed to belie the philosophy and the feelings which Anne Lindbergh expressed so eloquently in her writings, and people were shocked to think she might be the author of it.*

Certainly she seems to have been wholeheartedly behind her husband in the isolationist campaign which he was now launching, and it cannot have been easy for her. The Morrow family had been solidly pro-Ally in World War I, when the issues were less clear-cut. Anne Lindbergh must have known that her beloved father, Dwight Morrow, would have been in the forefront of the anti-Nazis in World War II. As for her mother, Betty Morrow had made it clear from the start where she stood in regard to the war, and it was not in the ranks of the isolationists. What made it even more awkward was that her younger sister, Constance, with whom her emotional ties were close, was now married to Aubrey Morgan, and that quiet, pleasant Welshman had now been

* The truth about the origin of the sentence will perhaps come when Anne Lindbergh publishes *her* diaries for 1936–41. A day-to-day comparison with her husband's entries will make intriguing reading.

THE BATTLE THE WRONG SIDE WON

made assistant chief of the British Information Services in New York. This was the organization (together with Jewish groups) which Lindbergh claimed was trying to trick America into the war.

It was bad enough to see her family on occasional visits, but at the end of October 1939 the Lindberghs' lease on the house at Lloyd Neck terminated. They moved temporarily to—where else?—Next Day Hill, the family home at Englewood. Constance and Aubrey Morgan were also there for several days of the week, and brought with them distinguished writers, artists, and personalities from Britain who had come over to do some propaganda. Betty Morrow had joined local and national Aid the Allies committees, and, indefatigable organizer that she was, filled the house with friends whom she exhorted to go out and spread the word that God and all decent Americans were on the side of the British.

Anne Lindbergh knew that every college friend she had ever made was pro-Allied and could not understand what her husband was up to and how she could possibly support him. They were shocked when they came over to help Betty Morrow pack food parcels or welcome refugees, and Anne refused to help them. It wouldn't be impartial, she said. What had impartiality to do with it? they asked, angrily. Did she and Charles really want the Nazis to win?

One of her closest friends was present when Betty Morrow rounded on her daughter, and tartly suggested that next time Charles Lindbergh made a radio speech he might at least express some sympathy toward the victims of the war, and his abhorrence of Nazi methods. Anne retorted that this would undermine Charles's desire not to take sides, to be regarded as an impartial observer, a sort of umpire of the war in Europe.

"I always understood," replied Mrs. Morrow, "that umpires have whistles and sometimes blow for a foul."

Charles Lindbergh seemed to be impervious to the fact that some of his friends were reluctantly crossing him off their lists. Even such close friends as Henry Breckenridge, his attorney, who had been through the kidnaping with him, and Harry Guggenheim, who had sponsored him so warmly after his transatlantic flight, were beginning to eye him warily, like castaways suspecting that one of their number is turning cannibal. But Lindbergh had the compensation of knowing that he was making hosts of new friends, and he seemed unconscious of the fact that he would not have deigned to speak to most of them had they not shared his suspicion of foreign entanglements and hatred of the Roosevelt Administration. Anne found it difficult to achieve any rapport whatsoever with their wives. As one of the Morrow relatives remarked:

"John Nance Garner is bad enough, but have you seen *Mrs.* John Nance Garner?"

It was difficult to know how she could constructively help her husband and demonstrate beyond all doubt that she was loyal to him. He was still extraordinarily vulnerable to criticism, and she had an example of it toward the end of fall, 1939. Lindbergh's speeches inferring that the English were decadent, incapable of standing up to the virile Germans, bound to be defeated (unless they could entice the Americans into coming to their rescue), had not unnaturally aroused some indignation in Britain. There were many ripostes in the press and in speeches. The particular piece which hurt and angered Charles Lindbergh came from Harold Nicolson, who wrote an article in *The Spectator* to "explain" the malaise from which his erstwhile friend was suffering.

Nicolson called him a man whose simplicity had become "musclebound," whose ideas had become rigid, "his self confidence thickened into arrogance and his convictions hardened into granite." It had all happened because of the murder of his child.

"The suffering which that dreadful crime entailed upon himself and those he loved pierced his armor," Nicolson wrote. "He identified the outrage to his private life first with the popular press and by inevitable association with freedom of speech, and then with freedom. He began to loathe democracy."

This meant, Nicolson went on, that by the time he came to Germany "he was not at all deterred by the suppression of free thought and free discussion. He admired the conditioning of a whole generation to the ideals of harsh self sacrifice." On the other hand, his rigid outlook, "hard as metal and as narrow as a chisel," made him blind to the qualities of the British. "The slow organic will-power of Britain eluded his observation, and he hoped we would run away before Marshal Göring could catch us."

It was the last passage, however, which wounded Lindbergh most, possibly because it hit the spot where he was most vulnerable:

"Let us not allow this incident," wrote Nicolson, "to blind us to the great qualities of Charles Lindbergh. He is and always will be not merely a schoolboy hero, but a schoolboy."

When he saw a reprint of the article in the New York *Times,* Lindbergh thought it "rather silly" and "expected something better of him" and bridled at the claim by Nicolson that he was the Lindberghs' friend. He admitted that they had rented Long Barn from Mrs. Nicolson but "at a very adequate price,"† and that he and Anne had visited them at Sissinghurst "two or three times for tea. But I do not feel that we ever really knew either of them, or they us." The association had been closer than that, and he knew it.

Anne Lindbergh watched her husband brooding over these slights to his self-confidence and self-importance and locked herself away to write something which would show—publicly to the world—how much she shared his views. The result was "A Prayer for Peace," which, when it was finished, read much more like a prayer for neutrality and a warning of fire and brimstone upon the British if they failed to end the war (inferentially, by submission) immediately, or at least by the Christmas season.

Lindbergh was touched and pleased by the gesture. He called up his Oxford Group friend, Jim Newton, who apparently had contacts at *Reader's Digest*, and asked him if he could place the article in the magazine. He wanted the largest possible circulation for the piece since "we both feel it is essential to get people in America thinking clearly about Europe and what is taking place there." He told himself that he was "reluctant" to involve his wife in the crusade, "but it is better to take part in preventing a catastrophe than to be dragged to the guillotine after it has taken place. . . . More than one artist has shouldered a gun to protect his art."

He added a fervent note of his gratitude to her:

"I don't believe a woman exists who is her equal—if one ever did."

Most of the January 1940 edition of *Reader's Digest* (which would appear on Christmas Day 1939) had already gone to press, but the magazine knew the selling power of the Lindbergh name and they were prepared to make space for it, sight unseen. They sent a messenger around for a copy, and telephoned to say they liked it, and would get it into the issue by taking out two other articles.

So that Anne Lindbergh could have plenty of time on the morrow to make last-minute changes in the article, they went to bed early that night. Tossing around in bed, Lindbergh decided that his wife would not be able to work on her piece if the secretary was typing it, and therefore would not be able to make those alterations which "like the strokes of an artist's brush, often make the difference between excellence and genius." He therefore whispered to her that he was restless and would sleep in another room so as not to disturb her. Then he crept upstairs to an office on the third floor and typed the article through the night, finishing at 6 A.M.

† Two hundred dollars a month.

"Fatigue never does catch up with you," he told himself with satisfaction, "if the goal is great enough, and I felt Anne's 'Prayer for Peace' is great enough."

Nineteen forty was an election year, and it was now certain that Franklin D. Roosevelt would stand for a third term. There were no more overtures to Lindbergh to stand as the Republican candidate, but he was asked to come to the Republican Convention in Philadelphia as a delegate. He refused on the grounds that this would compromise his "nonpartisan" stand against the war.

His status was equivocal at the moment. He had not so far attacked the President openly. He still remained a member of the Air Corps Reserve, technically under the orders of the Chief Executive, who was ipso facto Commander in Chief of the Armed Forces. His chief appeal to middle America, from most of whom came support for neutralist and isolationist sentiments in the nation, was that he *knew* what was going to happen in the war in Europe—knew better than the Administration, better than the generals, better than the combatants themselves.

He *knew* that Germany was going to win the war, and he was simply trying to prevent America from making the grave error of rushing to the aid of the losing side. Since Americans have always shown more reluctance than most people to backing or sympathizing with a loser, his advice made sense. Keep clear of involvement, and let them fight it out among themselves.

Early in 1940 a member of the No Foreign War Group sent him a poem, and he wrote back to its creator, whose name was Oliver Allstorm, to tell him that it exactly mirrored his sentiments about the present situation. It was a poem for audiences with tin ears, and it must have made Anne Lindbergh wince when she read it, but since it preceded many antiwar rallies and isolationist meetings in the United States during the first six months of 1940, the author reluctantly inflicts it upon his readers. It was called "The Lone Eagle's Litany" and it read as follows:

> George Washington said
> "Beware unto Dread
> All foreign snares."
> And he was quite right,
> We'll hold to our might
> By minding our own affairs.

We'll stay on this side
Of the rolling tide
Forever and still be true
To the snow-white stars and the red-white bars
Of our flag Red White and Blue!

"Over there" there's mud and shedding of blood
And tongues confusing and strange.
So why lend a hand to an alien land
Whose streams we can never change.

In France they'll be French and stick to a trench
As long as their banner flies,
They'll guard their Moselle with bullet and shell
Til the last brave *poilu* dies.

The Hun will be Hun while the blazing sun
Looks down from an ailing sky
And fathers and sons will fight with their guns
Til the River Rhine goes dry.

And England shall ring with "Long Live the King!"
While Tommy knows how to shout
She'll blast off her foes with death-telling blows
Til the sunlight flickers out.

They shout with their lungs in various tongues
And each strange lingo is grand
But to us it's all Greek for most of them speak
In ways we can not understand.

They scream it with lead and gas that is spread
And cannon balls grim and cold,
With bullets and bombs, and bugles and drums
And flags with tassels of gold.

"Away with this shindy!" cries Colonel Lindy
"We'll never be Allied tools,
Nor again parade in a foreign brigade
Like saps in a squad of fools.
We'll not join the kill in the murder mill
Of plunder, rape and despair,
Nor sink in the snag and stain our dear Flag
With the blood of serfs over there.
We'll not sound the knell of our Liberty Bell
Nor raze Independence Hall

Nor nail Betsy Ross to a foreign cross.
God gave us our land, we held His hand
And promised Him never to fail
To send up a cheer for Paul Revere
Or a tear for Nathan Hale!"

There's the Soviet bear in his Russian lair,
And China is still in her sleep,
And this land and that are all sitting pat
On top of an arsenal's heap.

But Lindy's Pa saw it all from afar,
Said, "Son, don't take up a gun,
Don't salvage the tea from an angry sea
Where Old Boston sent it down.
Europe may strut thro its bloody rut
And scheme with her Babel snares
But we'll stay at home this side of the foam
And mind our own affairs!"

It was not exactly "The Battle Hymn of the Republic," but Charles Lindbergh seemed to find it "rousing."

Norway and Denmark fell into Nazi hands. In May 1940 the German armies and Luftwaffe turned to the West, broke through into neutral Holland and Belgium, and then began the blitzkrieg against France. Once more, as Charles Lindbergh had forecast, the Nazi air arm had things all its own way. As the Allied armies fell back, the British toward Dunkirk, the French toward Paris, he could not help feeling a quiet satisfaction that his predictions were coming true. But he was troubled about the reactions of the "prowar" clique. "The press is hysterical," he wrote. "The newspapers give one the impression that the United States will be invaded next week!"

It was time to go on the radio again and warn America that more than ever now it was important to stand aside and let the strong conquer the weak, meanwhile making sure that America was strong enough to defend herself. But he scoffed at the idea that Göring's Luftwaffe could reach the United States, or even wished to do so.

He gave two radio talks over this period. Just before the first one, General Arnold called him in and said he was passing on a request from Secretary of War Woodring. Would he include in his speech some news of how the U. S. Army was building up its strength? Lindbergh refused, believing that it was a "clumsy effort" on the part of the Administration to "dull the edge of my talk." He also felt "quite certain that Arnold would not wish me to follow Woodring's suggestions," which, if true, would have been an odd attitude for Arnold to take. Did he not wish the people to know that the United States was rearming?

The speech was mainly devoted by Lindbergh (he spoke for thirteen minutes) to an attack on those who were alarmed at the advance of the German armies into France. He called upon his listeners to shut their ears "to this hysterical chatter of calamity and invasion which has been running rife these last few days." Next day there was a sharp rebuke for him in the New York *Times*, which wrote:

> The "hysterical chatter" is the talk now heard on every side in the democracies if France and Britain stand in danger of defeat by Germany. Colonel Lindbergh is a peculiar young man if he can contemplate this possibility in any other light than as a calamity for the American people. He is an ignorant young man if he trusts his own premise that it makes no difference to us whether we are deprived of the historic defense of British seapower in the Atlantic Ocean. He is a blind young man if he really believes we can live on terms of equal peace and happiness "regardless of which side wins this war" in Europe. Colonel Lindbergh remains a great flier."‡

He was careful in this talk not to make any overt attack on the Administration, but a few days afterward he heard some news which persuaded him to sharpen his attitude and go after Roosevelt more directly. Kay Smith telephoned him that she had some important news to tell him about her husband, and then came round to see him about it. The Administration had found out about Truman Smith's activities on Lindbergh's behalf and was "banishing" him from Washington to Fort Benning.

What had happened was that on May 27, 1940, the President's press secretary, Stephen T. Early, sent a message to Roosevelt's military secretary, General Edwin Martin Watson:

> Dear "Pa": Dwight Davis, former Secretary of War, told me Saturday afternoon he had good reason to believe that Lieut. Col. Truman Smith inspired Colonel Lindburgh [*sic*] to make his radio address last week, and collaborated with Lindburgh [*sic*] in preparing his remarks.

‡ New York *Times*, May 20, 1940.

Mr. Davis further stated that Colonel Smith described the President's Defense Message to Congress last week as "a hysterical speech."

The former Secretary of War also said that Lindburgh [sic] had been the personal guest of Colonel Smith; that Colonel Smith had served many years in Berlin as Military Attaché, and that he was known to be pro-Nazi.

Mr. Davis spoke to me in confidence and his name should be protected unless he is asked and gives his consent to the use of his name as my informant. I do not know whether he would be willing to do this. I did not ask him. S.T.E.*

Lindbergh was angry and convinced that Smith's banishment was a Roosevelt ploy to injure him (Lindbergh). Kay Smith told him that Secretary of the Treasury Henry Morgenthau, Jr., had even asked General George Marshall to discharge her husband from the Army, but Marshall had refused because "Truman was too valuable to him." Lindbergh added in his diary that night:

"Kay says the report is around Washington that the Administration is out to 'get me.' Well, it is not the first time, and it won't be the last."

He arranged to speak on the radio again on June 15. By that time, the German armies had entered Paris, and France was asking for an armistice. The British Army was escaping back to England from Dunkirk. Just before the broadcast, Lindbergh's close friend, mentor, and collaborator, Dr. Alexis Carrel, telephoned him. There had been a kind of estrangement between the two men recently, because Carrel loathed the Germans and felt that European civilization would be destroyed if France fell to them. Lindbergh, who did not share this opinion of the Germans at all, had told him that the Nazis were going to save Europe from Bolshevism. Now, as Carrel spoke, he was in tears. The hated swastika flew over the Eiffel Tower. His wife, whom he had left behind, was trapped in Brittany. He asked Lindbergh if he would include in his radio talk some friendly reference to France and the French people. His friend primly replied that "I would like to do so," but did not see how "I could appropriately include a reference to France in that address, since it was primarily an argument against our entry into the war."

This time he made a direct appeal to his listeners to bring pressure on Congress and "the minority" who were trying to involve the United States in the war. It was too late, he said. America's only hope was to put her faith in a hemispheric defense system, accompanied by a na-

* Stephen T. Early Papers, Franklin D. Roosevelt Library, Hyde Park, New York.

tional call-up of all young men for military service, and the elimination of war profits. He accused the Administration of "making gestures with an empty gun" and encouraging the Allies "to hope for help we cannot hope to send them." He added:

"There are men among us [pause] in addition to the sincere ones [pause] of less honesty who advocate us stepping closer and closer to war, knowing that there is a point beyond which there can be no turning back. They have baited the trap of war with requests for modest assistance. . . . This is a question of mortgaging the lives of our children and our grandchildren. [If they trap us into war] every family in the land will have its wounded and its dead."

Next night in Boston, a meeting of thirty thousand people acclaimed a proposal for the immediate shipment to the Allies of everything short of an expeditionary force. The gathering had been sponsored by the Boston branch of the Committee to Defend America by Aiding the Allies. Among the telegrams of support was one from Mrs. Dwight Morrow. The speakers included educators, former soldiers, lawyers, and business leaders. One of them cried:

"The blood-drenched Hitler is at our gates, and some people would like to invite him in. . . . But if France and England go down, we shall face the dictators alone. It is inconceivable that America can continue to exist as the only free nation in a world of conquering tyrants."

The speaker was Colonel Henry Breckenridge. Charles Lindbergh had lost another friend. But maybe there would be a reconciliation when the war was over, which, Lindbergh was certain, couldn't be long now.

But that was the trouble. As the weeks passed by, and defeated France was occupied by the Nazis, the stubborn British gave no sign of giving in to the victors. Lindbergh was annoyed. In a letter to a friend, he blamed "America's encouragement" of the British for complicating "the re-adjustment that had to take place in Europe."†

Charles Lindbergh's diary makes a fascinating study during this dramatic summer and fall of 1940, as much for what it leaves out as puts in. When important events are taking place in the world, he usually puts a short summary at the head of the day's entry (for instance, on June 17, 1940, he wrote: "The radio announces that France has asked for peace terms"). But there is no mention of the advent of Winston Churchill as the British premier and the fall of his much-admired appeaser, Neville Chamberlain. What is more extraordinary is that,

† Quoted by Wayne S. Cole in *Charles A. Lindbergh and the Battle Against American Intervention* (New York: Harcourt Brace Jovanovich, 1974).

around this time, both Alexis Carrel and his French pilot friend, Michel Detroyat, came to see him and ask his advice about what they should do now that France was defeated.

It was a moment when General Charles de Gaulle was making his famous appeal to Frenchmen everywhere to continue the fight and refuse to accept Marshal Henri Pétain's capitulation to the Germans, and one wonders what were Carrel's and Detroyat's reactions to the call. Detroyat would, in particular, have been a considerable asset to the Free French cause, for he was both a fine pilot and a highly skilled aeronaut. But as he recounts his friend's talks with him, Lindbergh makes no mention of De Gaulle at all, and the alternatives which he describes Detroyat as facing are "whether to go back to France, join the still-existing French armies in North Africa, or to volunteer his services to the British government."‡ Eventually, Carrel and Detroyat both told Lindbergh that they were returning to Occupied France. It was an unfortunate choice, as it turned out. Both of them were subsequently accused of collaborating with the Germans.

The most significant omission from the Lindbergh diaries is any coherent account of the Battle of Britain, which started between the Royal Air Force and the German Luftwaffe in August 1940, and raged all through that winter and the spring of 1941. The curious thing is that Lindbergh did not write about the Battle of Britain anywhere else, either. It was as if, like De Gaulle's advent, the event signaled the continuation of a resistance which he felt was unnecessary, and therefore tried to wipe it out of his consciousness.

Yet the Battle of Britain was surely an event (aside from the fact that it saved Britain from invasion by Germany) which should have merited Lindbergh's attention as a student of aeronautics, aircraft, and air warfare. This was the moment when the Luftwaffe, which he had always claimed would make Germany master of Europe, and maybe of the world, was pitting itself for the first time against a rival air arm of equal technical caliber. It is true that Lindbergh had never thought the RAF was in the same class, in terms of numbers or morale, but he must surely have been fascinated by the day-to-day clash of the rival forces, and interested in analyzing their claims.

Can it be that he refrained from doing so because he was not pleased when it became apparent that the wrong Air Force was winning? That may perhaps explain why he made only one comment about the battle, and a rather sour one at that:

‡ It is interesting that though Lindbergh remained fascinated with France's fate, and paid a visit to France at the end of the war, he does not once use De Gaulle's name in a thousand printed pages of diary, including a description of the postwar visit.

"It seems probable that the Germans are losing a few more planes than the English, because they are attacking," he wrote on August 14, 1940. "Also, the English save every man who jumps from his plane over England, while all the Germans who jump are naturally put in concentration camps."

"Concentration camps" was a curious description to use of the POW camps in which captured German pilots were held by the British, and treated strictly according to the Geneva Convention for prisoners of war. They were hardly to be equated with Auschwitz, Belsen, and Buchenwald and other camps where the Germans were now herding millions of Jews and other non-Aryans on their way to the gas ovens. It turned out, however, that when Charles Lindbergh referred to these later he did not call them concentration camps but "Nazi prison camps."

But no matter what the British were doing with their captured German pilots, he was convinced that it would not help them. Ambassador Joseph Kennedy had come back from Britain to report to President Roosevelt about conditions there, and Lindbergh called him up at the Waldorf Astoria Hotel in New York. He was invited over and took Anne Lindbergh with him. They emerged from their talk considerably reinforced in their judgment of the situation by Kennedy's candor.

"He feels, as we do, that the British position is hopeless," Lindbergh wrote later, "and that the best possible thing for them would be a negotiated peace in the near future."

Kennedy told them that only Churchill and the hope that America would come in were keeping the British going. If it were not for Churchill, in fact, the war would stop.

The ambassador told them he was coming back to fight tooth and nail against American involvement in the war. He didn't think it would help, anyway. The war was lost.

So why bother about the Battle of Britain?

CHAPTER

TWENTY-ONE

AMERICA FIRST

Anne Lindbergh gave birth twice in the fall of 1940, once to a baby and once to a book. The baby, her first daughter, was doubly welcomed by her family, who hoped its arrival would ease the rather strained relations which were now developing between Betty Morrow and her daughter and famous son-in-law.

Mrs. Morrow and most of her circle (as well as most of Anne Lindbergh's college friends) were now banded together in devoted support of "gallant Britain," and the fact that the Lindberghs were on the "other side" was arousing quite a lot of gossip in the press. Speculation about what conditions were like in the family when they spent a weekend together at Next Day Hill were fanned by a speech from William Allen White, chairman of the Committee to Defend America by Aiding Britain. He talked of "a rift" between mother and daughter, and hinted that Betty Morrow and her son-in-law had had arguments.

Arguments, in fact, were something which Mrs. Morrow, always impeccably behaved, went out of her way to avoid. But she was embarrassed. It was about this time that she sent a telegram to the President which hints at her feelings:

DEAR MR. PRESIDENT, I WAS DEEPLY IMPRESSED WITH YOUR SPEECH. IT SHOULD GREATLY HELP ALL THE COUNTRY'S EFFORTS FOR OUR DEFENSE AND FOR AID TO ENGLAND. I TRUST YOU WILL NOT MISUNDERSTAND IF I SAY THAT THIS IS FOR YOUR OWN EYE. MR. WHITE'S UNFORTUNATE SPEECH ABOUT ME AND MY SON-IN-LAW HAS MADE ME LOATHE TO ENTER THE LIPS [LISTS] PUB-

LICLY AGAIN AT THIS TIME. SINCERELY YOURS ELIZABETH C.
MORROW (MRS. DWIGHT MORROW).*

Everyone around her hoped that now Anne Lindbergh had a baby
daughter to take care of, she would be able to retire from her active
support of what they considered to be Charles Lindbergh's "disloyal"
campaign.

They were in for a shock. Her book was published shortly afterward,
and at once put Anne Lindbergh in the forefront of the fight for nonintervention. It was called *The Wave of the Future*. Reading it today, it
seems to be a strange amalgam of *faux-naïveté* and sentimentality,
cloudy, imprecise, and illogical. It demonstrates Anne Lindbergh's surprising capacity for self-deception, as, for instance, when she equates
the "sins" of the Nazis ("persecution, aggression, war and theft") with
the "sins" of the "Democracies"† ("blindness, selfishness, smugness,
lethargy and resistance to change"). The theme of the book was that
"the wave of the future" in the shape of nazism, fascism, and communism was sweeping inexorably over the world, and that those who
tried to hold it back were refusing to accept the inevitable. This was
silly of them because "to resist change is to sin against life itself."

The book almost immediately became a best seller, and if it did not
please the reviewers or convince the more thoughtful, it had a considerable impact upon others. Probably the most vitriolic attack upon it
came from the Secretary of the Interior in Roosevelt's Cabinet, Harold
L. Ickes, who had now appointed himself the gadfly of the Administration and would be stinging the Lindberghs regularly and painfully in
the future. He described *The Wave of the Future* as "the Bible of
every American Nazi, Fascist, Bundist and Appeaser."

A more reasoned reply to it came from Anne's favorite cousin,
Richard B. Scandrett, Jr., who wrote:

> Your book seems to me to be the effort of a troubled
> woman, aghast at current world horrors, eager to have their
> area restricted and to find a conception of duty towards the
> situation which, if accepted, might keep life running on much
> as usual in America. . . . I have read and reread your book
> several times and each rereading adds to my original impres-
> sion that it is, to an appreciable extent, a lyrical and silver-
> coated exposition of the views expressed by Charles. Both you

---

* Presidential Papers, Franklin D. Roosevelt Library, Hyde Park, New York.
† From this date onward, the Lindberghs always referred to Britain, France, and
the United States as "Democracies" (in quotes).

and Charles seem to me to have accepted the totalitarian
definition of a democracy as a static or decayed material concept.

It wasn't, he maintained, and they were wrong. It was "a dynamic
and spiritual faith."

He went on to ask how Anne and Charles could possibly have
thrown in their lot with the isolationists if they really believed in "the
wave of the future," in a willingness to change. Because, Scandrett declared, most of the supporters of nonintervention were "men and
women who have been horrified rather than pleased by the desire for social reform which has been manifesting itself here during the past
decade."‡

Anne's cousin made it clear that he was proud to be what Charles
and his fellow-neutralists called "a warmonger" because he believed:

> That the enemies whom England is fighting today are our
> enemies, and that their defeat is of fundamental and vital im-
> portance to us not only in a political and economic sense, but
> to the continuation of life. . . . If a majority of the American
> people have concluded (as now seems to me to be the case)
> that this assumption is warranted, then I believe that they
> should also arrive at the conclusion that we should declare
> ourselves to be in a state of war."*

Scandrett believed that a majority of the American people were now
in favor of voting for a state of war against Germany. The presidential
election results that fall seemed to justify his belief, for Franklin D.
Roosevelt was sent back for a third term with 27 million votes over his
Republican opponent, Wendell Willkie.

Charles Lindbergh was deeply depressed by the result, as much because it was a vote for Franklin Roosevelt himself as well as his policies,
and he could not conceal his dislike and distrust of him. His diary during this period is peppered with remarks like: "No one trusts the President" or "Everyone I meet thinks the President cannot be trusted,"
which is hardly surprising, since he was now meeting few people other
than isolationists. He had now thrown in his lot with the No Foreign
Wars Committee, and among its leaders were a considerable number of

‡ It was a shrewd point to make. Most of the isolationists were not just against
helping Britain; they were sworn enemies of the social reforms of the New Deal.
* A copy of this letter is in President Roosevelt's Personal File in the Franklin D.
Roosevelt Library, Hyde Park, New York.

demagogues and racists. The two chief activists were a young man named Verne Marshall and a leader of the American Legion, O. K. Armstrong. They were both, in the words of Wayne S. Cole, "energetic, impulsive, courageous, patriotic, aggressive, emotional, 'banty rooster' types."† They set out to upstage each other and vied for attention by scurrilous attacks on their opponents. As Cole puts it: "Passions mounted. Marshall's emotions became strained to the breaking point. He said things he should not have said."

This is a polite way of indicating that Marshall began making racial charges against Roosevelt and implying that the Aid Britain campaign was a Jewish plot, and it might be a good thing if the Nazis won and cleared things up. Meantime, another of Lindbergh's new associates was also turning out to be a fierce anti-Semite. This was a certain Lawrence Dennis, who had been brought to him by Truman Smith and recommended as an ally in the fight. He ran a profascist weekly and thought that Europe might be a better place if Hitler won and America more fit to live in if Jewish influences were curbed.

Lindbergh decided that it was a mistake to have been mixed up with such overemotional characters. He himself was becoming increasingly concerned about "Jewish influence" in the United States, but he was not yet ready to say so publicly. He had never allowed the No Foreign Wars Committee to put his name on its note paper,‡ and he was therefore able to claim, in a telegram to the wire services on January 16, 1941, that he had "no connection with the No Foreign Wars Committee" and found himself "unable to support the methods and policies adopted by the new organization."

He joined the America First Committee instead.

"From September, 1940, until December 7, 1941, the America First Committee was the most powerful isolationist or noninterventionist pressure group in the United States," writes Wayne S. Cole. "And from the time he joined, in April, 1941, until Pearl Harbor, nearly eight months later, Charles A. Lindbergh was the Committee's most controversial and popular speaker."*

The chairman of America First was a stanch American patriot named General Robert E. Wood, in professional life the national chairman of Sears, Roebuck. He had surrounded himself with some of the most powerful men in the land, most of them rich, many of them famous

† *Charles A. Lindbergh and the Battle Against American Intervention* (New York: Harcourt Brace Jovanovich, 1974).
‡ Though he had regularly taken part in its discussions.
* *Battle Against American Intervention.*

politicians, all of them dedicated to fighting Franklin D. Roosevelt and keeping America out of the war. They included such names as J. Stanford Otis, vice-president of the Central Republic Bank of Chicago; R. Douglas Stuart, Jr., son of the president of Quaker Oats Company; Hanford MacNider, a banker and former national commander of the American Legion; J. C. Hormill, of Hormill Packers, Austin, Minnesota; John T. Flynn, an economist and writer; Thomas McCarter, president of the Public Service Corporation of New Jersey; Chester Bowles, advertising man; and Edward Rickenbacker, air ace and aircraft manufacturer. They also had some distinguished female support in the persons of Kathleen Norris, the writer; Lillian Gish, film star; Alice Roosevelt Longworth, political hostess; and Mrs. John P. Marquand, the rich, wacky wife of the famous novelist. Youth was not particularly well represented on the management committee with the exception of two brilliant young men, Stuart, who was organizer, and Kingman Brewster, Jr., a Yale student.

Membership of the America First chapters numbered around 300,000 at the beginning of 1941 and grew to 800,000 after Charles Lindbergh joined them. They were mostly middle-aged, well-heeled, white Anglo-Saxon Protestants (including many Lutherans), and from the Middle West. On the whole they were decent, honest, sincere citizens who passionately believed that foreign entanglements were bad for the United States, and that if a menace to their safety came from overseas, they were better off meeting it alone. Inevitably, they had pro-Nazis, German Bundists, racists, and extremists who tried to attach themselves to the organization, but they did their best to rid themselves of these elements, whose principles they abhorred. Thanks to Charles Lindbergh's efforts, the motorcar tycoon Henry Ford joined the organization at the end of 1940 and sent in a hundred-dollar subscription. But the committee demanded and got his resignation when it was pointed out, shortly afterward, that Ford was a rabid anti-Semite. General Wood exhorted his supporters to "fight hard but fight clean," and when, at one period, someone mailed a scurrilous anti-Roosevelt pamphlet to America First members, he took steps to have the culprit drummed out of the organization and wrote to the President to apologize.

When it was revealed that Charles Lindbergh had teamed up with America First, President Roosevelt recognized it for the first time as the most serious opponent of his plans for helping Britain, and girded his forces to destroy it.

It was a moment when his prestige was riding high. Back in the White House with a landslide vote, he had immediately put into action his plans for defeating Germany. He now no longer made any secret of the fact that he considered National Socialism the prime enemy of the United States, and was willing to take risks in order to defeat it. He had promised Winston Churchill all-out aid. He had dubbed his nation the "arsenal of democracy" and likened America's attitude to Britain's peril as: "Supposing my neighbor's home catches fire, and I have a length of garden hose. Shall I refuse to lend it to him?"

He had already arranged for Britain to take over fifty out-of-commission U. S. Navy destroyers with which to carry on the antisubmarine war in the Atlantic, and now proposed to help Britain pay for other armaments and supplies through what came to be known as the Lend-Lease Bill. (The President's wife, Eleanor Roosevelt, had an inspiration and suggested that the bill be numbered H.R. 1776.) He also had other plans in mind for actions which would take the U. S. Navy into the war zone and shoot back at the Nazis if threatened.

Roosevelt was in a belligerent mood. Convinced by this time that America's safety depended on a British victory—or, at least, on British survival—he was prepared to take great risks to see that the Nazis did not crush America's ally. And he was prepared to destroy by any methods which came to hand any person or organization which got in his way. Hitherto, he had regarded Charles Lindbergh as a menace to his own prestige. Now he saw him as a danger to the security of the American state. Franklin D. Roosevelt was a great man and a great statesman, but he was also a skilled and ruthless politician. From the moment he made up his mind that Lindbergh was in the way, he was determined to eliminate him—and not necessarily with a clean shot between the eyes.

On January 23, 1941, Charles Lindbergh testified before the Congress of the United States against the President's Lend-Lease Bill. He was in a despondent mood. "Will America enter the war?" he had been asking himself recently. "Will our vanity, our blindness and our airy idealism throw us, too, into the conflict, heedless of the future? Must we fly mothlike into the flame of a war an entire ocean away? I know what we should do, but no one knows what we will do. Our thinking is confused; our direction is undecided; our leadership uncertain."

He had decided that he would "work against war, but lay plans for one."

To the Congress committee he said:

"Personally, I do not believe that England is in a position to win the war. If she does not win, or unless our aid is used in negotiating a better peace than could otherwise be obtained, we will be responsible for futilely prolonging the war and adding to the bloodshed and devastation of Europe, particularly among the democracies."

He was momentarily enlivened when the audience in the caucus room applauded him at the end of his testimony, but he came away with a feeling that his efforts to combat the bill had been abortive. (They had. Lend-Lease was voted by overwhelming majorities in both Houses.) He was plunged into depression again by the time he got home. Everything was going wrong. The radio speech Anne had made over Christmas asking the American people to force the British into relaxing their blockade of German-occupied Europe, so that food could be sent in, had fallen flat. Their terrier dog, Skeean had died, painfully, and the gallant old German shepherd, Thor, was ailing.

Anne Lindbergh was in bed and announced that she was too ill to dine with the Archibald Roosevelts and the J. P. Marquands. "I have chicken pox," she announced. "Nonsense," he said, "it's just a rash."

A few days later he was in bed with chicken pox himself. While he was tossing around uncomfortably in bed, trying to find a position in which he could read, *The Saturday Evening Post* telephoned to say that they couldn't use an article he had written called "A Letter to Americans," along his usual lines. Was it a straw in the wind?†

Through most of March 1941, he and Anne convalesced by sailing the Florida Keys and Everglades, and when he came back to New York he was refreshed, recovered, and ready to take on Roosevelt and anyone else. On April 23 he spoke at a mass meeting arranged by America First at the Manhattan Center, and there was something about the tenseness of his attitude, the rancor with which he talked about the British and the Administration which seemed to whip up his audience. He admitted himself in his diary account of the meeting that "there was considerable anti-British feeling." He put it down to the feelings of frustration among the American people, the fear that they were being pushed into war regardless of how they felt about it, and that "England is largely responsible for the mess we are being dragged into."

It was true that there was confusion in people's minds, and both sides were now beginning to exploit it. The Gallup Poll indicated that 80 per cent of the nation was against going to war against Hitler, but 73 per cent were in favor of having supplies to Britain escorted by American warships, and willing to see them shoot back at Nazi attacks. The White House mail makes an interesting study during this period, because its tone (for or against the Administration, pro-Roosevelt or pro-Lindbergh) was rising and the words used were getting rougher. "How

† It was eventually taken by *Collier's Weekly.*

can such an utterly disgusting yellow-bellied traitor as Charles A. Lindbergh be allowed to spew off at the mouth before the public," wrote a Texan who signed his name. "He should be tied with a long chain and dropped in the middle of the Atlantic, where his body will no longer contaminate the U.S.A." On the other hand, a Portland, Oregon, housewife wrote that Roosevelt was "so absorbed by alien influences that you do not seem to be aware of their sinister plot to destruct and destroy America. Yours is a Jew Deal." These kinds of letters were by no means exceptions. The nation was in a rancorous mood, friends were arguing, tempers rising.

The time had come, the President decided, when it was necessary to strike down his opponents before they succeeded in dividing the nation. By destroying Charles Lindbergh, he would leave them thrashing around like a snake without a head, and it was against him that he turned his sword. On April 25, 1941, two days after Lindbergh's Manhattan Center speech, there was a presidential press conference at the White House. Press Secretary Steve Early had already tipped off certain correspondents that if they asked questions along certain lines, they would probably elicit some illuminating answers.

Almost at once, a reporter rose to ask the President whether he had read the speech Colonel Charles Lindbergh had made in New York City the previous Wednesday night, when he declared that the United States could not win the war for England, no matter how much aid they extended. Had he also noted that Colonel Lindbergh had repeatedly asserted that Germany was bound to win the war, and criticized the United States for its anti-German foreign policy?

The President replied that he had read the speech.‡

Another reporter rose. Could the President say why Colonel Lindbergh, who was a reserve officer, had not so far been called into active service? (The inference of the question was that if he had been called up, as so many reserve officers were being at this time, he would be unable to make any more speeches.)

"In answer to this question," the Associated Press reported, in its account of the press conference, "Mr. Roosevelt said that during the Civil War numerous foreigners and liberty-loving people fought on both sides, and at the same time both sides let certain people go. That is, they were deliberately not called into service. The people thus ignored, he said, were Vallandighams.

‡ Presidential press conferences were not reported verbatim in the newspapers at this time.

The President explained that the Vallandighams were people who from 1863 urged immediate peace, arguing that the North could not win the War between the States. There were also many appeasers at Valley Forge, he went on, who urged George Washington to quit, arguing that the British could not be defeated. He urged that the newsmen read what Thomas Paine wrote at that time on the subject of quitting.

"Are you still talking about Colonel Lindbergh?" asked a reporter.

A simple and emphatic affirmative was the answer.

By this time the flashes had gone out over the tape machines, and rewrite men were busily digging into their history books to find out more about the Vallandighams, and what Tom Paine had said in 1776. It turned out that the Vallandighams were named after Senator Clement L. Vallandigham from Ohio. In 1863 he had been arrested by the military authorities for alleged treasonable utterances against the North, and had been deported to the southern states.

He had been dubbed the Leader of the Copperheads. A copperhead was an American species of snake.

As for Tom Paine, he had written: "These are times to try men's souls. The summer soldier and the sunshine patriot will, in this crisis, shrink from the service of their country; but he that stands it *now* deserves the love and thanks of man and woman. Tyranny, like hell, is not easily conquered."

PRESIDENT CALLS LINDY A COPPERHEAD ran the headlines in the evening papers that day, and the stories underneath it made it clear that in this case "copperhead" meant a traitor. When friends telephoned him to tell him about it, Lindbergh immediately sent for the newspapers. He was deeply distressed and bitterly angry at the unfairness of the attack, at the way in which the President had hit out not at his political stand but at his patriotism and his position in the Armed Forces. His commission in the Air Corps meant a great deal to him, and the hints of treachery and cowardice hurt.

"What luck it is," he wrote, "to find myself opposing my country's entrance into a war I *don't* believe in, when I would so much rather be fighting for my country in a war I *do* believe in."

It was particularly ironic, he told himself, that he was speechifying up and down the country with *pacifists*, "when there is no philosophy I disagree with more than that of the pacifist," and nothing he would rather be doing than flying with the Air Corps.

"If only the United States could be on the *right* side of an intelligent war!" he cried. But this one was wrong, and only chaos would result— "race riots, revolution, destruction."

He agonized for forty-eight hours, and then, on Sunday night April 27, 1941, sat down in his study and wrote a letter to the President (it was dated the following day, when it was put in the mail):

My dear Mr. President: Your remarks at the White House press conference on April 25th, involving my reserve commission in the United States Army Air Corps have, of course, disturbed me greatly. I had hoped that I might exercise my rights as an American citizen to place my viewpoint before the people of my country in time of peace without giving up the privilege of serving my country as an Air Corps officer in the event of war.

But since you, in your capacity of President of the United States and Commander-in-Chief of the Army, have clearly implied that I am no longer of use to this country as a reserve officer, and in view of other implications that you, my President and superior officer, have made concerning my loyalty to my country, my character and my motives, I can see no honorable alternative to tendering my resignation as colonel in the United States Army Air Corps. I am therefore forwarding my resignation to the Secretary of War. I take this action with the utmost regret, as my relationship with the Air Corps is one of the things that has meant most to me in life. I place it second only to my right as a citizen to speak freely to my fellow-countrymen and to discuss with them the issues of war and peace which confront our nation in this crisis.

I will continue to serve my country to the best of my ability as a private citizen. Respectfully, Charles A. Lindbergh.

It was a fatal move to have taken, and one which President Roosevelt had obviously deliberately set out to provoke, having sized up his opponent. A more astute antagonist, used to the ways of politicians, would have refused to fall into the trap which had been set for him, and held on to his commission. But Charles Lindbergh was still as naïve and vulnerable to political tricks now as he had been three years back in Germany, when the Nazis had led him up the garden path. The New York *Times* summed up the way his resignation would be interpreted in an editorial on April 29, 1941:

President Roosevelt spoke impetuously last Friday. He went back three-quarters of a century into the bitterness of the

Civil War to find a disparaging epithet for Charles A. Lindbergh. Mr. Lindbergh, in turn, shocked those who believed him to be a loyal American—though a sadly mistaken one—by his petulant action in relinquishing his commission in the Army Reserve. No evidence existed to justify the President's comparison of Mr. Lindbergh with Senator Vallandigham, who was banished into Confederate territory because his words, spoken in a military zone during active operations, were thought to give aid and comfort to the enemy. Nor is any American, from private to general officer, in service or on reserve, big enough to take the position that he will not serve his country because he has been, as he believes, unjustly reprimanded by his Commander-in-Chief or any other superior.

Only the America First Committee and such supporters in the press as the Chicago *Tribune* rushed to his rescue. America First issued a statement saying:

> President Roosevelt's remarks about Colonel Lindbergh do not exhibit the spirit of tolerance or the respect for freedom of conscience and freedom of belief that the American people have admired in him. Unlike the President, the American people know that Colonel Lindbergh is an American first, last and always.

The Chicago *Tribune* carried a cartoon showing a great crowd rallying to Lindbergh and only a small group of stripe-panted bankers looking toward Roosevelt, with the caption: "If Lindbergh is disloyal, so are a hundred million more Americans."

President Roosevelt had succeeded in polarizing the war situation into the "patriots," who supported his policy toward it, and the "Copperheads," who were against him. Henceforward, things would be rough, and the most wounding words about Lindbergh would come from his former friends.

"A Knight of Hitler's order of the German Eagle has urged us to stop our policy of aid, and everything will be all right," wrote William C. Bullitt. "We can have peace at the price of slavery. I think at that price we shall never have peace. I think that there was something that grew here long before the Knight of the German Eagle was born, and that was liberty."

Henry Breckenridge ("dear, devoted, loyal Henry," as Anne once called him) was even harsher:

> "Norway has its Quisling. France has its Laval. The United States has its equivalent. He who spreads the gospel of defeatism is an ally of Adolf Hitler. All those who are not with Hitler are against him."

The Lindberghs were living in the summer of 1941 in yet another rented house on the North Shore of Long Island, having been driven out of the Morrow home at Englewood by the disapprobation of the family. It was not that any of their relatives or in-laws had ever audibly reproached them. Aubrey Morgan, Constance's Welsh husband, assistant head of the British Information Service in New York, was as gentle and polite as ever to Charles Lindbergh. When reporters asked him for his opinions of his brother-in-law, he replied that he was "surely the eternal refutation of those who say that British propaganda is invincible." Betty Morrow made it clear that she was as deeply fond of her daughter as ever, and admired her son-in-law for all his qualities, if not for his political beliefs. All the same, the Lindberghs felt it was better for everyone if they lived in a home of their own.

It would be wrong to say that they had lost public sympathy, despite their stand, even from those who did not agree with them. But attitudes were changing. Some weeks after President Roosevelt's slur on Lindbergh's reliability, the New York *Times* carried an article by Roger Butterfield which amounted to an explanation, if not apologia, for his attitude, and seemed to be written with an amount of detail which could only have been supplied by sympathetic friends—what friends he had left.

> [Anne] has made desperate efforts to reconcile her own personal feelings, which are warmly pro-English, with his fatal inclination towards Germany and totalitarianism. He takes little part in the social life of [Lloyd] Neck, where social gatherings and cocktail parties are popular. As often with the Lindberghs, people seem to feel that they are lonely, especially as many of their old friends definitely disagree with their present activities. Colonel Henry Breckenridge, Lindbergh's attorney for many years, is actually actively opposing him. Harry Guggenheim, who sponsored Lindbergh's goodwill flight around the U.S. in 1927, disagrees with him and hasn't seen him for a long time. Recently a woman friend of Anne cornered

Thomas Lamont at a dinner party and asked him (a former partner of Anne's father): "Why don't you go and see the Lindberghs sometimes. They're lonely."

"I've nothing to do with them," Lamont replied.

To replace friends like these, the Lindberghs have been going to dinner with America First associates like Norman Thomas and John T. Flynn. On their travels they stay at the homes of other America Firsters. . . . In Washington, where the Administration is highly Lindbergh-conscious, his name is a danger signal to many old friends. Admiral Jerry Land, Chairman of the Maritime Commission, and cousin of Lindbergh's mother, used to put up the young flier, but when a mutual friend mentioned Lindbergh recently he exploded:

"I just can't talk about him any more. I think he's gotten into bad hands, and he's all wrong."

Lt. Colonel Truman Smith, Lindbergh's companion in Berlin, is under specific orders not to discuss Lindbergh with anybody, or to discuss military matters with Lindbergh.

Kay Smith had, in fact, already telephoned Charles Lindbergh to say that her husband felt they should not meet any more for the time being, and also asked him not to telephone.

"We believe our telephone is tapped," she said.

An FBI check was also now begun on Charles Lindbergh's activities. As early as February 1941, the Bureau had been looking into the background of the America First Committee, and on March 1 J. Edgar Hoover wrote to the President's press secretary, Steve Early:

Dear Steve: Reference is made to your communication of February 21st, 1941, to which was attached a memorandum directed to you on February 21, 1941, by the President. It is noted that there was attached to the memorandum from the President a circular distributed by the America First Committee.

With regard to the President's request for information as to the source of funds of the America First Committee, I am attaching hereto a memorandum dated March 1, 1941, which already furnishes the desired information but provides additional data concerning the America First Committee.

If it is the President's wish that a more exhaustive investigation be made relative to the means by which the America First Committee is being financed, I will not hesitate to call

upon it to provide such information. With my highest regards,
Sincerely yours, J. Edgar Hoover.*

The attached memorandum merely gave a detailed list of the committee's aims, management committee, and added that it was "financed
by those interested in the organization." In fact, President Roosevelt
could hardly have seriously believed that America First was being
financed by the Nazis. Most of its leading members were rich enough
to pay for the full-page ads in the newspapers and the millions of pamphlets they were now printing.†

But what about Lindbergh? Had he and Truman Smith brought
back with them from Berlin ties with the Nazis which might now be
compromising their loyalty to the United States?

It is difficult to find the specific documents which confirm what is
practically certain: that the check on Lindbergh began shortly after
Roosevelt had made his Copperhead accusation and the flier had
resigned his commission. On May 21, 1941, the President sent a
memorandum to Attorney General Robert Jackson. It was shortly before this that the Supreme Court had disapproved of tapping the telephone wires of private citizens, and this appears to have caused some
concern at the FBI and in the Justice Department. Roosevelt set out to
reassure them. He wrote:

> I have agreed with the broad purpose of the Supreme Court
> decision relating to wire tapping in investigations. The Court
> is undoubtedly sound . . . in its opinion that under ordinary
> and normal circumstances wire tapping should not be carried
> out by Government agents, for the excellent reason that it is
> almost bound to lead to abuse of civil rights.
>
> However, I am convinced that the Supreme Court never in-
> tended any dictum, in the particular case in which it decided,
> to apply to grave matters involving the defense of the nation.
>
> It is of course well known that certain other nations have
> been engaged in the organization of propaganda, of so-called
> "Fifth Columns" in other countries, and in preparation for
> sabotage as well as in actual sabotage.
>
> It is too late to do anything about it after sabotage, assassi-
> nations, "Fifth Column" activities are completed.

* Presidential Papers, Franklin D. Roosevelt Library, Hyde Park, New York.
† Though Nazi funds administered from the German embassy in Washington were
being paid out to certain labor leaders and politicians whose anti-Roosevelt activities
were not so scrupulously controlled as those of America First.

You are therefore authorized and directed in such cases as you may approve, after investigation of the need in each case, to authorize the necessary investigating agents that they are at liberty to secure information by listening devices direct to the conversation or other communications of persons suspected of subversive activities against the Government of the United States, including suspected spies. You are requested, furthermore, to limit these investigations so conducted to a minimum, and to limit them *insofar as possible* to aliens. F.D.R.‡

It was under this blanket permit that Truman Smith and Lindbergh were from now on put under surveillance. Lindbergh did not learn about it until July 7, 1941, when it had been in operation for some time. The America First organizer arrived to tell him that "friends" in the FBI had leaked him the fact that they were now tapping the Lindbergh telephones. They said they were "simply following out orders." Lindbergh told the organizer to tell the FBI that he had nothing to hide, and that if there was anything in his phone conversations that they didn't understand "I would be glad to give them additional information."

From this time onward, though, he increased the number of his speeches, the vigor of his delivery, the directness of his attacks on the Administration. On May 3, 1941, he spoke in St. Louis and justified his resignation from the Army.

"The President left me no honorable alternative," he cried. "In England, in France and now in my own country, we have listened to politicians and idealists calling upon the people for war, without hardly a thought of how that war is to be fought and won. I have seen France fall, I see England falling, and now America is being led into the same morass."

On May 9, he was in Minneapolis, one of the states where the America Firsters had their most powerful support. (He stayed in the "Nordic Suite" of the La Salle Hotel and commented: "What a press story that could make!") There he told a cheering audience:

If we intend to invade Europe in opposition to the same army and air force that broke the Maginot Line and broke the British forces in Norway, Flanders and Greece, then the United States must become a military nation. For many years

‡ Presidential Papers, Franklin D. Roosevelt Library, Hyde Park, New York.

to come we must become a regimented nation, a military nation that surpasses Germany herself in totalitarian efficiency.
In that case we must all realize that our way of life is a thing
of the past, that our children will be fortunate if they live long
enough to see it again. The conditions which exist in Germany today will seem moderate in comparison with those that
will result from a prolongation of this war. Men and women
of Minnesota, I say to you what my father said a quarter of a
century ago: the future of democracy depends upon your ability to govern our own country. It rests in the character of our
own people, in the welfare of our farmers and our workmen.
What happens in Europe is of little importance compared
with what happens in our own land. It is far more important
to have farms without mortgages, workmen with their own
homes, and young people who can afford families, than it is
for us to crusade abroad for freedoms that are tottering in our
own country.

Carl Sandburg sourly commented after he had read the speech:

Nowhere in the speeches and writings of the onetime flier
do we find any hint of the passion for freedom and equality of
opportunity that shook Lincoln . . . and the onetime flier's father. The father, as I noted him in the summer of 1917, speaking outdoors to a thousand farmers in a wheatfield outside the
city limits of St. Cloud, Minnesota, had a large mouth, a
touch of the Lincolnian, a deep and compelling baritone
voice, an Old Testament bitterness over the wrongs suffered
by the farmers of the Northwest. The son is something else.
The father had passion where the son has a precise mind, and
everything under control—the instrument board registering
like a mechanical brain, without bowels or solar plexus.

Nevertheless, America First was reporting considerable progress in
recruitment as a result of Lindbergh's speechmaking. If the FBI was
watching him on the President's behalf, they must have reported that
what was the most notable cause for concern was not his private activities but his public ones. As if galvanized by Roosevelt's slurs upon his
loyalty, he was fighting back. All over the country, particularly in the
Middle West, the masses were turning their eyes upon him, and quite a
few of them were now cheering him on.

On May 23, 1941, he addressed his most important audience yet, at

Madison Square Garden. There were 20,000 in the hall—"a much better type of people than you usually get in New York," Lindbergh commented—and another 14,000 outside. It was a highly excited and demonstrative audience, and violently partisan. When one speaker prophesied that Britain was going to lose the war, there were cheers. There were boos for Roosevelt, Secretary of the Navy Knox, and Secretary of War Stimson, for British Ambassador Lord Halifax and Winston Churchill. The hall was hung with a huge American flag, and small flags were handed to each seat-holder. The crowd fervently sang "America"* while they waited for the speeches to begin.

Anne Lindbergh sat beside her husband on the platform. "He rose several times and waved to the crowd," the New York *Times* reported. "He obviously relished being the cynosure of interest of the audience." He attacked the Administration even more rancorously than usual, and claimed that in the previous November's presidential election "we had no more chance to vote on the issue of peace than if we had been a totalitarian state ourselves."

He demanded "a change of leadership" in the country, and this was a point which most commentators took up afterward. What did he mean? There would not be another presidential election until 1944, more than three years away. As Westbrook Pegler put it in the New York *World Telegram*: "Is he thinking of having President Roosevelt impeached? In that case, look who he is going to get as the new President: Henry Wallace.† Or is he thinking of imposing it by other means, in which case we will probably get a Nazi."

Lindbergh immediately issued a statement denying that he had been referring to Franklin Roosevelt when he had asked for a change of leadership. What he had meant was a change in the "interventionists" who were surrounding and influencing the President.

"Neither I nor anyone else in the America First Committee advocate proceeding by anything but constitutional methods," he told the Baltimore *Sun*. A spokesman for the America First Committee stated that what Lindbergh had in mind was a new set of advisers surrounding the President, with John L. Lewis‡ as Secretary of Labor, James A. Farley as Secretary of War, Charles P. Taft as Secretary of the Navy, Thomas E. Dewey as Secretary at the Department of Justice, and Charles Lindbergh as Secretary for Air.

---

* It was later suggested that they did not sing "God Bless America" because it was written by a Jew.

† Henry Wallace was Vice-president.

‡ It was subsequently discovered that Lewis had accepted subventions from the Nazi embassy in Washington for fighting American entry into the war.

"This will unite America," he declared.

It hardly seemed so, since all of them would be isolationists, and the mass of the nation was still in favor of helping Britain even if it meant risking war.

In any case, Lindbergh had not really been telling the truth when he denied that his "change of leadership" statement did not apply to Roosevelt himself. In his diary for May 31, a few days later, he had a long conference with former President Herbert Hoover at the Waldorf Astoria in New York, and he said in the course of describing their talk:

"At one time during our conversation we discussed the possibility of Roosevelt being impeached before his term expires. We both feel it is possible but not probable."

It had now become apparent to the President and his advisers that Charles Lindbergh was shaping up into a dangerous opponent. They knew that behind the scenes he was seeing Truman Smith again, and that both of them were conferring with Hoover, Senator Burton K. Wheeler, and other anti-Roosevelt senators. His public speeches were having their effect upon those who had doubts about the situation, who were afraid of war, who feared foreign entanglements.

But how to stop him?

It was Harold L. Ickes who came to the Administration's rescue.

CHAPTER

TWENTY-TWO

DES MOINES

The Secretary of the Interior in President Roosevelt's Cabinet was a waspish little man whose sting had real poison in it. Unlike most other members of the Administration, who feared or resented Lindbergh but did not really believe him a Nazi, Ickes was convinced that he was planning to install a totalitarian regime inside America. He wrote of him later to the President:

> An analysis of Lindbergh's speeches and articles—I have a complete indexed collection of them—has convinced me that he is a ruthless and conscious fascist. Motivated by hatred for you personally and for democracy in general, his speeches show an astonishing identity with those of Berlin, and the similarity is not accidental. His actions have been coldly calculated with a view to obtaining ultimate power for himself— what he calls "new leadership."*

Ickes had a method of fighting which was not exactly according to Queensberry rules but was highly effective politically.

He had used it with telling effect against Wendell Willkie during the presidential election the previous fall. It consisted of a series of rabbit and kidney punches against his adversary's character ("Wendell Willkie, the barefoot boy from Wall Street" was a typical one), followed by a colossal wallop below the belt (accusations tying him in with convicted stock exchange swindlers). The idea was to knock him

* Presidential Papers, Franklin D. Roosevelt Library, Hyde Park, New York.

off balance and trap him into swinging wildly, laying his defenses open to a knockout blow.

In Willkie's case, Ickes was able to write gleefully to Franklin D. Roosevelt:

> Willkie's reaction to my speech shows how sensitive he is. And we ought to keep needling him. His denial he was ever a member of Tammany and his violent rebound when he was confronted with the high eulogy he had paid to Samuel Insull in 1935 shows that he lacks political seasoning, and is likely to get himself out on a limb.

In Lindbergh's case, Ickes decided that he had a more serious challenger to deal with. He saw something sinister in the way in which Charles Lindbergh, in every article he was writing and speech he was making at this time, kept stressing the fact that *now* was the time to change the leadership of America, though the election was only just over, and that "only people like us" could do it. He passed on with approval for the President's sight a letter which a reader had written on June 6, 1941, to the New York *Times* about Lindbergh's tactics:

> I agree heartily with the sentiment expressed in your editorial, "What 'New Leadership'?" in which you ask what Colonel Lindbergh is talking about when he says, as he has in all his recent public speeches, "It is time we begin to look about for new leadership" and "Is it not time for us to turn to new policies and to a new leadership?"
>
> May I call your attention to what seems to me perhaps the most sinister of all Colonel Lindbergh's remarks along this line. In his famous "Letter to Americans" published in Collier's magazine for March 29 and distributed throughout the country, he concludes with the statement that we can only become "a strong and victorious nation" and "preserve our ideals" ". . . if you, and I, and people like us, take the reins in hand once more, as our forefathers have done in times of crisis."
>
> At the time that letter was published these words escaped general notice, because at that time Colonel Lindbergh had not yet launched the "all out" campaign to inculcate in the American people the theories of the "Fuehrer-Prinzip" upon which he is now so busily engaged.
>
> But in the light of his subsequent repeated calls for "new

leadership" his earlier words assume an inescapable meaning. The only way I know of to "take the reins in hand" is to take them out of the hands of those who now hold them—in this case, the duly elected public officials whose leadership Colonel Lindbergh so vehemently attacks. As you point out in your editorial, the people of the United States have entrusted the reins to those public officials for the next two to four years. But Colonel Lindbergh insists that "now" is the time to change our leadership. The only way I know of to take the reins out of the hands of our duly elected public officials now is by revolution.

No doubt Colonel Lindbergh's friends will say that these words don't mean what they say. But from all reports his audiences understand them all too well. For whenever he calls for new leadership his audiences shout themselves hoarse in the chant: "We want Lindbergh!"

If Colonel Lindbergh himself doesn't mean what he says, it is about time the country knew it. If he does mean what he says, it is time that the country knew that, and, what's more, it's time that the country knew just whom he refers to as "those like us" who are to join with him in taking the reins. I would be very much surprised if any portion of his supporters will go along with him in any such proposal as this except those vociferous groups whom he professes to repudiate: the bundists, fascists and communists.

William C. Chanler
Corporation Counsel, City of New York

These were feelings which Harold Ickes completely shared, and nothing was too rough to say against a man whom he now seriously believed to be plotting to take over the country and unseat the legally elected Administration. Accordingly, he carefully worked out which portion of the Lindbergh persona was most vulnerable, and moved in, ready to batter away at the sensitive spot until his enemy began to bleed. From now on, in every speech he made on behalf of the Administration, he never referred to Charles Lindbergh by name but carefully and deliberately called him "the Knight of the German Eagle," a reference to the decoration he had received from Hermann Göring and never returned. And, as Ickes subsequently wrote, "that got him." Charles Lindbergh bled.

On July 16, 1941, he sat down in his study at Lloyd Neck, Long Island, and penned a letter to President Roosevelt. He put it in the ordinary post and at the same time called in the wire services and handed them a copy. So that next morning the President read in his morning newspapers the missive which he himself did not receive until the following day, an old Lindbergh ploy. He did not like the press, but he knew how to use them. The letter said:

My dear Mr. President: I address you, Sir, as an American citizen to his President. I write concerning statements made by an officer of your Cabinet, the Secretary of the Interior.

For many months, and on numerous occasions, your Secretary of the Interior has implied in public meetings that I am connected with the interests of a foreign government, and he has specifically criticized me for accepting a decoration from the German Government in 1938.

Mr. President, is it too much to ask that you inform your Secretary of the Interior that I was decorated by the German Government while I was carrying out the request of your Ambassador to that Government? Is it unfair of me to ask that you inform your Secretary that I received this decoration in the American Embassy, in the presence of your Ambassador, and that I was there at his request in order to assist in creating a better relationship between the American Embassy and the German Government, which your Ambassador desired at that time?

Mr. President, if the statements of your Secretary of the Interior are true, and if I have any connection with a foreign government, the American people have a right to be fully acquainted with the facts. On the other hand, if his statements and implications are false, I believe that I, as an American citizen, have a right to an apology from your Secretary.

Mr. President, I give you my word that I have no connection with any foreign government. I have had no communication, directly or indirectly, with anyone in Germany or Italy since I was last in Europe, in the spring of 1939. Prior to that time, my activities were well known to your Embassies in the countries where I lived and traveled. I always kept in close contact with your Embassies and your military attachés, as the records in your State Department and War Department will show.

Mr. President, I will willingly open my files to your investigation. I will willingly appear in person before any committee you appoint, and there is no question regarding my activities now, or at any time in the past, that I will not be glad to answer.

Mr. President, if there is a question in your mind, I ask that you give me the opportunity of answering any charges that may be made against me. But, Mr. President, unless charges are made and proved, I believe that the customs and traditions of our country give me, as an American citizen, the right to expect truth and justice from the members of your Cabinet. Respectfully, Charles A. Lindbergh.

The President never replied to Lindbergh's letter, and all he got instead was the following from the presidential secretary:

> July 19, 1941. Dear Mr. Lindbergh: I acknowledge the receipt of your letter dated July sixteenth. It was received at the White House at 11:22 a.m., July eighteenth. However, the text was in the possession of the Press on the morning of July seventeenth—more than twenty-four hours before it reached the White House.
>
> When the newspapermen advised me on the morning of July seventeenth that you had written the President, they said they already had the text of your letter. I told them, because of these circumstances, it appeared obvious that you had written the letter for the Press—that you merely addressed it to the President. This statement, I now repeat to you because, as you know, this is not the first instance of its kind. It has happened before.
>
> In keeping with time honored tradition the text of this letter will not be given to the Press, at least until you have received it. Since it is not written primarily for the Press, it is possible it may never be given to the newspapermen. Very sincerely yours, Stephen Early, Secretary to the President.†

Secretary Ickes was delighted at Lindbergh's response, and one can imagine that gadfly character doing victory rolls all over his office and buzzing: "I've got him, I've got him!" In his diary he wrote:

> On Wednesday Lindbergh wrote an open letter to the President. . . . Up to that time I had always admired Lindbergh in one respect. No matter how vigorously he had been attacked

† Presidential Papers, Franklin D. Roosevelt Library, Hyde Park, New York.

personally he had never attempted an answer. He had kept determinedly in the furrow that he was plowing. I had begun to think that no one could get under his skin enough to make him squeal. But at last I had succeeded.

He was confident that, having pierced the Lindbergh armor, things would begin to happen to him. He felt that "Lindbergh has slipped badly," and added:

He has now made it clear to the whole country that he still clings to this German decoration. He is now in the position where he is damned if he gives it back and damned if he doesn't. Moreover, he hasn't helped himself, in my opinion, by writing a querulous letter to "teacher." He should have slammed right back at me. For the first time he has allowed himself to be put on the defensive and that is always a weak position for anyone.

It was true. From this moment on, he grew increasingly sensitive, suspicious, no longer willing to accept that those who believed in helping Britain fight the Nazis were sincere, but that they were doing it for personal, and often malevolent, reasons. He now no longer trusted even those who were halfway convinced by his isolationist crusade, but not quite enough to come out on his side. One of these was Roy Howard of the Scripps-Howard newspaper chain. Howard had always been one of Lindbergh's most fervent admirers and had willingly given him a platform. But personally, Howard was sufficiently independent to want to go on arguing with Lindbergh, and, in his present mood, this was tantamount to being in the "warmongers'" camp. After a long discussion about the war in Europe with Howard on July 18, 1941, he complained that "these people" (meaning Howard) were "not used to *open* discussion" and that they were "always looking for something underneath what you say, something behind your motives."

Before, he had despised the tabloid press and the sensational newspapers, but now he preferred them to the New York *Times* and the New York *Herald Tribune*, because most of them, particularly the Chicago *Tribune* and the Hearst press, supported his no-war stand. On August 11 he gave a long interview to Larry Kelly of the Hearst papers in Chicago, and obviously felt guilty about it. He wrote in his diary that night that the Hearst press "has done things to me in the past which I cannot forgive from a personal standpoint," but they were on his side in favoring American neutrality and had "given us such good support in this issue."

He summed up his feelings in these words:

"I like to have men on my side on whom I can count to the last shot. There are few of them at present."

It was in this mood that he and Anne were gathering up their diaries, letters, records, and other writings and taking them over to Yale University, where they would henceforward be deposited in the Yale Library for safe keeping.

There was a touch of defiance about the way he wrote about it, pointing out that neither he nor his wife was "ashamed" of the way they had lived their lives, and there was nothing in their records that they feared to have known.‡ "I wonder how many of our accusers," he added, "would be willing to turn their complete files and records over to study in the future."

It was in this light—as one who was being "accused"—that he seemed to regard himself now. Unjustly accused, it goes without saying. A movement had now begun among the supporters of America First to promote a congressional investigation into the motion picture industry and the media to find out what "sinister" forces were behind so much of the pro-British, anti-Nazi propaganda in the country. John T. Flynn, of the America First management committee, had been conducting the "investigation" and he told Lindbergh over lunch on August 8 that he was getting "amazing results" and that "a strong undercover movement for war exists" and had infected the motion picture industry.

Two days later, in Washington, Lindbergh foregathered with his two trusted cronies, Kay and Truman Smith, and afterward they went on to Senator Gerald Nye's apartment, where Senators Burton K. Wheeler and D. Worth Clark (all isolationists) were waiting for them. They discussed the way the Administration was manipulating the media in order to create a climate in favor of war. No one mentioned the word "Jewish" when they spoke about prowar propaganda, but the word was increasingly in Lindbergh's mind. His conviction was hardening that there were Jewish influences in the country who were influencing Americans against their own best interests, and that the time was approaching when he must expose their dangerous machinations.

He said nothing to the management committee of America First about his plans, and only Anne Lindbergh, John T. Flynn, and the Truman Smiths knew what he was planning to include in his speech.

‡ He made it a condition of the deposit, however, that "these files will not be opened until after we are dead, [when] time will clothe the nakedness of their contents."

He chose September 11, 1941, as the date and Des Moines as the place where he would make it. The President was due to address the nation a few days earlier and urge them to face up to the war challenge that was looming before them. Charles Lindbergh's speech would be in the nature of a reply. Then, at the last moment, the President's mother died and Franklin Roosevelt postponed his speech for a few days. When the new date was announced, it was scheduled for the same evening, September 11. They would be fighting practically simultaneously for the nation's attention.

Charles Lindbergh had never regarded Franklin D. Roosevelt as much of a speaker, and did not really understand why most people's opinion of the President's oratory differed from his own. Listening to two of Roosevelt's radio speeches in 1932 had persuaded him that "I did not trust the man who gave them and that I did not want to see him President of the United States," and as a result he had voted for Herbert Hoover. But he realized that many other people regarded him as an "able speaker" with the ability to "arouse crowds," and that the Des Moines meeting would therefore have to face up to a difficult and unique situation. He was annoyed to discover on arriving in the city, moreover, that the local committee of America First, anxious to show their "fairness," had announced that audiences who came to hear Lindbergh would not have to miss the President, because they would broadcast his speech from the stage before their own proceedings began. It was too late to do anything about that, but Lindbergh did succeed in dissuading the committee from having the speakers sit on the stage while Roosevelt was speaking. They would wait in the wings and enter immediately afterward.

Roosevelt was in good fighting form, and though the 7,500 people who had crowded into the hall to hear Lindbergh presumably included a majority of isolationists, it was noted that they cheered the President eleven distinct times—in a speech which was an out-and-out attack on the Nazis, and included the statement that henceforward the U. S. Navy had been ordered to clear the sea of "enemy" warships wherever it was necessary for American interests. The entry of the America First speakers one minute after he had finished was something in the nature of an anticlimax, and for the first time since he had become a politician, Charles Lindbergh found himself greeted with more boos than cheers. He was in a very tense mood, smiled only once, and decided long before he rose to speak that the "opposition" had brought in "organized hecklers" who were "strategically located to be effective for the microphones."

He had learned his new trade in the course of recent months, and he had become an incisive and effective speaker. This was the Middle West, where isolationists were thick on the ground, and Lindbergh's thesis that America was being driven into a war she could not win aroused many sympathizers.

"England's position is desperate," he cried in ringing tones. "Her population is not large enough and her armies are not strong enough to invade the continent of Europe and win the war—which she declared against Germany. Her geographical position is such that she cannot win the war by aviation, regardless of how many planes we send her. Even if America enters the war, it is highly improbable that the Allied armies could invade Europe and overcome the might of the Axis forces."

He was cheered for that.

"If it were not for her hope," he went on, "that she can make the United States responsible for the war, financially as well as militarily, I believe that England would have negotiated a peace in Europe many months ago, and be better off for doing so."

They raised the rafters for that one, too.

There was a sudden hush in the hall as he began to talk about the Nazi regime.

"I can understand why the Jewish people wish to overthrow the Nazis," he said. "The persecution they have suffered in Germany would be sufficient to make bitter enemies of any race." He paused, then added simply: "No person with a sense of the dignity of mankind condones the persecution of the Jewish race in Germany. Certainly I and my friends do not."

He had the meeting with him now. This time when they cheered, there was an emotional note to it. If Charles Lindbergh had left it there and gone back to lashing out at the President and the Administration, it might have been the most effective speech of his campaign. But he could not leave well enough alone.

"But," he cried to the audience, "though I sympathize with the Jews, let me add a word of warning. No person of honesty and vision can look on their prowar policy here today without seeing the dangers involved in such a policy, both for us—and for them." Pause. He allowed the last words "and for them" to sink in, and then went on crisply:

"Instead of agitating for war, the Jewish groups in this country should be opposing it in every possible way, for they will be among the first to feel its consequences. Tolerance is a virtue that depends upon peace and strength. History shows that it cannot survive war and devastation. A few far-sighted Jewish people realize this, and stand opposed to intervention. But the majority still do not. Their greatest danger to this country lies in their large ownership and influence in our motion pictures, our press, our radio, and our Government. . . . We cannot blame them for looking out for what they believe to be their own interests, but we also must look out for ours. We cannot allow the natural passions and prejudices of other peoples to lead our country to destruction."

The audience cheered him, but the mood had changed again, and both the applause and the boos mingling with it had an undertone which had been missing before. In one short passage he had changed the quality of the meeting and the nature of his approach to America's problems.

It was all very well for his apologists to say later that Lindbergh had not attacked the Jews, but simply Jewish influence. In the charged atmosphere of the time, no one was prepared for an argument over semantics. They judged as they heard. Lindbergh was afterward to say that he knew full well what an uproar his charges were bound to cause. Before he died, he showed Wayne S. Cole a handwritten first draft of his Des Moines speech in which he had scribbled:

"I realize that in speaking this frankly I am entering in where angels fear to tread. I realize that tomorrow morning's headlines will say 'Lindbergh attacks Jews.' The ugly cry of anti-Semitism will be eagerly joyfully pounded upon and waved about my name. It is so much simpler to brand someone with a bad label than to take the trouble to read what he says. I call you people before me tonight to witness that I am not anti-Semitic nor have I attacked the Jews."*

He omitted these remarks from his final speech, possibly because even he realized the naïveté of them, especially to an audience which had just heard him denounce the Jews for using films, newspapers, radio, and government influence to involve the American people in "their" war. They had heard him hinting that the Jews would be the first to suffer unless they backed the America Firsters in opposing war, and there had been an undertone of "or else" in this passage of his speech which sounded uncomfortably like the threats of Nazi demagogues.

As Wayne Cole has written, some of the strongest denunciations of the speech came from New York, but it was refreshing and encouraging to opponents of racism to note that the rest of the country reacted just as angrily to the implications of Lindbergh's remarks: "They came from Jews, but also from Protestants and Catholics. They came from interventionists, but also from noninterventionists. They came from

* Wayne S. Cole, *Charles A. Lindbergh and the Battle Against American Intervention* (New York: Harcourt Brace Jovanovich, 1974), p. 173.

Democrats, but also from Republicans and Communists. They came from high government leaders, but also from grassroots America. They charged Lindbergh with anti-Semitism, Nazism, and sympathy for Hitler. They called on the America First Committee to repudiate him. They urged a congressional investigation. And individual letter writers wanted to send him back to Germany."

The press did not hold back, either. Charles Lindbergh, who was now disillusioned with the New York *Times*, could well have claimed that that newspaper's attack on him was understandable, since it was Jewish-owned, but he could hardly say that of the Des Moines *Register*, the Kansas City *Star*, the San Francisco *Chronicle* and the New York *Herald Tribune*, which wrote:

> We have sustained Mr. Lindbergh against attacks upon his patriotism, which we believe to be unwarranted by the facts. This was done in the conviction that the discussion of America's relation to the great world conflict was an American debate conducted by Americans who were resolved to maintain the American system, and differing only in their concept of how that is to be accomplished. But the Des Moines speech, marking the climax of a series of innuendoes and covert allusions by Isolationist leaders, opens new and ugly vistas, and seeks to inject into open debate subjects which all good Americans pray might be confined to the pages of the Voelkischer Beobachter and the addresses of Adolf Hitler.

President Roosevelt and Harold L. Ickes made no comment on the speech. But then they didn't need to. Lindbergh, and the outrage of ordinary, decent Americans, had done their work for them.

CHAPTER

TWENTY-THREE

FAREWELL TO

LINDBERGH?

"I know I'm just a stubborn Swede," Charles Lindbergh once told a New York *Times* reporter, and if that meant he would never admit it when he had made a mistake, it was true. Aside from the fact that he went on believing you could live with the Nazis, and that it was the Jews who were driving America into war with them, he also refused to admit that he had made a tactical error in bringing up the Jewish question at Des Moines. He was astounded when he discovered that General Wood, chairman of America First, had been so shocked by reaction to the speech that he was all for adjourning the committee's functions. He could not understand why people were resigning from America First. He lashed out angrily at John T. Flynn, who now told him he had thought from the first that "it was inadvisable to mention the Jewish problem." This from a man "who feels as strongly as I do" that "the Jews are among the major influences pushing this country toward war"! He lunched with Herbert Hoover, who told him he thought his attack on the Jews at Des Moines had been a mistake. Lindbergh insisted that what he had said was true, and was depressed when Hoover replied "that when you had been in politics long enough you learned not to say things just because they are true."

The whole incident seemed to have thrown him off balance, and now he was prepared to believe anything that bolstered his belief that Germany would win the war and that the Administration was a nest of unscrupulous conspirators. He lunched with Truman Smith and swallowed the assertion made by a fellow guest that reports in the newspapers of Allied successes were all false, but were printed because they boosted circulation. He seemed delighted with Smith's claim that the Russian armies were in a state of collapse.

His speeches were now becoming both more emotional and more extreme, and it was obvious to observers that the inner resentments now stirring him were driving him toward the more fanatic and sinister supporters of nonintervention. He appeared to believe that at any moment President Roosevelt planned to curb not only the powers of Congress but America's traditional freedom of speech. At Fort Wayne, Indiana, on October 3, 1941, he told his audience that he realized this speech might well be his last, inferring that there were plans to gag him.

"If free speech ends in this country," he cried, "it means we are no longer a free people. It means we are about to enter a dictatorship and probably a foreign war. . . . [The Administration] have been treating our Congress more and more as the German Reichstag has been treated under the Nazi regime. Congress like the Reichstag is not consulted. As a nation we've been led along like children with sugared promises and candied pills."

Even his sympathizers were now beginning to look at him askance, wondering where he was going next. As for the newspapers, the New York *Times* came out with an editorial headlined "Swan Song or Malice?" which spoke for a growing public sentiment:

> Mr. Lindbergh's warning that his speech on Friday night might well be his last because free speech in America is on the way out was coupled with the clear implication that President Roosevelt may abolish the elections next year. The first, with its explicit statement that he and those who hold his views may at any time be deprived of their freedom of speech, gives the impression that he may be building up a new case for himself in the role of a persecuted martyr. The second falls little short of a direct charge that the President is planning a coup d'etat, and intends to overthrow the American form of constitutional government for a dictatorship.
>
> Neither charge does credit to Mr. Lindbergh's intelligence or his patriotism. Both can serve only one purpose—to inflame fanatics and frighten the uninformed. Both are obviously appeals to prejudice, designed to arouse hatred and fear. Either Mr. Lindbergh is ignorant of the fact that the President has no power to suspend the constitutional guarantee of freedom of speech and that he has no control whatever over the Congressional elections or he is deliberately misrepresenting the situation. In either event his statements are a measure of political adolescence or a fundamental lack of a sense of responsibility. This is further borne out by the manner in which he

29. In January 1941 Lindbergh campaigned against a request from President Roosevelt that the embattled democracies in Europe be granted Lend-Lease aid in their fight against Nazi Germany. Here he is seen testifying against the measure before the House Foreign Affairs Committee.

30. In 1941 Lindbergh stumped the nation campaigning against America's entry into World War II, addressing meetings in every state of the Union. Here he is seen on the platform of an America First rally at Madison Square Garden on May 23, 1941. With him are Senator Burton K. Wheeler (left), novelist Kathleen Norris, and Socialist party leader Norman Thomas.

31. Lindbergh went into seclusion at the end of World War II, eschewing publicity while working on space and missile projects for the government. But
occasionally he emerged, as on this occasion, for a White House dinner given
by President Kennedy to welcome French Minister of Culture André Malraux.

32. The Lindberghs avoided public functions, but some they had to attend. This
one was taken at a dinner of the National Institute of Social Sciences, from whom
Lindbergh had received a medal for his services to conservation.

33. More and more in the years following World War II, Lindbergh gave his time — and prestige — to encouraging public consciousness of the importance of ecology. Here he is shown on a survey flight over Hawaii.

34. For Charles and Anne Morrow Lindbergh, busy though their lives were, separately and together, there was always time through the years for their children and grandchildren. Here Lindbergh and his son, Land, go over a map of Land's Montana ranch.

sought to give the impression that the refusals of halls to himself and his followers, and the attacks which have been made upon him, were inspired by the government in Washington. The cold truth is that they are the result of local disapproval of what he has said and stands for. They are signs of the extent to which the Eagle's prestige has fallen. The fact that the President's private secretary and that Mr. Ickes have gone out of their way to insult Mr. Lindbergh is a mark of their unfairness rather than an indication of an organized campaign by the Administration against him. Certainly Mr. Lindbergh's rebuttals have not been on a much higher plane.

The formal charge that the President may soon abridge the right to hold elections will stand beside the attempt to smear the Jews as proof of Mr. Lindbergh's disregard for American tradition and practices. As we pointed out two weeks ago, the President under the Constitution has no power or control, direct or indirect, over the holding of Congressional elections. He cannot prorogue Congress. He cannot prevent it from meeting as prescribed under the Constitution. He cannot suspend the Constitution or any part of it. If, therefore, he were to endeavor to prevent the Congressional elections from being held in 1942, he could do so only by the use of the armed forces of the United States. This would be revolution.

If Mr. Lindbergh doesn't realize this, it is time he learned it. If he doesn't know that to charge the President of the United States with planned revolution and with the deliberate destruction of the Constitution is to make inflammatory statements which can serve only one purpose—to bring aid and comfort to the enemies of democracy in this country and abroad—he is a strangely blind man. If he knows how his remarks will be interpreted, then he must forfeit the last shred of respect which his fellow citizens have for him.

He made one last big speech, this time at Madison Square Garden on October 30, 1941, before an excited audience of nearly 20,000. They gave him a fervent six-minute ovation, and when he studied their faces he decided that "they were *far* above the average of New York. These people are worth fighting for." He heard one member of the audience cry out "Hang Roosevelt!" but decided that he was "almost certainly an opposition 'plant.'"

A few days later, a reporter from the New York *Times* was having dinner in the Lafayette Hotel, on University Place and Ninth Street in

New York, when he noticed something missing from one of the walls. The Lafayette had been owned by Raymond Orteig, whose Orteig Prize and $25,000 had been awarded to Charles Lindbergh for his 1927 transatlantic flight. Ever since, the so-called Lindbergh Flag, an American banner which had flown to Paris with Lindbergh, had hung on the restaurant wall.

Now it was gone. When the reporter asked J. B. Orteig, son of the hotel-man and now operator of the hotel, why the flag had disappeared, he shrugged his shoulders.

"Too many pros and cons," he said. "When we hung it there in 1927 Lindy was an aviator and everyone was proud of him. But now he's talking politics, and lately, when people notice the flag, they start getting into arguments. So it seemed best simply to remove it."

It was down below in his private office, Orteig said. "I don't think it will stay there. You see, when the war is over, Lindy will realize he was wrong. Then he'll be himself again, and we'll replace the flag in the dining room. That's all. We just took it down for a while."

On December 7, 1941, Japan bombed Pearl Harbor, the United States was in the war, and the time for speeches was over.

Charles Lindbergh had a date to speak in Boston and telephoned to cancel it. General Wood was already there and spoke to him.

"Well," said Wood, "he got us in through the back door."

It was one of those moments in history when patriots decide to forget their fraternal differences and join together to meet the common danger from outside. There was no such spirit of reconciliation between Charles Lindbergh and Franklin D. Roosevelt.

Lindbergh's first reaction when he knew that his country was at war was to feel downcast and afraid, not for himself but for the United States. "Now all that I feared would happen has happened," he wrote. "We are at war with the world and we are unprepared for it from either a spiritual or material standpoint."

His second reaction was to volunteer for service at once. A man with less complicated emotions churning around in his mind would have marched to the nearest recruiting office and joined up. The gesture would have immediately restored his prestige and popularity, and even the meanest kind of politics would have been unable to prevent his inevitable apotheosis.

But for all his claim to be a direct and simple man, Charles Lindbergh did not think that way. He had to get devious about things, and it would have bitter consequences for him.

His first impulse was to sit down and write a letter to the President offering his services, pointing out that he "had not changed my convictions" but was prepared to "submerge my personal viewpoint" in the interests of national unity. But in the end he could not do this. He simply could not bring himself to trust the President ("I do not know a single man who has known Roosevelt, friend or enemy, who trusts what he says from one week to the next"). Besides, Roosevelt had the reputation of being vindictive. If he wrote to him at this time, he would probably make what use he could of "my offer from a standpoint of politics and publicity" and then assign him to an obscure post "where I would be completely ineffective."

It does not seem to have occurred to Lindbergh that, in the circumstances, he must expect to have to go through a certain amount of humiliation, justified or not, and that he must endure it in the interests of his country. In any case, once back in the forces, not even a vindictive President would be able to keep a man of his caliber down.

He havered around, talking to America Firsters, to friends in Washington, and it was not until the war was two weeks old that he got down to writing a letter to his old chief, General Arnold, of the U. S. Army Air Corps, offering his services. That was on December 20, 1941. On December 30 he read in the newspapers that he had volunteered for the Air Corps, but had heard nothing from his friend General Arnold. He decided that despite the war the Christmas-New Year holidays had got in the way, and he let it alone until he went down to Washington early in January. On January 10, 1942, he telephoned General Arnold at the War Department and was put to his aide, Major Beebe. Would he be able to see General Arnold over the weekend? There was a pause, and then Beebe asked him what he wanted to see General Arnold about. It was about whether he could be of assistance to the Air Corps, Lindbergh said.

Beebe advised him to go directly to the Secretary of War. "I am sure the Secretary of War will see you," he said, "if you call his office and ask for an appointment."

Lindbergh knew from the tone of Beebe's voice that it had been arranged for him to see the Secretary, and he phoned for an appointment. He was told that Secretary Henry L. Stimson would see him at 3:30 on Monday afternoon. He spent the weekend wondering what was in store for him.

What Lindbergh did not know was that Harold Ickes had seen the item in the newspapers on the previous December 30 saying that the flier had applied to rejoin the Air Corps, and he had immediately taken up his pen to write a memorandum to the President:

December 30, 1941. My dear Mr. President: I notice that Lindbergh has just offered his services to the Army Air Corps. I believe that, taking the long view, it is of the utmost importance that the offer should *not* be accepted.

An analysis of Lindbergh's speeches and articles—I have a complete indexed collection of them—has convinced me that he is a ruthless and conscious fascist. . . . His actions have been coldly calculated with a view to obtaining ultimate power for himself—what he calls "new leadership." Hence it is important for him to have a military service record.

It is a striking historical fact that every single dictator and half-dictator in postwar Europe had a military service record. Mussolini was a war veteran. Mustapha Kemal Pasha was a war veteran. Pilsudski was a war veteran. Horthy was a war veteran. Hitler was a war veteran. The same is true of the fascists. Leaders who never achieved power but came close to doing so: Colonel de la Rocque in France, Starhemberg in Austria, for example.

To accept Lindbergh's offer would be to grant this loyal friend of Hitler's a precious opportunity on a golden platter. It would, in my opinion, be a tragic disservice to American democracy to give one of its bitterest and most ruthless enemies a chance to gain a military record. I ardently hope that this convinced fascist will not be given the opportunity to wear the uniform of the United States.

He should be buried in merciful oblivion. Sincerely yours, Harold L. Ickes.

This was one of those times for Franklin D. Roosevelt to show his tremendous qualities as statesman and President and ignore the mean-minded memos of his acerbic Secretary of the Interior. It was true that there was a report in his office which purported to describe a "farewell" meeting of the America First Committee in New York, two weeks after the outbreak of war, at which Lindbergh had lashed out against the British as "the cause of all the trouble in the world today," and asserted that the United States and Germany should be fighting together against the "yellow hordes" of Japan and China, and the forces of communism.* It was also true that a number of congressmen and masses of ordinary citizens were bombarding the White House with letters urging the President to keep Lindbergh out of the Army.

But it was an opportunity for a President to demonstrate that there are times when great men are prepared to forgive and forget—and take risks—for the sake of the unity and common purpose of the nation. Only a politician could really have believed that Charles Lindbergh, once more flying in his country's Air Corps against its enemies, would be a danger to United States security.

It was as a politician that Franklin D. Roosevelt reacted. He penned a note in reply to the Ickes memorandum: "Dear Harold: What you say about Lindbergh and the potential danger of the man I agree with wholeheartedly. As ever, FDR."

On Monday, January 12, 1941, Charles Lindbergh took a cab to the Munitions Building in Washington and was shown into Secretary Stimson's office after a ten-minute wait. Stimson had already received a communication from President Roosevelt about his visitor. It consisted of a memorandum which the President had received some days before from Secretary of the Navy Knox, to which he had attached a comment. Knox's memorandum was as follows:

> January 1, 1942. Yesterday Steve Early at your request sent me a letter someone had written you concerning Lindberg's [sic] offer of his services to the Army. I read the thing over yesterday and again today, and I give you my sober reflection for what it may be worth. If I were in your place I would not become involved in discussion about Lindberg [sic] but would leave it to the Army to handle. If it were a Navy question and were put up to me, I would offer Lindberg [sic] an opportunity to enlist as an air cadet like anybody else would have to do. He has had no training as an officer and ought to earn his commission [!! The author's exclamation points]. Frank Knox.

To this the President had attached:

> January 12, 1942. Memorandum for the Secretary for War. I think Frank Knox is right. For the time being the matter can remain 'under consideration.' Please return for my files. FDR."

* Lindbergh certainly attended the meeting, but he denied making the statements—though they matched with those he had expressed in the past.

So Stimson was quite well aware of what was expected of him. He greeted Charles Lindbergh cordially and they talked for a few minutes about a favor the flier had once done the Secretary of War, at some inconvenience to himself. (It was Stimson who brought the matter up and showed that he was still grateful.) Then they passed on to more serious matters. Since his subsequent account of the conversation pretty well agrees with Lindbergh's diary entry, it will be used here as Stimson reported the following day to the President:

January 13, 1942. Dear Mr. President: As requested, I return to you herewith your memorandum in regard to Colonel [sic] Lindbergh, together with Knox's letter attached thereto. I am glad you have taken such an attitude towards this troublesome matter. I heartily agree with you.

Colonel Lindbergh having requested an interview with me, I saw him yesterday afternoon. I had previously inquired as to his past contacts with the War Department and found that several years ago, when we were extremely short of news as to the progress of aviation in Germany, he had rendered a really valuable service by placing at our disposal facts which he had acquired from his visit to Germany, and his examination of their airports and planes.

The Secretary went on:

When he came in yesterday, he told me that he was thinking of going into the business of airplane manufacture, but that he did not wish to do so until he had offered his Government to help it in the present emergency in any way that he could. I thanked him and told him of my own position on this matter, as announced the other day at my Press conference, namely that I would welcome any information or suggestions that might come to me from him or any other American which would help us in our work in the Department.

I told him that to that end I would arrange for his meeting with [General] Arnold and [Assistant Secretary] Lovett, to work out details with us. But I also told him that I would not be frank if I did not make it clear to him now that from my reading of his speeches, it was clear to me that he took a very different view of our friends and enemies in the present war from not only that of ourselves but from that of the great majority of our countrymen, and that he evidently lacked faith in the righteousness of our cause.

I told him that we were going to have a very difficult and hard war on our hands, and that I should be personally unwilling to place in command of our troops as a commissioned officer any man who had such a lack of faith in our cause, as he had shown in his speeches.

I then sent for Lovett and turned him over to Lovett to talk over his suggestions in detail. Though evidently rather set back by my frankness, he thanked me cordially for seeing him and for giving him this opportunity for even limited service. Faithfully yours, Henry L. Stimson, Secretary for War.

It says much for the basic humanity of Henry L. Stimson that he managed to make swallowable, if not palatable, the devastating humiliation of Charles Lindbergh's rejection. One can even detect a certain amount of sympathy for his visitor in his account of the session. But no matter how gentle the Secretary's manner, it came to the same thing: he had been turned down for service and found unfit to wear his country's uniform.

It was worse than that. Juan Trippe, of Pan American, told him he would be welcomed back into the company with open arms, to help with the wartime expansion which was inevitably coming. But a few days later he phoned to say "obstacles had been put in the way" and the offer was withdrawn. The same thing happened when he talked to United Aircraft and Curtiss-Wright. Each time it turned out that someone in the Administration, or Congress, or the Senate, showed hostility to the idea, and the directors backed down.

It was obvious that the Administration now had him where they wanted him, and were determined to keep him there. Unless he really groveled before Franklin Roosevelt, he decided, and did it in full public view, there would be no part in the war for him. And if groveling meant changing his opinions of the war and of the President, that he would not do, since, as he told Assistant Secretary Lovett, he thought the first was still wrong and the second still untrustworthy.

It must have been a bitter moment in his lifetime, but Anne was ill in bed and he did not wish to burden her with his troubles, and he was not the kind to bleed his heart into his diary. There is no mention in any of the entries made around this time of the pain he must have been feeling.

On the day he learned that Pan American had been pressured into turning him down, the only items in his diary concern extrapersonal events. He writes about going to see a film, about the death of a German general, about America's lack of enthusiasm for the war. And this choice paragraph:

> New York seems strange on a Sunday night now. Most of the show windows are dark, and only a few windows are lighted in the buildings. The streets remind me of London; much of the bustle is gone. As a matter of fact, I think I prefer New York this way. At last it has learned enough to go to bed at night, as a respectable city should.

There was one man in the United States, however, who could not be pressured. He loathed Roosevelt even more than Charles Lindbergh did. He also despised democracy, was anti-Semitic, and employed a ruthless thug to break the affiliations, the spirit, or the heads of those who got in his way. But not even the United States Government was strong enough to challenge him, or prevent him from saying or doing pretty well what he wished.

His name was Henry Ford. He had made his millions building cars for the people. Now he proposed to make even more millions building bombers for the war. And on Saturday, March 21, 1942, he sent a message to Charles Lindbergh and told him he wanted to see him.

Part
Six
The Mote and
the Beam

CHAPTER

TWENTY-FOUR

CIVILIAN AT

WAR

Charles Lindbergh and Henry Ford had known each other since 1927. They met when Lindbergh came to Detroit on the good-will tour which followed his transatlantic flight, and instantly found qualities to admire in each other. Ford's approval of the young flier was such that he agreed to take a flight with him, the first time he had ever been up in a plane. They quickly discovered in subsequent meetings that they had characteristics (and prejudices) in common: Both were lifelong teetotalers and nonsmokers, both believed in God and the puritan ethic, both admired the discipline and efficiency of the totalitarian regimes in Europe, both hated Roosevelt and his Administration for having got them into the wrong war on the wrong side, and both believed that sinister influences were at work in the nation to destroy the moral fiber of the people. Henry Ford came out loud with it and flatly blamed the Jews.

In addition to this, both of them were mechanical geniuses, sharing a great love for the internal-combustion engine. Over glasses of carrot juice (a beverage Ford had invented), they would talk for hours about the machine's infinite capacity for providing man with energy, saving his time, broadening the nature and length of his life, or, as in this case, winning his wars. Henry Ford was convinced that America should never have allowed herself to get involved in a war with Germany and Japan, but now that it had happened he was determined to provide America with more and better machines with which to bring it to a speedy conclusion.

Charles Lindbergh went to work for him as a technical consultant at the Willow Run bomber plant at Detroit on April 3, 1942, at a salary of $666 a month, and stayed with him until the fall of 1943. He worked with two of Ford's right-hand men, a pile-driving organizer named Harry Bennett, villain of some of the bloodiest antiunion battles in the history of American industry, and Charles Sorensen, a mass production expert who ate nuts and bolts, and inefficient workmen, for breakfast. They were loud, feisty types who were apt to settle an argument with a right cross to their opponent's nose, and Lindbergh was reminded of the lumberjacks he had known in his boyhood.

"Oh, we had some experiences in those days at Ford," he said later. "It was an extraordinary place to work. All kinds of things happening all the time. They even had fist fights among the staff. And Ford himself—a genius, a real genius, and an eccentric, those qualities seem to go together—was extraordinary. There never was a dull moment around him."

Between them, after some agonizing teething troubles, they got Willow Run's lines running with B-24 bombers in one of the most extraordinary mass production efforts of the war.

It was not his only effort to help fight the war. He moved out to the Mayo Clinic in Minnesota for a series of experiments in the clinic's pressure chambers, using his phenomenal lungpower and good blood pressure to test his capacity in altitude tests. He put the new P-47 Thunderbolt fighter through some grueling trials, and almost lost his life when his oxygen machine failed at 42,000 feet. Only his formidable physical fitness saved him.

It was a busy life and a productive one, but he found it zestless and lacking in a sense of achievement. The insults and rebuffs which he had had to suffer since the war had begun, and the deep wounds to his pride, could only be assuaged by something more uplifting than backroom conferences, clinical experiments, and flights (no matter how dangerous the altitude) over safe home territory. There was a war going on, but it was going on elsewhere. Men were once more flying out against the enemy and battling them in the skies. He wanted, needed, to be with them and fighting alongside them, just as he had longed to fly with "Tam o' the Scoots" over the western front in World War I.

He blamed Franklin D. Roosevelt for preventing him from doing so, and missed no opportunity of sniping at his speeches, his strategy, his conduct of the war. Everything that went wrong was the President's fault, the loss of Corregidor, the Japanese occupation of the Aleutians, rationing of gasoline, dimmed-out lights on automobiles, obstreperous workers, restive blacks, the general cheapening of life around him and what he called "moral decay."

He was surrounded by decay. Suddenly the brave old German shepherd, Thor, was beginning to fade away. He lay on the rug in the house they had rented in Detroit and made desperate attempts to move or bark when he thought that Anne or the children were in danger, but did not even succeed in rising to his feet. Charles Lindbergh went out, found a hillside near the house, and dug a grave.

"The ground was hard, and I did not finish until half-past ten at night," he wrote. He hated to dig the grave before the dog was dead, but who would do it if Thor died while he was away? The faithful shepherd, thoughtful to the last, made sure that his labors were not wasted, and died the following day. His mother was showing signs of old age, too, even if she was not yet moribund. They had not seen so much of each other since 1941, after Charles stepped up the vehemence of his antiwar campaign, possibly because Evangeline Lindbergh was a stanch pro-Ally and could not understand why her son preferred the Germans to the British. But now that hostilities had begun and America was fighting, and now that Charles was putting his back behind the war effort, all was forgiven. Only why didn't they let him go out there and really show them how to fight?

All Lindbergh's old affection and protectiveness welled up again when he saw how she had aged in the past two years (she was now in her middle sixties), and though she tried to conceal it, he did not fail to notice the terrible trembling of her hands. He began a campaign to persuade her to resign her job in school and take it easy, and meanwhile had her examined by a doctor. It was as he suspected, the first stage of Parkinson's disease, the creeping paralysis for which there was no cure.

He could comfort her with one thing, however. A new grandchild was on the way. Wars, holocausts, cosmic disasters, would never persuade Charles Lindbergh that this world was no place for children, and his ambition was still to have a quiverful. Anne had become pregnant again at the moment when bombs fell upon Pearl Harbor and her husband's political hopes and ambitions had crashed around his ears; he was in the worst moments of his humiliation when she told him what was to happen, and it was the only bright event in a gloomy prospect.

He had attended the birth of all of Anne's children, and at three o'clock in the morning of August 13, 1942, he rushed to the Henry Ford Hospital in Detroit, donned cap and gown and extra thick mask (he had a cold), and went into the operating room, where Anne was already in labor. She never took an anesthetic until the actual birth of the baby, preferring to concentrate her thoughts upon some symbol which she placed in front of her with which she could "share" and thus ameliorate her pain. Sometimes it was a sea shell or a feather. On this occasion it was a postcard photograph of a carved wooden deer with shells for eyes, made by Florida Indians long generations ago.

He had brought along her favorite madonna and an oval glass case which she considered a talisman, and this he slipped into her hand and felt her grip it hard. The child was born at 5:12 A.M. It was a boy, weighing seven and a half pounds, and later they named him Scott, after O. E. Scott, manager of Lambert Field, St. Louis, when Lindbergh had been an airmail pilot there.

He was forty years old, father of three sons and a daughter, and married to a woman he thought without equal in the world. But he would gladly have left them all to get in at the sharp end of the war. But thanks to Franklin D. Roosevelt, there was no hope of that.

News reached Ford officials in mid-September that the President would pay a secret visit to the Willow Run plant to see the famous bomber production line in operation. Everyone (friends and enemies) was there to greet him when he arrived on September 18, save Charles Lindbergh. He drove off into Bloomfield Hills and stayed there until the presidential party had been and gone.

It so happened that among those who were introduced to the President during his visit was a visiting British delegation of aircraft experts, headed by Miles (now Lord) Thomas. Thomas, an old World War I flier, barnstormer, and stuntman, was particularly anxious to meet Lindbergh, and asked Charlie Sorensen, who was conducting the presidential party over the plant, what had happened to him. Roosevelt overheard him and said, with a grin:

"He heard the devil was riding into town today, Miles, and took to the hills."

Thomas and his party were introduced to Lindbergh the following day. "Knowing what a keen air tactician and strategist he was," Thomas said, "I expected him to be full of questions about the Battle of Britain and the bombing of London. When all's said and done, we'd just come from the scene of the action, and I thought he would be burning with curiosity. But he was very formal and kept strictly to what was going on at Ford. When I told him that I was chiefly in America to buy tanks for the British Army, he seemed to lose all interest. He looked nervy to me, tired and distracted. I'd read all about that famous Lindbergh smile, and wondered where and when he'd buried it. In Washington, I expect, when America came into the war on our side."

In the next twelve months, Charles Lindbergh's status gradually changed. Though members of the Administration carefully avoided any contact with him, most of his old friends in the Armed Forces had begun to call him up and were willing to be seen lunching with him in Washington. There was a slight revulsion of feeling when a story appeared in the Minneapolis *State Journal* on October 12, 1943, which tried to tie him up with the fascist rump of the old America First Committee. This had been taken over by a way-out reactionary named the Reverend Gerald K. Smith, who garnered scare headlines by announcing that Charles Lindbergh would be the "spearhead" of America First's presidential drive for 1944. "Smith made it plain," the *Journal* announced, "that if the Republicans renominate Willkie or the Democrats renominate President Roosevelt, America First 'will jump into the field with its own candidates, Charles Lindbergh at the head.' "

Someone sent a copy of the story to the President, but even he did not appear to believe it. Lindbergh did not even bother to deny it. He had had a sickener of politics, and almost certainly would have rejected an offer even if it had come from respectable Republicans. It was so much nicer to be able to talk politics instead of being involved in them. He had even made his peace with his mother-in-law, and had begun staying with Anne and the family at Next Day Hill again. Aubrey and Constance Morgan and a colleague of Morgan's, John Wheeler-Bennett, were also there and they acted like family instead of polite strangers. (He did not tell them that he was thinking of secretly backing a history of the causes of the war, in which Britain's role would not exactly be favorably regarded, or perhaps the atmosphere might have curdled slightly.*)

It is true that not everyone had forgiven or forgotten. It was just about this time that George S. Kaufman and John P. Marquand were collaborating on the drama version of the latter's novel, *The Late George Apley*, for Broadway, and they had gathered together with their wives for a working weekend at the Kaufman home in Bucks County, Pennsylvania. The Marquands had both appeared on America First Committee lists, but the Kaufmans forgave them this "eccentricity," as they called it, even if they did not understand it. On the other hand, they felt quite differently about the Lindberghs, whose attacks on the Jews they could not excuse.

During the weekend Anne Lindbergh called Adelaide Marquand at the Kaufman home and left a message for her. Beatrice Kaufman was furious and tartly told Adelaide Marquand that if she wanted to call *that woman* back, she had better use someone else's phone. Adelaide Marquand angrily told her husband to take her away at once, and swept out. Beatrice Kaufman retired to her room in tears.

---

* The book, to be written by Harry Elmer Barnes, never came to anything.

Later John Marquand crept back to the house and joined his fellow collaborator. Writes Stephen Birmingham:

> There had been no discussion of the scene that had oc-
> curred, and quite obviously both men were somewhat embar-
> rassed by their respective wives' behavior, Kaufman for his
> wife's insulting a guest and John for Adelaide's poor taste in
> giving the Kaufmans' telephone number as the one where the
> Lindberghs could reach her. . . . The two stood in silence for
> a while, and finally Kaufman said, "John, why do you associ-
> ate with people like the Lindberghs?" Marquand thought for a
> moment and replied, "George, you've got to remember that
> all heroes are horses' asses."†

To judge by some of the correspondence which was still flowing into the White House about them, there were even stronger words for them. But in Service circles, word was spreading of the work he was doing ironing the kinks out of new planes, and his skill and understanding of the wartime pilot's job was building him both a reputation and good will. When he ventured to suggest at one Washington lunch table—at which Brigadier General Louis E. Wood of the Marines happened to be present—that someone with expert knowledge of the new Corsair ought to go out to the Pacific and see how it was behaving, Wood said:

"Why not you?"

"I'm not in the Service," said Lindbergh simply.

"What does that matter?" replied Wood. "Why can't you go as a ci-vilian?"

"The White House would never allow it," he said.

Wood: "Why does the White House have to know?"

On Monday April 2, 1944, he took a subway to the American Mu-seum and walked into the Hall of Ocean Life to look at the *Tingmas-sartoq*, the plane in which he and Anne had flown the polar route to Europe. Whenever he was sad, worried, downhearted, he would steal into the Smithsonian in Washington, and, hiding from the crowds behind the glass cases, gaze up at the *Spirit of St. Louis* hanging in mid-air. He used the *Spirit* to cheer him up and convince him that nothing was as desperate as it seemed. The *Tingmassartoq*, on the other hand, was his talisman when things were going well, and the prospects ahead were promising. Things looked promising now. There had been a kind of conspiracy in the Navy, and Admiral DeWitt C. Ramsey, assistant

---

† Stephen Birmingham, *The Late John Marquand* (Philadelphia: Lippincott, 1972).

chief of the Bureau of Aeronautics, had been brought in to provide a cover for Charles Lindbergh's new mission: to take a Corsair out to the combat areas of the South Pacific and demonstrate to pilots on active service how to get the best out of the machine in their fights with the Japanese.

He would go as a civilian technical assistant. The White House was not informed. Though he would be moving around under navy auspices, Secretary of the Navy Frank Knox was not told either.‡ So long as he could prevent a leak while he was still in the States, his mission would remain a secret—since there was a censorship on messages from the combat zones.

He went to Brooks Brothers to be fitted for a uniform; he would wear a navy officer's uniform without insignia. Then to the hospital for his inoculations.*

On April 24, 1944, he took off from North Island base, California, in a Douglas DC-3, spent ten days in Hawaii, and landed at Espíritu Santo, in the New Hebrides, on May 8. He carried an expanding canvas bag which contained his razor, soap, boot polish, chocolate bars, toothbrush, spare uniform and underwear, and one book, the New Testament ("the more I learn and the more I read, the less competition it has").

In Hawaii he had been greeted as a celebrity and had spent most of his time hobnobbing with admirals and generals, but here he was at the sharp end at last, and all the pilots cared about was not who he was but what he could do for them. As it turned out, he could do plenty.

Charles Lindbergh was four months in the South Pacific, and most of it was therapy to his soul. He was back in the world of flying and fliers, and it was just like old times—only better. There were not only planes to tinker with and planes to fly, but there was the terrain to explore as well. He fell in love with the tropical islands of the South Pacific at once, and became daily more beguiled by the beauty of the setting, the exotic nature of the flora, and the richness of the fauna around him. He went out on pigeon shoots with the pilots after operations, but found himself bird watching instead of using his gun; and he swam for hours around the coral reefs, savoring the shapes, maneuvers, and extraordinary numbers of multicolored fish.

On May 21 he was at Green Island, Guadalcanal, and that night in

‡ He died on April 28, 1944, and was replaced by James Vincent Forrestal.
* A tip-off from the hospital alerted the Associated Press that he had had a yellow fever shot, and they tried to contact him. He left word that he could not be reached.

the mess he told one of the flight commanders† that the best way for him to find out how the Corsairs were behaving in combat was to fly one in operations. He was invited to join the morning patrol over Japanese-held Rabaul the following day. He was waiting at the pilots' room after breakfast, and drew a .45 automatic, a leg knife, and parachute, life raft, and jungle-kit pack and joined the fliers for the briefing.

There were four Corsairs in his flight and he was assigned to fly wing on Major Alan J. Armstrong. They were to give cover for a raid on Japanese installations on Rabaul, and strafe targets on the way home if they met no opposition. This is what happened. The raid went through without any Japanese planes appearing, so the Corsairs turned back for Green Island and picked Japanese camps to rake with machine-gun fire en route. Lindbergh put a burst through a building, saw his tracers crash through the walls, and hoped only soldiers—and no women and children—were there. On another island he homed in on another building and came in at treetop level, only to see at the last second that he was aiming at a church. He swung clear just in time.

When he came back the commanding officer of the station was waiting, and he looked tense. He had been told Lindbergh would be flying over Green Island only, and learned only too late that he had flown on operations.

"You didn't fire your guns, did you?" he asked.

Lindbergh told him he had indeed fired them.

"But you should never have done that," the colonel said. "You're on civilian status. You have a right to observe combat, but not to fire guns. If you'd had to land, and the Japs caught you, you would have been shot."

Lindbergh crisply replied that from what he had heard, the Japs would shoot him anyway.

The other pilots had been listening. "Surely it's all right if he engages in target practice on the way back?"

The C.O. nodded. His tenseness had disappeared, and he had begun to relax. He shrugged his shoulders and smiled.

"Let's wait a few days and see if anyone kicks up a fuss," he said.

Two days later he was off on a patrol again. This time they arrived over New Ireland, where all natives as well as the occupying Japanese were regarded as unfriendly and legitimate targets. As Lindbergh's Corsair swept the beach, he saw a man coming out of the surf and, at one thousand yards, he knew he could not miss. He lined up his sight, calculating exactly where he would fire when the man began to run.

---

† Who, by a strange irony, had once been a member of the Illinois Chapter of the America First Committee.

Only he did not run. As Lindbergh's finger tensed on the trigger, he suddenly sensed that the man below him, though knowing what was coming, disdained to run. He walked up the beach with what seemed to be a sort of dignity—and he felt that formed a bond between them. "His life is worth more than the pressure of a trigger. I do not want to see him crumple on the beach." He eased his finger on the trigger and let the man live. And later he wrote:

"I shall never know who he was—Jap or native. But I realize that the life of this unknown stranger—probably an enemy—is worth a thousand times more to me than his death. I should never forgive myself if I had shot him—naked, courageous, defenseless, yet so unmistakably a man."

Word of his presence in the theater filtered down to General MacArthur's headquarters in Australia, and was confirmed when Lee van Atta, an INS war correspondent, told General George C. Kenney, who commanded MacArthur's air forces, that he had seen Lindbergh in Guadalcanal the day before.

"I was positive MacArthur's headquarters didn't have any official knowledge of it," Kenney said, "and I knew the old man tended to get suspicious of intruders. So I put out an order to have Lindbergh report to my office in Brisbane immediately. He arrived the next morning. I knew Slim from peacetime days, and I had the highest respect for his aviation know-how and his courage. But I also knew that he was a civilian, and that he had been flying combat with the army squadrons. That was not only illegal, and would get his head chopped off by the Japs if he was captured, but it was being done without MacArthur's permission—and that was worse. I asked him what the hell the Navy had been thinking of to allow him loose in our theater without asking first. It took about two minutes' conversation to confirm my suspicions he had no authorization to come into the theater, and that if I didn't fix up some orders to legalize his entry he could be in all kinds of trouble."

Kenney says that he took him in to see MacArthur, "who was the soul of cordiality," and after chatting awhile, asked if there was anything he could do for him.

"I butted in and said I had an important job for him to do," went on Kenney, "and it would keep him very busy for every minute he could spare. If anyone could fly a little monoplane from New York to Paris and have gas left over, he ought to be able to teach my P-38 pilots how to get more range out of their planes. . . . Lindbergh nodded with that kid grin of his that is one of his best assets. General MacArthur nodded his head and said: 'All right, Colonel, I'll just turn you over to General Kenney, but I warn you he's a slave driver.' I got him fixed up with pieces of paper, and then we talked about his job. He was quite enthusiastic."

Lindbergh's own version of this incident is different. It was General Richard K. Sutherland, MacArthur's chief of staff, who took him in to see his boss, and it was Lindbergh who suggested that he could train P-38 pilots in the combat theater to increase their range by at least one hundred miles. MacArthur said it would be a godsend if he could bring it off, and would be of tremendous importance to his campaign. Would he go back to New Guinea and start training the pilots right away?

"Nothing would please me more," Lindbergh said.

He took off from Brisbane in a borrowed fighter on July 14, 1944, and reported to Colonel Charles MacDonald's 475th Fighter Group in New Guinea three days later. Both MacArthur and Kenney had pleaded with him to preserve his "observer" status and not "get your head chopped off by the Japs" or "cause us any trouble at home," but had agreed that he could hardly tell combat pilots how to handle their planes if he kept out of combat himself.

On Friday, July 28, he was flying with MacDonald's wing when he found himself involved in a dogfight with Japanese fighters over Elpaputih Island. One of the Japanese planes suddenly swung round and came straight for him. They were one thousand feet apart and closing at five hundred miles an hour as Lindbergh (he was flying a P-38 Lightning) gave him a burst of cannon fire, and raked him with his machine gun. He saw the tracers slamming home as he pulled back on his controls. Simultaneously he realized that the Japanese had made the same maneuver and was zooming upward and still heading toward him. He banked and felt the jolt and heave of the slipstream as they missed each other by a few feet. When he looked around, he saw the enemy plane below him, wing over, out of control, plunging downward until it plunged into the sea in a fountain of spray.

He had shot down his first plane.

A few days later he came near to being shot down himself. Out over Babelthuap, a big Japanese base, MacDonald's wing ran into a force of Zeros. Lindbergh glanced in his mirror and saw a Zero diving on a comrade's Lightning and shouted the alarm over the intercom. The other plane banked away. Thwarted of its quarry by Lindbergh's signal, the Zero turned its attention to him. The Japanese plane was too high above him for Lindbergh to climb into him. He knew he didn't have the speed to run for it. He was too close to the ground to dive. All he could do was weave to prevent the Zero from getting in a deflection shot, and put his trust in his armor plating, and the possibility that one of the other members of the squadron would come to his rescue. He did not have much hope.

He crouched behind the armor plating in his cockpit and waited for the bullets to hit home. His thoughts were on Anne and the children, and he remembered later that his body was braced and tensed, that time seemed to stretch out to an eternity as he prepared for the sputtering of the engine, the fragments flying from his wing, the shattering of the glass on the instrument panel in front of him.

None of it happened. Colonel MacDonald had seen what had happened and forced off the Zero with a deflecting shot. Major Meryl M. Smith (to whose rescue Lindbergh had come a few days before) zoomed in on the enemy plane and gave him a second burst which started him smoking, but he succeeded in escaping into the shelter of a cloud. The wing formed up again and resumed their flight.

But next day news of the dogfight had spread through the American command and reached headquarters. Lindbergh had been told to keep out of trouble, and now here he was in the thick of it. It was bad enough to have him shooting down an enemy when he was only a civilian, but what if he had been shot down himself? What would they have said at home? What would the White House have said? He was recalled from the combat zone and told to report to General MacArthur at Brisbane.

Without exception, the men with whom he had flown in the past few months, Americans, New Zealanders, and Australians, were sorry to see him go. He had taken part in fifty combat missions and flown for 179 combat hours. Despite his age (and forty-two was old for a fighter pilot) he had proved that flying skill and instinct could more than make up for youthful reflexes. In battle, he had displayed courage and resource, and they were proud to have flown with him.

But he had also taught them a great deal about their own planes, and it would have a marked effect upon the course of the Pacific war. One afternoon during a patrol over Waigeo Island he had noticed his wingman circling, and when he asked what was the matter, the pilot replied that he was running short of gas and would not have enough to make base. Lindbergh asked how much he had in his tanks and was told 175 gallons.

"More than enough," said Lindbergh confidently, and instructed him to pull down his engine revs to 1,600, put his mixture control into "lean," and open his throttle wide enough to stay in loose formation with him. He then set course for Owi Island base at 185 mph with his wingman beside him. When they landed, the wingman had 70 gallons left, enough for another hour's flight at the speed they had been flying. But Lindbergh, who had started with the same load, had 260 gallons left. Like most of the combat pilots, the wingman was wasting gallons of fuel—and hours of flying—by pitching his engine revs too high and making his mixture too rich.

At the same time that he was taking part in operations, Lindbergh was running an intensive course in economic-flying instruction, and by the time he had finished he had altered the range of the P-38s in the Pacific. Hitherto fighter cover range had been limited to 570 miles. As he had predicted during his first meeting with MacArthur, he had changed that. The planes were now ranging over 700 and more miles—well beyond where the Japanese would expect to find them.

Back in Brisbane, he spent two hours talking to MacArthur on the evening of August 22, 1944. The first thing the general asked him was:

"How many Jap planes have you shot down?"

"One."

"Where was it?"

"Off the south coast of Ceram."

"Good, I'm glad you got one."

But he warned him to keep out of trouble in future. No more combat flying.

The conversation turned to politics, and MacArthur, who had just returned from Hawaii, told him of a session with Roosevelt.‡ The President was going forward for a fourth term, and his Republican opponent would be Thomas Dewey—"a nice little man," was the way Roosevelt described him—and indicated that he did not anticipate much trouble in defeating him. MacArthur said he was shocked at the President's frailty and hazarded the guess (which proved correct) that he would make no public appearance during the forthcoming campaign, in order to conceal how ill he was.

MacArthur made no mention of Lindbergh's personal position, though he must have known that two of his staff officers, at dinner the previous evening, had suggested that he take a commission as a colonel and come back as a member of MacArthur's staff. Lindbergh told them that there were "political complications" and that he would "hesitate to accept a commission under Roosevelt, even if I could obtain one."

He returned to the South Pacific a few days afterward, and arrrived back in the United States on September 16, 1944. When his train pulled in to the station in New York four days later, it was just like old times. Word had spread around that he had been in the Pacific, but no

‡ Who was on a visit to Pearl Harbor.

one in the United States knew quite what for. A horde of newspaper reporters was waiting for him.

"What can you say about your trip, Colonel Lindbergh?"

"I'd rather not say anything."

"But won't you tell us—?"

"I'm sorry, no, I have nothing to say."

The mission in the South Pacific may have made him feel like a different man, but in one thing he had not changed at all. All the old phobias about the press flooded back, and he had to stop himself from lashing out when a cameraman opened his car door to take a picture. He was furious. They had taken the edge off his homecoming.

"The average individual would be arrested in a few minutes," he declared, "if he created a fraction of the disturbance caused by pressmen."

CHAPTER

TWENTY-FIVE

RETURN TO

GERMANY

With the death of President Roosevelt in the last weeks of the war in Europe, it would be no exaggeration to say that Charles Lindbergh felt a load slip off his back. He was as unforgiving as his old adversary had been, and it was unlikely that there was much mourning in the Lindbergh household over the President's passing. For the world a great statesman and the architect of victory had disappeared from the scene, but that was not the way Lindbergh viewed the event. Rather did he feel that the American people were rid at last of the man who had tricked them into the war, and he himself of the mean-minded politician who had called him a Copperhead. If he had been a drinking man . . . but then, of course, he was not.

Early in the spring of 1945, United Aircraft, for whom he was working as an adviser, asked him if he would go to Europe to study German developments in aircraft and missiles, and he was attached to the U. S. Naval Technical Mission as a civilian consultant. He arrived in Paris on Sunday, May 13, just six days after the Germans had signed the official surrender terms with the Allies. It was six years and a week—and a whole war—since he had last been in the French capital, and as he wandered through the old familiar streets and stared at the people he was reminded of a great hospital, with all the inmates "recuperating from the illness of war."

Of three of the patients in whom he was interested, however, one had not survived, one had disappeared, and a third had departed. His old friend Dr. Alexis Carrel had died shortly after the liberation of Paris, some said of a broken heart after being accused of collaboration with the Germans. Lindbergh was bitter about the sad fate of his old scientific co-worker, and persuaded himself that it had been due more to his anti-Communist than to his pro-Nazi convictions. He remembered that Carrel had often declared that "if he had to choose between Fascism and Communism, he would take Fascism every time." Lindbergh appeared to believe that "leftist influence is now in control" in France, and Carrel had fallen a victim to their vengeance. In fact, General Charles de Gaulle was in full command of the situation in the country, and could hardly be called left-wing. But Lindbergh did not seem to be aware of this—or aware of De Gaulle either, for that matter.

His second old friend was the flier Michel Detroyat, but when he asked about him, the reply he got was:

"Oh, that is a very bad situation. He was supposed to be very friendly to the Germans."

When Lindberg angrily protested that Detroyat was a French patriot, his informants shrugged their shoulders.

"Of course," they said, "the Resistance can be wrong [in condemning him]. They have been wrong before."

His third friend was Madame Carrel, but she had sailed for the United States on the morning of his arrival, brokenhearted at her husband's shabby death, resolved never to live in France again.

He walked sadly through the neglected streets, gazing with a jaundiced eye at French and American planes performing aerobatics around the Eiffel Tower. Down below in the Place de la Concorde, French girls and Allied soldiers were dancing in the road to celebrate the great victory. He thought their gaiety was "forced" and he decided that "they were trying to get back to prewar times by going through the motions."

There was no elation in his heart, nor sense of victory. His spirits were low as he set out for Germany on May 17, 1945.

His mood got no lift from the sight of Munich, which Allied bombers had reduced to a heap of rubble, and he was intensely moved by the plight of the German people and soon angry at the way he considered they were being treated by the victorious Allies. He listened to stories of how the French had occupied Stuttgart and "indulged in loot, rape and murder," and was surprised and impressed by the fact that the passers-by in the Munich streets looked at Allied troops without hatred in their eyes. He was soon indignant at stories that "to destroy and loot is considered entirely proper" as far as GIs were concerned, though he took comfort from the fact that they looted "on a more civilized basis" than the Russians and the French; and he was very angry when he saw a German officer salute an American officer, "who sauntered by, obviously taking no notice whatever."

One of his first trips after arriving in Munich was to visit the Bavarian Motor Works with Commander Henry A. Seiller, USN, who wanted samples of BMW's jet-engine work to take back with him to Naval Technical Mission headquarters in Paris. They were putting pieces on one side and ticketing others when a British RAF officer, Lieutenant George Lea, came over and asked where they were taking them.

"The naval type said he was flying back to Paris with them that night," Lea said later, "and I said I couldn't allow that. I had strict orders to see that all engine parts taken out of the factory were sent directly to the Allied pool in England. There was this other type with the commander, a tall fellow in a sort of uniform with no tabs, and he suddenly said: 'Why England? Why should they go to England?' I said that was where they were being assembled, so that all the Allies could see and study them. The commander seemed to hesitate when I said that, but it was the other fellow who seemed to have the authority. He waved an arm to a Yank lorry that was standing by, and when it drew up he said: 'Load 'em up, sailor.' There wasn't very much I could do. I stood there looking at them as they piled the parts into the lorry. The naval type had the decency to appear a bit sheepish, but the other fellow carried on as if I wasn't there. When they took off, the naval type waved at me, but the other one just stared at me—or through me, really. After they'd gone, one of the Yanks said: 'Do you know who that guy was? That was Lindy himself—Charles Lindbergh!' Another of them said: 'He didn't seem to think much of you, did he, lootenant?' I said: 'Maybe it was my uniform he didn't like.' "

One of the main tasks Lindbergh had been charged with by United Aircraft was to find out as much as possible about German progress in jet engine development, and he was told that the best place to get the data was former German Air Headquarters at Zell am See, over the border in Austria. The following day he was joined by Colonel George Gifford of the U. S. Marines, who spoke fluent German and would act as his conducting officer on the trip. Gifford told him that there were two places around Munich that every GI and every visitor was anxious to see, one being the infamous concentration camp of Dachau, a matter of a few miles away, and the other Berchtesgaden, where Hitler had his Eagle's Nest, further down the road toward Austria. Lindbergh told him he preferred to miss Dachau, but would certainly like to visit Berchtesgaden. They made a detour and rode up the mountainside to Hitler's eyrie, where Lindbergh found himself drawn to the same spot by the picture window (its glass shattered, its surroundings wrecked by bombs) where Hitler was wont to contemplate the petty world below him. Gifford stood back while his companion gazed out across the valleys and the mountains, until, after a few moments, he turned and walked away without a word. It was almost as if, Gifford sensed, he had for a moment been in Hitler's skin, looking through that window and, as Lindbergh said later, "realizing the collapse of his dreams, still struggling against overwhelming odds."

This was the period, just after the end of hostilities, when fraternization with the defeated Germans was supposed to be forbidden, as was giving them food or gifts. Lindbergh told Gifford that he was impressed with the great dignity, the absence of hostility and resentment, and the "simple sadness" with which the Germans accepted this prohibition. Once, passing a group of defeated soldiers plodding homeward, he deliberately dropped a packet of his issue cigarettes in a spot where they would be sure to see it and pick it up.

He was soon outraged at the way in which American troops were eating high off the hog in the sight of hungry Germans, particularly hungry children. He felt ashamed of his people (and of himself, no doubt) as he ate with the GIs and felt the eyes of hungry children on them. "What right have we to stuff ourselves . . . what right have we to damn the Nazis and the Japs while we carry on with such callousness and hatred in our hearts?"

In fact, as most of those who were in Germany at the time will remember, not many German children hanging around American camps went hungry for long (or around British, French, or Russian camps, for that matter). In the author's experience, nonfraternization laws were broken from the start, and the troops billeted in German homes soon started sharing their rations with the people around them, and not always (as Lindbergh seemed to imagine) in order to "buy" the favors of a fräulein. After the first frenzies of anger were over (following the discovery of what the Germans had been doing to the inmates of the concentration camps), humanity kept breaking into the most formal relationships between victor and defeated. Among ordinary troops, the Germans were just people like themselves.

Charles Lindbergh was unfortunate in that he did not seem to see examples of this, and concluded that callousness toward the defeated enemy was the rule rather than the exception. He appeared surprised when he met an American officer who hated the behavior of some of his comrades, and honestly seemed to think that he was an exception. "He feels much as I do about our treatment of the people in Germany —disgusted with it," he wrote.

He could summon up no such feelings of sympathy toward the Russians, who, after all, had suffered in the war even worse than the Germans, and his subsequent conducting officers (Lieutenant E. H. Uellendahl and Lieutenant John B. Robinson) got the impression that he was icily antipathetic to all of them. At one moment during the trip he was asked to give a lift to a Russian officer who had strayed from his unit, and he decided at once that he didn't like the look of him. He was so convinced that he was "capable of anything" that he kept his right hand on his gun under his coat, ready to use it if the Russian tried anything. Yet even he, after a time, saw the ludicrousness of the situation, especially when the Russian fell asleep. He had his right hand on his gun, ready to shoot him, and his left hand on his shoulder strap, to keep him from falling out of the jeep and getting killed. "A truly Russian situation."

He was annoyed with the Russians. They were after German technicians and aeronautical information, just as the Americans and British were,* and German scientists, aware of the competition for their services, were expertly playing the one against the others. Official after official to whom Lindbergh talked took care to stress to him that the Russians were in the market, too—but that they, of course, preferred to deal with the Americans. One of them (Adolf Bäumker, former head of the German Aviation Experimental Institute) encapsulated their sales talk when he said to Lindbergh:

"Russian propaganda is very clever. Their radio is going all day long. They tell how establishments in their area are being opened up again. They say how well German scientists and workers are being treated—so much coffee, so much tea, so much food. For me, I wish to work with the Americans."

He decided that a quick trip back to Paris was necessary to emphasize the inroads the Russians were making, and asking that measures be devised (better treatment, opportunities in the United States) to combat it.

Back in Germany, he spent a night in Nuremberg and was shattered by the devastation he saw all around him. He felt surrounded by death. "Only in the sky is there hope," he told himself; "only in that which man has never touched and which God forbid he ever will."

He went on from there to see the famous stadium outside Nuremberg where Hitler and the Nazis had held their annual Party Day, and he climbed onto the dais from which Adolf Hitler used to speak. The conditions in the interior of the stadium shocked him, for released foreign prisoners of the Nazis (displaced persons, as they were called) had been camping out here, and the place was littered and filthy. To his

---

* "The British seem to be everywhere when there is any scientific or industrial information to be obtained," he complained.

nostrils it smelled like a box in which mice have raised their young, only worse.

This mousy smell seemed to assail him frequently from now on, whenever he came in the vicinity of "displaced persons." There were hordes of them wandering around Germany now: released prisoners, French, Belgian, Dutch slave labor, Russians, Poles, Slavs, gypsies, a few surviving Jews. As soon as they got near them, Lindbergh found, he noticed "that mousery smell," as he called it. He looked at one packed column of DPs from a distance, "an endless mass of humanity" who "I feel sure smell the same." They were in sharp contrast to the Germans, whom he found always clean and tidy, and he was moved when one German woman, to whom he gave a cake of soap, "cried a little."

It was with these impressions crowding his mind that he came (by accident) upon the only concentration camp he saw in Germany (or "ex-prison camp" as he called it). With Lieutenant Uellendahl and a GI, Sergeant Walker, they were on a visit to an underground aircraft factory tunneled into the Harz Mountains near Nordhausen. Lindbergh felt that it was no part of his mission to see the horrors which the Nazis had wrought upon lesser races who had come under their control, and he had sedulously avoided all of them. A few days earlier he had caught Sergeant Walker showing "some snapshots he had taken at one of the German prison camps" of a pit full of dead and starving bodies to a German air expert they were questioning. Walker had explained that the German "still thought the [Nazi] government was all right. I told him he'd better stop thinking so, or he might find himself behind bars." It was obvious that Lindbergh did not approve of such methods of chastening the Germans he was interviewing, and considered Nazi horrors had nothing to do either with himself or with the German officials with whom he was making contact.

Now suddenly, like it or not, he was confronted by an actual extermination center, and there was no way of avoiding it. The only way into the underground factory lay through Camp Dora, where worn-out "slave" labor was sent to the gas ovens after being worked to a standstill in the airless cavern beyond. The barracks where the SS had once held sway were now packed with displaced persons, and he sniffed the air and encountered that "smell of mousery" as they approached. He observed that the DPs had dirty clothing, but decided from the look of their bodies and faces that "they were not too badly fed."

Beyond lay Camp Dora. According to the records, 25,000 workers in the factory had been dispatched in the camp's incinerators. A young boy, so emaciated that he looked like an old man, showed them through the room where the cremating furnaces had operated, the steel stretchers for holding the bodies still sticking out of the open doors. He pointed to a shape lying on the straw on the floor. It looked exactly like him, a skeleton with skin on it, only this one was dead. The living one was a Pole, seventeen years old, a survivor of the camp after three and a half years. He did not explain how he had escaped when 25,000 others had died.

"It was terrible, three years of it," the young Pole said. He pointed to the emaciated body on the floor. "He was my friend, and he is *fat!*"

Lindbergh took out his diary that night and began to write in a somber mood. Ever since arriving in Germany, he had been obsessed with the way in which the defeated Germans were being humiliated by their conquerors, and he had spent an inordinate time listening to stories of Allied excesses against the Germans—Senegalese raping every female in Stuttgart between six and sixty, Red Army men on the rampage in Silesia. Now he was confronted by the organized bestiality of Nazism, and he was appalled by it. "Here was a place where men and life and death had reached the lowest form of degradation," he wrote, and asked how could anything faintly justify the setting up and operation of such a place.

But even with the dreadful and sordid reality of Camp Dora before his eyes, he was not yet prepared to swallow along with the stench and horror the real significance of it. He wrote in his diary that as he came to describe the human debris littered around the gas furnaces, dumped like ashes into a pit at home, "a strange sort of disturbance" entered his mind. He was suddenly taken back to the South Pacific. While he had flown with the U. S. Air Forces there he had listened to tales told him of GIs shooting Japanese soldiers who had tried to surrender to them, of Japanese troops killed in battle whose bodies had simply been dumped and left to rot, of troops starved into surrender and then shot, of soldiers who kept Japanese skulls for souvenirs and looted bodies for their gold teeth.

As he looked around the sickening carnage of Camp Dora, he was reminded of all this and he compared one with the other. It did not seem to matter to him that Camp Dora was part of a methodical, carefully orchestrated policy of planned murder on government order, whereas the others were isolated examples of individual human savagery committed in the heat of battle.

"Where had I felt like that before?" he wrote. "The South Pacific? Yes; those rotting Japanese bodies in the Biak caves; the load of garbage dumped on dead soldiers in a bomb crater; the green skulls set up to decorate ready rooms and tents. It seemed impossible that men— civilized men—could degenerate to such a level. Yet they had. Here at

Camp Dora in Germany; there in the coral caves of Biak. But there it was we Americans who had done such things, we who claimed to stand for something different. We, who claimed that the German was defiling humanity in his treatment of the Jew, were doing the same thing in our treatment of the Jap."

This quotation from *The Wartime Diaries of Charles A. Lindbergh* his literary executors have allowed me to use. But the passionate declaration which follows immediately upon it cannot be quoted here, because consent to reproduce it has been refused.

One wonders why, because no matter how one judges its wisdom, it does set forth Lindbergh's attitude toward war, and the evils it produces in men, with eloquent sincerity. In this passage of his diary, he insists that not only the Germans and Japanese were guilty of atrocities, but so were his fellow Americans—even if they had been "too civilized" and "too clever" to do it as crudely as the enemy. But we had "defiled ourselves" and had indulged in acts as barbaric as the enemy, and it was not just the enemy, but men of all nations "to whom this war has brought shame and degradation."†

The passage is a moving one, and so far as its sentiments about the brutishness and wickedness of war are concerned, all men of good will will approve it. But it was surely disingenuous of Lindbergh to equate the organized, state-controlled, mass killings of the Nazi concentration camps with the spontaneous brutality of the battlefield.

But Lindbergh wanted to make the point that all of it was due to the war: this tragic, terrible, unnecessary war which would never have taken place if he had had his way.

He flew back to the United States toward the end of June 1945, carrying with him long reports on German aviation and rocket developments, plus a list of names of German scientists and aeronauts whose immediate shipment to the United States he strongly recommended—before the Russians got them first.

He had hoped to stop over in England on the way home to talk to General Adolf Galland and other German jet-fighter pilots still under detention there, and Admiral Alan G. Kirk, head of U. S. Naval Forces in Europe, sent a request to the British through Admiral Harold R. Stark in London. The British authorities politely indicated that "for the time being" his presence in Britain would not exactly be welcome.

It is an indication of the naïve attitude he still took toward the war that he could not understand why the British felt that way about him.

† For the full text of this passage, the reader's attention is drawn to *The Wartime Diaries of Charles A. Lindbergh* (New York: Harcourt Brace Jovanovich, 1974), pp. 997–98.

Part Seven

Out of the Ashes

CHAPTER

TWENTY-SIX

A CHANGED

MAN?

The war was over, but for Charles Lindbergh and the America Firsters in many ways it was not. General Robert E. Wood, the former chairman, was all right. He simply went back to being chairman of the board of Sears, Roebuck. But the politicians in the movement suffered. The leading isolationists in Senate and Congress (Bennett Champ Clark of Missouri, Gerald P. Nye of North Dakota, Burton K. Wheeler of Montana, Henrik Shipstead of Minnesota, and Hamilton Fish of New York) were all defeated in elections just before or after the end of the war. Apologists for the movement have since claimed that these were acts of vengeance on the part of the interventionists, who poured in money to get them beaten, but that is to misread the feelings of the American voters. In any case, it was much simpler than that. The isolationists had backed the wrong horse, and when you do that, you lose.

Charles Lindbergh was not interested in political office, and all that happened to him was that the newspapers began to give him the silent treatment and ignored him—which, considering his passion for privacy, could hardly be considered a reprisal. His trouble was that he still burned with the conviction that he had been right, and longed for some sort of public vindication. He sublimated his feelings in the beginning by pleading for better treatment of the Germans, and condemning the trials at Nuremberg of the Nazi war criminals. If we were really a "Christian America," he insisted, such things would not be happening; and his repeated use of the phrase "Christian America" cannot have brought much comfort to non-Christian citizens who read his speeches.

But then a chain of circumstances persuaded him to change tactics and cut down his insistent harping on Germany's woes, which most people thought the Germans had brought upon themselves, anyway.

The Lindberghs had now bought themselves a house on the seashore at Scott's Cove, Darien, Connecticut, and he divided his time between there and an office in Washington, with travel to New Mexico and Minnesota in between. Anne Lindbergh had given birth to her sixth (and fifth living) child in the fall of 1945, a daughter they named Reeve, and though Charles Lindbergh still didn't think there were nearly enough of them, he was delighted with his family and eager to spend as much time as possible with them. They kept aloof from their neighbors, but a lot of old America Firsters came to see them, including the J. P. Marquands and, best of all, their old friends Kay and Truman Smith, who had taken a house farther up the Connecticut coast. Marquand had read some of the rough draft of the book which Lindbergh had been writing and rewriting over the years (later to be published under the title of *The Spirit of St. Louis*) and he kept urging his friend to get it finished. He was on the board of the Book-of-the-Month Club, he pointed out, and if the quality of the whole book turned out to be as high as the extracts he had read, he would recommend it to the committee.*

Truman Smith, on the other hand, wanted him to press on with another book project on which he was working. This was a collection of essays he was assembling on a variety of topics, such as his nearly fatal experiment with high-flying, when his oxygen apparatus failed, his narrow escape from being shot down by a Japanese fighter in the South Pacific, and his return to Germany in 1945. What interested Truman Smith most was the main essay in the book, on the Cold War, in which Lindbergh would make it clear that everyone had misunderstood the nature of his stand in the years before World War II. It was never that he had approved of the Nazis, but simply that he had believed that they were a bulwark against the forces of Bolshevism. Why had not his advice been taken, and the German and Russian armies allowed to turn upon each other and destroy each other? Wouldn't it have been better for the world?

As Smith pointed out on Lindbergh's behalf, most of the prophecies he had made in 1939–41 were now beginning to come true. The British Empire was in process of disintegration, as he had predicted. Half of Europe had come under the rigid, totalitarian control of Soviet Communism, and the rest of the Continent stayed free only because American troops remained in Europe to protect them. Meanwhile, in Asia, the Red hordes of China were sweeping their enemies into the sea.

Why, then, should he not now be recognized as the prophet who had

---

* It subsequently became a main choice of the club.

been maligned unjustly, and vilified only because he had insisted upon telling his fellow countrymen the truth? Truman Smith was a diabetic and believed that he had not long to live,† and he was anxious to see his friend (and himself) rehabilitated before he died.

In 1948 Charles Lindbergh published a book which gave a clear indication of the line he would be taking in future. It was called *Of Flight and Life*, and its main political essay strongly made the point that, despite World War II, alien hordes were still knocking at Western civilization's gate, just as they had been doing in 1939, only this time there was no longer a powerful German Army to hold them at bay. America was in greater danger than ever before, and only her trust in God and her strong right arm was going to see her through. Lindbergh pointed out that Russia was arming fast, that distances were shortening, and that two great powers have never lived within reach of each other without eventual war.

He was anxious for the future because "their spies and agitators are active in our country." There were chasms between the two powers so far as attitudes toward religion and human rights were concerned, and they could never be bridged. He pointed out that the right to live in freedom, to worship, and to speak were the qualities America held dearest, and these were the very qualities the Soviet Union denied "even to a greater extent than they were denied in Nazi Germany."

It was the language of those who would soon be known as Cold War warriors, but he had something for the racial supremacist, too, for he went on to state that America's greatness depended upon the quality rather than the equality of its people. "For Americans the doctrine of universal equality," he stated flatly, "is a doctrine of death." Why? Because if Americans accepted equality, he maintained, it would mean throwing open American borders to unrestricted immigration—though he did not explain why this followed—and this would mean the end of civilization as Americans knew it. They would be in competition with intruders with lower standards, who had different ideas—in short, they would be accepting a sort of world government in which they would have no means of law enforcement and would be bound by a foreign code of law.

The dire consequences of this seemed something of an anticlimax, the way he put it.

"It is unlikely," he wrote, "that a world government in which Asia cast one billion votes would maintain taxes, regulations, and freedom of action which would permit our American standards to go on."

† He is still alive in 1975.

But the greatest threat to America in 1948, as Lindbergh saw it, was the infiltration of "alien blood."

In a passage which must have been intended for the eyes of white readers only, he pointed out that Western civilization represented a balance achieved by "our forebears" through thousands of years of struggle. Americans, he said, were the offspring of marriages influenced by the culture of Greece, guided by the sermons of Christ, and fertilized by the blood of martyrs. They had been instructed by Western knowledge and protected by Western arms, *and if only one of those elements were changed, the nation would become a different people in mind, body, and spirit.* In the blood, bones, and brains of Americans ("our very tissues") were qualities which scores of generations and millions of lives had evolved, and they had grown up in a culture which had taken centuries to create. The only way to survive, Lindbergh declared, was to keep this balance. "To progress, we must improve it."

In some ways, *Of Flight and Life* was a moving as well as a revelatory book. It gave the first hint that his mind was turning away from science, that he feared that technologically the world was developing too fast, and there was a plea in several passages for a return to a simpler, less complicated life. But there were many readers who found disquieting passages, for they were those of a WASP philosopher with sometimes disturbing undertones of redneck.

But despite his concern over the galloping pace of technological development, nothing had impressed him more during his postwar visit to Germany than the enormous strides made there during the war by German scientists. Upon his return he collaborated on a report prepared by the Naval Technical Mission, and came pretty close in it to saying that if it had not been for blunders in the Nazi High Command, the enemy might well have won. The report stated, "Given a few more precious months, they could materially have changed the course of the war." The report went on:

> At the conclusion of the war, their technology was putting into action a formidable group of super-weapons. Among them were jet-propelled airplanes more than 100 mph faster than our best fighters, their remarkable V1 and V2 rockets, and similarly revolutionary weapons were being prepared for a much more effective use than terrorizing civilians. While we had been speculating about experimenting with supersonic speeds and probing within the realm of trans-sonic flight, the Germans for more than five years had been doing serious re-

search with supersonic wind tunnels. . . . In these wind tunnels were developed complete airplane designs, models and flight data at a speed of more than twice the speed of sound. These tunnels produced the V2. . . . There were detailed plans, calculations and launching platforms designed to put rocket projectiles into New York City. . . . The magnitude of this work was such as to provide the rapid expansion and development of 200 different designs and studies of guided missiles. One of the best developed at war's end was a ground-to-air rocket projected by a ground director into the air, and there an infrared homing device picked up the heat of the engine and directed it into the rear of its target. It was claimed that 74 four-engined bombers had been brought down with 75 of these guided missiles."‡

The report recommended that the United States devote itself as soon as possible to a program of organized research, with the aid of the best brains available in the nation. Not long afterward, Lindbergh was having dinner in Washington with General Carl Spaatz, then Chief of USAAF, and William Benton, president of the Encyclopaedia Britannica Company and an old friend from America First days. Spaatz mentioned that he had read the report, and that he wanted Lindbergh's services to co-ordinate research and help in other programs for the improvement of the American defensive system. Benton asked whether this meant Lindbergh would be given back his commission in the Army, with suitable promotion. Spaatz looked uncomfortable and said that it was beyond his powers to make any such promise, but that if Lindbergh wished he would forward a recommendation to the White House. Lindbergh shook his head emphatically. These were the days of the Truman Administration, and he did not expect to receive any gestures of reconciliation from that quarter.

Over Benton's protests, he said he would be willing to help the Armed Forces in any way he could, and felt he could be useful especially in the field of rocketry and space research. Spaatz said he would arrange for him to be made a civilian adviser at once, on a nominal salary of one dollar a year, and find him an office in Washington together with a plane for getting him around the country. Lindbergh asked only one thing in return. Spaatz, slightly apprehensive, asked what it was.

"Justice for Bob Goddard," Lindbergh said.

It was thanks to Dr. Robert H. Goddard that Charles Lindbergh

‡ U. S. Naval Technical Mission. A9-16 (3) (50/N) 1117 Tech. Rep. 373. Air Superiority. Summing Up German Technical Skills.

knew as much as he did about rockets. Goddard was an American rocket pioneer who had fired a liquid-powered missile one hundred feet into the air in a pasture in Auburn, Massachusetts, as early as 1929. Lindbergh, who was interested in rocketry as long ago as that, had him checked out by physicists at the Massachusetts Institute of Technology and later visited him at Clark University, where he was a professor. He learned that Goddard had been a believer in rockets since 1916 and was convinced they had a future as air carriers, weapons, and space probers, and at the end of an eight-hour talk he had convinced Lindbergh likewise.

The German Government was at this time (1929) conducting its own rocket experiments, and this was pointed out to the U. S. Defense Department, whose disinterest was profound. From lack of money, it looked as if Goddard would have to abandon his experiments. But then Charles Lindbergh persuaded his friend Harry Guggenheim that here was a promising project for one of his foundations to sponsor, and in the next nine years the Florence Guggenheim Foundation gave Goddard $140,000 to carry on his experiments, and enabled him to move his testing grounds to Roswell, New Mexico.

His work there still failed to stir the U. S. Armed Forces, but, on the other hand, excited great interest in Germany, where his patents for liquid-fuel rocketry were quietly annexed by scientists working at the proving grounds at Peenemünde and Rügen Island, in the Baltic. As Dr. Wernher von Braun, who built Nazi Germany's V2s and America's first space missiles, later said: "Goddard's experiments in liquid fuel saved us years of work, and enabled us to perfect the V2 years before it would otherwise have been possible."

The U. S. Government never did get around to using Goddard's talent and discoveries until well into World War II, and by that time he was a sick man. He died in 1945, largely unknown and unrecognized by his countrymen.

Now Charles Lindbergh made it clear that in exchange for his own help in bringing the United States up to date in rocketry, he expected to see some sort of recognition of his friend's pioneer labors, as well as financial recompense to the Guggenheim Foundation for its backing. He pointed out to General Spaatz that the Army was now simply proposing to steal Nazi Germany's missile systems, and should be reminded that they included many vital features of Goddard's work. While giving them expert advice, he would at the same time like to see them accept that the basic principles were of American origin and couldn't just be taken over as expropriated "enemy" inventions.

Spaatz promised to alert the right departments.*

Word of Lindbergh's activities on Goddard's behalf not unnaturally reached the ear of Harry Guggenheim, and, perhaps as Lindbergh had intended, the philanthropist contacted his erstwhile friend to express his thanks on behalf of the foundation. A reunion was arranged and their estrangement ended. On April 21, 1948, they stood on the same platform at a ceremony at the American Museum of Natural History to honor the memory of Robert H. Goddard. Relations between the two men would never be quite so warm as they had been before America First, but at least they were fraternizing again.

In the next few years, Charles Lindbergh was a kind of roving trouble shooter for the U. S. Air Force, as well as an adviser on rocketry and space matters. At the beginning of 1949 he was back in Germany again as a special adviser to U. S. Air Forces in Europe. The Soviet Government had clamped a ring around Berlin with the intention of starving this Western-controlled city into the Eastern bloc, and the Berlin Air Lift was organized to keep the city's inhabitants fed and warm (for it was midwinter and the weather was freezing). He was asked to give advice to Lieutenant General John K. Cannon and the tacticians at Air Lift Task Force Headquarters in Frankfurt about the most efficient way to run the operation, and how to keep it flying in the event that the Russians tried harassment either from the ground or in the air.

It was a mission after his own heart. Berlin was a Western outpost in Russian-controlled Eastern Europe, and a symbol of resistance to Bolshevik threats to the rest of the Continent. Correspondents remember that shortly after Lindbergh's arrival he gave a number of pep talks to American and British troops associated with the Air Lift and made it clear to them that in keeping West Berlin alive they were not just feeding Germans, but holding back the threatening tide of Communism. "If Berlin goes, it will be Western Germany's turn next, and after that France and Italy," he told one group in Hamburg.

He made at least a score of runs back and forth between Western Germany and Berlin across the East German Corridor, and on at least two other occasions rode herd on the transport shuttle in an American two-seater fighter (as a civilian, he could not take up the plane himself) at a moment when it was rumored that the Russians were planning buz-

* It was not, however, until August 4, 1960, that the U. S. Government decided to do justice to Goddard. He had already passed most of his patents over to the Florence Guggenheim Foundation, and after his death his widow ceded the remainder under an amicable arrangement. In 1960 the government announced that it would pay $1,000,000 in compensation to the foundation for infringement of Goddard's patents in their ballistic missile program.

zing and harrassing operations. He was disappointed when the Red fighters failed to show up.

There was only one incident to mar the exhilaration he felt during the Air Lift operation. That was when the city of Berlin decided to give a reception for a number of pilots and crews involved, at which the city mayor, Willy Brandt, acted as host. Lindbergh was invited along and it was proposed to present him to Mayor Brandt, as one of the brains behind the shuttle. When Brandt's advisers heard about it, they speedily made it clear that Lindbergh would shake the mayor's hand over their dead bodies. From their point of view, and that of the German public, Lindbergh was still the man who had admired the Nazis and taken a medal from Hermann Göring, and a picture of their Social-Democratic chief in friendly greeting with him would put lethal ammunition into the hands of Willy Brandt's critics both in Bonn and in Eastern Germany.

The mayor said he would be willing to see Lindbergh privately, but the invitation was never taken up, and the flier slipped away from the reception early.

Sometimes in this period of his life, Charles Lindbergh seemed like an actor in a small-town repertory theater who has to play most of the male parts in the script, one moment twirling his mustaches as the villain of the piece, a few minutes later reappearing as the blue-eyed hero.

To many people who met him in the first decade after the end of the war, he was the arch-apostle of anti-Bolshevism and white supremacy, and when the Cold War began in earnest he was right up there in the battle against the "spies and agitators active in our midst." Yet decency, compassion, concern for the quality of life—rather than the quality of the race—would keep breaking through. And, as time went on, it kept breaking through more often.

In 1949 he was presented with the Wright Brothers Memorial Trophy at the Washington Aero Club, Washington, D.C. The award was made for "significant public service of enduring evaluation to aviation and the United States," and he delivered in return one of the best speeches of his career. He took as his theme the way in which science was divorcing man from his old sense of independence and moral values, and he made a plea for a more equitable balance between the "hothouse" achievements of science and the "other qualities of life, qualities of body and spirit as well as those of the mind, qualities he cannot develop when he lets mechanics and luxury insulate him too greatly from the earth to which he was born. He must realize that even vision and judgment depend on the body as well as the mind."

It was a speech totally devoid of politics. Though it was an aviation occasion, Lindbergh did not once mention bombers or speak about the threat to "our country" from the forces of Communism. His remarks were restricted to a warning against allowing science to take over men and complicate their lives. In some ways, they were a precursor of what would be coming shortly, his crusade for ecological salvation.

The speech concluded with a short, emotional tribute to the Wright Brothers, and it sounded to those who heard it as if it genuinely came from the heart.

"In honoring the Wright Brothers," he said, "it is customary and proper to recognize their contribution to scientific progress. But I believe it is equally important to emphasize the qualities in their pioneering life and the character in man that such a life produced. The Wright Brothers balanced success with modesty, science with simplicity. At Kitty Hawk their intellects and senses worked in mutual support. They represented man in balance, and from that balance came wings to lift a world."

It was a balance he had not yet attained himself. But this was one of the occasions when it became manifest to everyone who heard him that he was trying.

In the early fifties, however, he was twirling his black mustaches again. This was the McCarthy period and while Lindbergh never voiced any overt approval of the egregious senator's inquisitorial methods, he remained complacent over the havoc he was wreaking in other people's lives. He could not raise much sympathy for people who hobnobbed with Communists. He was later to sum up his attitude at this time in a conversation with Wayne S. Cole:

> Lindbergh said he disliked both the "radical right" and "radical left." But he favored activity by the one to balance the other—provided neither got too strong. So far as Senator Joseph McCarthy was concerned, Lindbergh was "never impressed" by him. He did not like McCarthy's methods, but he did not think the Wisconsin Senator had enough ability to be a great danger.†

It was not exactly the reaction of a sensitive man to a shameful period in American history, but it is probably an honest summation of how he felt at the time. He was now fifty-two years of age, and giving

† Wayne S. Cole, *Charles A. Lindbergh and the Battle Against American Intervention* (New York: Harcourt Brace Jovanovich, 1974).

every sign of having become a stereotype middle-of-the-road Middle Western American, with a touch of what the British would have called blimpishness‡ about his reactions to people and events. Surprisingly enough, he had voted for Adlai Stevenson (a liberal Democrat) against Dwight D. Eisenhower (Republican) in the 1952 presidential elections. But that was probably a vote against Eisenhower (who would not see him when he went to Europe in 1945) rather than a vote for Stevenson, who seemed altogether too worldly, sophisticated, and urbane a character to have been Lindbergh's type.

He certainly voted for Eisenhower in 1956, but that was after the President had made up for his snub by summoning Lindbergh to Washington to tell him that he was—with his permission, of course—restoring his commission in the Armed Forces. On April 7, 1954, once more wearing his wings, he was sworn in as a brigadier general in the U. S. Air Force Reserve.

There was almost universal approval of the gesture, which was long overdue. But there was one commentary, in a letter to the New York *Times*, which was not inappropriate at a time when (thanks to McCarthy's smears) good men were being stripped of rank in government for past associations or aberrations:

> The President is to be congratulated on his nomination of Charles Lindbergh for promotion. It makes, however, a commentary on the inconsistency of public opinion that a Lindbergh can be forgiven his past associations and lack of judgment, while men with war records no less distinguished than Lindbergh's lost their jobs and are pilloried for having once attended a Communist meeting. David H. Rowan.

Anne Lindbergh was going through a crisis. She was a sensitive person and she had become rather more aware than her husband of the antagonisms and resentments which their joint stand against the war had engendered in those who had been their friends and admirers. She had made a trip to Europe for the *Saturday Evening Post* in 1947 and had been over several times since to see her sister and brother-in-law, Constance and Aubrey Morgan, in Wales and she had come back somewhat devastated by people's reactions. Even the Germans to whom she had talked had told her that her husband's attitude to the Nazis had been naïve and misguided, and her British friends had positively

‡ The word comes from a character in the cartoons of the late David Low, a die-hard reactionary ex-army type called Colonel Blimp.

snapped her head off for allowing her husband to be deceived so completely by the Nazis.

So far as she was concerned, enough was enough. She did not wish to hear about the war again, or about any war: World War II, the Korean War,* or the Cold War. She hated to think that anything she was now writing was being judged not on its intrinsic merit but because of her name and associations. She took it badly when a critic in *Saturday Review* attacked a volume of poems written by her which had just been published under the title of *The Unicorn and Other Poems.* The critic, John Ciardi, reviewed the volume in what *Time* magazine called "fifteen hundred sulphuric words," declaring that he had "nothing but contempt to offer" about her poems. "I must believe," Ciardi wrote, "that the art of poetry is more important than Mrs. Lindbergh or than you or me. I am compelled to believe that Mrs. Lindbergh has written an offensively bad book—inept, jingling, slovenly, illiterate even, and puffed up with a foolish afflatus, of a stereotype high seriousness, that species of aesthetic and human failure that would accept any shriek as a true high C."

He went on to pick out a stanza from the poems for a particularly mordant comment. The lines went: "Down at my feet / A weed has pressed / Its scarlet knife / Against my breast," and Ciardi described them as "the neatest trick of the literary season."

It was a cruel attack, and Anne Lindbergh not unnaturally suspected ulterior motives behind it, and refused to believe it when friends who knew the poet insisted that he was writing from the highest possible motives. (To have accepted that would, of course, have been even more hurtful.) She had once told Harold Nicolson at the beginning of her writing career that she was terribly afraid that "the papers will take it up as a Lindbergh stunt, and spoil it all for me," and now here it was again, though this time they were overreacting against her work where once they had tended to overpraise.

In fact, almost immediately after the criticism was published a flood of readers rushed to her defense, and Norman Cousins, editor of the *Saturday Review,* announced that Ciardi's attack had produced "the biggest storm of protest" in the history of the review. Most of the letters came from women. "How could any one individual be so cruel?" one of them cried. A man sent a telegram asking: "Why take a baseball bat to club a butterfly?" The Lindberghs, of course, made no reply. But Anne was hurt and miserable, and Charles angry, convinced that "they" were once more trying to get at him by hurting her.

* During which Lindbergh supported General MacArthur.

This was not really the case, as his own adventure into literature soon showed. Over the past twelve years, Charles Lindbergh had been working on a fragment of autobiography which would tell the full story of his transatlantic flight in 1927 and interweave into the narrative the story of his life to that date. He had written and rewritten it, polished and revised, in planes, trains, England, Germany, and the South Pacific jungles. Now he was satisfied with it at last. He called up his friend John P. Marquand and asked him to read it, and advise him on how to get it published. Marquand, who was a member of the editorial board of the Book-of-the-Month Club, found it an absorbing narrative (as did millions of other readers) and immediately recommended it to his colleagues at the BOMC, who promptly made it a main choice. He also introduced Lindbergh to his friend and agent, Carol Brandt.

"John brought him along one night in 1952 to the apartment at 1107 Fifth Avenue," said Mrs. Brandt. "It turned out that he didn't want an agent, but simply some tips about how to get the best market for the book. We sat before the fire and I gave him the best advice I could."

The advice was not only free but good. Shortly afterward it was announced that the *Saturday Evening Post* had paid $100,000 for the serial rights (a huge sum at that time). The book was published in 1953 under the title of *The Spirit of St. Louis* and became an immediate best seller. It deserved its enormous success. It was tightly written, had a driving narrative line, and made compulsive reading. No one was really surprised when it was shortly afterward announced that *The Spirit of St. Louis* had been bought for films for $1,000,000 and that James Stewart, one of the great stars of the day, would play the role of Charles Lindbergh.

From practically every point of view, the choice of Stewart was a shrewd one. He had been a passionate fan of Charles Lindbergh during his boyhood and later on shared most of his conservative opinions. They had dinner together and discussed the way to play the role but Stewart decided that "it was a little too late to ask for his autograph."

The film was to be directed by Billy Wilder and the script written by Leland Hayward, and Stewart suggested that it would help everybody if Lindbergh could meet them. He said he would get in touch next time he was in California.

"A few months later," Stewart said, "Lindbergh called from Pasadena, and agreed to come to Wilder's home, in Beverly Hills. Being Sunday, Leland Hayward's wife suggested that they stop by Lindbergh's Pasadena hotel and pick him up. But Hayward said: 'Oh no, he must have fifty cars and chauffeurs waiting to take him wherever he wants to go.' So everyone drove straight to Wilder's home. The time arranged for the meeting was 4 P.M. Lindbergh rang the bell at 4:03 P.M. He apologised profusely for being three minutes late. It turned out that he had come the twenty miles by streetcar and bus, and then walked to Wilder's house. He had calculated his arrival time to the minute, but those four blocks to the Wilder house from the bus stop were five times as long as the street map indicated, Lindbergh explained apologetically. Wilder said: 'But why didn't you tell me you had no car available?' He grinned and shrugged his shoulders. 'Oh,' he said, 'I like to ride on a bus.' "

It was typical of Lindbergh's loyalty to his old friends that he made one stipulation during the making of the film, and that was that his old barnstorming and parachutist comrade, Bud Gurney, should act as technical director. Through Gurney he kept a close control over the accuracy of the film.

"He only came on location once, though," Stewart said. "That was when we were making landing shots of Long Island with a plane that was the exact replica of the *Spirit of St. Louis*. He turned up unannounced one day and spent a long time discussing the performance of the substitute plane with the pilot, Stan Reaver. We were doing what was to be the final shot of the landing in Paris, and just before Reaver took off, Lindbergh said to him: 'Don't forget to slip in for a perfect three-point landing. Remember, I'm supposed to be flying that plane.' "

In the circumstances, it was ironic that the film turned out to be something of a box office flop. This, Stewart believes, was because Lindbergh was still a tarnished hero to many millions of middle-aged filmgoers, who resented his stand over the war, while to youngsters there was nothing particularly special about his transatlantic flight, in comparison with the feats of the air aces of World War II, then all the rage. The *New Yorker* summed it up in a cartoon showing a grownup and his small son emerging from a cinema showing *The Spirit of St. Louis*. The boy, looking bewildered, is asking his father: "If everyone thought what he did was so marvellous, how come he never got famous?"

In truth, the film came too soon. "It was a good film," said James Stewart recently, "and when the moment is right I think someone ought to revive it. I've always considered it one of the two best parts I've ever had in films, and I think I got right into Slim's character. I guess he thought so too. We became friends afterwards, and, of course, we used to meet a lot on air force occasions, both of us being in the Reserve. I think the failure of the film was a great disappointment to him—one more jolt he had to take on the chin from the great American public. Of course, he didn't help it any. He refused all requests for personal appearances and wouldn't talk to the press. A pity. He might just have turned the tide."

Almost at the same time that he came back into the Air Force, Charles Lindbergh was appointed to the board of the Air Force Scientific Advisory Board. It put an official stamp on work he had already been doing, but henceforward he spent an increasing amount of time at air force proving grounds in New Mexico and the Southwest, watching missile tests and sitting in on conferences on space projects. He got on well with Wernher von Braun, ex-Nazi rocket specialist, now in the United States to run the ballistic missile program, but he kept in closest contact with Adolf Bäumker, former chief of the Luftwaffe research and development program, afterward one of the most prized advisers in the United States defense project department. He had first met Bäumker in 1938 at the notorious American embassy dinner in Berlin, when Göring pinned a Nazi decoration on his lapel, and they had several conversations on the Luftwaffe building program. But at that time Bäumker had carefully avoided answering any questions about rockets.

They had met again in 1945, when Lindbergh went to Germany with the Naval Technical Mission, and Bäumker had demonstrated to the American's satisfaction that in spite of his high position (he had become head of the German Experimental Institute for Aviation), and his intimate association with Göring, Milch, and other party bigwigs, he had never been a Nazi. Bäumker had struck Lindbergh as being a very frightened man, bullied by Russian and American interrogating officers to spill his secrets, fearful of SS reprisals against him and his family. He gave him a can of fruit juice and two cigars, two packets of cigarettes to his wife, and a candy bar to his daughter (his ration for the week) and sent off Bäumker's name to headquarters in Paris as one of the experts worth shipping back to the United States.

Since that time, Bäumker and his chief aide, Dr. Helmuth Schelp, had turned over to the U. S. Government a complete history of rocket development in Germany.† When Lindbergh read it through, and realized how well developed in rocketry Germany had been even in 1938, he said to Bäumker:

"When I came to Germany, you promised to tell me everything. You didn't tell me half of it."

† There was a moment when Schelp hesitated to hand over his papers. His wife and child were being held by the Russians and he feared they would be used as hostages to persuade him to join the Red rocket program, in which many ex-Nazi scientists had already been enrolled. He was persuaded to opt for the Americans.

Bäumker laughed. "Did you really expect to get the truth out of us?" he asked.

"Yes," said Lindbergh, "I did."

One of Lindbergh's chief preoccupations after he joined the USAAF Scientific Advisory Board was manned space flight, and the problems the program was now facing in protecting and preparing aeronauts in the tests which were now being planned into space. Later on Michael Collins, Neil Armstrong, and Buzz Aldrin were all surprised when they talked to him and discovered how much he knew about space medicine.

"He talked to us about things like air stresses, acceleration tolerance, the so-called Oxygen Paradox as if the guy had spent hours in air pressure chambers himself," Armstrong said. "Turned out he had, too. He knew more about some of the problems than the doctors did."

It was a fact that Lindbergh was no stranger to the hazards and threats of survival in rarefied air. During World War II, following his rejection by Franklin D. Roosevelt, he had not only acted as a consultant for the Ford Motor Company's bomber program but also carried out a number of important experiments at the Aeromedical Unit at the Mayo Clinic in Rochester, Minnesota. He made several simulated parachute jumps from forty thousand feet in the laboratory pressure chamber, meticulously keeping note of nausea, anoxia,‡ and black-outs during "rapid descent."

In Germany with the Naval Technical Mission, he had compared notes on these experiments with members of the Luftwaffe's Medical Institute, but he missed the interviews the mission interrogators were at that time conducting with the institute's head, Dr. Hubertus Strughold. Reading through their reports, though, he noticed that Strughold, in 1942 a professor of air medicine at Heidelberg University, had been conducting almost exactly the same simulated parachute drops in Germany at almost exactly the same time as his own at the Mayo Clinic. He returned to America before he had time to talk to him.

Strughold was sent back to Heidelberg University after the war to write a study of German aviation medicine, but in 1947 he came to the United States to head a department of space medicine at the USAAF School of Aviation Medicine at Randolph Field, Texas, and Charles Lindbergh was one of those who recommended him for the job.

From that moment onward, Dr. Strughold was intimately involved with the care and cultivation of American astronauts, and most of them passed through his hands, especially after he moved to Brooks Air Force Base, San Antonio, Texas, at the end of 1958. He and Charles Lind-

‡ Loss of oxygen in the blood.

bergh often met and compared notes, and Lindbergh was one of those approached by investigators when Strughold made an application (which was granted) to become an American citizen in 1956. In 1959 allegations were made that Strughold had been involved in experiments on concentration camp prisoners at Dachau in 1942. This he strenuously denied, and during the private investigation which followed, Charles Lindbergh came to his defense. He pointed out that at the time Dr. Strughold was alleged to have been involved in a medical conference in Nuremberg (October 26 and 27, 1942), he was conducting experiments in simulated parachute drops at Heidelberg.

Lindbergh went on to point out that there was documentary evidence to show that Dr. Strughold's experimental method had always been to use volunteers for his tests, and these sometimes included himself. One member of his staff, Dr. Ulrich Henscke, when interrogated by the U. S. Naval Technical Mission, described experiments connected with acceleration limits of the human body. The tests were conducted on volunteers, among them six scientists from the German Air Force Medical Research Institute. One of these scientists was Dr. Strughold himself. U. S. Naval Technical Mission interrogation reports indicated, according to one report, that "in so far as could be determined, prisoners of war and displaced personnel were not used" in these experiments.

He went on to laud Dr. Strughold's work in the American space program.

"He was good and mad at the way they were trying to 'smear' the doctor," said a member of the department. " 'They're just trying to sabotage the program,' he said at one point. 'They'd do anything to prevent us from being first.' "

There was a danger during this period that Charles Lindbergh was solidifying into the archetypical, middle-aged, conservative American whose opinions on most questions of the day could have been fed into a computer and used for any situation that came up. He was more than half a century old, his hair gray, and his bald patch too big to be covered by the slick he combed over it. His face carried the worry lines of an active man of affairs who is anxious about the state of his business and the condition of his country.

Lindbergh had become a consultant again for Pan American Airways, and he spent much of his time traveling the company's routes around the world. These were not his only flying activities. He tested most of the Air Force's new jets. He rode on the B-52 bomber patrols over the Arctic to the edge of the Russian radar-scanning screens. He was also writing, mostly on aeronautical subjects at this time. So far as civil aviation was concerned, he was all for expansion: bigger planes (he was sitting in on construction plans for what became the Boeing 707), more routes, faster services. He was already planning for supersonic travel. With regard to the Air Force, he was the Pentagon's leading exponent of the need for more devastatingly destructive deterrents. Convinced that Communism was still the enemy, and that no rapprochement with Russia or China was possible, he campaigned for "a military position of such magnitude that if our enemies should strike us by surprise, annihilating hundreds of our bases, dozens of our cities, we can still exceed their power." America's only hope of survival, he asserted, lay in more and better armaments, rockets and planes.

"Our objective is the survival of Western civilization," he wrote, "and our policy must be dynamic. There is no longer such a thing as adequate defense. As long as a dangerous enemy exists, our security will lie in our indestructible power to destroy."*

It was his old contention brought up to date, that there was no defense against modern weaponry and that the only answer was to be more terrible than the enemy in attack. Other military strategists were quick to come forward to point out that he was almost certainly as wrong about this now as he had been in pre-World War II days. One of them was Major Alexander Peter Seversky, an old adversary, at that time a consultant with Republic Aircraft Corporation, and an adviser to the War Department. "Lindbergh's skill as an airman is as beyond question as his patriotism and his energy," Seversky wrote. "But aviation's skill, no matter how great, does not in itself guarantee a grasp of military facts."

Lindbergh, he pointed out, had been dangerously wrong on the basic concepts of national security at several critical junctures in America's recent history. He strongly attacked Lindbergh's contention that the most elaborate network of defense would not prevent a determined attack on the United States and that the hydrogen bomb and the supersonic missile had eliminated defensive security. Wrote Seversky:

> I am convinced that he is mistaken. Always, inevitably, the threat produces an adequate answer, which in time will tip the scales to give no less temporary superiority to defense. Before WW2 Lindbergh was saying that there was no adequate defense against air attack, yet the British air force, aided by radar, effected intolerable losses on Hitler's air armada and

* *Saturday Evening Post*, July 17, 1954.

staved off invasion. Lindbergh failed to realize—and we shall see that he repeats this failure in the context of [today]—that the balance between offense and defense shifts continually.†

To Anne Lindbergh all this was more of the same involvement in the same dreary and sterile arguments which she had hoped to be able to forget with the coming of peace; and this time she carefully and deliberately did not allow herself to get mixed up in the controversies which fizzed around her husband's name. In any case, there were domestic events which took up most of her time. The family was growing up.

Her second son, Land, was beginning to run around with girls, and in 1954 her eldest son, Jon, was married to a classmate while still a student at Stanford University. It would not be true to say that Charles Lindbergh opposed the marriage, but he certainly thought Jon was hitching himself up far too soon (he was twenty-two). One day he confided half-seriously to Sam Pryor, a director of Pan American Airways, that he suspected Jon was rushing his marriage because "he wants to get away from home ties." It wasn't true. Jon Lindbergh had grown up to be a levelheaded young man who appeared (and still does) to take every decision in his life after considerable careful thought. No one who has met his wife could possibly believe that she was simply an escape hatch.

Nevertheless, it was true that Charles Lindbergh at home—when he was at home—liked to run what Jon, after he joined the Navy, called "a tight ship" in which he was always and without question the captain. He was not the type who would ever have accepted what he would have called a softie or a physical coward for a son, and he had made it plain to both Jon and Land from the start that he expected them to become physically self-sufficient and capable of taking care of themselves in any fraught situation.

Luckily for him (and for Anne's peace of mind), both his elder sons accepted this as a challenge to their resourcefulness rather than a blight on their development. Jon has since confessed that the only time he thought his father was pushing him too hard was one afternoon when he was eight years old, and they set out together to swim from the shore of Lloyd Neck, Long Island, to a lighthouse about nine hundred yards offshore. He did very nicely until they were well out into the Sound, when the strong ebb tide began to make difficulties for Jon. He was resolved not to ask help from his father, and seriously thought he was going to go under from sheer exhaustion. Luckily, the lighthousekeeper

† New York *Herald Tribune*, December 12, 1954.

saw his plight, came out onto the rock, and threw him a rope and pulled him in. The keeper offered to row both Lindbergh and his son back to the shore, but Jon refused ("I knew the tide would be with us on the way back," he said later) and, after a tour of the lighthouse and a short rest, plunged into the sea and swam back home. He never did tell his father how close he thought he had come to drowning. Years later (after he was married) father and son swam together again in a sort of competition between the generations. By this time Jon had done a hitch in the Navy and specialized in diving techniques, and from his home in Puget Sound he suggested taking Charles Lindbergh for an underwater exploration some distance offshore.

The two men donned frogmen's suits and loaded themselves with weights for keeping them under when they began diving, and they set off to a buoy anchored some distance out into the Pacific. When they reached it, Jon turned to his father and indicated that this was where they began the descent to the sea bottom.

"You do, not me," Lindbergh said. "I'm bushed."

He said it so simply and frankly that Jon Lindbergh would have felt no sense of triumph even if he had been that sort of a son. Instead he was proud of his father for grinning and bearing so happily the fact that now the positions were reversed. When he came up to the surface again, he found his father patiently waiting for him and they swam in leisurely tandem back to the shore. Jon had no thought of mentioning what had occurred, but Charles Lindbergh himself brought it up over supper that evening and recounted with every evidence of pride how his son had outswum him earlier in the day.

"Father," said his youngest son, Scott, later on, "is the only King Stag in existence who makes you feel he's won by losing. He positively bugles."

Scott was the rebel in the family. He had come late and was less aware than his older brothers (or professed to be) that his father had once been the greatest hero of modern times. Jon learned to fly and jump by parachute in emulation of his father. Land went back to the land, like his Lindbergh ancestors, and became a rancher, a hunter, a crack-shot, a great outdoors type. In obvious ways (even though they liked it) they were measuring up to their father's stature and unconsciously seeking his approval. Scott was not that sort of character. The last thing he wanted to be when he grew up, he indicated, was a hero. Better to be a pop singer or a painter or a sculptor. He once told one of his aunts that the only thing in the house at Darien that he really admired was a head of his mother, a delicate piece which had been done in Paris in 1938 by Charles Despiau.

Most of the rows he was later to have with his father concerned the way he drove a car. Charles Lindbergh had always been a careful driver. (He was careful in his treatment of all mechanical objects: he never took up a plane or set out in a car without first making absolutely sure, even if it took minutes, that all controls were working perfectly.) He swore the first time he took a ride with Scott that "he made fuzz come out of my bald patch" because of the speed at which he took corners. He banned him from using a car again until he had been through a course of skid-control (father as professor) and proved that he could handle his vehicle in all weathers.

At this stage his daughters were no problem. They were pretty and though, in the coming years, they would both show that they knew exactly what they wanted out of life, and would not be thwarted by parental objections, for the moment they could twist their father around their fingers.

One of the regular trips the family took was to Detroit, where Charles's mother, Evangeline Lodge Lindbergh, still lived with her brother. But now she was dying of heart and Parkinson's disease, and it pained them all to see this once-proud, active woman regressing into a vegetable. Everyone was thankful when she finally lost the struggle in the fall of 1954. But her death hit Charles Lindbergh hard. His mother was one of the two people he loved, admired, and above all trusted more than any other human being (the other, of course, was his wife). He had not seen so much of her in recent years, but once she was dead he missed her badly.

Anne's mother, too, was ailing and she also died, in the first weeks of 1955. There had always been a certain love-hate relationship between Anne Lindbergh and Betty Morrow, and mixed up with Anne's adoration and admiration had been a certain resentment, because she envied her mother's indefatigability, her gregariousness, her overpowering personality, and her persistent, dogged cheerfulness. Now that she was gone, Anne was pervaded not just by a sense of loss but by a kind of guilt, because, despite family closeness, they had not always understood or sympathized with each other's feelings and problems.

It was a period of her life when Anne Lindbergh was at her most restless, vaguely unhappy, racked by a guilty sense of having missed out on something, and sick and tired of being wife to a husband who was never there, mother to sons who went off and married too soon, to younger children who behaved like fledglings in the nest, demanding constant food and continuous attention the moment Father was away. ("They behaved like model troops in the presence of a stern master sergeant while Charles was around," a friend said, "but relaxed and turned into normal American kids the moment he went through the door.")

It would not be true to say that she was bored. Nor was she homebound. She covered a good deal of mileage herself in the course of a year, sometimes with the family (they went to Paris, Switzerland, stayed with her sister in Wales), sometimes alone with Charles. They flew two or three times to stay with their friends the J. P. Marquands at the novelist's lovely rented retreat in the Bahamas, Treasure Island. But she was never alone, and she needed to be alone.

Shortly after her mother's death, she made up her mind that she was going to get away, away from home, husband, family, household chores, everything. She went to live on a southern seashore in a house on the beach, cooking her own simple meals, bird watching, searching the sands for shells, writing. At one point she was joined by her sister Constance, and they were transformed into schoolgirls again, romping and roistering along the beach like a couple of tomboys. It was a spring-cleaning of the body, mind, and nervous system, and the random notes with which she emerged from her "retreat" eventually became a small book called *Gift from the Sea*,‡ one of the biggest best sellers of the 1950s.

It had been written as therapy for her own state of mind, but when published it acted as an anodyne for masses of fretful women, and became a sort of Bible of the Middle American Housewife. Parts of it, designed to sustain a wife and mother weary of household drudgery ("meals, planning, marketing, bills . . . doctors, dentists, appointments, medicine, cod-liver oil, vitamins . . . car-pools, extra trips for basket ball or orchestra practice; tutoring; camps, camp equipment and transportation"), contained sentiments that would make today's American women's liberationists rise in scorn and anger. But there were also passages about the loneliness of the human condition and the dilemma of being a writer and housewife that were lyrically moving.

Her own family were impressed by the book, and somewhat chastened by its revelations of the turmoil going on in her mind. Back in what, in the book, she called "the oyster bed of middle-aged marriage, with its tireless adaptability and tenacity of purpose," she found her husband willing to stay around a little more often, and her children somewhat less exigent. They made it plain that they had missed her.

With the publication of *Gift from the Sea*, Anne Lindbergh found herself one of the most popular and successful writers in the United States. Her book stayed on the best-seller list for nearly half a year.

‡ Random House, 1955, republished by Vintage Books, 1965.

Both she and her husband were growing rich from their literary preoc-cupations, for Charles had earned nearly $1.5 million out of *The Spirit of St. Louis.*

Not that they needed to worry about money. When Betty Morrow's will was published, it revealed that she had left $9,359,000. Her be-quests included $100,000 each to Smith College and Amherst College, the respective alma maters of her and her husband; small endowments to a number of relatives and in-laws, including Charles Lindbergh, who got $10,000; and the rest to her three living children. Anne and her sister Constance received $50,000 each and life interests in trusts of one third of the estate; $50,000 and the residue of the other two thirds of the estate went to her son Dwight.

It was not the lion's share that Mrs. Morrow had left to her daugh-ters, but it was enough to keep them comfortable for the rest of their existence.

CHAPTER

TWENTY-SEVEN

TURNING POINT

Even with the Democrats they were now okay people. Charles Lindbergh voted for Richard Nixon in the presidential election of 1960, but,
once elected, John F. Kennedy put him and Anne on the lists of "beautiful people" to be invited to the big occasions at the White House. On
May 11, 1962, Jackie Kennedy gave a dinner to honor the visit of the
French writer André Malraux, at that time Minister of Culture in the
government of General Charles de Gaulle. Isaac Stern played for the
guests.

At one moment in the evening Anne Lindbergh found herself in an
animated conversation about French literature with the guest of honor,
and the President's wife, noticing Charles Lindbergh watching them,
took him over to be introduced to Malraux. Afterward, a French reporter asked Malraux what Lindbergh had said to him.

"He said, 'I'm sorry I don't speak French,'" said Malraux.

Pan American had now made him a director of the company, and he
had been to England several times to look over the prototype of the
Concorde supersonic airliner, which Pan American was then thinking
of buying for its air routes, when the plane became available in the
1970s. The more he saw and studied the developments, however, the
greater his doubts about the future of a plane which, as he pointed out,
would soon be capable of carrying passengers across the Atlantic "at the
speed of a rifle bullet."

Did the world really need such a plane? Could the world afford to
give it airspace?

For the moment he was not voicing his doubts out loud, for they
would hardly have been received with approbation from his fellow di-

rectors at Pan Am, and they would have raised hell in the board rooms of Boeing, Douglas, Lockheed, and North American, all of whom were still working at this time on plans for supersonic transport.

But he was worried. For the first time since the end of World War II —since 1938, even—he felt his priorities changing. He still believed that world communism was one of the greatest threats to the happiness and well-being of Western man, and he would never change in that. But now he saw other dangers looming, and these threatened all mankind and all living beings. Science was developing too fast. Gadgetry was taking over the world. Speed was becoming the god of man, and life was suffering because of it, mentally, spiritually, physically.

Anne and Charles Lindbergh had always been interested in nature. His love of wild places and his interest in animals and birds stemmed from his boyhood in the forests and along the river lands of Minnesota. A passion for the sea, the lakes, the woods, and the mountains was something the two of them had always shared and cherished, and since they had ceased flying the world together in small planes—two people involved with the elements—something had gone out of their lives, a zest out of their relationship. It was not something to be restored by putting more bird-feeding stations in their Darien garden or by occasional trips to the wilder places of Africa and Asia.

Lindbergh at this time was in a curious mood, and his friends remember that he walked around with a slight hunch to his tall figure— unusual for him—as if he was carrying some sort of a burden. His hurt resentment over the way his wartime attitudes had been "misunderstood" had driven him even more within himself, and it was rarely if ever that he unburdened himself of his secret thoughts. Friends doubted that he even shared his innermost emotions with his wife. She, on the other hand, gushed it all out, in her diaries and her books, and he read them avidly, in search of revelations, acutely sensitive to every mood and emotion she expressed.

Was there a revelation for him in *Gift from the Sea*, that evocation of the joys of simple living? And a warning for him, perhaps, that he was becoming like too many Americans of his age and background, relying too much on science, too interested in *rugged individualism, limitless growth, progress measured by size, wealth, and efficiency*.

Some of his associates say that after the publication of *Gift from the Sea*, Charles Lindbergh lost his interest in the Cold War ("the ice ran out of it for him," one of them said) and his passion for aeronautical development. He continued to go through the motions and attended all the meetings, but he seemed to have lost his dynamic. So far as the Cold War is concerned, about this time something happened that threw some light on the doubts and dilemmas which had begun to thrash around in his mind.

In 1967, in his capacity as brigadier general in USAAF, he arrived in Vietnam to visit personnel as part of a morale-boosting effort. His presence became known and reporters hung around his hotel in Saigon in the hope of getting a statement from him, but he curtly brushed them aside. But they did discover that he went along for the ride on several trips over the Ho Chi Minh Trail. Subsequently he took a side trip to Phnom Penh, the Laotian capital, and was introduced at an embassy reception to the British ambassador and his female companion. He did not realize that she was the local correspondent of one of the wire services.

"General Lindbergh," she said, "I hear you are not entirely happy with U.S. operations in Vietnam."

"I don't know who gave you that impression," he said crisply. "I approve of any operations which prevent the spread of communism in Asia."

"Then does that mean you're in favor of defoliation?" she asked. "I hear you flew over the rain forests? Didn't it horrify you—the way they've been destroyed? All those trees. All those animals. All those birds and people."

There was a silence. Then Lindbergh said:

"I should hate anyone to think I approve of that. Once upon a time I thought George Washington was a good hero for American children, because when he cut down the cherry tree he admitted it later on. Now I'd have the story omitted from American history books. Even owning up doesn't excuse cutting down a tree."

Later on he heard that his questioner was a correspondent, and that evening he telephoned her.

"If you quote me on that story, I'll deny it," he said.

"Don't worry about that," the correspondent said. "Just go on worrying about those trees."

His doubts about the way aviation was going seemed to date from around 1964. In that year he attended a long conference in the Pan Am Building in New York at which engineers from Curtiss-Wright, General Electric, and Pratt and Whitney met to discuss the technical options facing them in their plans for a supersonic plane. They were trying to decide the basic elements of an American model to compete with Concorde. Would they use fanjets or turbojets? What power and what pay load? How much above two thousand miles an hour should the plane fly?

As he listened to the arguments being batted back and forth, he experienced a sudden revulsion of feeling. It so happened that he had a rendezvous in Nairobi which he had postponed because of this meeting, but now he was filled with a compulsion to put as much space as possible between himself and all this talk of the glorious supersonic future. He took a cab to the airport and boarded a plane for Rome. He traveled as usual in tourist, on a ticket made out in another name. He carried a small case containing only one change of clothing, khaki-drill slacks and a bush shirt, plus underwear, a razor and toothbrush, a Bible and a camera. Changing planes in Rome, he catnapped across Africa until he landed in Kenya the following day, showing no signs of jet lag. He was greeted at the airport by his British friend, Ian Grimwood, chief Kenya game warden. Twenty-four hours later they were deep in the Africa bush.

The Lindberghs were no strangers to Kenya, or Africa, or African safaris. They had been to most of the game reserves, separately or together. Charles Lindbergh cherished as his most rewarding experience a foray four hours out of Addis Ababa, in Ethiopia, when he sat under a tree full of weaver birds and watched a herd of nearly a hundred hippopotami wallowing and lolloping in the warm water, at the confluence of a river and a hot stream. He later met Emperor Haile Selassie, an old airplane buff, who told him that his Atlantic flight had inspired him to buy planes and start the first air link in East Africa. He was asked to sign a French edition of *The Spirit of St. Louis*.

In Kenya he had quite a few friends, and not just among the game wardens. He had stayed on several occasions with Dr. Michael Wood, a flying doctor, who operated out of a farm on the slopes of Mount Kilimanjaro. The first time Wood took him for a ride in his jeep through the forest and brushland on the lower slopes of the mountain, they bumped for several hours along a painfully rough road.

"This reminds me," Lindbergh said, "of a story they tell of the early days of motoring in Minnesota. This city type arrives in Little Falls and he is riding with a farmer in his Model T along an atrocious highway. 'Which side of the road do you drive in Minnesota?' he asked. 'The best side,' said the farmer."

Lindbergh had first met Wood while on an early safari with one of Grimwood's assistants. He was still shooting animals at that time, and had permission to bag one rhino. In a Masai village they were taken to a hut where a warrior, one of a party who had been out hunting with spears, had been badly gored by a rhino and tossed on its horn, which had pierced through its stomach and come out of the man's back. The white hunter sent out a radio message and not long afterward Wood's plane touched down.

Lindbergh sat in on the operation, and marveled at the skill with which the British doctor tended and stitched the man's dreadful wound, and then loaded him aboard the plane for dispatch to the hospital. Before Wood took off, he invited Lindbergh to accompany him on his "rounds" on his next visit. They watched the plane disappear, and then the white hunter said:

"And now let's go and get your rhino. Perhaps it'll be the one that practically killed that poor bastard."

Lindbergh shook his head. "I've changed my mind. It would just be an eye for an eye, and a tooth for a tooth, and I gave that up after World War II."

Thereafter, when he went on safari, he used a camera.

Now he was back again, but this time he sensed that this was going to be a different experience. Somehow the overnight transference from that meeting on supersonic flight in New York to the unchanging, timeless life and landscape of the African bush seemed to have a catalytic effect upon Lindbergh. He had never before seen anything contradictory between his profession as an aviator and his passion for nature. What was wrong with building bigger, better, faster planes, and why was that aim incompatible with the preservation of the species? The answer to that came as he woke up at dawn on his first morning in the game lands, and it was a flash of revelation:

> Lying under an acacia tree, with the sounds of dawn around me, I realized more clearly, in fact, what man should never overlook: that the construction of an airplane, for instance, is simple when compared with the evolutionary achievement of a bird; that airplanes depend upon advanced civilization; and that where civilization is most advanced, few birds exist.
>
> I realized that if I had to choose, I would rather have birds than airplanes. I began to question the definition I had assigned to progress in New York.

He questioned it so sharply that not long after he returned to New York he switched the emphasis of his life. With the happy approval of Anne Lindbergh, he hung up his Cold War uniform and preached no more the doctrine of the big atomic stick. He still believed that the United States should have the capacity for massive retaliation against any atomic attack upon his country or its allies, and he still nurtured a deep hatred and suspicion of Russian and Chinese communism. But he now saw the need for some sort of détente instead of armed truce between the democracies and the Communists, to turn the possibility of atomic devastation into a remote and unlikely nightmare.

At the same time, he grew more and more apprehensive of the dangers, to man and to his environment, as he saw them, of fleets of supersonic airliners. Soon he emerged as an open opponent of the Anglo-French Concorde plane, as a polluter of the upper atmosphere, a waster of the planet's oil resources, and an all-round noisy menace. He told his fellow directors on the board of Pan American Airways that he was against following through their provisional order for Concordes, and felt that American companies would be making a mistake if they went on with their plans to build a rival supersonic plane.*

When the builders of the Anglo-French plane heard what was happening, there was consternation and dismay. Lindbergh had sat in on many of the discussions during the planning of the plane, and after its first prototype was produced he became a good friend of the chief French pilot, André Turcat. Turcat now sat down to write a letter to Lindbergh asking him if it was true that he had turned his back on the Concorde project, and pleading with him, if so, to think again. A long correspondence began between the two in which each passionately argued his point of view. Exactly what Lindbergh wrote cannot be reproduced here,† but the line he took followed that of a letter he later wrote to Congressman Sidney R. Yates (D., Ill.) and an article he did for the New York *Times*. In the letter to Yates he wrote that he did not "see any practical way to avoid disturbances that would be caused by regular sonic booms" and that an American supersonic plane was technically "but not economically or environmentally" viable. He added that "my vote will be against adding to the present noise level in any unnecessary way." In his article in the *Times* he made clear what Turcat and the Concorde builders suspected, that his opposition to supersonic flight was motivated as much by economic factors as by ecology, and the cynics among them wondered whether his opposition would have held if Pan American's accountants had figured out that they could make a supersonic service pay.

> Years ago [he wrote], I came to the conclusion that while we had sufficient technical knowledge to build supersonic transport, we could do so only at a cost that would be uneconomic for the airlines operating them, even if they were

---

* American manufacturers subsequently opted out of the race, but more for economic than environmental reasons.

† Turcat has been asked not to release the correspondence.

permitted to fly over populated areas regardless of sonic booms. Many airline operators have now come to similar conclusions.

He admitted that if subsidized foreign airlines began operating Concordes, American lines would be in a difficult position.

We could purchase Concordes in order to compete on equal footing with the foreign airlines operating them. This would require government financial assistance of major magnitude. It would force our acceptance of sonic booms and atmospheric contamination. It would also raise the question of starting another SST [supersonic transport] program of our own, regardless of environment and cost.

He was against it. With a ring of the old America First Lindbergh in his tone, he concluded:

To what extent do we control our own destiny, economically and environmentally? Having decided not to put SSTs into operation, must we still do so because of the pressure of foreign governments? . . . The supersonic transport symbolizes this issue. Our response to its challenge will indicate our future. Is the quality of life or the advancement of technology to guide us?

For me aviation is of value only to the extent that it contributes to the quality of the human life it serves. Supersonic flight is obviously of great importance and should continue.

But my personal conclusion is that the regular operation of SSTs in their present state of development will be disadvantageous both to aviation and to the peoples of the world.

I believe we should prohibit their operation on or above United States territory, as long as their effect on our overall environment remains unsatisfactory.‡

From now on, Lindbergh put his heart and mind into ecology. In some ways, this new preoccupation could not have come at a better moment, because his other great interest in life was growing up and away from him. He had once told Anne that he wanted twelve children, so that there would always be a young one around the house to be shown

‡ New York *Times*, July 7, 1942.

how to survive and thrive. She had firmly said no after her sixth, and of the five still living all but one had now flown the nest. Jon was married and running a company of oceanographers out of Puget Sound. Land had married a college mate and started a cattle ranch in Montana. Anne Spencer, the elder daughter, had married a young Frenchman, Julien Feydy, a childhood sweetheart, and they were now living in France. Scott was running around Europe and happily sowing wild oats.* Only the younger daughter, Reeve, was still around, and it would not be long before she, too, married and left the family home.† There was no one left at Scott's Cove to throw in the water or challenge to a race or teach how to shoot and fly a plane.

True, there were plenty of grandchildren coming along. Thwarted of a quiverful of his own, Charles Lindbergh hoped to see his offspring produce a whole alphabet of children among them (they have reached the letter J, for Johnny, so far), and he was proud and happy whenever he was with them. But it wasn't quite the same as having sons and daughters of his own to mold; he was careful not to interfere in the way their parents brought them up, and the doting grandparent dandling infants on his knee just wasn't his style. But what would Jon (or more important, Jon's wife) say if he took one of *his* sons by the ankle and swung him round his head?

The trip to Africa in 1964 had had a profound effect upon him, and when he got back he saw an article in the *Times* about the World Wild Life Fund.

"I couldn't find the organization in the phone book," he said later, "so I called the New York Zoological Society, of which I'm a member. They steered me to Dr. Ira Gabrielson in Washington, head of the Wildlife Management Institute and the grand old man of conservation. He'd taken on the presidency of the U.S. branch of the WWF and they were just getting under way. I made a small contribution."

The following year he joined the board of the WWF and then the executive committee.

"Since then I've been trying to build up conservation interest all round the world, which I am in a good condition to do since as a consultant to Pan Am I travel a great deal," he said.

In 1965 he joined the National Union for the Conservation of Nature and he was appointed its representative at the meeting of the In-

---

* He married a French artist, Monique Dubois (who paints under the name of Malika Watteau), at Châtaincourt, near Paris, in 1968. His parents did not come over for the wedding.

† She is now married and teaches school in Vermont, and has begun to write short stories.

ternational Whaling Commission in Peru in 1966. He was appalled when he learned what was happening to the blue and the humpbacked whale, and his feelings about the Russians and the Japanese were not exactly warmed when he learned that these two nations were the chief activists in the slaughter of them.

"Then I learned that Americans were also involved, and I was ashamed," he said. "I felt I had to do something about it."

After the commission's sessions were over, Lindbergh took a trip into the Peruvian Andes to try to see and photograph the rare vicuna, a llamalike animal. He was depressed to find that this, too, was threatened by hunters seeking to sell its silklike wool for expensive cloth. While he was in camp a message reached him that he was invited to lunch with the Peruvian President, Fernando Belaúnde Terry, at his palace in Lima.

"At lunch I talked to the President about the vicuna and about the blue and humpbacked whales," Lindbergh said. "They were then being constantly harpooned by hunters from a land station on the west coast of Peru."

President Terry said:

"If I make the arrangements, will you go out on a whaler and bring back a report to me?"

Lindbergh said he would eagerly do so. A few days later, he sailed out into the Pacific with the whaling fleet. This area is one of the principal gathering grounds for whales, and he was appalled not so much by the blood and stench and flies that go with offshore whaling but by the ruthless efficiency with which the great creatures were slaughtered. The killing rate was far above the production rate, and if it went on for much longer the herds would be destroyed.

When he talked to the captain of the whaler, he discovered that the company which controlled the fleet and ran the shore factory was, in fact, American. The parent company had its headquarters in Minneapolis, and its chairman of the board was a Swede whose family had come to the United States about the same time as his grandfather.

"When I wrote him a letter," Lindbergh said later, telling him why we wanted a ban on the harpooning of these endangered species, he, after consulting with his board, agreed with me. So the President of Peru was able to put into effect a voluntary ban on harpooning. This was a major step in saving the blue and the humpbacked whale. I think they'll come back now, that the herds will increase."‡

He was the kind of person for whom the WWF and its associated or-

‡ New York *Times,* June 23, 1969.

ganizations were looking. He had a network of friends all over the
world in influential positions. His fame commanded the attention of
heads of governments. When he spoke, people listened. When he asked
for funds, people gave. When he picked up the telephone and asked for
a President or a Prime Minister, he got the man or woman he asked for.
The invitations came crowding in for him to join the activists in the
ecology movement. Soon he was a committee member not only of
WWF, but of the International Union for the Conservation of Nature
and its Survival Service Commission, the Nature Conservancy, and the
Oceanic Foundation. He was asked for help in saving the polar bear in
Alaska, the one-horned rhinoceros in Java, marine life off Hawaii.

"I have not seen Charles so happy or excited for years," Anne told
her friends. "He's enjoying himself as much as he did when he flew his
first airplane. His whole outlook has changed, too."

It was true. The way his mind was turning can be gauged from an article he wrote for *Life* magazine in 1967:

> If I were entering adulthood now instead of in the environ-
> ment of fifty years ago, I would choose a career that kept me
> in touch with nature more than science. This is the choice an
> individual can still make—but no longer mankind in general.
> Too few natural areas remain; both by intent and indifference
> we have insulated ourselves from the wilderness that produced
> us. Our emphasis on science has resulted in an alarming rise in
> world populations, the demand and ever-increasing emphasis
> of science to improve their standards and maintain their vigor.
> I have been forced to the conclusion that an over-emphasis of
> science weakens character and upsets life's essential balance.

It was a revolutionary change in his thinking pattern, and from now
on it would dominate his life. Heretofore, he had always believed in the
wisdom and superiority of humankind. Not all humankind, of course.
He would never stop despising great masses of people, the types who
had made his life as a hero so much of a miserable torture. But hitherto
he had accepted the high place in the world of those whose background, breeding, and training had made them masters of their fellow
men. Now he had doubts. What if the masters, and the science they
controlled, were even more dangerous than the ordinary people?

After a trip into one of the remoter jungles of Indonesia, where he
was overwhelmed by the richness of the wildlife he found there, he
wrote:

Surrounded by wildness, representing the human lifestream
with diverse competing lifestreams close at hand, I start
doubting my superiority. I am struck by the perfection of competing species in contrast to my own. I'm amazed at the
beauty, health and balance nature has achieved through instinct's influence. I ask what intellect has done to warrant its
prestige. As earth's most messy, defective and destructive animal, man's record gives him little cause for pride.

He was still a consultant on the space program, and in December
1968 he went to the White House for a dinner President Lyndon
Baines Johnson gave for the astronauts just before they took off for the
first moonshot. Anne sat next to their old friend, William Benton, and
told him that moonshot day would be a happy one for Charles.

"When they land on the moon," she said, "it will be the fulfillment
of an old dream Charles has had ever since Bob Goddard died, to see
his friend's labors fulfilled. Goddard never wanted to see intercontinen-
tal missiles. He did want to see interplanetary ships, and he always
believed a moonshot was possible."

They were at Cape Kennedy when the astronauts took off for the
moon. Charles happily posed with Bormann for a Polaroid picture
which the astronaut then took with him into space. Dr. Hubertus
Strughold was there, and Lindbergh went across to shake his hand.
Anne wrinkled her nose at the spoliation of the Cape, which she and
Charles had known once as a nature reserve, full of flamingos and
heron, and she flinched over the gaudy roistering of the spectators. But
it was a triumphant occasion for her husband, and she was content for
him. Speaking about it later, Lindbergh said Goddard had told him as
early as 1929 that it would be possible to send a multistaged rocket to
the moon.

"Then he smiled a little bit," Lindbergh said, "and said the only
thing was, it would cost a million dollars—so of course that was out. I
would remind you that the Apollo moon landing is estimated to cost
$2.3 billion."*

Anne Lindbergh had bought a chalet, Le Monte de Corsier, overlooking Lake Geneva, in Switzerland, where she could entertain her daughter and her French husband and family, and also keep an eye on the
wandering Scott. It was also a favorite gathering point in Europe for
the other members of the family, and sometimes the chalet was filled
with children and grandchildren. Charles found it a convenient stop-

* Remarks to the Airline Pilots Association, 1969.

ping-off point during his world travels, and he had become a member of the Geneva committee of the WWF.

He liked the Swiss. They made no fuss of him when he walked through the streets. Their newspapers respected his privacy and rarely mentioned his presence in the country, except in connection with the WWF. They nearly all spoke English and he did not have to worry about language problems when he met them. His lack of facility with languages would always be one of the things that bugged him, but here it was no problem. At one small dinner party in Switzerland he was introduced to a famous Swiss historian, Dr. Karl Burckhardt. Burckhardt had been the League of Nations' High Commissioner in Danzig in the years leading up to World War II, and after they had shaken hands he pointed out to Lindbergh that they had seen each other before, when they were both guests at an aviation dinner at Potsdam in 1938.

"I told him that Hermann Göring said he was one of the best friends Germany had," Burckhardt said, "and he looked quite worried for a moment. I said: 'Don't worry, they said that about me, too, but I was just as much an anti-Nazi as you were.' I told him my home was not very far away, and asked him to come and visit me, but he never appeared."

It was at one of the Geneva meetings of the WWF that Lindbergh met up with a colorful Englishman named Tom Harrisson, who was one of the leading activitists for the Survival Service Commission, and it turned out to be the beginning of a fruitful association. Harrisson, a onetime anthropologist in Borneo, founder of Mass-Observation (an opinion-poll outfit), ex-wartime parachutist (he dropped into the Borneo jungle), expert on the habits and migratory patterns of the giant turtle, sometime professor at Cornell University and now Sussex University, England, was a type of Englishman Lindbergh had never met before, but one he took to almost at once.

What brought them together to begin with was that Harrisson was a passionate conservationist who had been working in the movement for years, and knew all the problems if not the answers.

"If it came to the crunch," he once said, "I'm more concerned with conservation than anything else. I can't make much contribution in politics because I chose to live in Borneo for twenty years, and it's too late. But I think I can, as a radical and progressive person, make a contribution on conservation. Animals are helpless creatures. They can't write to the New York *Times* for themselves. Someone has got to be in there thinking and planning for them. It's vital. If not, there won't *be* any animals left."

One of Lindbergh's objections to most of the Englishmen he had met was that they all seemed to have been to Eton and Oxford and patronized him in lah-di-dah voices, especially when they learned that he was a college dropout himself. He was pleased to discover that Harrisson had never completed college either, and did not hold it against him that he had been to Harrow when he learned that he had hated every moment of it.

They soon discovered that they were both natural rebels, suspicious of authority, ready to fight and stick for what they felt was right. Slowly, somewhat, it seemed to his own amazement, Lindbergh began singling out the Englishman at meetings and going off with him for a chat. Harrisson, a born raconteur, enlivened him with stories about the mating habits of the Kelabits in the rain forests of Borneo, and won his heart with a description of how the World Health Organization had decided to spray all the Borneo villagers' longhouses with insecticide to kill malarial mosquitoes and killed off all the cats as well. Result: a plague of rats. Remedy: Tom Harrisson collected two hundred alley cats from Sarawak, packed them in boxes, and parachuted them into the jungle villages.

They talked about Lindbergh's childhood, his memories of Mississippi Indians, duck and deer shooting in the backwoods, and went on to the flight patterns and routes of the Siberian yellow wagtail, the Japanese sparrowhawk and the longtailed munia. They exchanged mutual experiences as parachutists.

And then one day their association was cemented by an incident off the coast of New Jersey. Harrisson said:

"I had come up from Cornell to stay with Herb Mills, who was at that time chief director of the WWF, at his home on the Jersey shore, and among the people I found there was Charles Lindbergh. We were there to talk about a project for preserving the wetlands which lie along the Jersey shore south of Atlantic City. In the afternoon it was suggested that we all go out in a boat and cruise the waterways and take a look at the area. There were about six people in the party, dedicated conservationists, some of them so damned dedicated that they wouldn't kill anything, not even a partridge in the jungle for supper."

It was a still, hot, sticky day, and suddenly a swarm of painted lady flies, which have a painful bite, came swarming out of the swamps and began buzzing around the party.

"Now it so happens that I'm a very aggressive person in some ways," Harrisson said. "I can't bear horseflies or wasps or anything of that sort. I know it isn't a wise thing to do, and I know it isn't good conservation, but I have to hit out at them. Well, those painted ladies started coming at me, and I had to hit out. I discovered then that Lindbergh had exactly the same reaction. He had to hit out too. It was very interesting. He had seemed such a quiet, gentle, Quaker-like character, but now he was just like me, the aggressiveness bursting out of him. We stood together, swatting those damned flies. It created a sort of bond."

When they got back onshore, Harrisson said:

"Would you like to come out to the Philippines with me and save the tamarau?"

"Yes," said Lindbergh. "When do we go? What would you like me to do?"

Harrisson said later: "The marvelous thing was that I didn't even have to explain what a tamarau was. He knew."

The tamarau, a small, fierce buffalo, unique to the Philippines, lived in the mountains of the island of Mindoro, but had almost been wiped out by the hunting habits of Filipino sportsmen (who shot it from helicopters) and the land-clearing activities of ranchers (who turned machine guns on the herds). If it did not receive immediate protection, conservationists expected the animal to be extinct by the early 1970s.

Harrisson knew the haunts of the tamarau and how to save it.

"All we needed to do was persuade the Philippine Government to pass a law with real teeth in it," Harrisson said. "But that was easier said than done. The Filipino is a great man with a gun, and he doesn't like being stopped from using it. We knew that even some of the leading so-called local conservationists had been up in the mountains, helping to take part in the tamarau-slaughters."

Harrisson decided that what was needed was a big public relations exercise. "And that was where Lindbergh came in. There are certain characters in the WWF whose names and influence carry weight with heads of government. Prince Philip or Prince Bernhardt, for instance, can take time out during one of their official visits to draw the Prime Minister or President on one side and ask for national protection of this animal or that bird. They are listened to and it gets results. But in the Philippines, we knew we were not going to get anywhere until we got everyone talking about the tamarau—because we needed money as well as government help—and that meant publicity."

This was where Harrisson worried a bit. Knowing Lindbergh's festering hatred of the press, how would he react to having newspapermen going along with him, reporting his movements, expecting him to make statements?

He need not have worried. Charles Lindbergh had never objected to appearing in the press for what he called "legitimate" reasons.

"I'll call up the New York *Times*," he said. "They have always tried to be co-operative with me. They'll send someone along with us, I'm sure."†

Harrisson said:

"He was absolutely marvelous on the trip. He talked to the press and smiled and posed for photographs. For a man in his sixties, he was remarkably fit, and no matter what the heat or how high in the hills we were, he was always marching ahead of the whole lot of us, never showing any sign of fatigue. He not only got us the attention we needed in tamarau country, but he did his stuff at the other end. He was such a famous character that all his life he had been used to meeting top people, and we've learned in conservation that unless you get the top people interested, you get nowhere. Lindbergh in Manila asked to see President Ferdinand Marcos, and he saw President Marcos. He talked so persuasively that by the time he had finished, President Marcos had decreed that the tamarau was to be protected, and heaven help anyone who took a gun to one in future."

Shortly afterward, he approached the President about protecting the majestic monkey-eating eagle, of which only about thirty pairs were left in the islands, and Marcos issued another decree.

By this time the Englishman had become fascinated with Lindbergh. "He was a much more complicated character than he made out," he said. "For instance, he could doss down anywhere, in the jungle, on the floor of a plane, in a bug-ridden hut, and just go to sleep. He ate wild boar and picked fruit off the trees, and didn't ever seem to get worried about brackish water (though I must admit we mostly drank coconut juice). But when he got back to Manila, he instantly became the VIP again. He was of course invited to stay in the American embassy and was given the best suite in the joint, and he shrugged his shoulder ruefully over its grandeur. But I think he would have been annoyed, just the same, if he hadn't been given it."

His reactions to people interested Harrisson, too. "I'd wondered when I read some of his statements and listened to him talking whether he was one of those characters who believe in racial selection. You often find racialists among conservationists. They rationalize their dislike of the ordinary run of the human race by having this strong love of animals, or primitive tribes. I remember during our New Jersey trip one man in the party, who was a real color-bar character, said he thought the greatest menace to the world was overpopulation, and one of the best means of conservation would be to invent a liquid which you could spray on blacks and the like and they would wither away. Lindbergh

† They didn't that time, but they did later.

agreed that it would be a marvelous way of stopping overbreeding. I listened to them, appalled by the reactionary remarks they were making—even though I knew they weren't entirely serious. Finally, I said: 'Tell me, what *are* your politics, you two?' Lindbergh grinned. 'Tom,' he said, 'we're nothing but a couple of *black* Republicans. I'd never heard the expression before. I presumed he meant that they were a couple of old die-hards."

In the Philippines, though, Lindbergh was charming to the people and charmed by them. One of the main points of the exercise was to get the mayors of all the local villages in the tamarau areas on the side of conservation, and they made a tour by helicopter.

"It meant hopping out of the craft at every village, waving to the crowd, making speeches, and going through all sorts of boring ceremonials," Harrisson said. "Not only did Lindbergh do it all, but he looked positively happy doing it. In one village we took part in a tribal dance which is organized like a sort of standing musical chairs. The musicians strike up and you're supposed to dance around until they stop, and then you freeze. I've always been quite good at this sort of thing. I learned to keep still in the Borneo jungles when the Japs were looking for me. But Lindbergh was pretty good value for money, too. Soon we'd eliminated everyone in the village, and there were only the two of us left. I'm afraid I beat him in the end—I think a bug flew in his ear or something—but he didn't hold it against me. It was a good and successful trip. He had the expression of satisfaction on his face of a man who had found his métier."

In the midst of this new and happy absorption, however, something happened which almost wrecked the whole thing.

Harold Nicolson's first volume of diaries and letters had been published in the United States in 1966, before Charles Lindbergh really got launched into conservation and ecology. Lindbergh was, as has been made clear at the beginning of this book, deeply wounded and genuinely surprised by Nicolson's suggestion that he had been pro-Nazi and anti-American in the years before the beginning of World War II, and he poured out his anger and indignation in a series of painful letters.

Had he left it at that, all might have been well. But Nicolson's charges had opened up old wounds, and soon Anne Lindbergh saw, to her great distress, that her husband was not willing to bandage them up and wait for them to heal. Nicolson had stirred up all the old resentments, the need to justify himself, to be vindicated. She had thought that it was all over and forgotten, and here it was starting again.

Nigel Nicolson never heard from Charles Lindbergh again after the

35. Charles and Anne Morrow Lindbergh had five more children (three sons and two daughters) after the death of their firstborn, Charles Augustus, Jr. This is a picture of Jon, the eldest, taken on an oceanographic trip while he was a student at Stanford.

36. Jon Lindbergh now runs an underwater exploration company and conducts deep-sea ecological surveys off the West Coast of the United States at Puget Sound, Washington. Here he is shown with his father at a fish conservation project in which he is interested.

37. Lindbergh had always been interested in animals and plants, a passion dating from his boyhood in Minnesota, and in the last fifteen years of his life it occupied an increasing amount of his time. As a director of the World Wild Life Fund, one of his activities was saving the rare monkey-eating eagle of the Philippines. Here he is seen examining a tame specimen in a collection on Mindanao Island.

38. As a leading member of World Wild Life's Survival Service Commission and a director of Panamin (the Private Association for National Minorities) he became deeply involved with helping to preserve the threatened minority tribes of the Philippines. Here he is shown with members of a remarkable Stone Age group, the Tasadays, discovered on the Island of Mindanao. Seated is Manuel Elizalde, Jr., the Filipino president of Panamin.

39. Lindbergh's ecological activities took him to Africa, Asia, Indonesia, and South America as well as to the Philippines, and he was interested in the preservation of animals, birds, plants, trees, and people. Here he inspects a work project among a tribal minority in Southeast Asia.

40. Among the most important of Lindbergh's activities in his later years was a directorship with Pan American Airways, on whose behalf he traveled most of the world aboard the company's aircraft. The great aviation pioneer had come a long way.

emotional letter he had received from him on January 27, 1967. But that was because he had decided upon another method of securing vindication from the American people. He abandoned conservation for the moment, and went over to Yale University instead to immerse himself in his papers and go through the diaries which he himself had kept from 1938 through 1945. After reading them through again, he rang up his friend and publisher, William Jovanovich, of Harcourt Brace Jovanovich. It was agreed that except for certain excisions of names and events, and an editing for length, the diaries would be published as they had been written.

They appeared in the fall of 1970 under the title *The Wartime Journals of Charles A. Lindbergh*, and as an exercise in justification they could hardly be called a success. There was an air of defiance about Lindbergh's introduction which seemed almost deliberately intended to ruffle the feathers of his onetime opponents and provoke them into fighting him all over again. He pointed out that he found he still held the beliefs which he had set down in the journal's pages, and there was still not a word of criticism of the Nazi Government whose crimes he might have missed during his stay in Germany, but the horrors of which were now documented and proved.

He had not budged from his contention that the war had been wrong and that it had been fought against the wrong nation. In a challenging passage, he even denied that we had won World War II. Unfortunately, Lindbergh's literary executors have refused permission for the reproduction of this particular passage, which attracted much attention in the United States when the book was published, and was widely quoted.

In it Lindbergh maintained that the Allied victory had been one in a military sense only, and that otherwise none of the causes for which the war was waged had been won. In opposing Germany and Japan, we had aggrandized the Soviet Union and China. Poland had been lost. The British Empire had crumbled. France was in the grip of "a mild dictatorship."‡

If there was a rigidity in the opinions he expressed in his introduction, there were also some curious prejudices and *idées fixes* in the pages of the journals themselves which critics immediately seized upon. Jean Stafford in the *New York Review of Books* called him a "goony bird" about whom "the murk of prejudice and warmly nursed grievances obfuscates the message, unless the message is one too sinister to contemplate." Reed Whittemore's review in the *New Republic* was,

‡ For the full text, see *The Wartime Journals of Charles A. Lindbergh* (New York: Harcourt Brace Jovanovich, 1970), p. xv.

surprisingly enough, one of the few sympathetic ones and called his journals "extensive, diverse, full of variety and contradiction—and great honesty and humanity."

It was left to the New York *Times**** to sum up general feelings about the journals:

> Old controversies, like old soldiers, never die. They fade away only to return years later to be reargued in the narrative of historians and the memoirs of participants.
>
> The struggle from 1939 to 1941 to decide whether the United States would abandon its traditional isolationism and intervene in World War II was a historic controversy in the life of the nation. Charles A. Lindbergh was a vigorous, articulate spokesman for the isolationist side in that debate. In now publishing his wartime journals, Mr. Lindbergh is exercising his right to restate his opinions for the benefit of history and of a new generation. He is also indulging himself in the loser's prerogative of insisting that he was right after all.
>
> We do not believe that time has made Mr. Lindbergh's ideas more valid or that future historians will find them more persuasive than his contemporaries did. Like many civilized people in this country and abroad, he could not comprehend the radical evil of Nazism. Even in the retrospect of a quarter-century he is unable to grasp it. His analogy of Nazi genocide with alleged American excesses toward Japanese prisoners of war is grotesque.
>
> War brutalizes most men who engage in it, but there is simply no comparison between individual misdeeds of American soldiers toward dead or captured Japanese and the coldly planned, systematically executed German Government policy of murdering or enslaving Jews, Slavs, and other "inferior" people.
>
> "We won the war in a military sense; but in a broader sense it seems to me that we lost it, for our Western civilization is less respected and secure than it was before," Mr. Lindbergh writes.
>
> As his principal evidence for this astonishing conclusion, he points out that Russia and China have replaced Germany and Japan as even more menacing enemies.
>
> The world is admittedly not what Americans—or anyone

* September 6, 1970.

else—would like, but it is decidedly better than it would have been if the United States had not helped to defeat German and Japanese militarism. One has only to imagine how much worse the world would look like to Americans if a Nazi government, armed with nuclear weapons, ruled all Europe from the Urals to the English Channel, while a hostile Japan dominated the western Pacific to the very edge of Hawaii.

If any war can be said to be worth fighting and winning, it was World War II. Even vanquished nations gained, since Japan and Germany are far richer and freer today than they were in 1939.

There is no doubt who won the war. Mankind won it.

Far from vindicating Charles Lindbergh's stand, publication of his journals seemed to have had the opposite effect. Older people who had forgotten (or forgiven) were reminded of ancient quarrels, and bitter resentments were revived. Younger people, who knew him only as a legendary flying hero who had transformed himself into the apostle of a better and cleaner world, were astonished to learn that he was a diehard Republican with some very right-wing viewpoints.

There was much controversy over the book, but it did not sell. People seemed to spurn it. Anne Lindbergh, who was distressed that cupboards had been opened and skeletons brought out into the light, must have wished that it had never been published.

Much better to worry about the fate of the tamarau or other threatened species. She set out to persuade him to forget the whole thing and get his mind back on the future.

Not that Anne Lindbergh was averse to opening a few family cupboards herself, though when she did so there were different reasons for it, and what was revealed to the light were not so much skeletons but old dolls, souvenirs, and toys. In the early 1970s she began the publication of her own diaries covering the years from 1922 (when she was still in college) to 1935, when she and her husband fled to England to escape publicity, press persecution, and, they feared, the possible kidnaping of their second son, Jon.

It was a measure of the maturity of mind she had attained that she was willing to see published not only her thoughts and feelings during her courtship by Charles Lindbergh and her first years of marriage but also the black days and nights she had endured after the kidnaping and death of her baby. And not only that. She had reached a stage of peace and philosophical acceptance enough to be able to write introductions to each volume of her diaries, explaining and embellishing the entries, filling in the gaps, pointing out where she had made mistakes of judgment, been overconfident, too harsh, too kind, too sad, too happy. It is these introductions that give a special savor to the items which follow in the day-to-day descriptions of her daily life and thoughts.†

In one of the introductions there is a curious coincidence. Writing about her diary entries in the years 1922–28, she says (in *Bring Me a Unicorn*):

> There is, naturally, a distinction between diaries and letters. Letters are usually written not only to communicate with the recipient, but also to amuse or please him. So that the truth here is sometimes veiled or colored. Diaries are written for oneself and reveal the writer as he is when alone.

Anne Lindbergh wrote these words in 1971. If the reader will study Nigel Nicolson's letter to her husband written on January 31, 1967, he will find the same sentiments expressed in similar words.‡ This was the letter to which Charles Lindbergh never replied. But quite evidently some part of its contents stayed in Anne Lindbergh's mind, and, at least in her, the words struck a sympathetic chord.

† See *Bring Me a Unicorn* (1971–72), *Hour of Gold, Hour of Lead* (1973), *Locked Doors and Empty Rooms* (1974), all published by Harcourt Brace Jovanovich.
‡ See p. xxviii.

CHAPTER

TWENTY-EIGHT

LAST ADVENTURE

He was seventy years old in 1972, but he didn't look like an old man or act like one. It was true that there were lines under his eyes and his hair was thin, and he now had a slight hunch—since he was getting a bit deaf and had to lean down to hear what people, most of them shorter than himself, were saying to him—but his complexion was healthily ruddy and his step was vigorous and firm.

About this time he was working late one Saturday in an office Bill Jovanovich, his friend and publisher, had given him in the Harcourt Brace Jovanovich Building in New York. When he decided to call it a day, he discovered that everyone else had left. He turned out the lights and went into the elevator hall and pressed the "down" button, but nothing happened. The elevators had halted for the weekend.

He shouted, thumped on the elevator door. No one came. He turned back to the office door, but it had clicked closed behind him. He thought some sort of caretaker or patrolman would be sure to turn up soon, so he sat down on the floor in a corner to finish a letter he was writing to Russell Fridley, of the Minnesota Historical Society. But after a couple of hours he realized that he could well be trapped in the elevator hall over the whole weekend. That he was not prepared to accept. Rather than wait until Monday morning, he decided to get back somehow into the Harcourt Brace Jovanovich office, even if it meant breaking down the door.

The only trouble was, there was nothing with which to assault the door because the only thing in the hall was a large ceramic ashtray. "But I've got big feet and good shoulders," he scribbled to Fridley.

He stood back and then charged at the door and hit it with his shoulder, and promptly bounced off with no visible impact on the door and considerable pain in his shoulder. It was a method of breaking bones but not of getting back into the office. So he attacked it with his boot instead. For the first ten strikes, the door held firm. The eleventh time he kicked, he heard a crack. On the twentieth kick, the door flew open and he went inside.

Other men would then probably have sat down at a desk and telephoned for the help to come up and get him out of the building. Instead, Lindbergh opened a window and climbed down to Third Avenue by the fire escape. It was quite a feat for a man of his age. Back at Scott's Cove that night, he failed to tell Anne about his misadventure. She only learned about it later from Fridley.

Anne Lindbergh's persuasive efforts had succeeded, and the snub he had been given over his wartime journals was forgotten (or at least stowed away in the cellar of his mind) as he got back to conservation again. And this time he was on the brink of what he was later to describe as "one of the great experiences of life," quite evidently one that he put beside his famous flight. He discovered the Tasadays.

Though he was still traveling the world and was always popping up in Africa one week, Asia the next, he seemed, as Anne Lindbergh wrote to a friend, "to be more and more in . . . the Philippines, Japan, and Indonesia." His son Jon, who was running a salmon study off the West Coast of the United States, had got him interested in the protection of the Pacific's coral formations, and the setting up of marine preserves, but more and more the focus of his attention was on an island in the Philippines where a primitive tribe had been discovered in the rain forests.

His trip with Tom Harrisson to the haunts of the tamarau and the monkey-eating eagle had got him hooked on the Philippines, and he had been going back there ever since, fascinated as much by the tribes as the birds and the animals. In 1969 he had gone on a trip into the jungles of Mindoro to meet the aboriginal Batangans, and he made a long journey by jeep and on foot across Palawan Island to see the Batak and Bangwa peoples. He was best man at the wedding of a fifteen-year-old bride and groom, for which he stumped up the bride price of thirty pesos. The chief gave him a farewell gift of a strip of wood on which he wrote in his native script:

> We understand you are a good airplane pilot. We are grateful that you are able to visit our island of Palawan. We would appreciate it if you could teach us to fly, so we can visit your island some day.

As a result of these trips he became a friend and associate of an extraordinary young Filipino politician named Manuel Elizalde, Jr., a showy member of President Ferdinand Marcos's Cabinet who had decided to make a career out of protecting primitive peoples. Elizalde had once been known in a lot of night clubs and bordellos around the world as a drunken playboy, and he had been burning the candle at both ends and the middle ever since leaving Harvard. But then suddenly he went to a clinic and dried out, and abandoned booze and women for politics and conservation. Marcos had taken him into his administration and put him in charge of tribal minorities; and when Lindbergh came into Manila after the tamarau trip, the President introduced the two men. Elizalde had lost none of his old machismo, and he and Lindbergh were as unalike as an orchid and a daisy, but beneath the younger man's flamboyant manner the American sensed a sincere dedication to his job. After a few meetings with him, he consented to become a member of the committee of an organization which Elizalde had started for ensuring the survival of endangered tribes, called Panamin (Private Association for National Minorities). It was, as the name implies, backed by private donations, and Lindbergh made his own contribution.

By 1972 Panamin's main concern was saving the Tasadays from civilization.

The Tasadays had been discovered in the jungles of Mindanao Island several years earlier by a native hunter, who saw some footprints in the forest, followed them, and found three tiny men digging for roots. He made friends with them, and they took him back with them to their community. The Tasadays were naked except for a genital pouch made of leaves. They did not hunt nor cultivate the land, but lived on roots, grubs, dead animals, or frogs and crabs they fished in the rivers. They had no cloth, skins, metal, or pots, and made fire by spinning a wooden drill until it created sparks. They had crude stone tools, they swung through the trees like miniature Tarzans, and they lived in caves high up in steep cliffs reachable only by climbing tall trees and leaping into the entrance.

The Tasadays had no history, no horizons beyond the trees a few hundred yards away, no religion. Most remarkable and rewarding of all —especially in an island where fighting, bloodshed, pain, and cruelty are rampant—they had no words for war, enemy, murder, or even for indicating that someone is bad. They were a smiling and peaceable tribe which had been separated from outside influences possibly since the Stone Age and certainly for countless centuries.

But, as Elizalde explained to Lindbergh in the fall of 1971, the world was now threatening to move in on them.

Lindbergh knew what could happen to them in that case. Killing is practically a Filipino national pastime, but on Mindanao it is an industry. In the small towns there are more murderers, thieves, escaped prisoners, desperate outlaws, to the square yard than anywhere else in the republic, which is saying something. Armed gangs roam the hills, rustling cattle, raiding tribes and villages, kidnaping and raping women. Ranchers, lumberjacks, entrepreneurs, greedy for land, send mercenaries into the tribal areas to kill and torture until the tribesmen retreat and leave the territory to them, after which they move in to batter down the trees and level the land.

Lindbergh had had his own taste of the savagery of the terrain only a few months back, when visiting another area of the island with Elizalde. Resentment against the Filipino minister was bitter because he was impeding "progress" by protecting the tribes and their territory. One village mayor with ambitions for his region set a hundred-man ambush for the Elizalde-Lindbergh convoy as it came through. They emerged unscathed, but as Lindbergh remarked afterward, "just one shot could have triggered a blood bath."

If the Gentle Tasadays, as John Nance has called them, were to be saved from murder, rape, and dispersal (or from the more peaceful but no less pernicious intrusions of modern civilization), something had to be done quickly, because there were reports that gunmen were filtering through the rain forests and that meant the bulldozers could not be far behind.

Lindbergh agreed to accompany Elizalde on an expedition to Tasaday country, when they could decide how best to protect these peaceable relics from man's ancient past.

Toward the end of March 1972, an advance party made its way through the forest to the area where the Tasadays were living. It had been decided (in the face of Lindbergh's skepticism) that the best way to bring in the expedition was by helicopter. There were no clearings in which one could possibly land, so a small platform of wood and rope was constructed between trees one hundred feet high amid their topmost branches. Members of the party would either jump out of the hovering copter or be lowered by rope onto the platform.

For those who came in on the first flight (and they were young men) it was a difficult operation, because there was a jump of at least five feet to be made, and the platform swayed violently under the copter's downdraft.

They held their breath when Lindbergh's flight came in. A wind was already swaying the treetops, and the copter's downdraft set the platform rolling as if it were a rectangle of water with waves coming in. The familiar white hair and ruddy face appeared in the door, glanced down at the platform—which looked as small as a Ping-Pong table from above—at the green abyss below it, grimaced, and then Lindbergh jumped. As the copter pulled away he rocked for a moment on his feet, and then grinned with relief as hands reached out to steady him.

"Manda," he said to Manuel Elizalde shortly afterward, when he reached camp, "you've outdone yourself. That landing in the treetops was spectacular, just spectacular. It's a masterful piece of carpentry." He laughed and then added: "But I can't say I'd want to jump into it every day. Once is enough—but it was marvelous."

It was hard to believe he was seventy years old. He climbed the formidable cliff which lay between the green valley and the caves where the Tasadays lived, and showed few signs of fatigue. He was not fazed by rain, or heat, or by the leeches which attacked exposed parts of his arms and neck, simply borrowing a cigarette from Elizalde and burning them off. He was delighted with the Tasadays and pleased when they snuggled against him in sheer affection, or rode on his tall shoulders, or offered him live grubs as sweetmeats. He chewed on them solemnly and said to his fellow members of the expedition:

"Not too bad . . . like an oyster, a very tough oyster."

There was no doubt at all in his mind that these were a genuine Stone Age people, straight descendants of the original cavemen, and the only thing that puzzled him was why and how they had stayed this way, why there was no adventurous spirit among them who had insisted that they move a little beyond their caves and find out what was on the other side of the mountain. They just never had anyone among them with sufficient intellect to do so, and that had been their salvation.

"The rise of intellect has coincided with the decline of natural life," he told his companions, back on a now favorite subject. The human intellect's craving for adventure, its appetite for developing technology, had started man's decline toward the insatiable demands of commercialization and the inevitable pollution which had followed, he maintained, and was now in process of destroying the good things of the earth.

"And, in simple terms," he said, "this is the result of having stepped from where these people are now. . . . Now they have bitten the apple. There's no turning back, but great care can be taken in seeing that the Tasaday are not destroyed or allowed to destroy themselves." He did not add, but his listeners could hear his unspoken words: "As we are destroying ourselves."

He came out of the tent where he was sleeping one morning, brushed down the slacks and shirt in which he had lain, and set off for a walk through the forest. He was enchanted by the magic of the dawn, but when he looked around he saw that already the expedition had left traces of itself everywhere, in empty tins, discarded packages, the detritus of technological civilization.

"Man is the dirtiest creature on earth," he said. "I've always said that. Seen it everywhere. And now in this forest."

The Tasadays were a friendly tribe, and it took them only seven days to accept the expedition as friends and protectors. Soon they gave all the members nicknames (they called Lindbergh Kakay Shalo), and laughed, played with, and embraced them. Talks went on long into the night as to the best way of saving them from the encroachment of civilization. A radio call informed them an NBC crew had arrived in Manila and wanted to film the Stone Age people. Lindbergh was against it at first, instinctively cringing at the thought of all that publicity, unpleasant for him, dangerous for the Tasadays; and then he remembered that this was different, this was for a cause. He changed his mind and began urging Elizalde to get all the publicity he possibly could, but at a price. Make the *National Geographic* pay for being allowed to do a documentary and an article for their magazine. Allow NBC to come in to make a short sequence, but charge them high for it. This thing was worth hundreds of thousands of dollars, and it would all go into Panamin's coffers to help on the good work of protecting the Tasadays and others.

He was wearing a straw hat a tribesman had made for him and a bush shirt, and as the word "money" continually rolled off his lips he sounded like any old American salesman in the market place.

"I don't know, Charles," Elizalde kept saying, "I mean, wouldn't it look mercenary? You know, like we were using these people, or selling them?"

Lindbergh vigorously shook his head. No, he didn't think it mercenary. Many important organizations raised funds this way.

The NBC team flew in for a short visit, and they brought a sunshine crew with them whose members became immediately popular with the Tasadays. Not as popular as Lindbergh, though, who had had an inspiration, dug into his pack, and produced a magnet for one of the tribesmen, who went around attracting metal filings from rocks, but burst into tears when it wouldn't pull out leeches. Lindbergh took him in his arms and comforted him.

Something went wrong with the expedition's copter ("Our bird is sick," they told the Tasadays) and the company had to be flown out by a giant ship sent out from the USAAF base at Clark Field. The story got into the papers that Lindbergh had been "rescued" from the jungle and snatched out of terrible danger. That and prior publicity about the Tasadays sent the story all over the world. Five days after they all reached Manila (on April 6, 1972), President Marcos saw Elizalde and Lindbergh and afterward announced that 46,299 acres of Tasaday country was henceforward to be a reserve, banned from outside exploitation, entry, sale, or lease.

Critics of Marcos's regime criticized the proclamation (the whole story of the Tasadays, in fact) as a stunt to promote the President and Elizalde and win them elections. Lindbergh was angry. One night he was at an embassy dinner in Manila when he overheard a diplomat saying: "They're just ordinary little tribesmen, like thousands of others. But they're useful tools, my dear, for the President. If pygmies will bring him votes, he'll give them pygmies."

Lindbergh rounded on him, his eyes blazing with fury. "This is a clean story, and a heartening one," he said. "How dare you dirty it up with your snide remarks!"

He went back to the Tasadays for a second visit that May, and later helped to organize an exhibition about them at the Smithsonian, when Elizalde came over and spoke at the opening ceremony.

When he left the Tasadays in May 1972, he told one of them, an exuberant bachelor named Balayim:

"I will come back. I will always come back."

The Tasaday nodded, but there were tears in his eyes as he hugged the tall American for the last time. They all came to see him off.

He told Elizalde, too, when he was at the Smithsonian, that he would come back, and he kept in contact with him about Panamin. But somehow, for one reason or another, he did not come back, either to the Tasadays or to the Philippines.

It had been a rewarding experience, but it had also been his last great adventure.

CHAPTER

TWENTY-NINE

EAGLE'S NEST

In the fall of 1972, the Lindberghs' good friend, William Benton, president of the Encyclopaedia Britannica,* wrote to George Kennan and Bruce Gould to say he had just heard "with astonishment" that neither of his friends was a member of the National Institute of Arts and Letters. He thought this should be remedied immediately.

The Lindberghs heard about it, and both protested. Anne firmly declared that "I have never considered myself a writer in the way that most members of literary societies" consider themselves to be, but simply "a woman who has had an extraordinary life and have written in an attempt to understand it."

Charles Lindbergh pleaded with Benton not to get him involved in "another membership" because he just wanted "to live and work quietly, and have more time for reading and research and my family and friends." He insisted that he didn't want any more memberships, awards, regardless of how prestigious they were. He said he hoped "never again to have to attend a formal lunch or ceremony," and asked to be allowed to shell off social life and literary gatherings so that he could concentrate on his real interests. "It is just too easy to become submerged in the demands of modern life. I am determined not to do so."†

It was absurd of him to say that he wanted to "live and work quietly," of course, because he was not that sort of a man. By the time he wrote the letter to Benton, he had already been round the world six times that year. He was rarely at home in Connecticut for more than a

* He kept Lindbergh supplied with free copies of the new editions as they came out.
† Letter to William Benton, November 17, 1972.

week, but he caught up with Anne at Land's ranch in Montana, Jon's house on Puget Sound, or with his daughters at the chalet overlooking Lake Geneva.

He was gathering together the strands of his memories with the idea of writing his autobiography, and in going over old letters and old memories, he was stricken with one regret. His old friend Harry Guggenheim had died in 1971, and he hadn't been there. It troubled him. Guggenheim for many years had been his benefactor and good counselor, and they had never quite made up their differences over his stance during World War II. So when he got a letter from Nassau County (Long Island) authorities, asking a favor of him, he replied at once. Falaise, the Guggenheim estate on the North Shore, had been left to the county in Harry's will and was being turned into a park and museum. Charles Lindbergh said that he and Anne would be delighted to come along for the official opening.

It was a bright, sunny day in May, and quite a crowd of local politicians and landowners came along for the ceremony. There had been no prior announcement that Lindbergh was coming, but word soon got around. Officials, however, scurried around asking photographers and newsmen to lay off, and visitors to let the Lindberghs wander freely. They set off by themselves, first into the house and up to their old room overlooking the Sound, where they found signed copies of *We* and *The Spirit of St. Louis,* dedicated to Harry, lying on the dresser. Then they came down and wandered into the grounds and across to the old landing field from which they had secretly flown in their courting days.

It was obviously a sentimental occasion for both of them, and quite a few eyes were dabbed around the luncheon table later when Charles rose to make an unscheduled speech, and spoke warmly in praise of his old friend.

A few years earlier, Helen and William Benton had invited the Lindberghs to join them on their yacht for a Mediterranean cruise of the Greek islands and Turkey, but Anne had written their regrets. She told them that she and Charles were now building a small, simple house on a deserted part of Maui, in the Hawaiian Islands, and at the time the cruise was due to take place they would have to be there to make vital decisions, since they were eager to have their new home finished.

It was Sam Pryor, a friend from Pan Am, who had introduced Charles Lindbergh to the island of Maui. It is one of the smaller islands, and part of it has been turned into the Haleakala National Park. Lindbergh thought it was one of the most beautiful places he had ever seen. "There is nothing quite comparable when you think of waterfalls, natural swimming pools, and the ocean beyond," he said. When Pryor, who owned a large tract of land, offered to sell him four acres of forest, cliffs, and seashore, all of it remote and inaccessible, he accepted at once. Then he brought Anne to see it, and she fell in love at first sight. So they began to build a simple home of the kind she had conjured up in *Gift from the Sea,* a house with no modern amenities to it, no electric light, no air conditioning, a place where you could get back to the fundamentals of living and the closeness to nature and "wildness" which was now beginning to absorb her, too.

To begin with, they spent periods of six to eight weeks there every year, in between their other preoccupations. But as time went on, they planned to retreat there more and more for longer and longer. It was both a haven and a nest, and they had never felt safer or closer to each other than when they were there together.

In some ways, 1973 was the crucial year. It was as if Charles Lindbergh sensed that the sap was running out of him. He began writing to old friends he hadn't seen since before World War II, and with some of them he arranged meetings. No word was spoken about past differences, but it was obvious he was making a gesture of reconciliation toward those who had been hurt by his wartime opinions. To one Englishman whom he hadn't seen since 1941, who had been deeply hurt by his shabby remarks about his country and countrymen, he said:

"Everybody used to call me Silent Slim, but I guess there were times when I said a damn sight too much for my own good. Just a Hindleg Higginbottom, that was me."‡

The appearance at Falaise was not his only reaching back into the past. He went out to Little Falls, too, to open a new reception and lecture hall which had been built for visitors, beside his old home on the banks of the Mississippi. He stood on the stoop of the house and made an eloquent plea for the preservation of the flora and fauna of the United States.

"Few men have seen with their own eyes, as I have in the past fifty years," he said, "how serious is the breakdown of America's land surface. I have seen fencing pushing westward, enclosing once open land. I have seen bird and animal life disappear. I have seen towns and cities spring up where there were none before. Forest land converted into agriculture, farm land in turn become suburban subdivisions, mountains slashed through with power lines and superhighways, rivers and lakes

‡ A reference to a character in Kipling who talked the hind leg off a donkey.

fouled by pollution, the skies over even small towns hazed by smog—all evidence of human thoughtlessness about their environment. But there is still hope, if we take measures in time. The situation in many cases is reversible."

Several times that year he came to Washington and slipped into the Smithsonian Institution. It so happened that he had written the introduction to a book called *Carrying the Fire*, by Michael Collins, the astronaut, whose exploits in space he and Anne had followed from Cape Kennedy.

"You have experienced an aloneness unknown to man before," he wrote of Collins. "I believe you will find that it lets you think and sense with greater clarity."

Now Collins, working in the museum, caught sight of Lindbergh there. He would slip into the hall and hover behind a showcase, where visitors would not notice him, and then stare for minutes at a time at the *Spirit of St. Louis* hanging above him in the air. Collins wondered what he was thinking, but out of respect for the man's privacy did not go over and make himself known.

In the fall of 1973, Lindbergh, whose only illness had been chicken pox, came back from a trip to Asia and was bedded with a fever and what seemed to be a heat rash. The rash would not go away and the fever mounted. Doctors told him he had shingles. It was extremely painful, and, like most people who have never been ill, he took it badly and fretted and complained of his enforced inactivity. For the first time in his life, he lost his huge appetite and would not eat. Anne Lindbergh coaxed him with spoonfuls of porridge and ice cream, but by the beginning of 1974 his weight was down by twenty-four pounds and he looked skinny.

He rallied in the spring and put on weight, and no one but Anne and the doctors would have guessed that there was anything wrong with him. In March 1974 he resigned from the board of directors of Pan American Airways, told the World Wild Life Fund and associate organizations not to count on too many trips from him for the time being, and flew out to Maui to recuperate. He had a date in Brunei that year with Tom Harrisson, and wrote to tell the Englishman he would not be able to make it. Harrisson wrote back to express his regrets and sympathy.

"It's frustrating when illness or age get in one's way, isn't it?" he wrote. "I lie awake thinking of the clues I may have missed."

That summer, back in Darien, he began to cough and sweat, and came down with what was officially announced as a case of pneumonia. Those who knew him guessed that it was something quite different.

When his temperature rose to 104° he was taken from Darien to Columbia Presbyterian Hospital in New York, and a couple of weeks later his doctors told him what was really the matter with him. He had an advanced case of lymphatic cancer, and they did not give him long to live.

He was glad to know. He had never been afraid of death. He had faced it often enough in his lifetime to come to accept its inevitability. Except that it did get harder to bear, the older you got, especially if you had to lie there and wait for it.

He had always known how he wanted to die.

"Any coward can sit in his home and criticize a pilot for flying into a mountain in fog," he had once written. "But I would rather, by far, die on a mountainside than in bed. . . . What kind of a man would live where there is no daring? And is life so dear that we should blame men for dying in adventure? Is there a better way to die?"

Unfortunately, the hero's death he would have wished was beyond his strength. His body was no longer capable of taking up a plane and flying it into a mountainside, or out to sea until the gasoline ran out. All he had the strength to do was tell Anne and the doctors that he refused to die in a hospital bed, and that they must take him at once to Maui.

He was flown there in conditions of great secrecy on August 17, 1974, and like the methodical man that he was, he spent the last days of his life arranging his writings,* going over his will, and working out details of his death and funeral. And that, of course, was logical, since this was his last journey, and he was in no mood to make it without adequate preparation.

He had already said good-by to his two daughters. He spoke on the telephone to his three sons, and one of them, Land, came over from Montana to join him and his mother on the flight to Hawaii. For the next ten days, in between pain and coma, and moments in the sun staring at the birds and the crashing sea, he planned what he would wear for the burial (a simple drill shirt and pants) and what would be said and sung at the funeral.

He was anxious not to linger too long. Maybe he remembered how thoughtful his shepherd dog, Thor, had been after he had dug his grave on the hillside—dying next morning so that his efforts would not be wasted. He knew that local cowboys had already made him a coffin of plain eucalyptus wood. He knew that his burial site had been picked in the churchyard at Hana. He knew that a stateside clergyman from

---

* He left behind a thousand-page, so far unpublished memoir called *An Autobiography of Values*.

Burlingame, California (the Reverend John Tincher), had been told to stand by. He must not keep them waiting too long.

Accordingly, when all his instructions had been noted down, and his last farewell said to his beloved wife, he relapsed into a coma on the evening of August 25, 1974. Next morning, at 7:15, he took off on his final flight.

He had made a lot of mistakes in his lifetime, but not on the journeys he had made into the unknown. No word came of his safe arrival. But those who knew how carefully he prepared all his flights were pretty certain that he made it.

SOURCE NOTES

Any writer engaged on research into the life of a contemporary figure is naturally eager to consult not only documents and letters in archives or private possession in the countries his subject has visited, but also to record how his friends, acquaintances, and associates saw him. In the case of Charles Lindbergh, this is not so simple as it sounds. One swiftly discovers that although many of them are quite willing to talk about him, most are reluctant to have any of their remarks directly attributable to them. This is due to the danger, as they see it, of losing Lindbergh's friendship and respect when he was still alive, and that of his family since his death.

One close connection of Lindbergh put it this way:

"You ask me about Charles's friends. To be a friend of his, you could never afford to offend him or make a mistake with regard to him. I consider a friend as someone who can do or say something you hate, or even break a confidence about you, and you forgive him. But not Charles. Transgress one of his rules, and you were out. Talk about him to strangers, and you ceased to be his friend. Anne nowadays seems to follow the same rules, and has indicated that she will take it ill if anyone in her circle says anything. That's why you don't get many friends saying anything about either of them. Except anonymously, of course."

He went on to tell a story about Lillian Gish, the old-time silent film star who once sat on the America First Committee with Charles Lindbergh and got to know him and his wife well. Asked at a film party one night what she thought about Anne Lindbergh, she gushed:

"Oh, isn't she a wonderful person!" And then added in sudden panic: "But please, please, for heaven's sake don't quote me!"

With the exception of his mother and his wife, Charles Lindbergh had no women friends, but several old school and college mates of Anne's have known him since the days he was courting her in the 1920s, and some have been close observers during the great crises through which the couple has passed. They have much to tell, but except where they have given me specific permission to do so, I have refrained from using their names. Some of them obviously regret this.

"You know," said one of them, "it got to be a sort of sickness, this fear of publicity. I'm told that one night the Lindberghs and friends went out to dinner in Paris, and this girl came round doing sketches of the folks at the tables. Charles took one look at her and insisted that they leave. Luckily, they hadn't ordered, but one member of the party couldn't help saying: 'The kid was only trying to earn a few francs. What harm was she doing?' Charles said: 'She might have drawn us and sold the drawing to the newspapers.' This was 1971 and the kid wouldn't have known who he was even if he had told her. And which newspaper would have bought it, anyway? But he was still obsessed by intruders and by the press—and so was Anne."

As I have indicated in the Prologue to this book, it is the culmination of practically a lifetime of Lindbergh watching, and there are few places in the world where I haven't turned up a trace of him, a plaque, a record, a letter, a landing place, or a memory. There follows below a list, chapter by chapter, of the documents or books consulted, the memories culled, the places visited, the people to whom I have talked.

Prologue

It was during my visits to his family home in England (Sissinghurst Castle, Kent) that Mr. Nigel Nicolson provided me with the letters with which the Prologue primarily deals. Nicolson is, of course, editor of the journals and correspondence of both his parents, Sir Harold Nicolson and Vita Sackville-West, from which three volumes have so far emerged: *Diaries and Letters, 1930–39* (New York: Atheneum; London: Collins, 1966), *The War Years, 1939–45*, and *Portrait of a Marriage*. It is in the first of these three that Sir Harold wrote about his encounters with the Lindberghs both while he was writing the biography of Anne Lindbergh's father, Dwight Morrow, and later, when they rented his cottage, Long Barn, after they had fled from America to England. The correspondence which resulted between Charles Lindbergh and Nigel Nicolson after these extracts were published has been cut in certain places at the request of Mr. Nicolson, and Lindbergh's letters suppressed at the request of Mrs. Anne Lindbergh, but I think the flavor of the encounter has been retained.

The comments made by Anne Lindbergh about her husband's ubiquity ("someone suggested I should keep in touch with him by satellite") are described in the text as having been written to "a friend," and Charles Lindbergh once said that any story or comment about his family quoting "a friend" was usually "an unmitigated lie." There seems no harm in revealing that in this case "a friend" was the late Senator William Benton, with whom both Anne and Charles kept up a lively correspondence. Helen and Bill Benton became good friends with the Lindberghs when they all campaigned to keep the United States out of World War II. Benton considered Anne Lindbergh one of America's greatest writers ("She writes prose poetry," he told me during a conversation a few years ago), and he urged every professor of English he knew to include her works in their programs on American literature. As a member of the board of several universities and president of the Encyclopaedia Britannica he was not without his influence. Anne Lindbergh was somewhat embarrassed by this, especially his high opinion of her as a poet. She thought much of her own work was sentimental. "Sentimentality is natural to adolescence," she once told him, "and I had a phenomenally long one!" Benton kept Charles Lindbergh supplied with free copies of the encyclopaedia and was delighted when his friend confessed that he found parts of it "quite a bit over my head." The letter in which this remark was made so tickled Benton that he told Mary Gardner, his secretary, to have it framed. "That's a keepsake for posterity," he said.

Chapter One
Huckleberry Swede

The description of Charles Lindbergh's visit to his old home at Little Falls, Minnesota, was recounted by John T. Rivard, district manager of the Historic Sites Division of the Minnesota Historical Society, during one of my visits to Little Falls. Alden Whitman, who was with Lindbergh on the 1971 trip, also wrote an account of it in the *New York Times Magazine* for May 23, 1971. The new Interpretive Center which has now been opened on the banks of the Mississippi not many yards away from the Lindbergh house contains a library, charts, photographs, and a slide show, all devoted to a detailed documentation of Charles Lindbergh's ancestry, background, and flying career, and the house itself has been pretty well arranged so that it looks, inside, at least, as he must have known it during his childhood and early youth. The effectiveness of the reconstruction owes much to the devoted work of Russell W. Fridley, director of the Minnesota Historical Society, and it was he who persuaded Lindbergh to co-operate, a sure guarantee of its authenticity. Fridley is also responsible for persuading Charles Lindbergh to conjure back his own memories of life on the Little Falls farm, with the result that he wrote Fridley a remarkable series of evocative letters which do much to bring back the Minnesota world of 1910–20. The letters came from such disparate places as the Army and Navy Club in Manila, an airstrip in Northern Luzon, a British club in Hong Kong, an aircraft office in Frankfurt, the floor of the elevator hall in the office of Harcourt Brace Jovanovich in New York, and on an inaugural flight by Pan Am's new 747 between New York and London. (He stopped over for three and a half hours and came back by the next flight.) The letters have now been published in *Boyhood on the Upper Mississippi: A Reminiscent Letter*, by Charles A. Lindbergh (St. Paul: Minnesota Historical Society, 1972), and they are recommended reading for those who would like to savor what life was like in Minnesota when Lindbergh was young.

For details of the Lindbergh family background, I have had consulted the Family Papers in the Minnesota Historical Society, St. Paul, and found most useful and informative *The Lindberghs*, by Lynn and Dora B. Haines (New York: Vanguard, 1931), and *The Lindberghs: The Story of a Distinguished Family* (New York: International Press, 1935). Other useful books were *Minnesota: History of a State*, by Theodore C. Blegen (Minneapolis, 1963), and *A History of Minnesota*, 4 vols. (Minneapolis: University of Minnesota, 1921–32).

Chapter Two
Down on the Farm

Most if not all of Evangeline Land Lindbergh's contemporaries in Little Falls are now dead, but a number of their offspring are still around, and they mention that, after Charles became famous in 1927, their parents often told reporters and wandering magazine writers that she was "a gracious and neighborly lady" but were less complimentary among themselves. She figures in many of the clippings in the files of the Minneapolis *Tribune*, the St. Louis *Globe-Democrat*, and the Detroit *Free Press* (Detroit was her home town), and the Little Falls storekeeper, Martin Engstrom, is often quoted in stories about her; in practically every Little Falls story about Charles, too, for that matter. The consensus of Little Falls opinion seems to be that she was a proud, beautiful, forthright, and sometimes arrogant woman with a definite sense of her own superiority, particularly over the "Swede farmers," as she called them, who were her neighbors. Charles Lindbergh's feelings toward her are made clear in his reminiscent letters, and his protective instincts toward her are implicit in his description of the shooting incidents at the farm which he describes in *Boyhood on the Upper Mississippi*. When Bruce L. Larson was writing a life of his father, he asked Charles about his mother and he described her as "a woman of rapidly changing moods" whose "emotions were highly charged and often unpredictable, giving her a temperament not well suited to that of her husband." Lindbergh told Larson that it was for this reason, rather than the difference in their ages, or the collapse of his father's political career, which caused his parents to separate. "Their relationship was a tragic situation," he said, and implicit in his words are hints of his own emotional injuries suffered as a result of the strained relationship. See *Lindbergh of Minnesota: A Political Biography*, by Bruce L. Larson (New York: Harcourt Brace Jovanovich, 1971.)

For the picture of Charles Lindbergh's father I have had access to the Family Papers, and a selection of documents and books on the period, including *Minnesota Biographies* (St. Paul, 1912); *Midwestern Progressive Politics: A Historical Study of Its Origins and Developments, 1870–1958*, by Russell B. Nye (New York: Harper & Row, 1965); *Minnesota in the War with Germany*, by Franklin F. Holbrook and Livia Appel (St. Paul, 1928); *Why Is Your Country at War and What Happens to You After the War*, by Charles A. Lindbergh, Sr. (Washington, D.C., 1917); *Banking and Currency and the Money Trust*, by Charles A. Lindbergh, Sr. (Washington, D.C., 1913), both the latter books in the National Archives; *The Congressional Record* (64th Congress); and *The Progressive Era in Minnesota, 1899–1918*, by Carl H. Chrislock (St. Paul, 1971).

Lindbergh's own reminiscent letters to the Minnesota Historical Society and the documents and photographs in the Interpretive Center at Little Falls are still the best source for the details of his own life on the farm, his travels by car through the Minnesota backwoods with his father during his political campaigns, and his adventurous drive with his mother to California.

Chapter Three
Barnstorming

Charles Lindbergh's stay at the University of Wisconsin before he dropped out in 1921 has been admirably documented by Kenneth S.

Davis in *The Hero* (Garden City: Doubleday, 1959). Davis had the opportunity of talking to one of Lindbergh's college friends, Delos Dudley, and to the widow of another, Mrs. Richard (Eunice Rogers) Plummer, and files of the Madison (Wis.) *Capital Times*, the *Wisconsin State Journal* (Wisconsin Historical Society), and those of the Wisconsin University *Daily Cardinal* (in the university library) give the flavor of student life at the time. It was Delos Dudley who recalled Lindbergh's breakneck motorbike exploits, and two of his professors, R. F. Brosius and James Hyland, who described his work progress, his attitudes, and the circumstances of his dropping out. His mother's remarks when he told her he was leaving are to be found in Lindbergh's book *The Spirit of St. Louis* (New York: Scribner's, 1953), as are his father's attitudes and warnings against a flying career.

Charles Lindbergh's felicitous phrases about a newcomer's reaction to flying ("The novice has a poet's eye," etc.) are taken from his book *The Spirit of St. Louis*. He has written himself at considerable length about these early days of learning to fly, and of the setbacks he encountered while being tutored by his first flying instructor, Ira Biffle. But I have also consulted the New York *Times* files for the reaction of others who were there when it was happening, particularly a story from Lincoln, Nebraska, on May 21, 1927, in which Ray Page, who was then president of the Nebraska Aircraft Corporation, described his reactions to young Lindbergh's arrival and his difficulty in prizing lessons out of Biffle. The New York *Times* reported on March 30, 1934, that Biffle was lying near death in Chicago and without funds, and that Lindbergh (who bore him no grudge for the trouble he caused him) had sent him a fifty-dollar check and a note to the hospital doctor: "Please accept this contribution to the fund being raised for Biffle. Also tell him I'm extremely sorry to hear he is not well and that I hope he makes a fast recovery." Both Lindbergh and Ray Page have provided details of how the would-be flier eventually teamed up with Erold Bahl.

Chapter Four
Catharsis by Rip Cord

I flew over Lincoln, Nebraska, in a small plane to get some idea of how it might have looked to Charles Lindbergh when he took his first flight on April 9, 1922, but I did not go so far as to bale out in order to imitate his first parachute jump. It was an experience which had a tremendous emotional impact upon him, and he devoted quite a lot of space to it in both his books, *We* (New York: Putnam's, 1927) and

The Spirit of St. Louis. Ray Page and Harlan (Bud) Gurney have also talked about it, and Gurney said that when Lindbergh landed safely after showing every sign of roman-candling into the ground, he brushed a tear out of his eye, because he thought he was going to lose a kid about whom he already felt like a brother.

I tried to trace the professional parachutists, Kathryn and Charlie Hardin, having heard that Kathryn was almost certainly alive. There was a story that she had lost the sight of one eye, the eyeball having flooded with blood from the shock of too many stand-up landings, and killed the optic nerve. She was rumored to be in Chicago, but I failed to find her. The photographs of her taken at the time Lindbergh was using the parachutes she folded for him show her as a most fetching young woman, and it might have been interesting to get her reactions to the young flier, who, it appears, took absolutely no notice of her whatsoever.

To get some impression of what barnstorming across the Southwest of the United States was like in the early 1920s, my companion and I did some thousands of miles of small-plane flying through Minnesota, Kansas, Nebraska, and Missouri, and though one could see what Lindbergh meant when he talked about the "urban blight" spreading across the United States, there were still thousands of small towns and millions of square miles of open countryside to enable us to imagine that we were in a Jenny hedgehopping from state fair to state fair. At one point, near Brainerd, in Minnesota, we even came low enough to see from a housewife's washing which way the wind would be blowing when we landed, as Lindbergh often did.

The story of Fred A. Fair's encounter with the young barnstormer in Boulder, Colorado, comes from the Colorado Railroads Museum, Golden, Colorado (director: Bob Richardson).

The nine hundred dollars which Charles Lindbergh borrowed from the Little Falls branch of the People's National Bank of Shakopee, Minnesota, with which to buy his first Jenny remained outstanding until after he came back from his transatlantic flight. He then wrote to the cashier asking him to send the note to his backers in St. Louis. He had, in fact, paid off fifty dollars of the debt, but never earned enough from his barnstorming and wing-walking to stump up the remainder plus interest.

The description of Charles's flight with his father during the political campaign of 1923, and the crash on June 8, is told in some detail by Bruce L. Larson in his biography of the elder Lindbergh (op. cit.). The circumstances in which Lindbergh, Sr., died and the scattering of his ashes were described by his daughter, Eva, in interviews she gave after

Charles's transatlantic flight. Eva was born to Lindbergh, Sr.'s, first wife and was always the one closest to her father. In 1916 she married a young newspaperman, George Christie, and between them they founded the Red Lake Falls *Gazette*.

Chapter Five
Fireworks

Not many of the pilots who knew Charles Lindbergh in his barn-storming days are still around, but one of them is Bud Gurney, a life-time friend, who does not remember him keeping a list of "character factors" by which to live, but was only too well aware of the fact that his friend was guided by the most puritanical principles. "He could make you feel mighty guilty after the third beer," he said ruefully, "and didn't approve at all of girl-chasing, which was something every other youngster around indulged in. On the other hand, he was always a great one for risqué jokes, and some of them he told came quite close to the bone."

The remarks he made about his "character factors" were given in an interview he granted in London in 1927 after he came over from Paris on the tour which followed his transatlantic flight. The interview was apparently originally given to a writer from *Everybody's Weekly*, but the original cannot be checked because some of the early files of this magazine were destroyed in the bombing of London in World War II.

Charles Lindbergh's journey across the Southwest on a barnstorming trip with his mother was described by her in letters to Eva Lindbergh Christie, her stepdaughter. It is also mentioned in *The Spirit of St. Louis*. Both Bud Gurney and the late Marvin Northrop talked about his visit to the International Air Races at Lambert Field, St. Louis, and Northrop wrote an article about "the lonely kid" in *Western Flying* (May 1937). Accounts of his experiences in the Army Air Force are to be found in *Swedes in America, 1638–1938* (New Haven: Yale University Press, 1938), by John Goldstrom, and the official reports of his collision are to be found in the Aeronautics Section of the Science and Technology Division of the Library of Congress. Philip R. Love, who was flying with the formation and later became a fellow pilot with Lindbergh on the airmail run, is quoted frequently in the files of the St. Louis *Globe-Democrat* and in Associated Press dispatches after 1927 about life in the Army and Lindbergh's predilection for practical joking. His officers' reports on his record as a flier and a person are to be found through the Military Section of the National Archives, and I would like to thank John Taylor for helping me to dig them out.

Chapter Six
Mail Run

The development of the airmail service in the United States is told in *Airways*, by H. L. Smith (New York: Knopf, 1942) but has never yet been adequately chronicled (a good subject, one would have thought, for a Ph.D. thesis). Charles Lindbergh's association with Bill and Frank Robertson in the service which they ran between Lambert Field, St. Louis, and Chicago in 1926 has been described by both brothers, by Red Love and Thomas P. (Nellie) Nelson, who flew with him, and by Lindbergh himself in *We* and *The Spirit of St. Louis*, but still lacks a historian who could bring all of it together and compare it with other services in other parts of the United States. On each flight which Lindbergh made it was necessary for him to write a log, and it is from these official reports that his parachute escapes are described. The reports were forwarded to the Post Office in Washington and are now in the National Archives. Love, Nelson, and Bud Gurney all tell their separate stories of Lindbergh's penchant for practical jokes. Gurney bears no grudge against his long-time friend that in giving him kerosene to drink he all but killed him.

Chapter Seven
Promotion

The files of American, British, and French newspapers for 1926 and 1927 carry running stories about the Raymond Orteig Prize, and in the Bibliothèque Nationale in Paris there are some interesting interviews with the French contenders, René Fonck, and Nungesser and Coli. In a statement to *Le Petit Parisien* Fonck refers to Lindbergh's entry as a "derisory" fact, and Nungesser, when told just before he and his fellow pilot took off that Lindbergh was flying in from California, told *Paris-Soir:* "Cable him to stay in St. Louis. We will tell him all about it when we come there on our tour."

In both *We* and *The Spirit of St. Louis*, Charles Lindbergh told his side of the story of how he got backers, plane, and his entry accepted, and of the trials and tribulations through which he went. His backers, particularly Harry Knight, have also told their all in a succession of interviews, and the St. Louis *Globe-Democrat* files are full of stories (though, amusingly enough, when I visited their offices in 1974, I found a surprising lack of enthusiasm among the editorial staff about their association, and a glazed look came into several reporters' eyes when I brought up the name Lindbergh). But the best way to follow the *Spirit of St. Louis* enterprise from conception to delivery is by visiting the Lindbergh Museum in the Jefferson Memorial in St. Louis. Checks, notes, letters, are to be found among the hundreds of gifts Lindbergh received after the flight was made, and they are the fascinating artifacts of a remarkable story.

The stories quoted of the misadventures of Lindbergh's rivals while he was overseeing the building of his plane in San Diego come from the Los Angeles *Times* and the New York *Times*. Donald Hall described how he designed the Ryan monoplane and sat in with Lindbergh while it was building, and Franklin Mahoney, president of Ryan aircraft, wrote a memorandum about the final tests. He also recounted the incident when they heard that Nungesser and Coli were on their way across the Atlantic, and all their efforts to be ready in time looked like being in vain. It is Lindbergh's own personal account of all this—his bitterness over his dealings with Levine, his resentment at his rejection by the St. Louis *Post-Dispatch*, a newspaper he admired, his desperate race to be in New York before someone won the Orteig Prize before him, his quiet confidence that he would make it, providing he was ever allowed to take off—which colors and provides the drama for this period.

On my third visit to the Lindbergh Museum in the Jefferson Memorial, St. Louis, there was a Christmas sale going on in the basement where the exhibits were housed, which made concentration difficult. At one moment I gave up and went across to a table where a woman was selling dolls, and she said: "I saw you looking at the Lindbergh show. Isn't it something? You know, I once saw Lindbergh himself come in to see it. He was with Miss Beauregard." (Miss Beauregard was one of the curators and arranged the Lindbergh exhibit.) "I rushed out and told my driver to get downtown fast and buy a copy of *The Spirit of St. Louis* and get it back to me before Lindbergh left. He made it in time, and I went up to them, said hello to Miss Beauregard, and then asked him to sign his book for me. He asked me if I'd read it and when I confessed I hadn't, he said: 'You give it to Miss Beauregard when you have, and she'll send it on to me and I'll sign it for you.'" She paused and then giggled. "You know, I forgot all about it. I've never got around to reading it yet."

Chapter Eight
The Flying Fool

For the atmosphere of huckstering, mounting hysteria, and the day-by-day, hour-by-hour, minute-by-minute accounts of what happened up to 7:45 A.M. on May 20, 1927, when Charles Lindbergh took off for Paris, I have relied upon the files of the New York *Times*, the New York *Herald Tribune*, the New York *Daily News*, the New York *Daily Mirror*, magazine accounts, and recollections written later by those who were there in the form of articles or books. It is nearly fifty years ago, and participants are now pretty thin on the ground, and their memories are either vague or colored by what they have read or heard since. Dick Blythe's experiences were later recorded by his colleague and associate Harry A. Bruno in an article for the *Saturday Evening Post*, "Lindbergh, the Famous Unknown" (October 21, 1933), and Ken Lane, an engineer for Wright, who was around most of the time, did a piece for the Wright Aeronautical Corporation's house journal, *Tradewinds*. Harry F. Guggenheim remembered his first encounter with Lindbergh just before the flight in his book *The Seven Skies* (New York: Putnam's, 1930). Lindbergh himself has a lot to say about these final waiting moments both in *We* and in *The Spirit of St. Louis*, and sometimes his accounts differ from those of others who were there at the same time. For instance, Lindbergh says he posted a friend outside his door in the hotel the final night to protect him from visitors, and that he came in and woke him up with a stupid question; whereas the friend in question, Lieutenant George Stumpf, always maintained that he was sleeping in the same room, woke up to find he was chewing something, and realized that Lindbergh, who was awake, had dropped a stick of chewing gum in his mouth. They went down into the lobby of the hotel together. There, according to the New York *Times*, Lindbergh's rivals (Chamberlain and Bertaud) were already in the lounge, studying maps, and still hoping to get Levine's permission to take off before Lindbergh.

Chapter Nine
The Flight

Anyone writing about Lindbergh's New York to Paris flight must inevitably rely upon his own accounts of it in *We* and *The Spirit of St. Louis*, because from the moment he took off until the moment he landed, he was the only one who was there. The account in *We* is quite evidently a rush job, and in fact the account of the actual flight takes up only fifteen out of more than two hundred pages, and lacks both zest and immediacy. On the other hand, *The Spirit of St. Louis* was over twenty years in the making, and in its scenes over the Atlantic it certainly makes you feel as if you were there. It is a masterly reconstruction, and not only shows how formidable was Lindbergh's memory, but how much the incidents on his flight burned their way into his brain.

For what was happening on the ground while he was flying I have gone to contemporary accounts in the files of American newspapers, including the Detroit *Free Press*, whose reporters were keeping tabs on Mrs. Evangeline Lindbergh while she waited to discover whether her son had landed. Of the general atmosphere of the time, and of the impact made by the flight on the public, I have used the impressions of newspapermen who were around at the time, like the late Heywood Broun and my neighbor in France, Paul Gallico, and writers like John O'Hara and Frederick Lewis Allen in *Only Yesterday* (New York: Harper, 1931).

Chapter Ten
Hero

I always remember a veteran American newspaperman telling me how he broke through the traffic jam and got to Le Bourget airfield in time to see Lindbergh land after his Atlantic flight. He put his girl friend in the back seat of his open tourer, stuffed a cushion up her skirt, told her to make as if she were writhing in pain, and then persuaded other cars to give way by shouting: *"Femme enceinte! Femme enceinte!"* ("Pregnant woman!"). So far as the French were concerned, even Lindbergh's imminent arrival didn't take precedence over a baby's, and they let him through.

The best stories of what it was like in Paris after the landing are told by Waverley Root, a well-known newspaperman, now retired and living in France, who was on the staff of the Paris edition of the Chicago *Tribune* at the time. B. J. Kosposth, city editor of the paper, a character who, Root says, "had a peculiar laugh midway between the whinny of a soprano horse and a short blast from a rusty machine gun," didn't believe that the "crazy fool" would make it, and left no real space in the paper to cover the story if he did, with the result that next morning the

Tribune in Paris was the only newspaper in the world to carry the news of Lindbergh's triumph under a measly two-column headline.

Root doesn't share Herrick's impression that Lindbergh was "normal and comfortable in every situation," and maintains that at every press conference the flier gave he was in the viselike grip of the ambassador and a representative of the Wright Aeronautical Corporation, either one of whom answered all questions Lindbergh was asked. The only time they were stumped was when Hank Wales, the chief Chicago *Tribune* correspondent in Paris, "speaking from the hole in the corner of his mouth where he usually kept his cigar," asked: "Say, Lindy, did you have a crapper in that plane?" Not even Lindbergh answered that one.

Ambassador Herrick's opinions about Lindbergh are taken from his dispatches to President Coolidge, subsequently published in *The Flight of Captain Charles A. Lindbergh from New York to Paris, May 20–21, as Compiled from the Official Records of the Department of State* (U. S. Government Printing Office, 1927). He was a genuine admirer and the feeling was mutual. The two became great friends, and the Lindberghs kept up a close relationship with the Herricks after the flier came back to America and got married.

The story of Lindbergh's encounter with King George V, and Lindbergh's own comments on it, comes from hitherto unpublished portions of the diaries of the late Sir Harold Nicolson, kindly passed on to me by his son and literary executor, Nigel Nicolson.

Accounts of the growing hysteria in the United States as the public awaited the hero's return are taken from contemporary newspaper reports, and the exchanges between Herrick and Coolidge from *The Flight of Captain Charles A. Lindbergh*. Harry Bruno in *Lindbergh, the Famous Unknown* tells the story of the offers which now came pouring in on the flier, and of Dick Blythe's arguments with Lindbergh about what he should wear when he came ashore from the *Memphis*. At Blythe's suggestion, Lindbergh had accepted an offer from Putnam to write a "quickie" book about his transatlantic trip and his early life, and a writer named Fitzhugh Green was commissioned to fill out the page length by describing the flier's triumphant reception in Paris, Brussels, London, Washington, New York, and St. Louis. (This book, subsequently titled *We*, had a foreword by Ambassador Herrick.) It is upon Green that I have based my account of Lindbergh's American tour, supplemented by contemporary newspaper accounts. The description of some of the gifts he and his mother received are based on my own examination of the exhibitions in the Jefferson Memorial. The verse comparing Lindbergh and his father was subsequently published in the Minneapolis *Tribune.*

Chapter Eleven
"Who? Little Me?"

On the other hand, the description in this chapter of the Lindbergh Museum at St. Louis comes from an unpublished letter written by the late Sir Harold Nicolson to his wife, Vita Sackville-West, and reproduced with the permission of Nigel Nicolson. Nicolson was on his way to Mexico with Mrs. Betty Morrow (he was still writing Dwight Morrow's biography at the time), and they had stopped off in St. Louis (uncoupling their private car from the southbound train) in order to see the exhibit.

My account of Harry Guggenheim's friendship with Lindbergh is based on Guggenheim's own (see *The Seven Skies*), records at Falaise, the family home (now a museum), and contemporary accounts. The description of Falaise itself is based on my own visits to the house at Sands Point, for the furnishings and surroundings have (under family supervision) been left pretty much as they were in the days when Lindbergh was first invited there. The only exception is a garish one. On the dressing table in the room which was, after his first visit, always regarded as the Lindbergh Bedroom, is a copy of the New York *Daily News* with the full front-page headline: LINDY DEAD. I don't think he would have liked that at all.

The names of those who attended the parties Guggenheim gave for Lindbergh come from the society-page columns of the New York *Times,* the New York *Herald Tribune,* and other papers.

Dwight Morrow's family background and his own career are drawn from Harold Nicolson's biography, *Dwight Morrow* (New York: Harcourt, Brace & Co., 1935). His appearance is judged by contemporary photographs and descriptions of him by his daughters.

The visit to Mexico was well reported in newspapers at the time, and accurately so far as Lindbergh's official engagements were concerned. But the reports were wildly wrong about his private preoccupations. The accounts of his stay in the embassy in Mexico City with the Morrows which I have used come from the memories of people close to Anne Morrow Lindbergh who would be embarrassed if they were specified here. Not that they are revealing any secrets, but simply throwing a new light on a period about which Anne Lindbergh herself has written frankly and fully in *Bring Me a Unicorn: The Diaries and*

Letters of Anne Morrow Lindbergh, 1922–28 (New York: Harcourt Brace Jovanovich, 1971).

The account of the incident in Washington when Lindbergh was coming away from a visit to President Coolidge with Lieutenant Lester Maitland is told by Maitland himself in a newspaper report (the newspaper unfortunately not specified) in the Wray Scrapbook in the Minnesota Historical Society, St. Paul. (My associate who saw it hazards a guess that it came from the New York *Herald Tribune.*) From now on newspapers are increasingly preoccupied with Lindbergh's relations with them, and with the general public, and many columnists begin to comment on his "war" with the press. But he was still big news, and, of course, his endorsement of Herbert Hoover in 1928 was a front-page story.

The details of the courtship of Charles Lindbergh and Anne Morrow are based on the memories of those close to her, and, of course, they have been checked against Anne Lindbergh's own account of the bizarre circumstances in which perforce her wooing took place.

Chapter Twelve
A Life of Relentless Action

The description of the first months of Anne and Charles Lindbergh's married life has been fleshed out by accounts from friends and others close to them, based mostly on what she told them. The incident between Lindbergh and reporters at a Long Island airport was reported in the press at the time, and Lindbergh himself angrily described how he and his wife had been harassed during their honeymoon. The incident during the evening in Hollywood, described by Amelia Earhart, comes from *Soaring Wings: A Biography of Amelia Earhart,* by George Palmer Putnam (New York: Harcourt, Brace & Co., 1930). That at the airport in New York when Anne and Charles Lindbergh flew in from the Coast was told me later by Lady Rena Terrington, who was there as a reporter at the time.

Chapter Thirteen
The Fat Lamb Is Stolen

Charles Lindbergh was always completely frank about his financial affairs, and made a practice of paying slightly more income tax than he calculated he owed, just in case he had underestimated. Details of his income come from a memorandum he subsequently prepared for the U. S. Government which is in the National Archives in Washington. Of course he got tips and prior information from his influential business friends in ways which would have caused a great scandal if they had happened today, but in the early 1930s the "big boys" looked after their own, and gave them the first bite before the ordinary people could get at the apple, and they had by this time taken Lindbergh to their bosom and were happy to make him rich. To Anne Lindbergh, of course, it was a normal way of accumulating wealth; growing up as the daughter of a Morgan partner, she had never known anything else.

The description of the Lindberghs' journey to China is based on accounts in contemporary newspapers, and on Anne Lindbergh's own accounts of it in *North to the Orient* (New York: Harcourt, Brace & Co., 1935) and *Hour of Gold, Hour of Lead: Diaries and Letters, 1929–32* (New York: Harcourt Brace Jovanovich, 1973).

For the circumstances in which their son, Charles Augustus, Jr., was kidnaped, I have been through the reports of the New Jersey Police, ploughed through millions of words in the files of the New York *Times*, closely re-examined the transcript of the subsequent trial. In addition, since I always had a special interest in the case, I talked on several occasions and at length with the late Brigadier General Norman Schwarzkopf, whose path crossed mine in various parts of the world during and after World War II. I have also since spoken to Lewis J. Bornmann, a recently retired New Jersey State Police captain, but then one of the first patrolmen on the scene after Lindbergh telephoned to report the disappearance of his son. He mentioned that even during the investigation Lindbergh never lost his gargantuan appetite. He and the butler once caught him in the kitchen stealing a leg off a broiling chicken for a between-meals snack. "Don't worry, Ollie [Oliver Whately]," he said. "I'll be back to dine with the family." And then, of course, there were my conversations with Betty Gow as we crossed the Atlantic in the *Berengaria*.

Both Schwarzkopf and Bornmann confirmed the fact that Lindbergh took an active part in the investigation, and showed no squeamishness when theories were discussed about what might be happening to his child, or, after its body had been discovered, how it had been killed. Anne Lindbergh, on the other hand, kept away from the hordes of police in and around the house, and was only occasionally seen wandering like a distracted ghost between the rooms. For her own reactions, see *Hour of Gold, Hour of Lead*.

Chapter Fourteen
Lost Faith

Charles Lindbergh's statement asking for privacy was issued to the news agencies and prominently published in all newspapers. Harry Guggenheim's wise counsel to them on how to live with press and public intrusion was given when the Lindberghs came to stay the weekend at Falaise in June 1932. But his good advice was not only not taken but slightly resented, as Anne Lindbergh makes clear in her diaries.

The circumstances in which Thor, the German shepherd, was purchased have been described by Joseph Weber, its original owner, by Anne and Charles Lindbergh separately, and by Harold Nicolson. Their decision not to go back to their Hopewell home and the psychological results of going to live in the Morrow household were apparent to Harold Nicolson when he was a visitor there, and many of Anne's women friends thought it unwise at the time. It was not until later that she herself seemed to realize the inner conflicts it was bound to set up between her and her mother and her and Charles.

The exchange of telegrams between the Lindberghs and President Roosevelt at the end of their Atlantic flight together is in the President's Official Files at the Franklin D. Roosevelt Library, Hyde Park, New York.

For the background to the airmail controversy and the first clash which resulted between Lindbergh and President Roosevelt, I have read many books and reports, including H. L. Smith's *Airways, The Coming of the New Deal*, by Arthur M. Schlesinger (Boston: Houghton Mifflin, 1959), and *Global Mission*, by General H. H. (Hap) Arnold (New York: Harper and Brothers, 1949), as well as reports of the hearings of the Senate Post Office Committee (the Black Committee), *Revision of Airmail Laws: Hearings* (73rd Cong., 2 sessions, 1934, 114, 124, 220), the House Post Office Committee, *Airmail: Hearings* (73rd Cong., 2 sessions, 1934, 382–88), and papers in the President's Personal File at the Franklin D. Roosevelt Library. The telegrams and letters quoted come from the Black Committee's hearings and from the Library of Congress.

Chapter Fifteen
Ordeal by Trial

The description of Lindbergh's aviation interests and activities comes from contemporary press reports. That Anne Lindbergh thought she was pregnant again at this time and was disappointed when it proved to be a "false alarm" is information from someone close to her, as is the background to the trip to California to stay with her sister, Elisabeth.

The short exchange of words between Charles Lindbergh and his wife after the arrest of Bruno Richard Hauptmann was heard by a family friend.

As I have mentioned in the foreword to this book, I was present at the trial of Bruno Richard Hauptmann for the murder of Charles Augustus Lindbergh, Jr., and it was an experience I will never forget. I have also read most of the books on the subject, including *Kidnap*, by George Waller, which deals with both crime and trial (New York: Daily Press; London: Hamish Hamilton, 1961), *The Trial of Bruno Richard Hauptmann*, by Sidney B. Whipple, which gives a complete transcript of the proceedings (New York: Doubleday, 1937), and *Jafsie Tells All!* by Dr. John F. Condon, the go-between and deliverer of the ransom money (New York: Jonathan Lee Publishing Corp., 1936), which is a naïve but nevertheless fascinating account of the crime and the trial.

When it became known that I was writing this book, I was made aware that a good many people around the world still believe that Bruno Richard Hauptmann did not kidnap or kill the Lindbergh child. Most of them were cranks but there were some serious investigators among them. One letter said in part: "I have been interested in the Lindbergh case since reading George Waller's book, *Kidnap*, in 1961. I corresponded with him for some years, but he has lost interest since I became committed to the cause of Hauptmann's vindication. He doesn't wish to lose his neutrality. In 1965 I contacted Mrs. Hauptmann through the Mayor of Markgröningen, her home town (in Germany), and we became friends. In 1968 and 1970 I spent two weeks with her in Markgröningen. She lives in America but visits her relatives every two years or so." The writer then went on to describe why she was certain of Hauptmann's innocence, bringing up the question of the "Fisch letters," copies of which are in the district attorney's office in the Bronx, but were never produced at the trial. These letters, the writer of the letter insisted, would prove Hauptmann's innocence. They do not, in fact.

Another writer sent me a copy of two long discussions he had with David Wilentz, who was chief prosecutor at Hauptmann's trial, during which he tried to convince Wilentz that the Lindbergh child was still alive. He told Wilentz that the baby had been stolen by the Mafia as a revenge against Lindbergh who, in Prohibition days, "was in charge of a squadron of so-called bounty pilots whose job was to fly low over the countryside and spot illicit stills. For every one they spotted they received a bounty. These activities naturally displeased the Mafia." Wilentz replied that anyone who suggested that the boy was still living was "committing a vile crime by bringing all the agony of the time back to Lindbergh," and said he would not hesitate to "go after such sensation-reporters or writers."

The description of the family's reaction to the guilty verdict on Hauptmann comes from Harold Nicolson's *Diaries and Letters* with a slight addition. In the published version, his editor omitted the bracketed "A-tishoos", which give an extra touch to a brilliantly painted picture of a distressing moment.

It is on Nicolson, too, that I have relied for the description of life at Next Day Hill after the trial, and of his introduction to the formidable Thor. The description of Betty Morrow's departure for California to see her dying daughter comes from the hitherto-unpublished section of the diaries and letters. Anne Lindbergh's opinion of Nicolson comes from *Hour of Gold, Hour of Lead*.

Charles Lindbergh's tough attitude toward his second son, Jon, was recalled for me by family friends, as was the background to their decision to leave for England.

Chapter Sixteen
Surcease

The editorial commenting on the departure of the Lindberghs from the United States appeared in the New York *Herald Tribune*. The details of their arrival in England and the circumstances in which they settled at Long Barn come from contemporary newspaper accounts and from the diaries and letters of Harold Nicolson. The request Lindbergh made to Nicolson about a spiritualistic medium is from one of the hitherto-unpublished sections of his diary. Since Nicolson was, to a certain extent, acting as midwife to the Lindberghs' entree into English society, I have quoted freely in this section from his comments about the young couple.

The letters which thereafter began to pass between Charles Lindbergh and Major Truman Smith, prior to the visits by the Lindberghs to Germany, are printed by permission of Yale University Library, where they are part of the Papers of Truman Smith. I am grateful to Ms. Judith A. Schiff, Chief Research Archivist, Manuscripts and Archives at Yale, for helping me to assemble them.

I am also grateful to my old friend F. G. (Freddy) Miles for giving me details of his meetings with Charles Lindbergh and his wife, and of the aircraft which he built for them while they were in England.

Chapter Seventeen
Hooked

The character of Dr. William Edward Dodd as a sincere, liberal-minded American diplomat was well known to newspapermen in the Berlin of the 1930s. There are excellent examples of the way in which his mind worked in two books, *Through Embassy Eyes*, by Martha Dodd, his daughter (New York: Harcourt, Brace & Co., 1939) and *Ambassador Dodd's Diary, 1933–38*, by Martha Dodd and William Dodd, Jr. (New York: Harcourt, Brace & Co., 1941). The quotations from *The Winds of War* are by Herman Wouk (London: Collins, 1971).

Of the Lindberghs' first visit to Germany I have relied for details on reports in the Nazi press, in the New York *Times*, on the memories of old British and American newspaper hands in Germany, and my own researches into Nazi documents.

My picture of Dr. Alexis Carrel is based on two interviews I had with him, one in Paris in 1936 and one in New York in 1937, and an article I wrote in that year for *Everybody's Weekly*. Carrel spoke with great admiration and fondness of Charles Lindbergh, and was proud of the fact that he was working with him as assistant in his experiments. I have also, of course, referred to his famous book *Man, the Unknown*.

By the time Betty Morrow arrived in England to visit the Lindberghs at Long Barn, in the fall of 1936, there was another reason for the visit, in addition to seeing Anne, Charles, and her grandson. Her younger daughter, Constance, who came with her, had long since held the amiable Welshman, Aubrey Neil Morgan, in warm affection. But he had married her eldest sister, Elisabeth. Elisabeth's death brought the two of them together and mutual sympathy ripened into something deeper. By the fall of 1936 they were engaged and early the following year they married.

I have given Harold Nicolson's diary entries concerning Lindbergh a full flow in this chapter, because they give a revealing glimpse of the way his mind was moving so far as Britain, Germany, and Europe were concerned. The extracts here come from *Diaries and Letters*.

The remark by Mrs. Betty Morrow to Charles Lindbergh after the birth of his second son in London was repeated to the veteran correspondent H. R. Knickerbocker by a family friend and used in his book *Is Tomorrow Hitler's?* (New York: Reynal and Hitchcock, 1941).

I was not yet in Germany during the Lindberghs' second visit there in the fall of 1937, but I heard much about it afterward from my friend, Capitaine (later General) Paul Stehlin, who was then assistant air attaché at the French embassy in Berlin and the resident Deuxième Bureau (Intelligence) officer. Stehlin first met Lindbergh at the Lilienthal Aeronautical Congress in Munich, and they talked flying. Stehlin had his own plane in Germany and had taken it into Eastern Europe and the Balkans, a tour Lindbergh was also planning to make, and he passed on useful information about the conditions the American would encounter. He found Lindbergh charming and congenial, but though he did not say so to him, he was worried by the faith which Lindbergh seemed to have in the judgment of Major Truman Smith. Stehlin considered that Smith was not well-informed so far as German air developments were concerned, and that his admiration for the discipline and order of the Nazi regime was inclined to make him put too much faith in the declarations of the ministers and air force officers he encountered. Stehlin was a good friend of Ernst Udet's, the Luftwaffe's technical director, and liked him as a man and a flier, but he would have no more believed him when he talked about the program of the Luftwaffe than he would have believed Hitler when he said he had no more territorial claims in Europe. On the other hand, Smith seemed to have persuaded Lindbergh that Udet was incapable of lying or exaggerating. The Nazis had already succeeded in terrifying the French chief of air staff, General George Vuillemin, by putting on mass bombing displays during his visit to Germany, and the panic this had caused in Paris would only be reinforced, and French will to resist paralyzed, if Lindbergh was equally impressed by the Nazis and spread the gospel of despair. Stehlin pointed out in many of his dispatches that the Nazis were not as powerful as they made themselves out to be. "But who was I against Vuillemin and Lindbergh?" he said later.

As we now know from the Luftwaffe's own documents (see the statistics in the Luftwaffe Quartermaster General 6th Abteilung returns, now with the German Military History Research Bureau, Speciality Group 6), the strength of their air forces when Lindbergh was being mightily impressed by them in 1938 was 3,315 planes, of which only 2,835 were serviceable and only 1,019 were bombers, plus 227 dive bombers. Lindbergh believed they had around 5,000 serviceable bombers at this time, whereas they did not possess an air force capable of fighting a war so long as the alliance between France, Britain, and Czechoslovakia stood firm. And, proportionate with the Franco-British building program, the situation did not improve in the next two years. But Lindbergh refused to believe that the Germans were lying to him. He did not even believe it after World War II, when it was discovered that Ernst Udet had not died in an airplane accident in 1941 but had committed suicide, because he had completely botched the Luftwaffe building program and faked the production figures.

The quotation from Harold Nicolson's *Diaries and Letters* after the Lindberghs visited him and talked of the terror of the Luftwaffe, in the summer of 1938, is the famous one to which Lindbergh took such vehement objection when it was published in the 1960s. It was in his own Journal that Lindbergh charged Nicolson with being "very anti-German."

His subsequent talks with British ministers, and his famous dinner in Paris as a guest of William C. Bullitt, the U.S. ambassador to France, and his talks with Joseph P. Kennedy, U.S. ambassador to Britain, are to be found in British Foreign Office documents, and the dispatches of the two envoys on these talks in State Department documents in the National Archives. For the story of these encounters in greater detail and documentation, see my book *On Borrowed Time: How World War Two Began* (New York: Random House; London: Weidenfeld and Nicolson, 1969).

The letter to Ambassador Kennedy from Charles Lindbergh, dated September 22, 1938, in which the flier makes his most sensationally inaccurate estimate of the Luftwaffe's strength and capability, is taken from the Papers of Truman Smith, Yale University Library.

Chapter Eighteen
The Albatross

Details of Charles Lindbergh's third visit to Berlin are based on my own observations and dispatches at the time, but the account of the famous dinner party at which Hermann Göring pinned a medal on Charles Lindbergh is taken wholly from the Papers of Truman Smith, who includes the letter from Ambassador Wilson and Lindbergh's own postscript in 1955 among his documentation.

As for Lindbergh's plan to find a home in Berlin for himself and his family at the end of 1938, I talked about this to Herr Albert Speer when I was researching my biography of Hermann Göring. Speer later became one of the most powerful men in the Nazi Reich, but in 1938 he was chief architect of Hitler's grandiose plans for rebuilding the German capital in the image of the all-powerful Reich. He never actually did see Lindbergh but he remembered being rung up by Wendland about him, and told his staff to look at suitable sites for a house for the

Lindbergh family. "I laugh now when I think of it," he said. "Imagine an American planning to bring his family to live in Berlin in 1938–39! He must have been very naïve."

The equally naïve project which Lindbergh sponsored of a Franco-German aircraft first became known when Paul Stehlin revealed it in his book about his intelligence activities in Berlin, *Témoignage pour l'Histoire* (Paris: Laffont, 1964), a good and fascinating book which has never been translated into English. He talked to me about it at considerable length later on, but asked me not to quote him on his criticisms of Truman Smith and his amazement at Lindbergh's naïveté, but I feel that his recent tragic death releases me from that obligation. General Stehlin was a splendid servant of France who always told his government the truth, and was only too often not believed. It was he who, through his close contacts with Göring, first warned Paris of the imminent Soviet-German Pact of 1939 which made war inevitable. But of course Paris thought it was too fantastic to be true.

The correspondence between Ambassador Bullitt and President Roosevelt about the Project Fieseler Storch is taken from *Personal and Secret: For the Eyes of the President*, a selection of the envoy's dispatches edited by Orville H. Bullitt (Boston: Houghton Mifflin, 1972).

Lindbergh's increasing disenchantment with England at this period is reflected in his daily entries in *The Wartime Journals of Charles A. Lindbergh* (New York: Harcourt Brace Jovanovich, 1970). Anne was also writing to friends to say that they were finding Europe "difficult" and were thinking of returning to America. Lindbergh went first, and I have summarized his own account of his journey in the *Aquitania* and his reaction to the press in New York and Washington.

Chapter Nineteen
Portrait of an Isolationist

For background to my account of Lindbergh's return to the Army Air Force and of his reaction to conditions in America in 1939 I have relied on conversations with a number of officers who flew with him or met him about this time, as well as friends of Anne Lindbergh. The account of the party at Wright Field was given by a member of General George H. Brett's staff, and General Brett also remembered the incident. Lindbergh himself wrote later: "One of the women had taken too many cocktails and was in a disgraceful condition. She insisted on heading for me at every opportunity and made the evening rather difficult." He always had precise ideas of a woman's place, and it was never upright (or weaving) with a glass in her hand.

For accounts of the meetings, activities, and movements of Charles Lindbergh, Kay and Truman Smith, Hugh Wilson, and others associated with them, I have from now on relied upon various sources. One of them is the German military attaché in Washington, General Friedrich von Boetticher, whose dispatches are to be found in the National Archives and Record Service, Washington, D.C. (where Dr. Robert Wolfe is an indefatigable guide and helpmate), in T-179 Records of German Embassies, *The Interrogation of General Friedrich von Boetticher*, U. S. State Department Documents, 1945–46, as well as in the Militärgeschichtliches Forschungsamt in Germany. General von Boetticher makes frequent approving references to what he called "the Lindbergh Group" and includes other names in it, among them Congressman George H. Tinkham, Senator Burton K. Wheeler, Rear Admiral Stanford C. Cooper, Major (later General) A. C. Wedemeyer, Alford J. Williams (a former Marine flier), and Carl B. Allen, an aviation writer. He regards Smith's presence as the central figure of this group as a particular bit of luck for Germany, since his bitter opposition to Roosevelt and his friendship and admiration for Germany were well known. Boetticher considered that, as an intelligence officer on friendly terms with many powerful senior officers, Smith was in a choice position to know what the Administration was planning, and could be relied upon to do his best through his influential friends to thwart the President's plans. He never, however, suggests that Smith was anything other than a patriotic American working to sabotage policies he considered inimical to the best interests of the United States. And the author, though strongly disagreeing with Major Truman Smith's activities and attitudes in Germany and the United States during this period, is convinced that he acted always in the sincere belief that he was helping rather than hindering the best interests of his country. Boetticher's particular contacts in the Lindbergh Group were Williams and Allen, both of whom at one time or another did "research" work for him, he reported. Lindbergh certainly knew Williams, and he frequently appeared at meetings with others in the list the military attaché named, but only Allen could have been called a close friend. They had known each other since 1927, when Allen covered the transatlantic flight for the New York *World*. He was now a member of the Federal Air Safety Board (and later became assistant to the president of the Martin Aircraft Company). In his journals, Lindbergh records several conversations with him over the war situation (Allen shared his intense opposition to

Roosevelt's policies), and Boetticher obviously thought highly of him as a source of information, and it is he who mentioned that, to prevent snooping by pro-Roosevelt forces, the members of the group had adopted a simple communication code. How it worked comes from another source.

I have also relied to a large extent on papers in the Franklin D. Roosevelt Library at Hyde Park, New York, and I should like to thank Mr. Joseph W. Marshall, MSLS, and all members of his research room staff for the unflagging help they gave me during my stay there. The documents I studied were in the President's Official File; the President's Personal File; the President's Secretary's File; the President's Secret Service File (1934–45); the Herbert Claiborne Pell Papers (he was Minister to Portugal, 1937–41, Minister to Hungary, 1941, member of the United Nations commission on war crimes); the Henry M. Morgenthau, Jr., Papers; the Lowell Mellett Papers (he was administrative assistant to the President), 1938–44; and the Stephen Early Papers.

In the fall of 1974, in Washington, I was introduced to the late Senator Burton K. Wheeler, still a sharp, hale character of ninety-one when I saw him. I asked him about Charles Lindbergh and he chuckled and said, "He was a great fighter, but he didn't know when to keep his mouth shut. I do." Later I was referred to a statement he had made on his ninetieth birthday, when, asked about his anti-Roosevelt campaign, he said, "I thought I was right then and I still do. I said that if we got into war, we'd make the world safe for the Communists, and that's what we're doing."

The mystery of the offer to Lindbergh of a job in the Roosevelt Administration as Secretary for Air is one that I tried hard to elucidate. But of those concerned in it, Arnold and Woodring are dead, and Truman Smith is too old and ill to answer questions. I failed to find any correspondence about it in the Roosevelt Papers. I did hear that Chester Bowles, at that time an America Firster and an occasional associate of Lindbergh, had been in Washington at the time and knew about the offer, but when I spoke to him at his home in Connecticut, all he would say was: "Lindbergh? He was a *strange* feller." So one must rely upon the only written record of the incident, Lindbergh's own, and when it is carefully analyzed it makes a very peculiar story indeed.

The extract from Lindbergh's radio speech comes from accounts published in the next day's newspapers.

Chapter Twenty
The Battle the Wrong Side Won

I spent a weekend in England recently with a friend who lives in Henry James's old house at Rye, in Sussex, and another guest was an old friend of Anne Lindbergh's. She told me that Anne was reluctant to continue publication of her diaries and letters, since they would henceforth take her into the bitterly controversial period of the America First campaigns and World War II. However, before he died, Charles Lindbergh had urged her to publish them in order to vindicate the attitude they took toward Germany and the democracies. I told my fellow guest I couldn't wait to see them. "Neither can I," she said dryly. When they do appear, one hopes they will finally elucidate whether Anne Lindbergh really did insert the cruel sentence ("as impersonal as a surgeon with his knife") into her husband's first radio speech. For the background to the writing of her article, A Prayer for Peace, which appeared in Reader's Digest in January 1940, I have relied on information from Mr. Kenneth Payne and from Lindbergh's journals. The article by Harold Nicolson appeared in the October 20, 1939, issue of the Spectator, London.

The poem by Oliver Allstorm, "The Lone Eagle's Litany," is among an FBI folder of America First literature in the Franklin D. Roosevelt Library at Hyde Park. I have made many inquiries in an attempt to track down Oliver Allstorm, to no avail.

The New York Times's response to Lindbergh's second radio speech was printed in the issue of May 20, 1940. Stephen Early's letter about the speech (to General Edward Martin Watson) is in the Stephen Early Papers, Franklin D. Roosevelt Library, Hyde Park.

The report of the Boston meeting comes from the Boston Globe.

The letter to a friend about America's encouragement of British resistance is quoted in Charles A. Lindbergh and the Battle Against American Intervention in World War II, by Wayne S. Cole (New York: Harcourt Brace Jovanovich, 1974). Mr. Cole, a well-known writer on personalities involved in the America First campaign, about which he has written with sympathy and understanding, was allowed limited access to the Lindbergh papers under the supervision of Charles Lindbergh himself. He says in his introduction to it: "It has been my custom in each of the three volumes [about various aspects of nonintervention policy] not to ask any of the principals to read the manuscripts in advance. Thus General Lindbergh did not read the manuscript of this book. The publisher, however, did ask him to read the galley proofs. The General prepared comments on the galleys, and the publisher sent them to me. As a result, I made minor factual corrections in seven instances, but I made no changes in analysis and interpretation. . . ."

The omission of any reference to General Charles de Gaulle in Lindbergh's journals can be attributed to a variety of reasons, none of them particularly pleasant. The general's decision to fight on, instead of allowing France to accept the German defeat, quite evidently did not please Lindbergh, nor did he seem to have much faith in De Gaulle's chances. He would hardly have sent his two best French friends back to Occupied France, otherwise. He must have realized that if De Gaulle and Free France won, there would obviously be created for his friends the difficulty of explaining why they were unwilling to fight on, too.

There is evidence of the same sort of pique (it could hardly have been guilt-feeling) over the survival of England and the outcome of the Battle of Britain. It is not easy to swallow the fact that your loudly publicized predictions have been completely refuted. All the same, it seems strange that Lindbergh the airman, fascinated as he was by air warfare, whose hero had been a Briton, Tam o' the Scoots in World War II, never got around to writing any serious study of what happened during the Battle of Britain, and why it changed the course of the war.

Chapter Twenty-One
America First

The background to the situation in the Morrow household at Next Day Hill when the Lindberghs moved back there comes, as may be guessed, from family friends and those close to Anne. Mrs. Morrow's telegram to President Roosevelt comes from the Presidential Papers (Personal File), Franklin D. Roosevelt Library. So does the letter to Anne Lindbergh from her cousin, Richard B. Scandrett, Jr., because someone sent a copy of it to the President. The quote from Ickes comes from *The Secret Diaries of Harold L. Ickes, 1939–41* (New York: Simon and Schuster; London: Weidenfeld and Nicolson, 1955).

Background to the activities of Verne Marshall, O. K. Armstrong, and other fringe members of the America First campaigners comes from Cole's *The Battle Against Intervention*, and there are further interesting revelations in *Prophets on the Right*, by Ronald Radosh (New York: Simon and Schuster, 1975). For the general activities and purposes of the America First Committee itself, I have relied upon documents in the Personal and Official Files of the Presidential Papers, Franklin D. Roosevelt Library, particularly reports from J. Edgar Hoover, who investigated the organization at the request of the administration, and to Wayne S. Cole's four studies of the movement and its personalities: *America First: The Battle Against Intervention, 1940–41* (New York: Octagon, reprint of 1953 ed.), *Senator Gerald P. Nye and American Foreign Relations* (Minneapolis: University of Minnesota Press, 1962), *An Interpretive History of American Foreign Relations,* rev. ed. (Homewood, Ill.: Dorsey, 1974), and *Charles A. Lindbergh and the Battle Against American Intervention in World War II* (New York: Harcourt Brace Jovanovich, 1974).

The text of Lindbergh's testimony to the congressional committee in which he forecast that Britain could not win the war is from the *Congressional Record.* The correspondence that resulted is in the Personal Papers at the Franklin D. Roosevelt Library.

The account of the President's famous "copperhead" press conference is taken from contemporary newspaper reports. Lindbergh's letter in response is from the Presidential Papers (Personal File). The New York *Times* editorial comment appeared on April 29, 1941. America First's statement was distributed by the Associated Press. William C. Bullitt's comment was reported in the New York *Herald Tribune,* as was Henry Breckenridge's speech.

The article about the Lindberghs' living pattern about this time was printed in the New York *Times.* It mentions Thomas Lamont's unwillingness to communicate with the Lindberghs. Lamont had been one of Dwight Morrow's closest friends and a doting godfather of Anne Lindbergh. He wrote several letters both to Betty Morrow and to Anne Lindbergh at this time, but it is believed that the correspondence has been destroyed.

The letter from Edgar Hoover to Stephen Early comes from the Presidential Papers (Official File), Franklin D. Roosevelt Library. So does Roosevelt's memorandum to Attorney General Robert Jackson.

Lindbergh's speeches at this time are taken from reports in the daily newspapers.

Chapter Twenty-Two
Des Moines

Secretary Ickes's critique of Lindbergh's articles and speeches is reprinted in *The Secret Diary.* His memorandum about Willkie is in the Presidential Papers (Personal File), Franklin D. Roosevelt Library. William Chandler's letter was written to the New York *Times* on June 6, 1941. Lindbergh's reply to Ickes in his missive to the President dated July 16, 1941, is taken from daily newspaper reports and checked against the original in the Presidential Papers (Personal File) together with Stephen Early's reply. Ickes's remarks are in *The Secret Diary*.

The account of the meeting between Lindbergh, the Truman Smiths, Senators Wheeler and Clark at Senator Nye's apartment comes from an FBI report in the Presidential Papers. Lindbergh's journal confirms it.

For the account of the Des Moines meeting I have relied upon contemporary newspaper reports, and I have used the reactions cited by Wayne S. Cole in *The Battle Against Intervention* and a pro-Lindbergh source to show that even his sympathizers were stunned or devastated by the tone of his speech. Ordinary comment did not hold back, as is seen from the editorials quoted.

Chapter Twenty-Three
Farewell to Lindbergh?

Lindbergh made the remark about being a "stubborn Swede" to Alden Whitman, of the New York *Times*. From the moment he saw the nationwide reaction to Lindbergh's attack on the Jews, John T. Flynn backtracked rapidly and Lindbergh, as his diaries show, resented it. Friends of Herbert Hoover leaked his remark to Lindbergh ("when you have been in politics long enough") to the press.

Lindbergh's subsequent speeches are taken from contemporary reports. So is the story of the taking down of the Lindbergh Flag at the Lafayette Hotel.

Shortly after the Des Moines speech, General Wood, seeing his "clean" campaign against Roosevelt threatened by dirty racial infighting, wanted to call a halt to America First's activities. Senator William Benton, a firm and loyal Lindbergh fan even in those days, was not in favor of going so far, but he did send a telegram on September 22, 1941, to Lindbergh saying:

> I AM HOPEFUL YOU MAY BE IN TOWN WEDNESDAY OR THURSDAY FOR LUNCH WITH MR. [CHESTER] BOWLES AND ME. IT WOULD BE AGREEABLE TOO IF I INCLUDED SMITH RICHARD QUERY. I HAVE BEEN TALKING TO HIM THIS WEEK ABOUT YOUR DES MOINES SPEECH. WE FAVOR AN UNEQUIVOCAL STATEMENT FROM THE

COMMITTEE. RICHARDSON IS SEEING FLYNN TODAY. STEWART
TELLS ME STATEMENT DUE WITHIN FEW DAYS. . . . I HOPE TO
SEE GENERAL WOOD ON MY RETURN TO CHICAGO. I MAY BE TALK-
ING TO HIM BY PHONE. BILL BENTON 444 MADISON AVENUE NYC.

The result of this meeting was that the America First Committee
continued in business. But feelings were muted and there was a growing
feeling that something drastic ought to be done against the Administration's policy. This happened in early September when someone in
the U. S. Army Intelligence Department stole a top secret document
out of the files detailing the program the government was planning for
meeting the menace of the Axis, including rearmament and recruitment. The program was delivered to Senator Burton K. Wheeler, who
proceeded to leak it to a correspondent of the Chicago *Tribune*. The
purloined document appeared on December 4, 1941, as evidence of the
U. S. Government's belligerent attitude and determination to involve
the American people in war. Three days later the Japanese attacked
Pearl Harbor.

The account of Lindbergh's attempts to get a job after war began
come from the Presidential Papers (Personal and Official Files) and so
does Ickes's memorandum to the President. The President's reply,
Knox's memorandum, and Stimson's report on his interview with Lindbergh are also in these files. What happened next is recounted in Lindbergh's journals.

Chapter Twenty-Four
Civilian at War

The accounts of Charles Lindbergh's activities at the Ford Motor
Company and in Minnesota come from several sources, including the
Ford Company's records, the National Archives, Lord (Miles) Thomas.
Lindbergh's remarks about working at Ford ("Oh, we had some extraordinary experiences") were made to John Nance in the Philippines
and quoted in *The Gentle Tasaday* (New York: Harcourt Brace
Jovanovich, 1975). It was Lord Thomas who overheard the President's
remark to Charlie Sorensen about Lindbergh's absence during his visit
to Willow Run.

For a time, Lindbergh was very eager for a history of America's involvement in war to be written as seen from the point of view of the
isolationists, and he wrote several letters to Henry Ford advocating the
employment of Harry Elmer Barnes on the project. The letters are not
available.

The remark by John P. Marquand to George S. Kaufman is quoted from *The Late John Marquand*, by Stephen Birmingham (Philadelphia: Lippincott, 1972).

The accounts of Lindbergh's civilian war against the Japanese in the Pacific are taken from interviews with General George C. Kenney, a delayed report subsequently published by International News Service correspondent Lee van Atta, an interview by Colonel Charles MacDonald, and Lindbergh's journal.

Chapter Twenty-Five
Return to Germany

I am particularly grateful to the director and his staff at the Naval Archives, U. S. Navy Dockyard, Washington, D.C., for extending their fullest facilities during my visits in 1974, and allowing me to examine the reports of the Naval Technical Mission which Charles Lindbergh accompanied to Germany in 1945. Although Lindbergh's name is not mentioned in these reports (he was attached as a civilian consultant employed by United Aircraft), it is possible to tie him in with certain reports and interrogations by comparing dates in his journals. For instance, a report (File A9-16 (3N) (50/VON) Serial 693 Tech. Rep. 172-45, signed by S. T. Robinson) of an interrogation of Dip. Ing. Helmuth Schelp turns out to be the same interview that Lindbergh describes in his journal entry for May 22, 1945. There are many others, including interrogations of Messerschmidt and Baeumker, for instance. By this means it is also possible to see some reports and activities in which he participated which do not appear in the journal.

Chapter Twenty-Six
A Changed Man?

Of Flight and Life, to which reference is made in this chapter, was published by Charles Scribner's Sons, New York, 1948.

The report on German technical skills on which he gave help and advice and from which quotation is made was made available to me by the director of the Naval Technical Archives, U. S. Navy Dockyard, Washington, D.C., and is: U. S. Naval Technical Mission. A9-16 (3) (50/N) 1117 Tech. Rep. 373. Air Superiority. Summing Up of German Technical Skills.

The account of the meeting with General Carl Spaatz and William Benton comes from a source which does not wish to be identified.

For further information about the rocket experiments of the late Dr. Robert H. Goddard, and Lindbergh's association with them, I recommend *This High Man: The Life of Robert H. Goddard* (New York: Farrar, Straus, 1963). Lindbergh wrote a preface to the book, his first public acknowledgment of his association with rocketry.

Details of Lindbergh's peregrinations over the first decade after the end of the war come from air force records, Pan American Airways, and contemporary newspaper reports. His comments on the McCarthy era come from *The Battle Against American Intervention.*

The review of Anne Lindbergh's book of poems by John Ciardi appeared in *Saturday Review*, February 11, 1950, and the letters in reply to it were printed in the following weeks.

Ms. Carol Brandt told me the story of Lindbergh's visit with John P. Marquand to her apartment in 1952 to discuss his forthcoming book, *The Spirit of St. Louis.* James Stewart, who stars in the film, told the story of how the film of it was made. In London in the summer of 1975 (he was performing in a revival of *Harvey*) he confirmed that he still thought it a good film, a perfect part for himself, and that it came too soon. One of the women who was present and remembered the film said, "You know, when Lindbergh died and they printed his picture, I was surprised. I'd always thought of him as looking like Jimmy."

Details of Lindbergh's work in rocketry and space medicine come from armed forces sources which have asked not to be specified.

His article on the need for bigger and better deterrents was written for the *Saturday Evening Post*, July 17, 1954. Alexander Seversky's reply to it was in the New York *Herald Tribune*, December 12, 1954.

Background on the Lindbergh domestic life with their children comes from sources close to the family.

Chapter Twenty-Seven
Turning Point

The story about Lindbergh and André Malraux comes from André Malraux.

The story about Lindbergh's trip to Southeast Asia and his comments about George Washington and the trees was told me by other newspapermen covering the Vietnam War, to whom it was recounted later. Curiously enough, Anne Lindbergh used the cherry tree analogy in a speech about ecology some years later.

His experiences in East Africa were pieced together from various sources: from Ian Grimwood, of the Kenya Game Parks; from Kebbede

Mikael, then chief of the Ethiopian Imperial Archives, who was present at the interview with Haile Selassie; and from friends of Dr. Michael Wood, of Kilimanjaro, Tanzania. The passage he wrote about "lying under an acacia tree" appeared in *Reader's Digest*, July 1964.

André Turcat, chief French pilot of the Anglo-French supersonic plane, the Concorde, has been asked not to release the correspondence which he carried on with Lindbergh after the latter turned against supersonic travel. The letter to Congressman Sidney Yates was issued shortly before the appearance of the article against commercial supersonic planes which Lindbergh wrote for the New York *Times* on July 7, 1972.

Details given here of the Lindbergh family come from friends and those close to them.

Lindbergh explained how he came to join the World Wild Life Fund in a statement to the New York *Times* on May 23, 1971 (though he joined the WWF in 1965). The article which he wrote on the environment for *Life* appeared in that magazine's Christmas issue, 1967.

Lindbergh's remarks about the cost of the first lunar program and Goddard's estimate of it were made at a meeting of the Airline Pilots Association in 1969.

The information about Anne Lindbergh's chalet in Switzerland and the family sojourns there comes from sources close to them. Dr. Karl Burckhardt, who died in 1974 but was a friend for many years, told the story about Lindbergh when I was consulting him for information for my biography of Hermann Göring. Tom Harrisson is another old friend, and his stories of his association with Lindbergh were told me during talks at his home in Brussels, and during visits to my home in the South of France.

The exposition of his standpoint on World War II as he saw it in the light of what has happened since ("We won in a military sense but") come from Lindbergh's introduction to *The Wartime Journals of Charles A. Lindbergh* (op. cit.). The riposte from the New York *Times* appeared on September 6, 1970.

Chapter Twenty-Eight
Last Adventure

Charles Lindbergh recounted the incident when he was locked in the Harcourt Brace Jovanovich Building in a letter to Russell Fridley, of the Minnesota Historical Society, dated December 27, 1969.

The account of his trips to the Philippines come from various sources: from the bulletins of the Survival Service Commission of the International Union for the Conservation of Nature, from Survival International, from Elizalde's own accounts in his long reports to Panamin, from Lindbergh's own statements to the New York *Times*, from various articles and magazines, and from a splendid book about the Stone Age tribes of Mindanao, *The Gentle Tasaday*, by John Nance (New York: Harcourt Brace Jovanovich, 1975). An introduction to this book was the last published work that Lindbergh wrote. He finished it in Hawaii five months before he died.

Chapter Twenty-Nine
Eagle's Nest

William Benton's attempts to get his friends to agree to become members of the National Institute of Art and Letters are detailed in his papers, and Lindbergh replied to him on November 17, 1972. The Lindberghs' visit to Falaise on the day of its opening as a museum was described by my neighbors at Glen Head, Long Island, where I was living during the researching of this book. They were also there at the invitation of Nassau County.

Lindbergh's remarks about the urban sprawl that America was becoming ("few men have seen with their own eyes") were made to visitors and guests invited to the opening ceremony of the new Center at the Lindbergh home in Little Falls. Details of his illness come from informants at Columbia Presbyterian Hospital, and his attitude to death appeared in an item he wrote in his journals while on a trip to Russia in 1938.

The burial service was conducted by the Reverend John M. Tincher, of the United Methodist Church of Burlingame, California. It took place a few hours after Lindbergh died, on August 26, 1974, when Rev. Tincher read the words:

> "We commit the body of General Charles A. Lindbergh to
> its final resting place, but his spirit we commend to Almighty
> God, knowing that death is but a new adventure in existence
> and remembering how Jesus said upon the cross, 'Father, into
> Thy hands I commend my spirit.'"

Tincher talked with Anne Lindbergh about her husband's death and wrote later, in a letter to me, "Mrs. Lindbergh helped me to understand the tremendous grasp of death and the willingness to accept the inevitable, both of which were expressed in the last few days of Charles Lindbergh's life."

Anne Lindbergh wore a plain simple dress to the funeral ceremony and a single string of pearls. The color of the dress was purple, her favorite color and, when she wore it, his.

INDEX

A CATALOG OF SELECTED
DOVER BOOKS
IN ALL FIELDS OF INTEREST

A CATALOG OF SELECTED DOVER BOOKS IN ALL FIELDS OF INTEREST

CONCERNING THE SPIRITUAL IN ART, Wassily Kandinsky. Pioneering work by father of abstract art. Thoughts on color theory, nature of art. Analysis of earlier masters. 12 illustrations. 80pp. of text. 5⅜ x 8½.   23411-8 Pa. $4.95

ANIMALS: 1,419 Copyright-Free Illustrations of Mammals, Birds, Fish, Insects, etc., Jim Harter (ed.). Clear wood engravings present, in extremely lifelike poses, over 1,000 species of animals. One of the most extensive pictorial sourcebooks of its kind. Captions. Index. 284pp. 9 x 12.   23766-4 Pa. $14.95

CELTIC ART: The Methods of Construction, George Bain. Simple geometric techniques for making Celtic interlacements, spirals, Kells-type initials, animals, humans, etc. Over 500 illustrations. 160pp. 9 x 12. (USO)   22923-8 Pa. $9.95

AN ATLAS OF ANATOMY FOR ARTISTS, Fritz Schider. Most thorough reference work on art anatomy in the world. Hundreds of illustrations, including selections from works by Vesalius, Leonardo, Goya, Ingres, Michelangelo, others. 593 illustrations. 192pp. 7⅛ x 10¼.   20241-0 Pa. $9.95

CELTIC HAND STROKE-BY-STROKE (Irish Half-Uncial from "The Book of Kells"): An Arthur Baker Calligraphy Manual, Arthur Baker. Complete guide to creating each letter of the alphabet in distinctive Celtic manner. Covers hand position, strokes, pens, inks, paper, more. Illustrated. 48pp. 8¼ x 11.   24336-2 Pa. $3.95

EASY ORIGAMI, John Montroll. Charming collection of 32 projects (hat, cup, pelican, piano, swan, many more) specially designed for the novice origami hobbyist. Clearly illustrated easy-to-follow instructions insure that even beginning papercrafters will achieve successful results. 48pp. 8¼ x 11.   27298-2 Pa. $3.50

THE COMPLETE BOOK OF BIRDHOUSE CONSTRUCTION FOR WOODWORKERS, Scott D. Campbell. Detailed instructions, illustrations, tables. Also data on bird habitat and instinct patterns. Bibliography. 3 tables. 63 illustrations in 15 figures. 48pp. 5¼ x 8½.   24407-5 Pa. $2.50

BLOOMINGDALE'S ILLUSTRATED 1886 CATALOG: Fashions, Dry Goods and Housewares, Bloomingdale Brothers. Famed merchants' extremely rare catalog depicting about 1,700 products: clothing, housewares, firearms, dry goods, jewelry, more. Invaluable for dating, identifying vintage items. Also, copyright-free graphics for artists, designers. Co-published with Henry Ford Museum & Greenfield Village. 160pp. 8¼ x 11.   25780-0 Pa. $10.95

HISTORIC COSTUME IN PICTURES, Braun & Schneider. Over 1,450 costumed figures in clearly detailed engravings–from dawn of civilization to end of 19th century. Captions. Many folk costumes. 256pp. 8⅜ x 11¾.   23150-X Pa. $12.95

THE BEST TALES OF HOFFMANN, E. T. A. Hoffmann. 10 of Hoffmann's most important stories: "Nutcracker and the King of Mice," "The Golden Flowerpot," etc. 458pp. 5⅜ x 8½. 21793-0 Pa. $9.95

FROM FETISH TO GOD IN ANCIENT EGYPT, E. A. Wallis Budge. Rich detailed survey of Egyptian conception of "God" and gods, magic, cult of animals, Osiris, more. Also, superb English translations of hymns and legends. 240 illustrations. 545pp. 5⅜ x 8½. 25803-3 Pa. $13.95

FRENCH STORIES/CONTES FRANÇAIS: A Dual-Language Book, Wallace Fowlie. Ten stories by French masters, Voltaire to Camus: "Micromegas" by Voltaire; "The Atheist's Mass" by Balzac; "Minuet" by de Maupassant; "The Guest" by Camus, six more. Excellent English translations on facing pages. Also French-English vocabulary list, exercises, more. 352pp. 5⅜ x 8½. 26443-2 Pa. $9.95

CHICAGO AT THE TURN OF THE CENTURY IN PHOTOGRAPHS: 122 Historic Views from the Collections of the Chicago Historical Society, Larry A. Viskochil. Rare large-format prints offer detailed views of City Hall, State Street, the Loop, Hull House, Union Station, many other landmarks, circa 1904-1913. Introduction. Captions. Maps. 144pp. 9⅜ x 12¼. 24656-6 Pa. $12.95

OLD BROOKLYN IN EARLY PHOTOGRAPHS, 1865-1929, William Lee Younger. Luna Park, Gravesend race track, construction of Grand Army Plaza, moving of Hotel Brighton, etc. 157 previously unpublished photographs. 165pp. 8⅞ x 11¾. 23587-4 Pa. $13.95

THE MYTHS OF THE NORTH AMERICAN INDIANS, Lewis Spence. Rich anthology of the myths and legends of the Algonquins, Iroquois, Pawnees and Sioux, prefaced by an extensive historical and ethnological commentary. 36 illustrations. 480pp. 5⅜ x 8½. 25967-6 Pa. $10.95

AN ENCYCLOPEDIA OF BATTLES: Accounts of Over 1,560 Battles from 1479 B.C. to the Present, David Eggenberger. Essential details of every major battle in recorded history from the first battle of Megiddo in 1479 B.C. to Grenada in 1984. List of Battle Maps. New Appendix covering the years 1967-1984. Index. 99 illustrations. 544pp. 6½ x 9¼. 24913-1 Pa. $16.95

SAILING ALONE AROUND THE WORLD, Captain Joshua Slocum. First man to sail around the world, alone, in small boat. One of great feats of seamanship told in delightful manner. 67 illustrations. 294pp. 5⅜ x 8½. 20326-3 Pa. $6.95

ANARCHISM AND OTHER ESSAYS, Emma Goldman. Powerful, penetrating, prophetic essays on direct action, role of minorities, prison reform, puritan hypocrisy, violence, etc. 271pp. 5⅜ x 8½. 22484-8 Pa. $7.95

MYTHS OF THE HINDUS AND BUDDHISTS, Ananda K. Coomaraswamy and Sister Nivedita. Great stories of the epics; deeds of Krishna, Shiva, taken from puranas, Vedas, folk tales; etc. 32 illustrations. 400pp. 5⅜ x 8½. 21759-0 Pa. $12.95

BEYOND PSYCHOLOGY, Otto Rank. Fear of death, desire of immortality, nature of sexuality, social organization, creativity, according to Rankian system. 291pp. 5⅜ x 8½. 20485-5 Pa. $8.95

A THEOLOGICO-POLITICAL TREATISE, Benedict Spinoza. Also contains unfinished Political Treatise. Great classic on religious liberty, theory of government on common consent. R. Elwes translation. Total of 421pp. 5⅜ x 8½. 20249-6 Pa. $9.95

MY BONDAGE AND MY FREEDOM, Frederick Douglass. Born a slave, Douglass became outspoken force in antislavery movement. The best of Douglass' autobiographies. Graphic description of slave life. 464pp. 5⅜ x 8½. 22457-0 Pa. $8.95

FOLLOWING THE EQUATOR: A Journey Around the World, Mark Twain. Fascinating humorous account of 1897 voyage to Hawaii, Australia, India, New Zealand, etc. Ironic, bemused reports on peoples, customs, climate, flora and fauna, politics, much more. 197 illustrations. 720pp. 5⅜ x 8½. 26113-1 Pa. $15.95

THE PEOPLE CALLED SHAKERS, Edward D. Andrews. Definitive study of Shakers: origins, beliefs, practices, dances, social organization, furniture and crafts, etc. 33 illustrations. 351pp. 5⅜ x 8½. 21081-2 Pa. $8.95

THE MYTHS OF GREECE AND ROME, H. A. Guerber. A classic of mythology, generously illustrated, long prized for its simple, graphic, accurate retelling of the principal myths of Greece and Rome, and for its commentary on their origins and significance. With 64 illustrations by Michelangelo, Raphael, Titian, Rubens, Canova, Bernini and others. 480pp. 5⅜ x 8½. 27584-1 Pa. $9.95

PSYCHOLOGY OF MUSIC, Carl E. Seashore. Classic work discusses music as a medium from psychological viewpoint. Clear treatment of physical acoustics, auditory apparatus, sound perception, development of musical skills, nature of musical feeling, host of other topics. 88 figures. 408pp. 5⅜ x 8½. 21851-1 Pa. $11.95

THE PHILOSOPHY OF HISTORY, Georg W. Hegel. Great classic of Western thought develops concept that history is not chance but rational process, the evolution of freedom. 457pp. 5⅜ x 8½. 20112-0 Pa. $9.95

THE BOOK OF TEA, Kakuzo Okakura. Minor classic of the Orient: entertaining, charming explanation, interpretation of traditional Japanese culture in terms of tea ceremony. 94pp. 5⅜ x 8½. 20070-1 Pa. $3.95

LIFE IN ANCIENT EGYPT, Adolf Erman. Fullest, most thorough, detailed older account with much not in more recent books, domestic life, religion, magic, medicine, commerce, much more. Many illustrations reproduce tomb paintings, carvings, hieroglyphs, etc. 597pp. 5⅜ x 8½. 22632-8 Pa. $12.95

SUNDIALS, Their Theory and Construction, Albert Waugh. Far and away the best, most thorough coverage of ideas, mathematics concerned, types, construction, adjusting anywhere. Simple, nontechnical treatment allows even children to build several of these dials. Over 100 illustrations. 230pp. 5⅜ x 8½. 22947-5 Pa. $8.95

DYNAMICS OF FLUIDS IN POROUS MEDIA, Jacob Bear. For advanced students of ground water hydrology, soil mechanics and physics, drainage and irrigation engineering, and more. 335 illustrations. Exercises, with answers. 784pp. 6⅛ x 9¼. 65675-6 Pa. $19.95

SONGS OF EXPERIENCE: Facsimile Reproduction with 26 Plates in Full Color, William Blake. 26 full-color plates from a rare 1826 edition. Includes "TheTyger," "London," "Holy Thursday," and other poems. Printed text of poems. 48pp. 5¼ x 7. 24636-1 Pa. $4.95

OLD-TIME VIGNETTES IN FULL COLOR, Carol Belanger Grafton (ed.). Over 390 charming, often sentimental illustrations, selected from archives of Victorian graphics—pretty women posing, children playing, food, flowers, kittens and puppies, smiling cherubs, birds and butterflies, much more. All copyright-free. 48pp. 9¼ x 12¼. 27269-9 Pa. $7.95

PERSPECTIVE FOR ARTISTS, Rex Vicat Cole. Depth, perspective of sky and sea, shadows, much more, not usually covered. 391 diagrams, 81 reproductions of drawings and paintings. 279pp. 5⅜ x 8½. 22487-2 Pa. $7.95

DRAWING THE LIVING FIGURE, Joseph Sheppard. Innovative approach to artistic anatomy focuses on specifics of surface anatomy, rather than muscles and bones. Over 170 drawings of live models in front, back and side views, and in widely varying poses. Accompanying diagrams. 177 illustrations. Introduction. Index. 144pp. 8⅜ x11¼. 26723-7 Pa. $8.95

GOTHIC AND OLD ENGLISH ALPHABETS: 100 Complete Fonts, Dan X. Solo. Add power, elegance to posters, signs, other graphics with 100 stunning copyright-free alphabets: Blackstone, Dolbey, Germania, 97 more–including many lower-case, numerals, punctuation marks. 104pp. 8⅛ x 11. 24695-7 Pa. $8.95

HOW TO DO BEADWORK, Mary White. Fundamental book on craft from simple projects to five-bead chains and woven works. 106 illustrations. 142pp. 5⅜ x 8. 20697-1 Pa. $5.95

THE BOOK OF WOOD CARVING, Charles Marshall Sayers. Finest book for beginners discusses fundamentals and offers 34 designs. "Absolutely first rate . . . well thought out and well executed."–E. J. Tangerman. 118pp. 7¾ x 10⅝. 23654-4 Pa. $7.95

ILLUSTRATED CATALOG OF CIVIL WAR MILITARY GOODS: Union Army Weapons, Insignia, Uniform Accessories, and Other Equipment, Schuyler, Hartley, and Graham. Rare, profusely illustrated 1846 catalog includes Union Army uniform and dress regulations, arms and ammunition, coats, insignia, flags, swords, rifles, etc. 226 illustrations. 160pp. 9 x 12. 24939-5 Pa. $10.95

WOMEN'S FASHIONS OF THE EARLY 1900s: An Unabridged Republication of "New York Fashions, 1909," National Cloak & Suit Co. Rare catalog of mail-order fashions documents women's and children's clothing styles shortly after the turn of the century. Captions offer full descriptions, prices. Invaluable resource for fashion, costume historians. Approximately 725 illustrations. 128pp. 8⅜ x 11¼. 27276-1 Pa. $11.95

THE 1912 AND 1915 GUSTAV STICKLEY FURNITURE CATALOGS, Gustav Stickley. With over 200 detailed illustrations and descriptions, these two catalogs are essential reading and reference materials and identification guides for Stickley furniture. Captions cite materials, dimensions and prices. 112pp. 6½ x 9¼. 26676-1 Pa. $9.95

EARLY AMERICAN LOCOMOTIVES, John H. White, Jr. Finest locomotive engravings from early 19th century: historical (1804–74), main-line (after 1870), special, foreign, etc. 147 plates. 142pp. 11⅜ x 8¼. 22772-3 Pa. $10.95

THE TALL SHIPS OF TODAY IN PHOTOGRAPHS, Frank O. Braynard. Lavishly illustrated tribute to nearly 100 majestic contemporary sailing vessels: Amerigo Vespucci, Clearwater, Constitution, Eagle, Mayflower, Sea Cloud, Victory, many more. Authoritative captions provide statistics, background on each ship. 190 black-and-white photographs and illustrations. Introduction. 128pp. 8⅞ x 11¾. 27163-3 Pa. $14.95

EARLY NINETEENTH-CENTURY CRAFTS AND TRADES, Peter Stockham (ed.). Extremely rare 1807 volume describes to youngsters the crafts and trades of the day: brickmaker, weaver, dressmaker, bookbinder, ropemaker, saddler, many more. Quaint prose, charming illustrations for each craft. 20 black-and-white line illustrations. 192pp. 4⅝ x 6. 27293-1 Pa. $4.95

VICTORIAN FASHIONS AND COSTUMES FROM HARPER'S BAZAR, 1867–1898, Stella Blum (ed.). Day costumes, evening wear, sports clothes, shoes, hats, other accessories in over 1,000 detailed engravings. 320pp. 9⅜ x 12¼. 22990-4 Pa. $15.95

GUSTAV STICKLEY, THE CRAFTSMAN, Mary Ann Smith. Superb study surveys broad scope of Stickley's achievement, especially in architecture. Design philosophy, rise and fall of the Craftsman empire, descriptions and floor plans for many Craftsman houses, more. 86 black-and-white halftones. 31 line illustrations. Introduction 208pp. 6½ x 9¼. 27210-9 Pa. $9.95

THE LONG ISLAND RAIL ROAD IN EARLY PHOTOGRAPHS, Ron Ziel. Over 220 rare photos, informative text document origin (1844) and development of rail service on Long Island. Vintage views of early trains, locomotives, stations, passengers, crews, much more. Captions. 8⅞ x 11¾. 26301-0 Pa. $13.95

THE BOOK OF OLD SHIPS: From Egyptian Galleys to Clipper Ships, Henry B. Culver. Superb, authoritative history of sailing vessels, with 80 magnificent line illustrations. Galley, bark, caravel, longship, whaler, many more. Detailed, informative text on each vessel by noted naval historian. Introduction. 256pp. 5⅜ x 8½. 27332-6 Pa. $7.95

TEN BOOKS ON ARCHITECTURE, Vitruvius. The most important book ever written on architecture. Early Roman aesthetics, technology, classical orders, site selection, all other aspects. Morgan translation. 331pp. 5⅜ x 8½. 20645-9 Pa. $8.95

THE HUMAN FIGURE IN MOTION, Eadweard Muybridge. More than 4,500 stopped-action photos, in action series, showing undraped men, women, children jumping, lying down, throwing, sitting, wrestling, carrying, etc. 390pp. 7⅞ x 10⅝. 20204-6 Clothbd. $27.95

TREES OF THE EASTERN AND CENTRAL UNITED STATES AND CANADA, William M. Harlow. Best one-volume guide to 140 trees. Full descriptions, woodlore, range, etc. Over 600 illustrations. Handy size. 288pp. 4½ x 6⅜. 20395-6 Pa. $6.95

SONGS OF WESTERN BIRDS, Dr. Donald J. Borror. Complete song and call repertoire of 60 western species, including flycatchers, juncoes, cactus wrens, many more—includes fully illustrated booklet. Cassette and manual 99913-0 $8.95

GROWING AND USING HERBS AND SPICES, Milo Miloradovich. Versatile handbook provides all the information needed for cultivation and use of all the herbs and spices available in North America. 4 illustrations. Index. Glossary. 236pp. 5⅜ x 8½. 25058-X Pa. $7.95

BIG BOOK OF MAZES AND LABYRINTHS, Walter Shepherd. 50 mazes and labyrinths in all—classical, solid, ripple, and more—in one great volume. Perfect inexpensive puzzler for clever youngsters. Full solutions. 112pp. 8⅛ x 11. 22951-3 Pa. $4.95

PIANO TUNING, J. Cree Fischer. Clearest, best book for beginner, amateur. Simple repairs, raising dropped notes, tuning by easy method of flattened fifths. No previous skills needed. 4 illustrations. 201pp. 5⅜ x 8½.   23267-0 Pa. $6.95

A SOURCE BOOK IN THEATRICAL HISTORY, A. M. Nagler. Contemporary observers on acting, directing, make-up, costuming, stage props, machinery, scene design, from Ancient Greece to Chekhov. 611pp. 5⅜ x 8½.   20515-0 Pa. $12.95

THE COMPLETE NONSENSE OF EDWARD LEAR, Edward Lear. All nonsense limericks, zany alphabets, Owl and Pussycat, songs, nonsense botany, etc., illustrated by Lear. Total of 320pp. 5⅜ x 8½. (USO)   20167-8 Pa. $7.95

VICTORIAN PARLOUR POETRY: An Annotated Anthology, Michael R. Turner. 117 gems by Longfellow, Tennyson, Browning, many lesser-known poets. "The Village Blacksmith," "Curfew Must Not Ring Tonight," "Only a Baby Small," dozens more, often difficult to find elsewhere. Index of poets, titles, first lines. xxiii + 325pp. 5⅜ x 8¼.   27044-0 Pa. $8.95

DUBLINERS, James Joyce. Fifteen stories offer vivid, tightly focused observations of the lives of Dublin's poorer classes. At least one, "The Dead," is considered a masterpiece. Reprinted complete and unabridged from standard edition. 160pp. 5³⁄₁₆ x 8¼.   26870-5 Pa. $1.00

THE HAUNTED MONASTERY and THE CHINESE MAZE MURDERS, Robert van Gulik. Two full novels by van Gulik, set in 7th-century China, continue adventures of Judge Dee and his companions. An evil Taoist monastery, seemingly supernatural events; overgrown topiary maze hides strange crimes. 27 illustrations. 328pp. 5⅜ x 8½.   23502-5 Pa. $8.95

THE BOOK OF THE SACRED MAGIC OF ABRAMELIN THE MAGE, translated by S. MacGregor Mathers. Medieval manuscript of ceremonial magic. Basic document in Aleister Crowley, Golden Dawn groups. 268pp. 5⅜ x 8½.   23211-5 Pa. $9.95

NEW RUSSIAN-ENGLISH AND ENGLISH-RUSSIAN DICTIONARY, M. A. O'Brien. This is a remarkably handy Russian dictionary, containing a surprising amount of information, including over 70,000 entries. 366pp. 4½ x 6⅛.   20208-9 Pa. $10.95

HISTORIC HOMES OF THE AMERICAN PRESIDENTS, Second, Revised Edition, Irvin Haas. A traveler's guide to American Presidential homes, most open to the public, depicting and describing homes occupied by every American President from George Washington to George Bush. With visiting hours, admission charges, travel routes. 175 photographs. Index. 160pp. 8¼ x 11.   26751-2 Pa. $11.95

NEW YORK IN THE FORTIES, Andreas Feininger. 162 brilliant photographs by the well-known photographer, formerly with *Life* magazine. Commuters, shoppers, Times Square at night, much else from city at its peak. Captions by John von Hartz. 181pp. 9¼ x 10¾.   23585-8 Pa. $13.95

INDIAN SIGN LANGUAGE, William Tomkins. Over 525 signs developed by Sioux and other tribes. Written instructions and diagrams. Also 290 pictographs. 111pp. 6⅛ x 9¼.   22029-X Pa. $3.95

ANATOMY: A Complete Guide for Artists, Joseph Sheppard. A master of figure drawing shows artists how to render human anatomy convincingly. Over 460 illustrations. 224pp. 8⅜ x 11¼. 27279-6 Pa. $11.95

MEDIEVAL CALLIGRAPHY: Its History and Technique, Marc Drogin. Spirited history, comprehensive instruction manual covers 13 styles (ca. 4th century thru 15th). Excellent photographs; directions for duplicating medieval techniques with modern tools. 224pp. 8⅜ x 11¼. 26142-5 Pa. $12.95

DRIED FLOWERS: How to Prepare Them, Sarah Whitlock and Martha Rankin. Complete instructions on how to use silica gel, meal and borax, perlite aggregate, sand and borax, glycerine and water to create attractive permanent flower arrangements. 12 illustrations. 32pp. 5⅜ x 8½. 21802-3 Pa. $1.00

EASY-TO-MAKE BIRD FEEDERS FOR WOODWORKERS, Scott D. Campbell. Detailed, simple-to-use guide for designing, constructing, caring for and using feeders. Text, illustrations for 12 classic and contemporary designs. 96pp. 5⅜ x 8½. 25847-5 Pa. $3.95

SCOTTISH WONDER TALES FROM MYTH AND LEGEND, Donald A. Mackenzie. 16 lively tales tell of giants rumbling down mountainsides, of a magic wand that turns stone pillars into warriors, of gods and goddesses, evil hags, powerful forces and more. 240pp. 5⅜ x 8½. 29677-6 Pa. $6.95

THE HISTORY OF UNDERCLOTHES, C. Willett Cunnington and Phyllis Cunnington. Fascinating, well-documented survey covering six centuries of English undergarments, enhanced with over 100 illustrations: 12th-century laced-up bodice, footed long drawers (1795), 19th-century bustles, 19th-century corsets for men, Victorian "bust improvers," much more. 272pp. 5⅜ x 8¼. 27124-2 Pa. $9.95

ARTS AND CRAFTS FURNITURE: The Complete Brooks Catalog of 1912, Brooks Manufacturing Co. Photos and detailed descriptions of more than 150 now very collectible furniture designs from the Arts and Crafts movement depict davenports, settees, buffets, desks, tables, chairs, bedsteads, dressers and more, all built of solid, quarter-sawed oak. Invaluable for students and enthusiasts of antiques, Americana and the decorative arts. 80pp. 6½ x 9¼. 27471-3 Pa. $8.95

HOW WE INVENTED THE AIRPLANE: An Illustrated History, Orville Wright. Fascinating firsthand account covers early experiments, construction of planes and motors, first flights, much more. Introduction and commentary by Fred C. Kelly. 76 photographs. 96pp. 8¼ x 11. 25662-6 Pa. $8.95

THE ARTS OF THE SAILOR: Knotting, Splicing and Ropework, Hervey Garrett Smith. Indispensable shipboard reference covers tools, basic knots and useful hitches; handsewing and canvas work, more. Over 100 illustrations. Delightful reading for sea lovers. 256pp. 5⅜ x 8½. 26440-8 Pa. $8.95

FRANK LLOYD WRIGHT'S FALLINGWATER: The House and Its History, Second, Revised Edition, Donald Hoffmann. A total revision–both in text and illustrations–of the standard document on Fallingwater, the boldest, most personal architectural statement of Wright's mature years, updated with valuable new material from the recently opened Frank Lloyd Wright Archives. "Fascinating"–*The New York Times*. 116 illustrations. 128pp. 9¼ x 10¾. 27430-6 Pa. $12.95

PHOTOGRAPHIC SKETCHBOOK OF THE CIVIL WAR, Alexander Gardner. 100 photos taken on field during the Civil War. Famous shots of Manassas Harper's Ferry, Lincoln, Richmond, slave pens, etc. 244pp. 10⅝ x 8¼.　22731-6 Pa. $10.95

FIVE ACRES AND INDEPENDENCE, Maurice G. Kains. Great back-to-the-land classic explains basics of self-sufficient farming. The one book to get. 95 illustrations. 397pp. 5⅜ x 8½.　20974-1 Pa. $7.95

SONGS OF EASTERN BIRDS, Dr. Donald J. Borror. Songs and calls of 60 species most common to eastern U.S.: warblers, woodpeckers, flycatchers, thrushes, larks, many more in high-quality recording.　Cassette and manual 99912-2 $9.95

A MODERN HERBAL, Margaret Grieve. Much the fullest, most exact, most useful compilation of herbal material. Gigantic alphabetical encyclopedia, from aconite to zedoary, gives botanical information, medical properties, folklore, economic uses, much else. Indispensable to serious reader. 161 illustrations. 888pp. 6½ x 9¼. 2-vol. set. (USO)
Vol. I: 22798-7 Pa. $9.95
Vol. II: 22799-5 Pa. $9.95

HIDDEN TREASURE MAZE BOOK, Dave Phillips. Solve 34 challenging mazes accompanied by heroic tales of adventure. Evil dragons, people-eating plants, blood-thirsty giants, many more dangerous adversaries lurk at every twist and turn. 34 mazes, stories, solutions. 48pp. 8¼ x 11.　24566-7 Pa. $2.95

LETTERS OF W. A. MOZART, Wolfgang A. Mozart. Remarkable letters show bawdy wit, humor, imagination, musical insights, contemporary musical world; includes some letters from Leopold Mozart. 276pp. 5⅜ x 8½.　22859-2 Pa. $7.95

BASIC PRINCIPLES OF CLASSICAL BALLET, Agrippina Vaganova. Great Russian theoretician, teacher explains methods for teaching classical ballet. 118 illustrations. 175pp. 5⅜ x 8½.　22036-2 Pa. $5.95

THE JUMPING FROG, Mark Twain. Revenge edition. The original story of The Celebrated Jumping Frog of Calaveras County, a hapless French translation, and Twain's hilarious "retranslation" from the French. 12 illustrations. 66pp. 5⅜ x 8½.
22686-7 Pa. $3.95

BEST REMEMBERED POEMS, Martin Gardner (ed.). The 126 poems in this superb collection of 19th- and 20th-century British and American verse range from Shelley's "To a Skylark" to the impassioned "Renascence" of Edna St. Vincent Millay and to Edward Lear's whimsical "The Owl and the Pussycat." 224pp. 5⅜ x 8½.
27165-X Pa. $5.95

COMPLETE SONNETS, William Shakespeare. Over 150 exquisite poems deal with love, friendship, the tyranny of time, beauty's evanescence, death and other themes in language of remarkable power, precision and beauty. Glossary of archaic terms. 80pp. 5³⁄₁₆ x 8¼.　26686-9 Pa. $1.00

BODIES IN A BOOKSHOP, R. T. Campbell. Challenging mystery of blackmail and murder with ingenious plot and superbly drawn characters. In the best tradition of British suspense fiction. 192pp. 5⅜ x 8½.　24720-1 Pa. $6.95

THE WIT AND HUMOR OF OSCAR WILDE, Alvin Redman (ed.). More than 1,000 ripostes, paradoxes, wisecracks: Work is the curse of the drinking classes; I can resist everything except temptation; etc. 258pp. 5⅜ x 8½. 20602-5 Pa. $6.95

SHAKESPEARE LEXICON AND QUOTATION DICTIONARY, Alexander Schmidt. Full definitions, locations, shades of meaning in every word in plays and poems. More than 50,000 exact quotations. 1,485pp. 6½ x 9¼. 2-vol. set.
Vol. 1: 22726-X Pa. $17.95
Vol. 2: 22727-8 Pa. $17.95

SELECTED POEMS, Emily Dickinson. Over 100 best-known, best-loved poems by one of America's foremost poets, reprinted from authoritative early editions. No comparable edition at this price. Index of first lines. 64pp. 5³⁄₁₆ x 8¼. 26466-1 Pa. $1.00

CELEBRATED CASES OF JUDGE DEE (DEE GOONG AN), translated by Robert van Gulik. Authentic 18th-century Chinese detective novel; Dee and associates solve three interlocked cases. Led to van Gulik's own stories with same characters. Extensive introduction. 9 illustrations. 237pp. 5⅜ x 8½. 23337-5 Pa. $7.95

THE MALLEUS MALEFICARUM OF KRAMER AND SPRENGER, translated by Montague Summers. Full text of most important witchhunter's "bible," used by both Catholics and Protestants. 278pp. 6⅝ x 10. 22802-9 Pa. $12.95

SPANISH STORIES/CUENTOS ESPAÑOLES: A Dual-Language Book, Angel Flores (ed.). Unique format offers 13 great stories in Spanish by Cervantes, Borges, others. Faithful English translations on facing pages. 352pp. 5⅜ x 8½. 25399-6 Pa. $8.95

THE CHICAGO WORLD'S FAIR OF 1893: A Photographic Record, Stanley Appelbaum (ed.). 128 rare photos show 200 buildings, Beaux-Arts architecture, Midway, original Ferris Wheel, Edison's kinetoscope, more. Architectural emphasis; full text. 116pp. 8¼ x 11. 23990-X Pa. $9.95

OLD QUEENS, N.Y., IN EARLY PHOTOGRAPHS, Vincent F. Seyfried and William Asadorian. Over 160 rare photographs of Maspeth, Jamaica, Jackson Heights, and other areas. Vintage views of DeWitt Clinton mansion, 1939 World's Fair and more. Captions. 192pp. 8⅞ x 11. 26358-4 Pa. $12.95

CAPTURED BY THE INDIANS: 15 Firsthand Accounts, 1750-1870, Frederick Drimmer. Astounding true historical accounts of grisly torture, bloody conflicts, relentless pursuits, miraculous escapes and more, by people who lived to tell the tale. 384pp. 5⅜ x 8½. 24901-8 Pa. $8.95

THE WORLD'S GREAT SPEECHES, Lewis Copeland and Lawrence W. Lamm (eds.). Vast collection of 278 speeches of Greeks to 1970. Powerful and effective models; unique look at history. 842pp. 5⅜ x 8½. 20468-5 Pa. $14.95

THE BOOK OF THE SWORD, Sir Richard F. Burton. Great Victorian scholar/adventurer's eloquent, erudite history of the "queen of weapons"–from prehistory to early Roman Empire. Evolution and development of early swords, variations (sabre, broadsword, cutlass, scimitar, etc.), much more. 336pp. 6⅛ x 9¼. 25434-8 Pa. $9.95

THE INFLUENCE OF SEA POWER UPON HISTORY, 1660–1783, A. T. Mahan. Influential classic of naval history and tactics still used as text in war colleges. First paperback edition. 4 maps. 24 battle plans. 640pp. 5⅜ x 8½. 25509-3 Pa. $14.95

THE STORY OF THE TITANIC AS TOLD BY ITS SURVIVORS, Jack Winocour (ed.). What it was really like. Panic, despair, shocking inefficiency, and a little hero-ism. More thrilling than any fictional account. 26 illustrations. 320pp. 5⅜ x 8½. 20610-6 Pa. $8.95

FAIRY AND FOLK TALES OF THE IRISH PEASANTRY, William Butler Yeats (ed.). Treasury of 64 tales from the twilight world of Celtic myth and legend: "The Soul Cages," "The Kildare Pooka," "King O'Toole and his Goose," many more. Introduction and Notes by W. B. Yeats. 352pp. 5⅜ x 8½. 26941-8 Pa. $8.95

BUDDHIST MAHAYANA TEXTS, E. B. Cowell and Others (eds.). Superb, accu-rate translations of basic documents in Mahayana Buddhism, highly important in his-tory of religions. The Buddha-karita of Asvaghosha, Larger Sukhavativyuha, more. 448pp. 5⅜ x 8½. 25552-2 Pa. $12.95

ONE TWO THREE . . . INFINITY: Facts and Speculations of Science, George Gamow. Great physicist's fascinating, readable overview of contemporary science: number theory, relativity, fourth dimension, entropy, genes, atomic structure, much more. 128 illustrations. Index. 352pp. 5⅜ x 8½. 25664-2 Pa. $8.95

ENGINEERING IN HISTORY, Richard Shelton Kirby, et al. Broad, nontechnical survey of history's major technological advances: birth of Greek science, industrial revolution, electricity and applied science, 20th-century automation, much more. 181 illustrations. ". . . excellent . . ."–*Isis*. Bibliography. vii + 530pp. 5⅜ x 8¼. 26412-2 Pa. $14.95

DALÍ ON MODERN ART: The Cuckolds of Antiquated Modern Art, Salvador Dalí. Influential painter skewers modern art and its practitioners. Outrageous evalu-ations of Picasso, Cézanne, Turner, more. 15 renderings of paintings discussed. 44 calligraphic decorations by Dalí. 96pp. 5⅜ x 8½. (USO) 29220-7 Pa. $4.95

ANTIQUE PLAYING CARDS: A Pictorial History, Henry René D'Allemagne. Over 900 elaborate, decorative images from rare playing cards (14th–20th centuries): Bacchus, death, dancing dogs, hunting scenes, royal coats of arms, players cheating, much more. 96pp. 9¼ x 12¼. 29265-7 Pa. $12.95

MAKING FURNITURE MASTERPIECES: 30 Projects with Measured Drawings, Franklin H. Gottshall. Step-by-step instructions, illustrations for constructing hand-some, useful pieces, among them a Sheraton desk, Chippendale chair, Spanish desk, Queen Anne table and a William and Mary dressing mirror. 224pp. 8⅛ x 11¼. 29338-6 Pa. $13.95

THE FOSSIL BOOK: A Record of Prehistoric Life, Patricia V. Rich et al. Profusely illustrated definitive guide covers everything from single-celled organisms and dinosaurs to birds and mammals and the interplay between climate and man. Over 1,500 illustrations. 760pp. 7½ x 10⅛. 29371-8 Pa. $29.95

Prices subject to change without notice.

Available at your book dealer or write for free catalog to Dept. GI, Dover Publications, Inc., 31 East 2nd St., Mineola, N.Y. 11501. Dover publishes more than 500 books each year on science, elementary and advanced mathematics, biology, music, art, literary history, social sciences and other areas.